COMPARING
ASIAN
POLITICS

THIRD EDITION

COMPARING
ASIAN
POLITICS

INDIA, CHINA, AND JAPAN

SUE ELLEN M. CHARLTON

COLORADO STATE UNIVERSITY

A Member of the Perseus Books Group

Published by Westview Press,
A Member of the Perseus Books Group

Find us on the World Wide Web at www.westviewpress.com.

Every effort has been made to secure required permissions to use all images, maps, and other art included in this volume.

Westview Press books are available at special discounts for bulk purchases in the United States by corporations, institutions, and other organizations. For more information, please contact the Special Markets Department at the Perseus Books Group, 2300 Chestnut Street, Suite 200, Philadelphia, PA 19103, or call (800) 810-4145, ext. 5000, or e-mail special.markets@perseus books.com.

Designed by Trish Wilkinson
Set in 10.5-point Adobe Garamond

Library of Congress Cataloging-in-Publication Data

Charlton, Sue Ellen M.
    Comparing Asian politics : India, China, and Japan / Sue Ellen M. Charlton. — 3rd ed.
        p.   cm.
    Includes bibliographical references and index.
    ISBN 978-0-8133-4414-0 (pbk. : alk. paper) 1. Asia—Politics and government—Case studies.   2. India—Politics and government. 3. China—Politics and government. 4. Japan—Politics and government. I. Title.
JQ24.C48 2009
320.3095—dc22   2009021643

10 9 8 7 6 5 4 3 2

To
James W. Boyd
In appreciation for who he is
and what he does

Contents

Tables and Illustrations

Photos

Focus Boxes

Preface to the First Edition

All books begin with an author's conviction that there is something new to say or that something old can be said better. So it is with *Comparing Asian Politics*. Some twenty-five years of teaching Asian politics to undergraduates and arguing with friends and family members about the intrinsic interest and value of understanding political processes in Asia finally prompted what has been an ambitious and lengthy project—far too lengthy, judging by the comments of those around me.

The length of this project can be explained by common problems that beset most writers, including competing work and family obligations. One of the delightful, if insidious, reasons for the delay in completion has been the temptation to spend time exploring Asia in person rather than staying home to read, think, and write. For the opportunity to work in Japan in 1991 and 1993, I am especially grateful to the Center for Women's Studies, Tokyo Woman's Christian University; and for making possible my stay in India in 1992, I thank the American Institute for Indian Studies. Travel support to both Japan and India, as well as to China in 1995, was also provided by the College of Liberal Arts, Colorado State University.

One of the most important goals of this book is to provide nonspecialized readers with a balanced discussion of contemporary Asian politics that is sensitive to historical and cultural contexts. Insofar as this sensitivity has been realized, it is due in large part to the generations of scholars whose research has helped to inform this book. Any successes are also due to numerous colleagues, friends, hosts, and passing acquaintances in Asia. They have caused me to learn, to rethink what I was sure I understood, and to help me see their world through their lenses, not mine. They may have difficulty understanding how their patience and, occasionally, impatience touched me, but they should know that without them, this book would have been the poorer. I am deeply grateful to the following people: Marcia

M. Allen, Karuna Ambarasen, Sonja Arntzen, Tsuyoshi Awaya, Surinder and Gunit Ghuman, Janet Gilligan and John Waples, the Ishibashi Family, Yasuko Muramatsu, Anup and Raji Nair, Yukiko Oda, and Irene Tong.

Scholar-writers need support networks, and I am no exception. The network includes colleagues, especially those in the Asian Studies Program at Colorado State University, who have sustained my interests over the years, who answer my questions and correct my mistakes, particularly Loren Crabtree, Bill Griswold, and Kai-Ho Mah. I owe a debt of appreciation also to two special friends: Jana Everett, University of Colorado at Denver, for her knowledge, friendship, and encouragement in trying times; and the late Betsy Moen of the University of Colorado at Boulder, whose premature death cast a lingering shadow over this book.

My students in several sections of Asian politics have served as test-subjects for the book's ideas and organizational scheme. Over a period of several years, some of them took on the project of reading and critiquing the chapters in various drafts. Their help was invaluable in my efforts to avoid jargon and make sure that the writing was clear and interesting. The network also includes two particularly knowledgeable and patient editors at Westview Press: Susan McEachern, who supported the project early on, and Laura Parsons, who saw it through.

Best of all has been my immediate family network: my parents, who lent their "cabin on the Hill" so that I could think and write with minimal interruption and to whom this book is dedicated; and Jim Boyd, who never lost faith, who read and commented on endless drafts—colleague, friend, and *compagnon de route*.

Sue Ellen M. Charlton

Preface to the Second Edition

Every day, hundreds of people stop at a Starbucks next to the Kamo River in downtown Kyoto. The coffee shop backs up to a small, old Japanese rice-cracker store that sells traditional snacks. On the other side of the coffee shop, windows overlook the river, a microcosm of urban life in Japan. Picturesque at first glance (especially by moonlight), the river represents the commitment to control nature. Concrete walks and banks, small dams and stepping stones across the river bottom—all are designed to prevent recurrence of a disastrous flood. Young couples, parents and children, and the retired stop to read, play, talk, or just watch. And if you look carefully from the same Starbucks, the homeless, with their bright blue tarps, are also visible under the bridge.

Scenes like these are found across Asia, where globalization and modernization confront the local and traditional, and wealth is juxtaposed with poverty. We are pressed to ask: What has really changed? This new edition of *Comparing Asian Politics* is driven largely by this question, in recognition of the many obvious changes that have occurred since the mid-1990s. Changes abound not just in the mix of urban buildings, the new brands, fashions, and hairstyles but also in the way these physical attributes raise questions about economic growth, government policies, and national identity.

In addition to substantial revisions to accommodate political changes and new scholarship, this edition seeks to be more sensitive to comparative issues and illustrations from other Asian countries, although the central focus on India, China, and Japan remains. The book also retains the structure and themes of the first edition. I have dropped some material in favor of expanding the analysis of linkages between domestic and international politics, and between national issues and global political and economic currents. An illustration of this new material is a section on the Kashmir dispute between India and Pakistan at the end of the chapter on Indian political history. A new chapter uses human rights to explore the impact of global political currents; this chapter also proposes ways we might learn from Asia in order to enrich our thinking about comparative politics. The glossary has been revised, and new tables, photos, and figures have been added to enhance the book's clarity and usefulness.

The most important shared feature between the original and revised editions is the central goal of generating interest in the complexities that mark contemporary Asian politics. Many topics are not discussed or are discussed in aggravating brevity, but I trust that the questions that are raised will prompt readers to launch their own explorations of the paradoxes of politics, not just in Asia, but elsewhere.

I continue to be indebted to those who have encouraged my project by providing material, suggesting sources, and lending moral support. Many of these individuals were acknowledged in the preface to the first edition, and their influence continues in this revision. In addition, I am indebted to Sonoko Bayes, Jennifer and Fritz Galt, Jeffrey Hester, Stuart Sargent, and Yang Zhong; the Fulbright Commission for supporting a Colorado State University group project in India; Dean Hajime Yamamoto and the staff of the Center for International Education at Kansai Gaidai University; and especially my twenty Japanese students from whom I learned so much. I am grateful to Colorado State University for sabbatical leave, and the University of Tennessee for providing a welcome environment for writing. The latter would not have been possible without the professional and personal support of Chancellor Loren Crabtree, Monica Christen, the Department of Political Science, and the Cartographic Services Laboratory at the University of Tennessee. A good book needs a good editor, and Steve Catalano of Westview Press is thoughtful, engaging, and supportive.

None of this would have been possible without the commitment of James W. Boyd—lifelong student and scholar of Asia, indefatigable proofreader, tireless traveler, and photographer "on command."

Sue Ellen M. Charlton

Preface to the Third Edition

In the fifteen years since the first edition of this book, Asian countries have been through two major economic recessions; India has held four major national elections and hundreds of state and local elections; China has seen two major, smooth leadership transitions and hosted a spectacular Summer Olympics; and Japan's much-vaunted economy and the quasi-monopoly of the Liberal Democratic Party have both been enfeebled, even as its popular culture inspires imitations around the globe. A new generation of Asia scholars and students has come of age.

Despite the many changes that have taken place since the mid-1990s, the fundamental questions that motivate this book are the same. What is the relevance of history and culture for studying the politics of India, China, and Japan? Where are there enduring political patterns, and where are there significant changes? What are some of the implications of these changes for ordinary citizens? How do Asian countries help shape the course of globalization? *Comparing Asian Politics* attempts to address these types of questions by looking at India, China, and Japan individually, in their unique contexts, and comparatively, in order to highlight common elements about political processes.

The third edition of *Comparing Asian Politics* includes updated information and new photos, but the most significant changes are the insertion of focus boxes and "Exploring Further" notes. A focus box is found in most chapters; it may emphasize a general theme in comparative politics or highlight countries not otherwise included in the book. The boxes are set off from the main text and are designed to enrich the primary elements discussed in the chapter.

A paragraph called "Exploring Further" has been added to a number of chapters to suggest reading or films that might interest some readers to engage the main points from the chapter. The choices of what to suggest are eclectic, even eccentric in some cases. I have drawn from students, colleagues, and friends, as well as my own interests, to make suggestions. These short paragraphs avoid mention of the most common websites and academic sources, which often are quickly outdated. Rather, I have included sources that readers may not know about or have thought about in terms of their political dimensions. Ideally, these recommendations will stimulate other ideas and suggestions.

Many of the individuals mentioned in the first and second editions of this book have continued to be sources of support, information, and clarification. Ping Dou, Martha Denney, and Mary Littrell have given me permission to use their photographs, for which I am grateful. To my students, who both learn and teach, thank you—with a special note of appreciation for Travis Hall, a diligent reader and critic of the second edition. Five anonymous reviewers took valuable time to comment and make recommendations that were used to craft many of the changes in this edition, and their efforts are appreciated. Robert Zimdahl offered his expertise to comment on Chapter 13, which is new to this edition. Elizabeth Perry Bonnema generously and cheerfully gave her time and expertise to facilitate handling of the photos, and Nano Bliss Molloy, of the College of Liberal Arts, Colorado State University, provided invaluable help on the tables and diagrams.

Books represent a team effort, and the acquisition, editorial, and production teams at Westview are excellent. I particularly appreciate the patience shown by Brooke Kush and Laura Stine in answering numerous e-mail queries.

A special acknowledgment is due to my friends and family members who have been placed on "hold" too often while I scrambled to meet deadlines. You are special and I owe much to your long-term support and friendship.

Sue Ellen M. Charlton

1

Introduction:
Themes in Asian Politics

Why Asia?

In August 2008, China took the world stage with its spectacular staging of the Summer Olympics. By hosting the games, the Chinese government could justly claim that the humiliations of the nineteenth and twentieth centuries, when the country was subjected to invasion and defeats by Western countries as well as Japan, had been erased. China was now a new regional superpower. Who could deny that the twenty-first century would be China's century, or at least the "Asian century"?

The Olympic spotlight was so bright that it was easy to overlook undercurrents of political and economic tension in China. It was even easier to overlook the rest of Asia: the renewed conflict in Kashmir and political uncertainty in Pakistan; Japan's struggle to regain economic and political prominence; rebellions in southern Thailand and the Philippines; the launching of a constitutional monarchy in tiny Bhutan; and, above all, the day-to-day lives of millions of people working to earn a living, feed their children, and move up in the world (see Figure 1.1).

This book explores the richness and diversity of politics in South Asia and East Asia by looking at these and many other issues. The emphasis, as in earlier editions, will be on India, China, and Japan. For different reasons, these three countries have much to teach us about the political process. One measure of their importance is size: China and India are the two most populous nations in the world, and this fact alone suggests that their systems of governing, their political

1

FIGURE 1.1 Map of Asia.

choices, and their crises should interest outside observers. China and Japan have long weighed heavily on our calculations about military and economic power in the Pacific Rim region, whereas India has become more important in strategic thinking about South and West Asia since the September 2001 terrorist attacks on the United States.

Studied individually, Indian, Chinese, and Japanese politics are as rich and as fascinating as any countries in the world. Taken together, they raise provocative questions that can best be studied in a comparative framework. Studying China, for example, may help us understand what happens when a government pursues apparently contradictory political and economic goals, such as encouraging competition in one arena (the economic) and not in another (the political). The study of Japan raises questions about the adaptation of an East Asian civilization to Western technology, political institutions, and popular culture. In recent decades, the comparative study of Japanese politics has invited inquiry into the connection between economic and military power and the linkage of both of these to international political influence.

Despite its significance as a nuclear power in an unstable region of the world, India is too frequently overlooked in comparative political studies. However, it has much to teach us about the most important political dilemmas of our age. Issues that dominate Indian politics are central to Western nations. For example, what is the appropriate balance between communities and individuals for fostering human freedom and social order? How do we reconcile the tensions between demands for regional autonomy and the need for national cohesion and stability? How have economic and social changes altered the balance of power between central and regional governments? Finally, it is in India, not China or Japan, where one of the most important political debates of the early twenty-first century is occurring—the debate over what it means to have a secular political system.

Ultimately, what draws many students and scholars to Asia is the conviction that the traditions of the region have much to offer us as we try to define and answer the great questions of human experience, including those of our political life.

Themes in Asian Politics: Culture and Tradition

For purposes of comparison, seven themes run through the chapters in this book. These themes reflect the author's assumptions about what is most important and most interesting in the study of Asian politics, and they also reflect the motivating question behind the book: What can we learn about politics by studying other countries, particularly those in Asia? The discussion that follows in this section introduces the first three themes, which are historically interwoven. The next section then takes up a second group of themes that builds on the first group and focuses specifically on contemporary issues of development, the role of the state, and national identity in the rapidly shifting global order of the twenty-first century.

The first theme is that of the *endurance of traditional cultures* that are unique for their ancient roots as well as for their richness in literature, the arts, and philosophy. Especially in India and China, history is measured not only by decades and centuries but also by millennia. Of particular significance for our study is the fact that both countries have ancient political texts, historical figures, and representational symbols that modern politicians lay claim to. Thus, Chinese Communist leaders in the 1960s and 1970s staked out their ideological territory by referring to ancient political figures and debates. In India, a modern political party uses the lotus as a party symbol, thus consciously drawing on an artistic and religious tradition that dates back at least 2,500 years (see Figure 1.2). Even Japan, a relatively young country by contrast, claims the oldest monarchy in the world.

It is not just the age or durability of these traditions but their legitimacy in the eyes of today's citizens that gives them political significance. This legitimacy is reinforced by the existence of ancient texts, architectural monuments, and artistic works that are daily reminders of traditional values and accomplishments. Despite traumatic historical events in the modern era, including colonial conquest (India), war and revolution (China), and war and military occupation (Japan), much of the traditional culture endures and influences politics. The question to be asked, then, is this: How significant for politics and government is this cultural continuity?

The second theme is an extension of the first and may seem at first glance to contradict it. This theme is the *intermingling and grafting of the Asian traditions*, meaning the way in which the Asian traditions have moved across the continent and influenced one another. The most striking cultural and human migrations have moved from west to east: the expansion of ancient Persian influence from West to South Asia; the spread of Islam to South and East Asia; the migration of Buddhism from India to South, Southeast, and East Asia; and the influence of Confucianism, Chinese language, and other aspects of culture in Korea, Japan,

FIGURE 1.2 Lotus symbol

and much of Southeast Asia. The cultural movement has continued into the twenty-first century, often with today's traders converging by airplane in Mumbai (Bombay), Shanghai, and Fukuoka rather than by the ships of past centuries. Hindi movies are broadcast in Hong Kong, Chinese restaurants proliferate in India, workers from throughout Asia enjoy Tokyo parks on Sunday afternoons, and transnational sex trafficking takes place throughout the region.

The political significance of this intermingling varies and may be both direct and indirect. It is direct when an old politician such as Lee Kuan Yew, the former prime minister of Singapore, calls for an official national ideology of Confucianism and asserts the superiority of Confucian over Western political and social values.[1] It is direct also when religious and ethnic minorities, such as Chinese populations in Southeast Asia, Muslims in the Philippines, or Indian Tamils in Sri Lanka, become a political force or a "problem" to be "dealt with." It is both direct and indirect when a Japanese feminist works with Koreans, Chinese, and Filipinos to organize an international tribunal publicizing Japan's World War II military sexual slavery, and the participants gradually become aware of each other's perceptions.[2] Likewise, it is both direct and indirect when Japan's newest national museum in Kyushu explicitly portrays Japanese history in the context of cultural influences from China and Korea (see Photo 1.1).

PHOTO 1.1 **Kyushu National Museum. Photo courtesy of James W. Boyd.**

The third theme is the *influence of Western values and institutions in Asia*. We may date the origins of Western influence from the first great period of European exploration and conquest, the fifteenth to the seventeenth centuries. The remnants linger in place-names such as Macao and Goa (Portuguese) and Pondicherry (French). Other footprints of the early Europeans mark the historical passage through the Asian experience. There are hidden memories of Christian converts in early Japan; our English word "caste" comes from the Portuguese term "casta," used to describe the Indian social organization encountered by early Portuguese traders. We have all heard of the early spice trade that prompted the explorations. Fewer have heard about the privileged status of a European missionary who served as a scientific adviser at the Chinese imperial court in the mid–seventeenth century,[3] or know the term "Dutch learning," which described Western knowledge in Japan for two centuries.

The second sweep of Western expansion, from the late eighteenth to the early twentieth centuries, caused many of the political tremors that linger even at the beginning of the twenty-first century. To this period belong the direct British conquest of most of South Asia; the creation of a French empire in Indo-China (today's Vietnam, Laos, and Cambodia); American merchant and naval ships in Japanese harbors, cracking the isolation of the Tokugawa order; the carving up of coastal Chinese territory by the Russians, French, British, Americans, and, ultimately, the Japanese; and the replacement of Spanish colonialism with American colonialism in the Philippines. It is to this period that we must look for the origins of modern Asian nationalism, which helps us understand in turn the preoccupation of today's Asian governments with strong state institutions and national integrity.

For the purposes of this book, the most important aspects of the Western impact occur in the area of political institutions and ideas, including the idea of development. The Western lineage is direct, if different, for all three of the countries under study. The Indian Constitution draws directly on documents from the colonial period, and India's national parliamentary institutions largely replicate the British. Western impact on Japanese politics dates to the early Meiji period (1860s–1870s) and was consolidated during the post–World War II U.S. occupation (1945–1952). China, seemingly the nonconforming case, actually borrowed from a different European tradition, combining Marxist-Leninist ideology with Leninist Communist party and state organizations. All three countries lead Asia in paying homage to concepts of development that have their roots in European history.

Taken together, these three themes suggest that we need to be alert to evidence of both the distinct influence and the intersection of culture and institutions based in the indigenous traditions of India, China, and Japan; the role of other

Asian thought systems, conventions, and institutions; and, of course, the Western impact. These relationships can be illustrated in concrete terms, a good example being the political relationships found in contemporary Japan. What is the mixture of traditional norms (such as factional loyalty in the political parties), bureaucratic prerogative (inherited from the Confucian tradition), and (Western) parliamentary convention in public policy decision-making? Similar questions will be asked about Chinese and Indian politics as well.

As important as the flow and overlap among these three sets of influences is the fissure, or conflict, that may occur among them. A striking example of such conflict emerged in Indian politics in the 1980s and continues today with the public debate over the appropriateness of (Western) secular institutions and ideology in what some political leaders have argued is and should be a traditional Hindu nation. Similarly, China has questioned the appropriateness of Western definitions of human rights in non-Western contexts, where the primary concern is to improve standards of living.

The point of questions of this sort is not to measure the exact input of a particular factor in a specific political moment. Rather, it is to remind us that, even where indigenous traditions are strong, politics also mirrors foreign history and culture. Political institutions are permeable to external influences. The very fact of this permeability, in turn, may inspire national political resistance and controversy, as happens periodically throughout Asia.

Themes in Asian Politics: Development, State, and Nation in International Context

The fourth theme that runs through this book is that of *socioeconomic development and political change*. The very notion of development, as the word is used here, is Western, the concept having been brought to Asia in the nineteenth and twentieth centuries. Development carries with it the assumption of linear, progressive change. It is linear in its future-oriented perspective and in its assumption that history means progress. Progress in turn means material advancement in the broad sense: higher material standards of living, accompanied by longer life expectancies and the spread of wealth to increased numbers of people.

One of the most distinctive features of development in the early twenty-first century is that it constitutes a political mandate for Asian governments. A handful of exceptions notwithstanding, Asian politicians (like their European and American counterparts) are almost universally preoccupied with development. For example, what policies will stimulate growth in the context of globalized economic institutions and processes, and who gains and who loses under these policies are issues found on every government agenda. Politics both responds to socioeconomic change and seeks to direct it.

Development cannot be fully understood without recognizing its relationship to the political concepts of *state* and *nation*. Often these two words are linked, as in *nation-state*, to refer to the territorially based political units that came to cover the globe in the nineteenth and twentieth centuries. It is useful to remember, however, that the two words reflect distinct, though complementary, concepts. Historically, the word *state* refers to the authoritative legal order that controls and governs the territory. *Nation*, in contrast, refers to the cultural, ideological, and emotional bonds that link the population of the territory to each other, to the territory itself, and to the state. Because these words have different meanings and implications, they are linked to issues of development in different ways. To explain these linkages, we need to turn to the fifth and sixth themes of the book.

The fifth theme is that of the *relationship between individuals and institutions of the state*. For a variety of reasons, state authorities in Asia (like those elsewhere) have sought to expand the influence and control of their policies and institutions. This expansion has been a response to both internal and external pressures. For example, Western imperialism propelled Chinese, Indian, and Japanese leaders to modernize the civilian and military bureaucracies of their states in order to counter and eliminate external threats. The preoccupation with internal and external threats has also defined the primary goals of the new political elites who came into power in the twentieth century: unity and state sovereignty, domestic civil order, economic self-sufficiency, and development. The implementation of these goals has called for building up state authority and capability.

What have been the consequences of this process for ordinary citizens? Obviously, the consequences vary by time and place and also depend on the citizens in question. Some pay more taxes than others or receive better services. Expanded police authority affects the poor, illiterate, and female more than others. Those advantaged by traditional sources of power are better placed to convert their power into "modern" influence through new institutions such as political parties. One of the tasks of this book is to look at ways in which individuals and the state interact, the linkages between them, and the kinds of parties and groups that offer opportunities for citizen influence.

The sixth major theme is that of *national identity and nationalism*. Before the nineteenth century, national identity was seldom a concern—if it existed at all— except for intellectuals or those in the highest levels of state leadership. By the early twentieth century, nationalist elites throughout Asia began to see national identity and cohesion as a tool to be used in eliminating Western colonialism and imperialism. Nationalism begat nationalism: Some Asian politicians were deeply influenced by the schooling in nationalist theories and ideologies they received in Europe and America. As successful nationalist movements in Asia arose, they inspired other Asian movements.

In several ways, the focus on national identity links the earlier themes. Asian nationalism cannot be understood without reference to the flow and mixing of indigenous, Asian, and Western cultures. Many have argued that socioeconomic development facilitates the growth and spread of nationalist sentiment and loyalty, as when public schools are established, roads built, and computers distributed. A strong sense of national identity and cohesion also facilitates the implementation of development policies insofar as individuals feel loyalty toward the state institutions charged with formulating and executing those policies. For this reason, elites charged with enhancing state independence and wealth typically seek to nurture nationalism at the same time.

All six themes are linked by a seventh that is implied by the preceding discussion. This theme is the *importance of the international context.* "Globalization" is the contemporary term for the transnational economic interrelationships of market economics that have deeply influenced—and been influenced by—Asian nation-states. But there is much more to the international context of Asian politics than this form of globalization. For example, organizations such as the United Nations and nongovernmental organizations (NGOs) are part of a process of internationalization that has transformed domestic issues, such as the treatment of prisoners and child labor, into transnational political matters.

Lenses

It is important to reflect on our role as outsiders trying to understand the inside of Asian politics. The author is one such outsider, as will be most of the readers of this book. We must therefore look for and even create bridges between our external, non-Asian positions and the internal realities of Indian, Chinese, and Japanese politics. We cannot hope to understand Asian politics without building on the work of those who have preceded us as students and scholars—but at the same time, and in many ways, our understanding is biased by our predecessors.

Lenses clarify and magnify; they also distort and color. At the very least, when we look through them, we see some things and not others. So it is with intellectual lenses: They make it possible for us to see things we would otherwise miss, but when this happens, our focus becomes selective and often distorted.

There are numerous ways in which our knowledge and hence our understanding of Asian politics have been filtered. For example, during the past thirty years, scholars have debated the impact of "Orientalism" on Western learning about Asia.

Orientalism means a Eurocentric bias in accounts of Eastern history and society. In its crudest form, this bias results in stereotypes such as brutality (Mongol hordes), inscrutability (East Asians), terrorists (Muslims), or exotic (Asian women).

In the late 1970s, Edward Said argued in his book *Orientalism* that the idea of the Orient was in effect a European invention. The Orient, he claimed, has existed as part of a dualistic mindset that juxtaposes Us and Other (or We and They), West and East. Further, the historical relationship between West and East has been one of power and, as suggested above in the sketch of Western colonialism and imperialism, frequently of Western domination of Eastern territories, peoples, and cultures. Examples of the attitudes and interpretations that have accompanied Western hegemony would range from those that explicitly postulate the superiority of Western values to the stereotypes mentioned above.[4]

The attack on Orientalism by Said and others is a reminder that our (Western) understanding of Asia's history and cultures has been filtered through the lenses of our own history and culture. These lenses have magnified some phenomena and excluded others, giving a focus to the Western scholarship that enables comparative study of Asian politics, while simultaneously inculcating biases that are so pervasive we barely notice them.[5] To illustrate: It is commonplace to write and talk about the "Middle East" and "Far East," which are clearly Eurocentric terms because they reflect Asian geographic regions as seen from Europe. A more neutral, geographically accurate way of referring to those areas is West, South, and East Asia. Although some scholars maintain that the orientalist bias in Western thinking has dramatically declined, others suggest that the preoccupation with terrorism after September 2001 renewed the stereotyping and dualistic mindset characteristic of Orientalism.

In addition to the widespread impact of Eurocentrism, our knowledge about Asian politics has been filtered in other ways that are important for this book. One is a clearly identifiable political or ideological bias in researching, interpreting, or reporting facts. The second is the distortion that often results from the process of translating one language (and its inevitable cultural context) into another.

Scholarship, Politics, and "Truth"

Sometimes the political bias in the development of knowledge is immediate and explicit and manifests itself through political control that clearly serves the interests of a ruling ideology or party or the government in general. Examples of such control are almost universal. It was illegal for Americans, including scholars, to travel to China in the 1960s. The Chinese Communist Party (CCP) and government, in turn, long restricted the scope and focus of research and publication, particularly on political and social questions. India bans objectionable books or films, particularly those likely to cause conflict between Hindus and Muslims; in Thailand, it is a matter of *lèse majesté* (a criminal offense against the monarch) to write, say, or do anything that appears to insult the king; and North Korea offers an extreme case of controlled information. One of the most notable instances of the relationship between scholarship, politics, and truth is found in school text-books (see Focus Box 1).

It may be difficult to identify political or ideological bias, particularly if there is no overt government control. Scholars themselves may not recognize their bias or may not admit the way it affects their research. If research is sponsored by a government agency or another organization with a vested interest in the research findings (such as a private corporation), the scholarly lenses may be suspect. International relations may directly influence not only the access scholars have but also their interpretations.

A good illustration of these issues is found in American scholarship on China, beginning with charges in the 1940s and 1950s that American officials and jour-nalists working in China had failed to understand the "true" nature and inten-tions of the Communist Chinese movement. These gullible Americans, their detractors charged, were too sympathetic with the Communists, who were locked in civil war with the Nationalist Chinese forces under Chiang Kai-shek; they con-sequently contributed to the "loss" of China to the Communists. In retrospect, we can see that China-watching, whether conducted by U.S. State Department analysts, journalists, or academics, was heavily influenced by Cold War politics.

The debate over the nature of the pre-1949 Communist movement is echoed in the shifts of opinion since 1949, and these debates continue to affect both popular and scholarly views of China. Some Chinese policies, such as those on birth con-trol, the repression of demonstrations in Tibet or of the Falun Gong movement in the early twenty-first century, or even the tight controls exercised during the 2008 Olympics, have contributed to controversy over the nature of Chinese politics.

The real problem with our lenses is that they are either black or white, leaving little room for the gray truths of Chinese politics and policies. Even the best-trained scholars have been influenced by the cycles of romanticism and cynicism, idealization or condemnation that color the broader climate of opinion. These cycles are rooted in the nineteenth century and have characterized American ap-proaches to China up to the present century, with the result that scholars should be particularly sensitive about the way the political climate continues to influ-ence our China-watching.[6]

Sometimes our understanding of political events and processes is so embed-ded in a worldview conditioned by national identity that it is difficult to discern

```
┌──────────────┐
│ FOCUS BOX 1  │
└──────────────┘
```

TEXTBOOK "TRUTHS"

Textbooks are an ideal vehicle for conveying images about peoples and places. They offer the opportunity to implant a particular understanding of history that reinforces national identity and may endure for decades.

Japanese textbooks are notorious for provoking political controversy in East Asia. Central to the controversy is the account of Japan's military expansion in the first half of the twentieth century. The key topics in the debate have been the Nanjing Massacre, military sexual slavery ("comfort women"), and the treatment of Okinawans near the end of World War II.

The Ministry of Education (MOE) approves all books to be considered for school use. Some scholars have fought MOE control over textbook content, arguing that a full exposure of Japanese wartime atrocities is necessary to foster democracy and peace in East Asia. Noted historian Ienaga Saburo (1913–2002), for example, fought three court cases demanding the right to describe Japanese war crimes in history textbooks.

Resisting the efforts of Ienaga and those who shared his views, the Society for History Textbook Reform has promoted its own so-called "revisionist" version of national history. The society's textbook, which minimizes Japanese wartime aggression, was approved by the MOE in 2001. Although few schools adopted the book, MOE approval provoked a storm of protest in China and Korea.

The Japanese textbook debate stands out for its international political consequences, but it is certainly not the only example in Asia—or elsewhere—of governments, groups, and individuals using school materials to advance a particular ideology. Chinese textbooks are routinely screened, if not written, by government agencies, and anti-Japanese rhetoric and the selective recounting of history serve China's nationalist agenda. Until 2003, South Korea used a single government modern history textbook, but subsequently it approved privately published history texts for secondary schools. These have drawn criticism from conservatives who—much as in Japan—find their portrayals of Korean history too negative.[1] In Indonesia, new research over the origins of a failed 1965 coup that led to the thirty-two-year rule of former President Suharto resulted in the drafting of a new school curriculum in 2004, but the curriculum was challenged in 2006 by a new government with ties to the old regime. In India, the writing of history has fallen prey to the debate over the country's identity as secular or Hindu, and in 2008 the state of Goa withdrew a textbook after protests over the book's alleged anti-Hindu bias.

---

1. Choe Sang-Hun, "Unflattering Textbooks Add Heat to a Debate About South Korea's History," *New York Times*, November 18, 2008.

factual truth. This is the case with historical research on the Nanjing Massacre and World War II more generally, where the questions of exactly what happened and how to think about the implications of events in the 1930s and 1940s affect political debates decades later.

The Nanjing Massacre (or "Rape of Nanjing") refers to the mass killing of Chinese people by Japanese troops in the city and environs of Nanjing during the winter of 1937–1938. For Chinese, both in China and abroad, the cultivated memory of the killings is a unifying event that "brings together all who identify with China and/or oppose Japan."[7]

In Japan, opinion has been more divided, although the parties to the debate understand its implications for national identity. Progressives have sought to research and reveal the extent of Japanese aggression in the 1930s and 1940s as part of a necessary historical accounting to Japan's citizens and its East Asian neighbors. In contrast, influential conservatives deny the established accounts of Japan's World War II role, especially the Nanjing Massacre (which they refer to as the "Nanjing Incident"), seeing these accounts as masochistic, apologetic, and destructive of national pride.[8]

Within this context, the question of national history as transmitted in writing, but also as memorialized at public events and in museums, becomes a political matter. In Nanjing, the commemorative memorial to the victims of the Nanjing Massacre provides an official interpretation of the event, including the sacrosanct number of victims (300,000). In Japan, the question of whether Japan sees itself as an aggressor or victim (of American bombing) continues to generate controversy about World War II museum exhibits.

It is important to remind ourselves that contentious debates over historical meaning are not unique to East Asia. As the cartoon shown in Figure 1.3 suggests, the truth of World War II varies with the national lens of the viewer. This was brought home to Americans in the mid-1990s when the Smithsonian's National Air and Space Museum displayed components of the American bomber, nicknamed *Enola Gay*, used to drop the atomic bomb on Hiroshima in 1945. The museum originally planned to include in the exhibit historical materials showing the civilian destruction caused by the bomb, but a political campaign led by veterans' organizations forced the museum to restructure the exhibit.[9]

Language

In addition to various kinds of political and cultural biases, language itself constitutes a lens that illuminates or distorts our understanding of Asian politics. As noted earlier, the Asian countries highlighted here draw on ancient traditions of literacy.

FIGURE 1.3 "Different Views of History," by Bill Mutranowski. *Japan Times Weekly,* September 21, 2002. Used by permission of the *Japan Times Weekly.*

They offer an abundance of philosophical, literary, political, and legal texts for scholars to translate and study. The process of translation of an Asian language itself constitutes a study, as it does with any language. In the cases of China, India, and Japan, however, translation encompasses the additional steps of transliteration and romanization. Words that are written in the characters of one alphabet are written in the characters of another alphabet (transliterated) in order to approximate the same sounds or words. To "romanize" means to write the characters from the different alphabets (and scripts) in the Roman alphabet, which is used for English and other Western languages. Because romanization is often only an approximation of the original sound, different spellings of the same word are common—such as Moghul/Mughal, Moslem/Muslim, or Sanscrit/Sanskrit.[10]

Chinese and Japanese (or Arabic, for West Asian scholars) alphabets present comparable technical and interpretive problems. The case of Japanese is further complicated by the use of three traditional systems of characters: Along with the Chinese characters (*kanji*) are found Hiragana and Katakana alphabets, each with a different script. Figure 1.4 illustrates these alphabets with the word *manga*. The problems confronted by the casual visitor to Asia are multiplied for the scholar, who must both understand the various translations possible for characters and then be able to translate with the greatest accuracy the meaning that is consistent with the context of the word. The challenge is even greater when words change meaning through time.[11]

Two words illustrate the political relevance of language issues. The word *dharma* refers to a traditional Hindu concept that embraces a number of English words, including righteousness, duty, law, nature, religious merit, principle, and right.[12] Frequently, *dharma* is not translated into English because of its multiple and complex meanings, which change through time and context, but when there is no English synonym, the political or philosophical implications of the word remain ambiguous.

The Japanese word *kami,* which is often translated (even by Japanese) as "god(s)," "deity," or "divinity," causes more problems when these English words

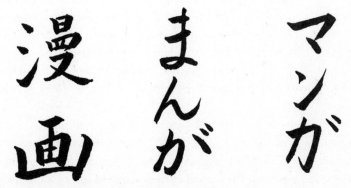

FIGURE 1.4 **Japanese scripts for the word** *manga*: **kanji, hiragana, and katakana. Calligraphy courtesy of Nakanishi Masako.**

are used. Words such as *god* immediately conjure associations with Western religious notions of transcendence. But in Japanese Shinto, the gap between the human and divine is much less clear than in a Western religion such as Christianity or Islam. The ambiguity of the term *kami* is part of the controversy over the status of the emperor, who is presumed to have renounced his "divinity" at the end of World War II, but who, in so doing, was not denying that he had *kami* nature. The error is in translating *kami* from one cultural context to another.[13]

The point of using these examples to emphasize the lenses that filter our understanding of Asian politics is not to deter study but to encourage us to be more thoughtful in our comparative work.

Organization and Approach

This book is divided into four parts. Chapters 2–4 in Part One, "People and Politics," introduce the populations of India, China, and Japan, with particular attention paid to those qualitative features, such as gender and ethnic diversity, that are especially significant for contemporary politics. Part Two, "The Foundation of Politics," includes Chapters 5–7, which examine the growth of nationalism and the contemporary state structures of the three countries under study. Each of these chapters, like those in Part One, focuses on a single country.

Part Three, titled "Government Structures: Form and Substance," includes comparisons of the constitutions of the three countries (Chapter 8), the national governments of India and Japan (Chapter 9), and China's party and state structures (Chapter 10). Chapter 11 compares the subnational levels of government in the three countries, paying particular attention to issues of decentralization.

Part Four looks more closely at the relations between individuals and the state and is titled accordingly. Chapter 12 contrasts the decay of the Congress, Liberal Democratic, and Chinese Communist parties and looks at their alternatives. Chapter 13 casts a broader comparative focus by examining the debate over the meaning of development and its consequences for governance and civil society. Chapter 14 suggests ways in which globalization has affected Asian politics, and also the ways in which the study of Asia enriches our understanding of comparative politics.

Readers will note that Chapters 2–7 are essentially country studies that lay the basis for other approaches to comparative politics undertaken in the succeeding chapters. The shifting nature of comparison between (and sometimes within) the later chapters reflects a deliberate choice. The treatment of India and Japan in Chapter 9, for example, is synchronic, focusing on similarities and differences across national boundaries in roughly the same time period. Chapter 10 on China, in contrast, contains diachronic comparison of one political system over time.

No one book can contain all that is important or interesting about the politics of three countries as complex as Japan, China, and India. The purpose of the approach used here is to encourage readers to explore more fully the individual countries in Asia. The organization of the book is also designed to raise comparative questions that are relevant not just to Asian politics but to other regions as well, so illustrations from other countries are used where appropriate. The focus boxes illustrate these broader perspectives. I hope that readers will move quickly beyond the questions raised here to others that they find equally or more relevant to their thinking about politics.

The discussions in this book place a relatively heavy emphasis on history and culture in the belief that these are unfamiliar areas for most of us raised outside the Asian traditions. Although studying culture and history often leads to the assumption that countries are unique and therefore their political systems are not subject to valid comparison, such an assumption ignores the extensive cross-fertilization among Asian countries and among Asia, Europe, and the rest of the world. Hence, both that which is unique and that which is shared are found in this book.

As the comparative journey begins, a note about romanization of words from the Indian, Chinese, and Japanese languages is in order. There are numerous scholarly conventions about alternative forms of transliteration and romanization, as explained earlier. Those that have become the most widely accepted in recent decades and that readers are the most likely to encounter in the library or on the Internet are the ones used here. The most confusion generally arises over transliteration of Chinese words because the People's Republic of China (PRC) uses the *pinyin* system in preference to other spellings. When the PRC shifted to *pinyin*, transliteration became a matter of politics, and the Chinese government of Taiwan retained one of the earlier systems, called Wade-Giles (after two nineteenth-century Englishmen) in translations to English. Thus, readers will find, for example, that the revolutionary Chinese leader, Mao Zedong (*pinyin*), is called Mao Tse-tung in older publications and anywhere the Wade-Giles system is used. Where necessary, endnotes are added to clarify confusing situations.

Finally, there is the subject of personal names. East Asians generally place their surname, or family name, first; for example, Mao Zedong's family name is Mao. This convention has been observed in translations to English for writings on China and is followed here. The Japanese also place their family name first, but this has not been carried over consistently to English. Many widely read English-language materials published in Japan (such as newspapers) have adopted the

European name order. Nonetheless, the traditional name order (surname first) is used for Japanese names in this book in order to be consistent. Indian names are given in the Western order, which is the convention in India. Macrons (short lines over vowels) and other marks that are used as aids for pronouncing words transliterated from the Indian and Japanese languages have been omitted in order to facilitate reading.

Exploring Further

An old, but revealing, classic treatment of American lenses is Harold Isaacs, *Scratches on Our Minds: American Images of China and India* (New York: John Day, 1958). The website *History News Network*, based at George Mason University (http://hnn.us/), contains articles about history teaching and textbooks. Readers should also explore the dozens of English-language online news sources based in Asia, including *Asia Times Online* (www.atimes.com).

Notes

1. Fareed Zakaria, "Culture Is Destiny: A Conversation with Lee Kuan Yew," *Foreign Affairs* 73, no. 2 (March/April 1994), 109–126. In a 2007 interview, Lee admitted that these values had been diluted by globalization and that change was inevitable. See Seth Mydens and Wayne Arnold, "Lee Kuan Yew, Founder of Singapore, Changing with Times," *International Herald Tribune*, August 29, 2007, at www.iht.com, retrieved August 15, 2008.

2. The feminist referred to is Matsui Yayori, a key organizer of the December 2000 Women's International War Crimes Tribunal for the Trial of Japanese Military Sexual Slavery. See the discussion of "comfort women" in Chapter 4.

3. Jonathan D. Spence, *The Search for Modern China* (New York: W. W. Norton, 1990), 43.

4. Edward W. Said, *Orientalism* (New York: Vintage Books, 1979), 11.

5. For a criticism of Said and an analysis of the political and scholarly biases of the (anti-) Orientalist argument, see Bernard Lewis, *Islam and the West* (Oxford: Oxford University Press, 1993), chapter 6.

6. Carola McGiffert, ed., *China in the American Political Imagination* (Washington, D.C.: Center for Strategic and International Studies, 2003), particularly chapters 4–6.

7. Mark Eykholt, "Aggression, Victimization, and Chinese Historiography of the Nanjing Massacre," in *The Nanjing Massacre in History and Historiography*, ed. Joshua A. Fogel (Berkeley: University of California Press, 2000), 57.

8. Takashi Yoshida, "A Battle over History: The Nanjing Massacre in Japan," in Fogel, *The Nanjing Massacre*, 107–108. For a discussion of the multiple historical narratives about World War II, see Takashi Inoguchi, "How to Assess World War II in World History: One Japanese Perspective," in *Legacies of World War II in South and East Asia*, ed. David Koh Wee Hock (Singapore: Institute of Southeast Asian Studies, 2007), 138–151.

9. Similar tensions confront the telling of Confederate history in southern museums. See Edward Rothstein, "Away Down South, 2 Museums Grapple with the Civil War Story," *New York Times*, September 3, 2008, E1.

10. In these examples transliterated from the North Indian Devanagari script, the second version of each word has replaced the first as the preferred romanized form for scholars.

11. Bernard Lewis has illustrated the problems of translating Arabic as they are magnified across time. The word *siyasa*, for example, in a thirteenth-century text meant "severe discretionary punishment"—hardly synonymous with its contemporary translation as "politics" or "policy." Lewis, 66–67.

12. See the discussion in Wendy Doniger's introduction to *The Laws of Manu*, trans. Wendy Doniger with Brian K. Smith (London: Penguin Books, 1991), liv–lviii, lxxvi–lxxvii.

13. Norman Havens, "Immanent Legitimation: Reflections on the 'Kami' Concept," in *Kami*, ed. Inoue Nobutaka (Tokyo: Kokugakuin University, Institute for Japanese Culture and Classics, 1998), 237–239.

PART ONE

People and Politics

We are a few years into the twenty-first century, and the population of the world is almost 7 billion and growing; 60 percent of the global population lives in Asia. India and China alone are home to more than 2.4 billion people. Put differently, two-thirds of Asians and nearly two of every five people in the world are Chinese or Indian.

Politics is about people, and the size and composition of a country's population has important implications for politics. For example, countries that are relatively overpopulated find that their resources are stretched thin and the demands for government services typically far exceed the ability of the government to provide even minimal services for citizens. In response to population pressures, governments often initiate policies in areas such as birth control and abortion. In Asia, China and India provide obvious case studies on the dynamics of extremely large numbers of people and on high-population density, and in both cases, the governments have had long-standing population policies. At the same time, both countries are aware that aging populations also present a challenge, although the challenge is not as dramatic as in Japan, South Korea, or Taiwan.

Both the size (the quantity) and the composition (the qualitative features) of a country's population have consequences for politics and government. An example of the direct significance for politics of a country's demographic makeup is its degree of ethnic and religious heterogeneity. Near the end of the twentieth century, the map of Europe was transformed with the disintegration of the Soviet Union and Yugoslavia. By comparison, the national boundaries in Asia were stable, although demands for subnational identity seemed to be growing from Pakistan in the west to the Philippines in the southeast. To varying degrees, India, Nepal, Sri Lanka, Thailand, Indonesia, and China confronted destabilizing pressures from autonomy movements. In contrast, the high degree of ethnic

21

homogeneity in Japan has often been cited as a contributing factor in that nation's political stability.

Like many countries in the world—and in marked contrast to North America and Western Europe—most Asian countries are predominantly rural, although the rate of urbanization is increasing. Approximately 40 percent of Asia is considered urban, but this percentage is projected to increase to 60 percent by mid-century. Countries as diverse as Pakistan, Nepal, and Laos still have at least two-thirds of their people living in rural areas. At the same time, some of the highest concentrations of people in the world are found in Asia: Twelve of the world's twenty largest urban agglomerations are in South and East Asia, including six that are in India and China (Kolkata, Mumbai, Delhi, Beijing, Shanghai, and Tianjin).

Differences between urban and rural areas are economically, socially, and politically important in all three countries that are examined in this book. Even in Japan, where the rural population has declined to 21 percent, farming and fishing communities, which account for most of the rural families, continue to wield political power. Urbanization throughout Asia tends to increase pressures on governments by concentrating the demands for public facilities or infrastructure, such as roads, sewers, and water lines. Urban agglomerations may also become "flash points" for conflicts among politically mobilized groups.

The geographic distribution of people is made more important by the qualitative features of a country's population. Are ethnic or religious groups concentrated in one region, or are they spread throughout the country? Has rural-to-urban migration skewed the age and gender composition of some regions, for example, by leaving disproportionate numbers of women, children, and older people in the countryside? Has international migration created pockets of foreigners whose presence becomes contentious? Are poverty and its companions, such as unemployment, illiteracy, and hunger, concentrated in urban or rural areas? Do diseases such as AIDS affect some population groups more than others?

The following discussion makes no attempt to provide an in-depth demographic analysis of Asia. Rather, it offers a general overview and then emphasizes those factors that seem to be of both immediate and long-term political significance. Three criteria were used to select illustrative cases: the usefulness of the cases as examples of the themes introduced in Chapter 1, the clarity of the political implications as gleaned from both academic scholarship and media coverage, and the issues gauged to be of particular interest to general readers. We begin with India, in many ways the most complex case.

2

India

Population Size and Distribution

India's 2001 census confirmed that the country's population had surpassed the billion mark, increasing in ten years from 844 million to 1.02 billion. By 2008, the population was more than 1.1 billion, and recent projections suggest that the country will surpass China to become the most populous in the world by 2030.[1]

The nation is gradually becoming more urbanized, both because of the natural reproduction of city dwellers and as a result of migration from the rural areas. Between the 1981 census and that of 2001, the number of cities with a population more than one million nearly tripled, growing from twelve to thirty-five. The number of cities with a population between 100,000 and one million had similarly increased. Although many of the people who are newcomers to the cities end up living in slums or on sidewalks, they will almost all stay in the cities, where opportunities are better than in the villages they left. Despite these changes, three-fourths of Indians still live in rural areas, and this is likely to remain the case until the middle of the twenty-first century.[2]

Another feature of the distribution of India's population is its varied density throughout the regions and states of the country. India has twenty-eight states, in addition to a number of smaller Union Territories that are administered directly by the central government (see Figure 2.1). As in many federal systems, including those of the United States and Canada, the Indian states range in size from the small ones in the Northeast (Sikkim, Tripura, and so on) to the largest states of Madhya Pradesh and Rajasthan. The states that have traditionally had the lowest population density are either mountainous (Jammu and Kashmir, Himalchal Pradesh), have a large desert (Rajasthan), or are tropical rain forests (the

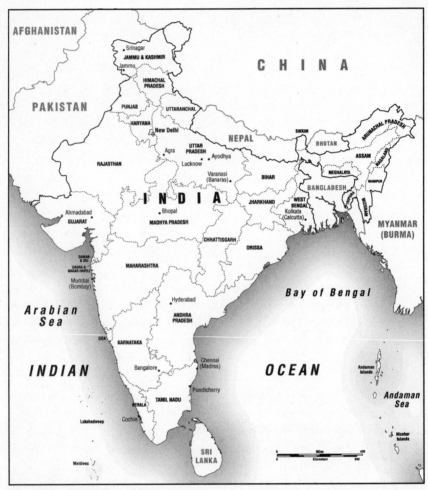

FIGURE 2.1 Map of India. The University of Tennessee Cartographic Services Laboratory; Will Fontanez, cartographer.

states in the northeastern region). Some of these states, however, have experienced a fast increase in population density in recent years that, in turn, has caused political controversy. For example, illegal immigration from Bangladesh across the porous 4000-kilometer border with India has changed the demographic makeup of several border states, with political consequences. The new residents are largely Muslim and poor, with the result that the tension between religious communities of Hindus and Muslims is exacerbated. There have been charges that the immigrants are diluting the cultural heritage of Assam, in particular, that they occupy scarce land and jobs, that they have packed the electoral roles against longtime citizens, and that many are linked to extremist Muslim causes.[3]

The rhythm of life varies dramatically between urban and rural areas. Urban culture and modern technology are transforming every corner of India, but the pace and the nature of the changes are uneven. In some rural areas, one may still see scenes like the one in Photo 2.1, in which the women and young children of a family are riding to a market or temple in a cart drawn by a camel. The men and older boys walk; the women and older girls are careful to cover their faces most of the time (particularly in the presence of strangers). In contrast, urban areas showcase the latest consumer goods in glitzy shopping malls, such as those in Gurgaon, a suburb of New Delhi (see Photo 2.2). Poor laborers live side-by-side with the affluent who enjoy all the advantages of a consumer culture. For all, however, political news is easily accessible through the broadcast media, the Internet, and newspapers, where competition is vigorous among both indigenous-and English-language papers.

The importance of mass communications and the difference between urban and rural peoples cannot be overestimated, for the literacy rate in India is still relatively low. Moreover, despite the rise in literacy in recent decades, the absolute

PHOTO 2.1 Camel-drawn cart, Rajasthan. Photo courtesy of James W. Boyd.

PHOTO 2.2 New shopping center, Gurgaon. Photo courtesy of James W. Boyd.

number of illiterates continues to increase—another example of the problems associated with India's continually growing population. The literacy rate increased from roughly 16 percent in 1951 (the first census after India's independence from Great Britain) to 65 percent in 2001, but there are still tens of millions of illiterate people throughout the country.

TABLE 2.1 Male and Female Literacy in Five Indian States (2001 Census)

State	Percent Male	Percent Female	Literate*
Kerala	94.2	87.86	90.92
Bihar	60.32	33.57	48.53
Madhya Pradesh	76.80	50.28	64.11
Rajasthan	76.46	44.34	60.13
Uttar Pradesh	70.23	42.98	57.36

*Percentage of literates to estimated population.
Source: Adapted from Government of India, *Census of India 2001*, http:censusindia.net.

Gender

Discussion about literacy leads into issues that pertain not just to the size or density of India's population but to its composition and diversity as well. In the case of literacy, for example, there are differences among the populations of literates and illiterates that are significant for politics in both the short and long run. The most important differences are related to gender and to geographic regions. As an example, the southwestern state of Kerala, with its combined male-female literacy rate of 91 percent and female literacy rate of 88 percent, has long been seen as giving higher status to women than other Indian states.[4] Four major states in the northern half of the country (Bihar, Madhya Pradesh, Rajasthan, and Uttar Pradesh) have literacy rates of 64 percent or less. More striking is the gap in male-female literacy, as seen in Table 2.1: On average, 57 percent of the women in these four large states (which constitute 36 percent of India's population and have the fastest growing populations) are illiterate. Women's roles tend to be very traditional in these areas, as is suggested by the rural scene just discussed in Photo 2.1, which was taken in Rajasthan.

When literacy rates are linked to another characteristic of India's population—the declining sex ratio—we can start to answer questions that are relevant to every comparative politics study, such as who participates in political life and why. The sex ratio is the proportion of females to males in a population. In most of the world's populations, females outnumber males, even though more males are born. The higher male birth rate is neutralized by a higher male mortality rate. The declining sex ratio in India means the proportion of females to males is declining, thereby raising questions about increasing mortality rates for girls and women. Table 2.2 illustrates this point more clearly: An equal sex ratio would be 1,000; that is, there would be 1,000 females for every 1,000 males. In 1901, the sex ratio in India was 972; it had dropped to 929 by 1991.

TABLE 2.2 India's Declining Sex Ratios (females per thousand males)

Selected Census Years	*Sex Ratio*
1901	972
1921	955
1951	946
1971	930
1991	929
2001	933

Source: Adapted from Government of India, *Census of India 2001*, http:censusindia.net.

The 2001 census showed a rise in the ratio to 933, but the absolute deficit of females increased by about three million, for a total of over thirty-five million. More troubling was the fact that the sex ratio for children below six years old had declined from 945 in 1991 to 927 in 2001, suggesting that India could expect a sharp rise in the deficit of females over time. In the 1970s, studies suggested that the reasons for the skewed sex ratio were under-enumeration of females and poorer health care for infant girls, but recent evidence shows that although women are now living longer, the sex ratio at birth is increasingly unfavorable to females.[5] Sex-selective abortion is the primary reason for the discrepancy, and despite the fact that it is illegal in India, the practice is widespread, particularly in urban and wealthier areas where couples have easier access to prenatal tests.[6]

Both in India and in China, the availability of fetal sex-determination tests combined with the traditional cultural preference for boys and the acceptability of abortion is responsible for sex-selective abortion. Growing public awareness, government concern, and more aggressive legal penalties have not stopped the practice, although by 2008 there were a few signs of progress in reversing the trend.[7]

The declining sex ratio is the most obvious statistical evidence of the advantages accorded Indian men that begin at birth and cut across all aspects of life, affecting health, access to education, employment, and, of course, politics. It is not surprising, therefore, that high-ranking formal political positions (in the government bureaucracy, legislatures, and courts) are overwhelmingly held by men. Less than 10 percent of the national legislature is female, only two of the top thirty cabinet positions were held by women in 2008, and none of the twenty-five Indian Supreme Court judges is female. Although there have been several female chief ministers at the state level, women in high-level state positions continue to be a small minority. Nonetheless, one of Asia's most powerful political leaders in the past half century was Indira Gandhi, India's prime minister from 1966 to 1977 and again from 1980 to 1984, and there has been speculation that the female chief minister of India's most populous state, Uttar Pradesh, may be well-placed to be a future prime minister (see next section).

The issues of gender and politics go beyond formal political roles, however. One of the oldest and most diverse women's movements in the world is found in India. Self-styled women's rights activists and feminists today range from upper-class matrons active in social welfare causes to poor rural and urban women who have assumed leadership roles in grassroots political groups committed to radical change. Women's groups have taken the lead in debating and changing conditions of employment in urban slums and have addressed such diverse issues as the environmental damage caused by large-scale development projects and the physical abuse of women. These activities represent an impressive level of political commitment in a country where most women are disadvantaged by socioeconomic conditions and historically are discouraged from public activity.

Caste and Class

Caste is intrinsic to Hinduism, the principal religion in India. Even communities whose origins stem from a different worldview, such as Christian communities, are marked by caste divisions. In the dominant Hindu view, caste is inherent in the nature of human society: Relations between human beings are and should be defined by the behavioral norms and roles that are ascribed to one's caste. Caste, like gender, marks people at birth; traditionally, it was only with great difficulty that individuals could escape the attributes and roles of their caste.[8]

For non-Indians, caste and class are probably the hardest qualities of Indian society to understand.[9] The English word *caste* is derived from the word that the seventeenth-century Portuguese used to describe the Hindu social groups they found in India. They called these groups *castas*, meaning tribes, clans, or families. The term *caste* has come to include two kinds of social divisions that, though different, are closely related. The larger of these divisions is known by its Sanskrit name *varna*, or "color," and has been loosely translated as both class and caste, which adds to the confusion.

A number of scholars believe that *varna* came to India when Aryan tribes began invading the subcontinent from the northwest around 4,000 years ago, a period about which historians know comparatively little.[10] Much of what is known about the origins of caste in *varna* is actually extrapolated from literary texts, the most famous of which is the *Rig Veda*, one of the world's great historical documents. The *Rig Veda* was originally a collection of hymns to be sung in praise of the gods of the early tribes that entered India as part of the Aryan invasion. The memorization and recitation of these and other Vedic hymns was the exclusive prerogative of the priestly class of these tribes. The most important of these tribes, the Bharatas, gave its name to India: Bharata (both in Sanskrit, the original Indo-European language of the Aryans, and Hindi, its most important modern derivative). This root word appears in other contexts in this book. It is found, for example, in the name of one of India's most important political parties, the Bharatiya Janata Party (BJP), or Indian People's Party.

The original priestly class of the Bharatas and other tribes became the highest *varna* in the social order that was gradually created in what we now call India. Three additional *varna* gradually crystallized during the period of the *Rig Veda* and have survived to the present era. Beneath the priestly *varna* (the *brahmana*, or Brahmins) were the warriors, rulers, and administrators (Kshatriyas); traders, merchants, and farmers (Vaishyas); and, at the bottom, peasants, serfs, or servants (Shudras).

As the Aryans settled among the darker-skinned peoples who were the original inhabitants of India, the meaning of color seems to have become more important, and the Aryans laid more stress on purity of blood.[11] Gradually the indigenous groups sank in the social scale, class divisions hardened, and the system of *varna* was given religious sanction. The people most disadvantaged by this system were actually outside the *varna*, or outside the caste system, and were called by the pejorative term "outcastes." Constituting almost 20 percent of the population of modern India, these people were also known as "untouchables" because they were viewed as so inferior that it would be ritually polluting for people in higher castes to touch them.[12]

Varna is one kind of social division included in the term *caste*. The other is known also by its Sanskrit name, *jati*. Generally, when the term *caste* is used here (as in "caste politics"), it means *jati*. *Varna*, as well as the "untouchables," are heterogeneous groups, fractured by multiple *jati*. India has several thousand *jati*, and *jati* is the social group that matters the most in the day-to-day lives of Indian women and men. Originally, *jati* may have emerged from the intermingling of all kinds of tribal groups, and historical evidence suggests that early *jati* were associated with different village trades or crafts, such as pottery. This would help account for the fact that in contemporary village India, caste (*jati*) often continues to be an occupational grouping. In urban areas, trades and occupations as a defining characteristic of caste tend to break down more rapidly, as do customs of ritual purification and pollution.[13]

Castes are historically endogamous; that is, their members marry within their own group. That this feature is very much alive can be seen in one of the most interesting features of modern Indian newspapers and the Internet, the matrimonial ads. Families in search of appropriate marriage partners for their sons and daughters place an ad in the matrimonial classifieds and often specify the caste of the family, making it clear they are looking for a potential bride or groom of the same caste. The following example, which is a composite of several classifieds, identifies caste and illustrates the preference for fair-skinned marriage candidates: "Suitable match 4 Brahmin boy. 1983 born, 5'7" colour fair. Seeks any BR Girl Fair Veg above 5'2". Contact [e-mail]."

Caste is also very much alive in politics. Many people thought that the importance of caste, particularly its most negative features, such as discrimination against lower caste groups and "untouchables," would decline after India received its independence from Great Britain. One reason for this assumption was that one of India's great nationalist leaders during the first half of the twentieth century, Mohandas K. Gandhi, rejected the discriminatory features of the traditional caste system. The Mahatma (or "the Great Soul"), as Gandhi has become known, insisted that his followers, no matter what their caste, share such tasks as cleaning latrines. This would be viewed as polluting, and therefore repugnant, to all but the lowliest Hindus. Mahatma Gandhi also used the word *harijans* ("children of God") for untouchables, thereby indicating their special importance in his view of the ideal society to be created after the British were driven from India. It should be noted that Gandhi was partially responding to pressure from another brilliant Indian leader, Dr. B. R. Ambedkar. Like Gandhi, Ambedkar was a British-trained lawyer. Unlike Gandhi, he was an untouchable who had experienced firsthand the discrimination against "outcastes."

Gandhi succeeded in forcing many to rethink the role of caste in Indian society. He was a committed Hindu who believed that untouchability was an abhorrent corruption of Hinduism and should be eliminated. In contrast, Ambedkar called for the destruction of the entire caste system and attacked Hinduism itself, which he argued was the foundation of caste.[14] The Indian Constitution represents a compromise between these positions. For example, Article 17 proclaims that untouchability is abolished "and its practice in any form is forbidden." Caste, however, is not abolished, although Article 15 prohibits discrimination against any citizen on the basis of caste (as well as on the basis of race, sex, or religion). It may be argued, in fact, that the constitution actually sanctified caste and ensured its enduring impact on Indian politics. The First Amendment to the constitution in 1951 added to Article 15 the provision that nothing in the article prohibiting discrimination "shall prevent the State from making any special provision for the advancement of any socially and educationally backward classes or for the Scheduled Castes and the Scheduled Tribes." The castes and tribes in question are the former untouchable *jati* and indigenous tribes, whose names were first placed on a schedule or list by the British rulers in 1935 and 1936. The special provisions called for in the constitution included, for example, the reservation of legislative seats and university positions for the Scheduled Castes and Tribes.[15] Such provisions created a precedent for Indian-style positive discrimination or "affirmative action" measures to help the most disadvantaged citizens, and these measures are today the subject of intense political debate and conflict (see Focus Box 2).

Caste has become politically salient for other reasons. It provides one of the most important organizational bases in India's intense, combative elections. So-called vote banks (groups of voters mobilized for a particular candidate) may be organized along caste lines, and prominent politicians, especially at the state and

POLITICAL REPRESENTATION:
QUOTAS AND RESERVATIONS

Many governments have devised policies designed to address social, economic, or political inequalities among their citizens. In the United States, these are usually referred to as affirmative action policies. Although vilified by some Americans, explicit quotas, most often for elected political positions, have been adopted by a wide variety of countries around the world. Thus these policies raise interesting questions about the nature of political representation.

Quotas for women are found on every continent, with more than ninety countries using some variant of quotas to increase the number of women in politics. In some cases, the requirements are imbedded in constitutions, but more commonly they are stipulated in election laws for parliaments or political parties. Some mandate a percentage or number of *seats* to be held; others call for a certain percentage of *candidates* to be female and male. There is a great deal of debate among scholars and activists about both the desirability and efficacy (in terms of policy changes) of these provisions, but in Asia at least ten countries have adopted some variant of quotas, including South Korea, Nepal, Pakistan, Taiwan, Thailand, Indonesia, and India.[1]

Special allocations for ethnic, linguistic, or racial minorities tend to be more specific. Whereas political party quotas for candidates are common for women, seat quotas in legislatures are characteristic of strategies to enhance minority representation. These different approaches reflect the crosscutting nature of gender, with men and women belonging to all political parties and classes, whereas ethnicity tends to be "coinciding"—for example, concentrated in a particular class or geographic region. Consequently, the demands for representation take different forms: for women, it is political inclusion, but for minorities it is recognition of difference, an acknowledgment and legitimizing of particularism.[2] Thus different conceptualizations of representation are operating.

India has a long-standing policy of using quotas, called reservations, to compensate for historical discrimination against Scheduled Castes and Scheduled Tribes. Reservations exist both for the lower house of parliament, the Lok Sabha (House of the People), and the state legislative assemblies. Reservations are also used in local government bodies, for government employment, and for public colleges and universities. Constant demands to expand reservations to Other Backward Classes frequently provoke political conflicts, sometimes resulting in violence.

continues

| FOCUS BOX 2 |

The 73rd and 74th amendments to the Indian constitution, adopted in 1993, established a reservation of 33 percent of seats for women in local governments. Research to date suggests that the inclusion of women has both legitimized their public political presence and had some policy impact.[3] Comparable proposals for female reservations in state assemblies and the Lok Sabha have stalled, both due to lack of unity among proponents and opposition from vested political interests.

1. International Institute for Democracy and Electoral Assistance (IDEA), "Global Database of Quotas for Women," A Joint Project of International IDEA and Stockholm University. See www.quotaproject.org, and also the Inter-Parliamentary Union website, www.ipu.org.
2. Mala Htun, "Is Gender Like Ethnicity? The Political Representation of Identity Groups," *Perspectives on Politics 2*, no. 3 (September 2004), 439–458.
3. Medha Nanivadekar, "Are Quotas a Good Idea? The Indian Experience with Reserved Seats for Women," *Politics and Gender 2* (2006), 119–128.

local levels, are often identified by their association with a particular caste. Caste has also become more important in recent decades because the lowest castes, consisting primarily of those formerly considered untouchables, have increasingly mobilized in order to press their political demands and combat discrimination. They have chosen to call themselves by the name *Dalit*, meaning "oppressed" or "downtrodden," to signify their commitment to political activism. Although discrimination against Dalits continues to be widespread, elections have provided the vehicle for some Dalit representatives to rise to prominence. One such example is Mayawati Kumari, generally referred to just as Mayawati, the chief minister of Uttar Pradesh. Mayawati helped form the Bahujan Samaj Party (BSP) in 1984. She served as chief minister in three short-term coalition governments, and in 2007 began a fourth term when the BSP won an absolute majority in the state legislature. Called by many the "Queen of the Dalits," Mayawati announced in 2008 that she intended to become a candidate for prime minister of India.

In view of the long-term social and cultural importance of both *varna* and *jati*, it is not surprising that class as conventionally understood in Western democracies (as a group of people marked by socioeconomic status) cannot be understood in isolation from caste. Particularly in Indian villages, class is *jati*. Even though most Indians still live in villages, urbanization persistently changes the country's socioeconomic landscape. In some cities, industrialization has created an urban working class. Long-standing problems of underemployment and unemployment radicalize men in particular (including many from traditionally high-status castes) against policies they see as favoring lower castes. At the same time, there is a huge middle class whose tastes and lifestyles fuel an expanding consumer economy. Put differently, development hurts some but can provide opportunities for others, including those disadvantaged by the traditional social order.

Finally, one additional social category must be introduced here—the Backward Classes (BCs). The word *backward*, as used in the Indian context, is distinctive and refers to a large, mixed category of people who are economically and socially deprived. The Backward Classes are not classes in the Western sense but rather are a combination of caste and class, although the precise mixture of criteria for establishing the category is controversial. Together, the Backward Classes include the Scheduled Castes and Tribes, along with the Other Backward Classes (OBCs), whose ritual and occupational status are above the former "untouchables," but who are economically and socially depressed. The OBCs are a residual category, and the question of establishing the boundaries of this group for purposes of determining government benefits has been one of India's most hotly contested political issues.

Language

Indians routinely identify themselves as northerners or southerners. One major reason for this distinction is that the northern and southern parts of the country are dominated by different families of spoken and written languages. There are five major language families in India, but the most important are the Dravidian languages in the South and the Indo-European or Sanskrit-based languages in the North.[16] The Dravidian peoples inhabited North India before the Aryan invasions, and as the Aryan tribes came in, it is thought that many Dravidians moved south. Today, Dravidian-based languages dominate four southern states: Andhra Pradesh, Karnataka, Kerala, and Tamil Nadu.

Although there are important differences among these four languages, the fact that they are part of the same linguistic family contributes to a sense of regional identity in the South. This sense of identity has taken on clear political importance in the individual states as political parties have formed to assert the distinctiveness of regional culture and problems. The Dravida Munnetra Kazhagam (DMK, Dravidian Progressive Federation) is a good example of this development. Originally, the DMK urged the secession of the Dravidian South from India, arguing that the South is racially and culturally distinctive and that it has been dominated economically and politically by the North. The DMK and its offshoot, the AIADMK (the All-India Anna DMK), have dominated politics in the state of Tamil Nadu since independence.

When the Aryans first came to India, they brought their own language, Sanskrit, with them. Sanskrit is no longer commonly spoken, but it remains the basis for the languages that dominate North India, much as numerous West European languages are rooted in Latin. The most important of the Sanskrit-based languages, Hindi, is widespread in North India (hence southerners may refer to the "Hindi North").

When the Muslims began to occupy India in the thirteenth century, their rulers and administrators spoke Persian and Arabic (Persian was used for official purposes until the nineteenth century). Ultimately, a new language called Urdu emerged from the combination of Hindi, Persian, and Arabic. Urdu subsequently became the court language of the Mughals, who ruled India from the sixteenth to the nineteenth centuries.[17] Today it is spoken principally in North India and is especially important in Kashmir.

Like the Sanskrit languages and Urdu, English is also historically associated with an "invasion" or conquest—that of the British. English was introduced into the Indian school system in the early nineteenth century by the British colonial rulers and for most of the past two centuries has been associated with India's educated elite. Although fewer than 5 percent of Indians are fluent in English, the language retains an importance far beyond what is suggested by this low percentage. As a language of the elite, English is spoken by national-level politicians, administrators, and businesspeople. Because many of the Indian languages are mutually unintelligible, English is the only language spoken throughout India. Far from disappearing, as most independence leaders assumed it would, English has been "Indianized": It has taken on its own accents and idioms, reflecting the cultural context in which it evolved. The uniqueness of Indian English is perpetuated not only in oral communication but also throughout the English print and broadcast media. Despite the widespread importance of English, however, in the late twentieth century, a movement to "Indianize" geographic terms led to changing the names of several well-known cities: Madras became Chennai, Bombay became Mumbai, and Calcutta became Kolkata.

In all, there are over one dozen major languages in India, each spoken by millions of people. There are many more languages with smaller numbers of speakers and still more regional dialects. The multiple scripts of these languages add further confusion. The Sanskrit-based and Dravidian-based languages have different scripts, and there are even different scripts, grammar, and pronunciation rules within these families.

Part 17 of the Indian Constitution is devoted to the issue of language. It declares Hindi in Devanagari script (the script in which Sanskrit is written) to be the country's official language and includes the provision that English would also be an official national language for fifteen years after the constitution went into effect in 1950 (Article 343). All laws, court, and legislative proceedings, until otherwise determined by Parliament, would also be in English (Article 348). The constitution further provides for the establishment of official state languages. All of India's major languages, including Hindi but not English, are recognized in a list appended to the constitution. This list, the Eighth Schedule of the constitution, serves to legitimize the importance of these languages, even as the constitution tries to give special prominence to Hindi.

One-fourth to one-third of Indians speak Hindi as their first or second language—and that is a large minority of the population, but far from a majority. This is one reason that Hindi has never truly become *the* national language. Another reason is the strong resistance to Hindi by the southern states, where most people do not read, speak, or understand Hindi. Consequently, alongside Hindi, English continues to be the second official language.

As a practical matter, Indian elites are generally at least bilingual, if not trilingual. High-level administrators and politicians who come from a state outside the northern "Hindi belt" speak their own regional language (Bengali, Kannada, Tamil, and so on), along with Hindi and English. In many states, migration from the countryside creates communities of people who speak one language in cities dominated by another language. These migrants will pick up some of the dominant languages in their new home but may never become linguistically integrated into their new region. Thus, urbanization has only partly eroded the divisions of language in India.

Religion

Almost every major religion in the world has its adherents in India, and religion is central to many of India's most enduring political conflicts. One of the best-known of these was a conflict that resulted in the destruction, in 1992, of an old Muslim mosque called the Babri Masjid, in the North Indian town of Ayodhya. The mosque's destruction was followed by Hindu-Muslim riots in numerous cities, recalling the persistent tensions between the two largest and most important religious communities in India. The events surrounding Ayodhya will be discussed in more detail in Chapter 5 because they illustrate the confluence of so many contemporary political issues in India, including the politicization of Hinduism.

For Westerners, religion is defined primarily as a set of beliefs that are accompanied by an institutionalized authority and recognizable ritual practices. Religion may be an important part of people's lives, but for most individuals in our secularized societies, it is just one part of a much larger whole. In contrast, for most Indians, religion is much more: It is an all-embracing worldview and "attitude of mind that helps individuals order their universe and their place in it."[18] Religion is the source of meaning for life, not a distinguishable "part" of it. This is especially true of Hinduism, the dominant religion in India both in terms of numbers of identifiable Hindus and in terms of its impact on Indian society and culture. Gandhi and Ambedkar, it will be recalled, had to confront the central place of Hinduism in India when they sought to reform (Gandhi) or eliminate (Ambedkar) the caste system, for Hinduism and caste are inextricably intertwined. Put differently, Hinduism and India's fundamental social structure are inseparable.

Hinduism is more easily understood as a worldview and social system than as a single religion in the conventional sense used by most Westerners.[19] One school of philosophical Hinduism affirms that the belief in an all-pervasive, absolute, formless Reality coexists with the belief in one or more superhuman manifestations of this absolute One. These manifestations constitute a plurality that expresses the richness of the One, and they are anthropomorphized, meaning that they take human shapes and display human characteristics. Although these gods and goddesses take different forms and are called by different names, they are accepted and recognized across the regions and languages of India. They become real to children through symbols, pictures, and stories; they are celebrated in temples and homes; and their representations are found everywhere: in stores, taxis, and even political cartoons. Much of the language and symbolism of politics draws from the tradition of this popularized Hinduism.

Philosophical Hinduism focuses on understanding and realizing an individual's oneness with the essence of life—the ultimate Reality, usually called Brahman (not to be confused with the priestly caste called Brahmin[20]). Much of the diversity of Hinduism stems from the acceptance of many ways of reaching oneness with Brahman. A commonly held belief, however, is that the soul must be reborn through countless lives, as one struggles to be reborn at higher levels of both caste and spiritual purity. As a practical matter, this process means that all individuals are expected to observe the norms and rituals prescribed by caste, as adapted for gender and age. The highest caste groupings (*varna*) are called "twice-born" castes, and their members rank higher in spiritual and social attainment than low castes and untouchables. They constitute the traditional religious, social, and political elites of India.

At the family and village level, most Hindus practice popular, devotional, *bhakti* Hinduism. The *bhakti* traditions are as diverse as the people of India and include many colorful practices that are unfamiliar to Westerners: They range from protecting cows and decorating them for festivals to slaughtering goats, to dressing and undressing temple "gods" when waking them in the morning and putting them to bed at night. But behind this diversity are profound assumptions and beliefs that provide cohesion for the Hindu worldview.[21] For example, Hindus often accept the superiority of spiritual insight and intuition over the linear, scientific, and secular thought that has come to dominate Western culture. Photo 2.3 shows a Hindu pilgrim in the holy city of Varanasi, or Banaras.

Approximately 80 percent of Indians are Hindus and more than 13 percent are Muslim, or followers of Islam. Islam means submission to God's command, the Moral Law. God's message was revealed to his prophet, Muhammad ibn Abdullah (the son of Abd Allah), who was born in Arabia in 570 C.E.[22] The divine revelations continued for more than two decades in the early seventh century, when they were collected and written down in the Qur'an (*The Recitation*). Thus Islam, like Christianity, is a revealed religion whose truth is found in its Book.

PHOTO 2.3 Hindu pilgrim in Varanasi. Photo courtesy of James W. Boyd.

The first Muslims arriving in India were Arabs, who came soon after Muhammad's death in 632 C.E. But it was only three centuries later that the invasions and migrations from the northwest set the stage for a long period of Muslim political and military dominance. The sultanate of Delhi, established in 1206, inaugurated a period of Muslim control in North India, and in the sixteenth century, the Mughal Empire expanded this control to most of the subcontinent. Under the Mughal Empire, some Hindu temples were destroyed and replaced by Muslim mosques. One such mosque at Ayodhya, as noted earlier, was torn down in 1992 by a crowd of Hindus who claimed that it had been built on the site of an older Hindu temple.

The total number of Arab, Persian, Afghan, Turkish, and Mongol Muslim invaders who resided in India was never more than 1 or 2 percent of the subcontinent's population, but through intermarriage with Hindus and conversions, Muslims came to constitute one-fourth of India's population by the nineteenth century.[23] After Partition, the division of the Indian subcontinent into the independent states of Pakistan and India in 1947, and the migration of millions of Muslims to Pakistan, the proportion of Indian Muslims declined dramatically, although the number has continued to grow and now stands at more than 150 million, making India the second-largest Muslim country in the world after Indonesia (see Photo 2.4).

The importance of Islam in India is established not only by its history as the religion of the Mughal Empire, but by the size of the Muslim population, a population growth rate that is slightly higher than that of Hindus, and by the disadvantages that come with being part of a religious minority. On balance, Muslims are poorer, less educated, have worse jobs and fewer government positions than Hindus or other minorities, with the exception of Dalits. In 2006, a government commission studied extensively the status of India's Muslim population with the goal of crafting public policies to address their problems.[24] A key political issue is the demand of many Muslims (and also Christians) that they be accorded the same access to preferential policies as Dalits because they suffer from the same disadvantages. In fact, since the 1950s, many Muslim social groups have been recognized as backward classes, although not as Scheduled Castes.

Competition over scarce resources (here in the form of government policies) contributes to the tension between Hindus and Muslims. Seen from the perspective of some Hindus, in fact, India stands in the middle of an Islamic belt that stretches from North Africa to Indonesia and the southern Philippines. In this geographic context, there is pressure to define the Indian nation as a *Hindu* nation. Increasingly frequent terrorist bombings throughout India in the past few years have contributed to this pressure.[25]

PHOTO 2.4 Muslim in Mumbai. Photo courtesy
of James W. Boyd.

For Muslims also, the question of community identity and security is at stake
in the conflict with Hindus. One of Islam's central tenets holds that a power or
state exalted above God is a corrupt wasteland. Hence, the political ideal for an
Islamic community is an Islamic state. An Indian Muslim community that cannot fulfill itself in statehood (as Pakistan has done) risks assimilation with Hinduism or accommodation with a secular order that ultimately enfeebles the
essence of Islamic teaching.

In short, both Hindus and Muslims can and do lay claim to the greatness of
Indian civilization; both feel threatened by "minority" status, either in Asia as a
whole or in India, and both communities are seeking to redefine themselves vis-
à-vis the other and in distinction to Western values and influences.

After Muslims, Christians and Sikhs constitute the largest religious minorities
in India. Christians constitute about 2.3 percent of the population, and Sikhs,
1.8 percent. Christianity in India dates back 1,500 years and includes some of

the earliest Christian communities established anywhere in the world. Originally, the Christian church was rooted in the southwest state of Kerala, and today about 25 percent of Kerala's population is Christian. To this early Christian community have been added the later Indian converts of Portuguese and French Catholics, British Anglicans, and American and European Protestants.

Christianity has influenced Indian politics in selected and often indirect ways. For example, missionaries were critical to the introduction of Western education in India under British rule. Western-educated men and women were responsible for a number of social reforms, including some that were especially important for women, such as the suppression of *sati* (the self-immolation of Hindu widows on their husbands' funeral pyres). Some nineteenth-century Hindu social reformers drew a great deal of inspiration from Christian social ethics. In recent years, Christians have become embroiled in political controversy, for some of the same reasons as Muslims. They are clustered among the most disadvantaged of India's populations, and many Dalits, seeking to avoid the stigmas of the Hindu caste system, have converted to Christianity (and Islam). These conversions have provoked resentment, often from Hindus who do not have the access to medical and educational services that Christians do. In 2008, this resentment led to violent attacks against Christians in the eastern state of Orissa.

The history of Sikhs in India is very different from that of Christians, partly because of their indigenous roots and partly because of their geographic concentration in the northwest state of Punjab. Sikhism was founded in the sixteenth century by Nanak, who became the first guru (teacher) of the Sikhs. Guru Nanak sought to create a synthesis of Hinduism and Islam in order to reform both. In the seventeenth century, after the fifth guru was executed by the Mughal emperor, the Sikhs became increasingly militant in order to protect their faith from Muslim demands to convert to Islam. Sikh followers were required to adhere to certain symbolic distinctions; for example, the vast majority of Sikh boys and men keep their beards and hair unshorn, and the men wear a distinctive turban that is easily recognizable not only in India but also in the many cities around the world where Sikhs have settled. Photo 2.5 shows Sikhs visiting a gurdwara (or temple) in New Delhi.

Gradually, the Sikhs established an independent state and were only conquered by the British in the 1840s. Under the British Raj (rule), the Sikh's military skills were put to the service of the empire, and Sikh men became prominent in the army. This tradition carried over into the postindependence period, and even today the Sikhs constitute a disproportionately high percentage of both the enlisted troops and the officer corps.[26]

PHOTO 2.5 Sikhs visiting a gurdwara. Photo courtesy of James W. Boyd.

The importance of Sikhs in Indian politics far outstrips the small proportion of the population they represent. Not only are Sikhs prominent in the military (and civil) services, but they stand out in a number of urban occupations and have been successful farmers in their home state of Punjab. A nationalist Sikh movement with roots in the nineteenth century developed in the twentieth century, leading both to the creation of a separatist political party in Punjab and to a terrorist movement. One of the most important consequences of rising Sikh nationalism after independence and partition was the demand for a separate Punjabi-speaking Sikh state within India. The demand was finally accepted in the mid-1960s, and the large Punjab state was divided into two smaller states, one called Punjab, where Sikhs are in the bare majority, and another, Haryana, where Hindi-speaking Hindus dominate.[27]

The religions in India with the smallest number of adherents, Zoroastrianism, Jainism, and Buddhism, each compose well under 1 percent of India's population. The Parsis, or followers of the ancient Zoroastrian religion, are descendants of Persians who fled to India in the tenth century to escape Muslim invasions. Settling on the western coast, the Parsis are now important in India mainly as an economic force. They constitute one of the leading business communities and are especially important in the city of Mumbai, India's primary financial and commercial metropolis.

Jainism and Buddhism, like Sikhism, are indigenous to India and grew out of movements seeking, in part, to reform Hinduism. Both date back about 2,500 years and are credited as important sources of the ethical model of *ahimsa* (non-violence), a theme in Indian political and social thought. Mahatma Gandhi, who used fasting as a technique of *ahimsa* and who was a committed vegetarian, grew up around Jains and was clearly influenced by Jain principles.[28]

As a philosophy of life and religion as well as a political force, Buddhism is far more significant today outside India than in the land of its birth. Its primary political importance in recent decades has been as a refuge for untouchables seeking to escape their inferior status within Hinduism. In 1956, not long before his death, B. R. Ambedkar and thousands of his followers denounced Hinduism and embraced Buddhism as a faith standing for equality and unity.

Summary

India's population is not only the second largest in the world, but it is arguably the most diverse. The difference between rural and urban peoples and the gaps between men and women make India similar to many other countries; but in other ways, the differences among Indian citizens are unique. Caste structures society and the day-to-day contacts among people. Caste has also been the subject of intense political debate since the independence movement. India's constitution sets out the legal and philosophical context for government policies designed to improve the status and well-being of those most disadvantaged by the caste system. We will also see in future chapters that caste is an important basis for political competition.

Caste is intrinsic to Hinduism, the dominant religion or worldview in India. But both caste and Hinduism influence India's other religions, such as Islam and Christianity. The conflict between Hindus and Muslims is a central theme in national Indian politics, and religion has also played a role in regional conflicts, such as those in Punjab, where the Sikhs are the largest religious group, and in Kashmir (see Chapter 5). In recent years, caste and religious conflicts have fused over the issue of low-caste conversions to different religions, especially Christianity but also Islam and Buddhism, and these conversions are an additional source of communal tension.[29]

Cutting across the differences of religion is the diversity of language and, along with it, ethnicity. One of the most difficult hurdles to national unity in

India is the low literacy rate and the absence of any truly national language that is used and understood by a majority of people in every part of the country. As we will see in Chapter 11, language differences also partly account for the organization of the states in India's federal system.

This overwhelming diversity undergirds modern Indian politics and affects almost every political institution and public policy. Yet we must be cautious about prejudging this impact, for two reasons. First, so much diversity suggests that Indian politics must be anarchic, but this is not the case. Systems and structures have been put in place over the last sixty years to accommodate, but also transcend, the differences among Indians, and these also constitute part of the political picture. Second, the traditional cultural divisions among Indians should not blind us to the role of socioeconomic and political changes in altering the boundaries between communities and, in particular, in creating new social groups and political movements. These groups may benefit from or be disadvantaged by both the changes and the government policies that accompany them.

Exploring Further

One of the most engaging introductions to Indian culture is found in "Bollywood" films, which often may be rented from Indian food stores. In recent years, crossover films have become popular in North America. Especially recommended for portrayals of caste and class are Mira Nair's 2001 film *Monsoon Wedding* and the 2008 film *Slumdog Millionaire. The Story of India* (2009), a six-part series produced by PBS and BBC and narrated by Michael Wood, offers a wide-ranging, colorful introduction to India.

Notes

1. For details of India's population, see the Government of India's website *Census of India 2001* at http://censusindia.net. The projection is in Carl Haub and O. P. Sharma, "India's Population Reality: Reconciling Change and Tradition," *Population Bulletin* 61, no. 3 (September 2006), 3, 18.

2. Tim Dyson and Pravin Visaria, "Migration and Urbanization: Retrospect and Prospects," in *Twenty-first Century India: Population, Economy, Human Development, and the Environment*, eds. Tim Dyson, Robert Cassen, and Leela Visaria (Oxford: Oxford University Press, 2004), 108–129.

3. Such assertions are widespread in the Indian media and on the Internet. See, for example, Mitali De, "Illegal Immigration: India's Ticking Time Bomb," *East India Watch*, May 20, 2008, from www.eastindiawatch.blogspot.com, retrieved September 8, 2008.

4. William M. Alexander, "Normal Kerala Within Abnormal India: Reflections on Gender and Sustainability," in *Kerala: The Development Experience*, ed. Govindan Parayil (London: Zed Books, 2000), 139–156.

5. Peter Meyer agrees that the sex ratio likely will continue to fall, but he also notes that female life expectancy exceeded men's by the late twentieth century, thus creating a "mortality paradox." "India's Falling Sex Ratios," *Population and Development Review* 25, no. 2 (1999), 323–343.

6. Haub and Sharma.

7. The sex ratio improvement was noted in the northern state of Haryana from 2004 to 2006. O. P. Sharma and Carl Haub, "Sex Ratio at Birth Begins to Improve in India," *Population Reference Bureau* (2008), retrieved September 8, 2008, from www.prb.org/Articles/2008/indiasexratio.

8. The relative status of a caste may improve over time. See the writings of the Indian social anthropologist M. N. Srinivas, for example, his *Caste in Modern India* (Bombay: Asian Publishing House, 1962).

9. There are many descriptions of caste. For different interpretations, see A. L. Basham, *The Wonder That Was India: A Survey of the Culture of the Indian Sub-Continent Before the Coming of the Muslims* (New York: Grove Press, 1954), chaps. 2, 5; Morton Klass, *Caste: The Emergence of the South Asian Social System* (Philadelphia: ISHI Publishers, 1980); and the works of M. N. Srinivas (see n. 8).

10. There continues to be scholarly debate about events during this early historical period and about the origins of caste. Contrast, for example, the discussions by Basham and Klass (see n. 9); Klaus K. Klostermaier, *Hinduism: A Short History* (Oxford: One World, 2000), chap. 3; and Deepak Lal, *The Hindu Equilibrium, Vol. I: Cultural Stability and Economic Stagnation: India c. 1500 B.C.–A.D. 1980* (Oxford: Clarendon Press, 1988), chaps. 1–3.

11. This is Basham's interpretation, 35. Skin color is still important in India, despite centuries of ethnic intermixing: matrimonial classifieds advertise prospective brides and grooms as "fair," marketing of consumer products relies on lighter-skinned models, and so on.

12. There are numerous websites run by and for Dalits, such as the *International Dalit Solidarity Network*, at www.idsn.org. See also Robert Deliège, *The Untouchables of India*, trans. Nora Scott (Oxford: Berg Publishers, 1999).

13. An important feature of caste that developed through the centuries was proper observance of rituals connected to eating, cleansing, and contacts with people of other *jati*. The physical closeness of urban life often makes it impossible to observe these rituals.

14. For a flavor of the debate between Gandhi and Ambedkar, see M. K. Gandhi, *The Removal of Untouchability*, comp. and ed. Bharatan Kumarappa (Ahmedabad,

Gujarat: Navajivan Publishing House, 1954); and B. R. Ambedkar, *Annihilation of Caste, with a Reply to Mahatma Gandhi* (Jullundur City, Punjab: Bheem Patrika Publications, 1971).

15. For an insider's view of the operation of a university reserved-seat system, see Kancha Ilaiah, "India's Caste/Class Culture: An Andhra Pradesh Perspective," in *Democracy in India: A Hollow Shell*, eds. Arthur Bonner et al. (Washington, D.C.: American University Press, 1994), 49–64.

16. Ashok K. Dutt and M. Margaret Geib, *Atlas of South Asia* (Boulder: Westview Press, 1987), 110ff.

17. The word "Mughal" (or "Moghul") is the Indianized version of Mongol. The founder of the Mughal dynasty was descended from the famous thirteenth-century Mongol, Genghis Khan. The Mughals were not the first Muslim rulers in India; their name is given only to the rule that began with Babur in 1526. Many of North India's architectural wonders date from the period of Mughal rule.

18. Subrata Kumar Mitra, "Desecularising the State: Religion and Politics in India After Independence," *Comparative Studies in Society and History* 33, no. 4 (October 1991), 775.

19. Note that the word *Hinduism* is the name that foreigners used for the people beyond the river Sindhu or Indus, and for this indigenous religion.

20. The name for the priestly caste is sometimes transliterated as "Brahman." I have chosen to use "Brahmin" in order to clarify the distinction between that and the concept of Brahman. See also Diana L. Eck, *Banaras: The City of Light* (New York: Alfred A. Knopf, 1982), 370.

21. For an excellent introduction to the visual and spiritual importance of popular images, see Diana L. Eck, *Darśan: Seeing the Divine Image in India*, 2nd ed. (Chambersburg, Pa.: Anima Books, 1985).

22. The abbreviations B.C.E. (before the common era) and C.E. (common era) are used in this book in preference to B.C. (before Christ) and A.D. (Anno Domini, the year of the Lord), reflecting the recent scholarly effort to avoid emphasizing Christian tradition when a majority of the world's peoples are not Christian. Other calendars, such as the Jewish, Chinese, Japanese, and Islamic, derive from different traditions. Admittedly, the point of distinction is still the life of Jesus.

23. Stanley Wolpert, *India* (Berkeley: University of California Press, 1991), 99.

24. See *Social, Economic and Educational Status of the Muslim Community of India*, Prime Minister's High Level Committee Report, Issued November 2006, retrieved September 15, 2008, from http://minorityaffairs.gov.in/newsite/sachar/sachar_comm.pdf. (The report is popularly known as the Sachar Report after the committee chairman, Rajindar Sachar.) It is interesting to note that although Muslim girls are particularly

disadvantaged by low educational levels, the sex ratio is higher (more equitable) among Muslims than any other religious community in India.

25. In 2008 alone, there were bombings in the southern city of Hyderabad (Andhra Pradesh), the ancient holy city of Varanasi (Banaras, Uttar Pradesh), Ahmedabad (Gujarat), Jaipur (Rajasthan), New Delhi, and a major attack by Muslim gunmen in Mumbai.

26. Enlisted forces have tended to be around 10 percent, and the army officer corps higher. Sikhs, along with Gurkhas, have been the only minority with homogenous regiments. Omar Khalidi, "Ethnic Group Recruitment in the Indian Army: The Contrasting Cases of Sikhs, Muslims, Gurkhas and Others," retrieved September 8, 2008, from www.defenceindia.com/def_common/ethnic_group_recruitment.html.

27. Spoken Punjabi and Hindi are similar, but Punjabi is written in Gurmukhi, the script of the Sikh holy books. Punjab's Hindus, whose mother tongue is Punjabi, write in Urdu or Devanagari script. Thus, religion and written language together contribute to the Hindu-Sikh distinctions in Northwest India.

28. Gandhi came from the west-coast state of Gujarat, where Jain populations are concentrated. See Mohandas K. Gandhi, *Autobiography: The Story of My Experiments with Truth* (New York: Dover Publications, 1983), 18.

29. Dalit conversion has continued into the twenty-first century. In October 2006, mass conversions were held to commemorate the 50th anniversary of Ambedkar's conversion to Buddhism. Justin Huggler, "India's Untouchables Turn to Buddhism in Protest at Discrimination by Hindus," *The Independent*, retrieved October 13, 2006, from http://news.independent.co.uk/world/asia/article1868080.ece. By 2008, at least six states had passed laws restricting conversions of Hindus to Christianity, Islam, or Buddhism. See the analysis in Laura Dudley Jenkins, "Legal Limits on Religious Conversion in India," *Law and Contemporary Problems* 71 (2008): 109–127.

3

China

Population Size and Distribution

More has been written and said about population matters in China than in any other Asian country. In part this reflects the size of the population, currently the largest in the world. But it also reflects strong, sometimes coercive family planning policies and the controversy that has surrounded them.

China's demographic reality has changed, often dramatically, in the past few decades. The total population, in 2009 estimated at approximately 1.35 billion, continues to grow. The growth rate, however, is substantially lower than India's: For China, the rate of natural increase is 0.5 percent, and for India it is 1.6. With almost three times as much territory, China's average population density is much less than India's.[1] This comparison, however, does not take into account the concentration of people in the eastern part of the country, where the population density may be as much as one hundred times greater than in the sparsely populated western and northwestern regions. The eastern region, traditionally called "Inner China," is the site of the origins of Chinese civilization in a settled agricultural economy. In recent decades, the eastern part of the country has also become the home of the largest concentrations of industry.

As in India, much of the thinly populated area consists of mountains or desert that cannot support a large population. This "Outer China" is where most of China's ethnic minorities lived for centuries in relative isolation from the ethnic Chinese, or Han people. Politically, much of this area has been organized into autonomous regions since the 1949 revolution. Figure 3.1 shows the administrative divisions of modern China. As a consequence of this uneven distribution of people and the limited amount of arable land, there is less land

50

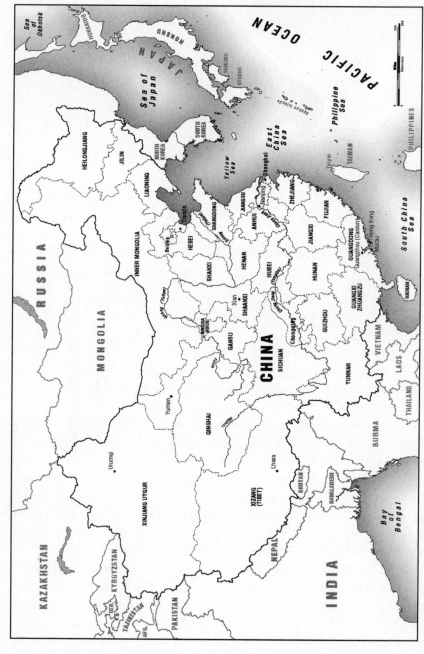

FIGURE 3.1 Map of China. The University of Tennessee Cartographic Services Laboratory; Will Fontanez, cartographer.

PHOTO 3.1 Beijing skyline. Photo courtesy of James W. Boyd.

available for cultivation in China than in either India or Japan.[2] The diversity of climate and topography also means that China, like India, has many different farming systems, family structures, and regional cuisines.

China has been urbanizing more rapidly than India. In the past half century, the proportion of China's urban population has increased from 13 percent to 45 percent, with no indication that the rate of urban growth will slow. For some time, the government controlled internal migration to the cities, for example by restricting registration for permanent urban residents. By the late twentieth century, however, the government had conceded the inevitability of rural-to-urban migration and gradually loosened restrictions.[3] Major urban centers such as Shanghai and Beijing now glitter with skyscrapers and lavish department stores (see Photo 3.1).

Other cities reflect the environmental and aesthetic costs of the push for modernization: They have long been "relentlessly growing, nondescript, drab industrial centers."[4] In all of China's cities, like those elsewhere in Asia, many people struggle with a precarious economic existence.

Urbanization is important for several reasons. First, it represents the government's commitment to socioeconomic modernization and industrialization and all that these efforts entail, including lower fertility rates and higher standards of living. But the obvious improvement in urban and suburban standards of living masks much of the poverty and tradition that continue to dominate the rural areas, where millions of Chinese still live. Thus China, like India, is marked by the gap between urban and rural values and lifestyles.

There is also a long tradition of political rebellion rooted in the cities, a tradition that includes the Tiananmen Square democracy movement of 1989. Not surprisingly, this history reflects the urban concentration of educated middle classes, students, intellectuals, and factory workers, and these are the people who have been at the forefront of demands for political and social change in China and who, more recently, have protested worker layoffs that have accompanied economic restructuring. The potential for civil instability grows when migration from rural areas, along with unemployment, swells the ranks of the dissatisfied. In analyzing the 1989 movement, for example, one scholar noted that economic problems in the countryside were driving hundreds of thousands of young men to the cities, where they had difficulty finding jobs and where their presence made possible the linking of social disorder born of economic dissatisfaction and the students' protest movement.[5] By the turn of the century, reports of worker unrest in numerous Chinese cities had become common.[6] Increasingly, this was accompanied by citizen protests over corruption, environmental issues, and illegal land-grabs (see Chapter 13).

Urban growth, unemployment, and even political instability are all part of the much larger picture of concern with China's population—both its size and its growth rate. From the government's point of view, nearly every policy goal is affected by the numbers of people whose lives are supposed to be improved through modernization. Even so, the government's commitment to birth control since the late 1970s represents a change in Chinese Communist thinking about the advantages and disadvantages of a large population. Because China's population policies have attracted so much attention, the issue warrants discussion.

Population Policies

Policies designed to limit population growth go back several decades in both India and China, but the Chinese policies have generated far more political controversy.[7]

Debates about the significance of the country's population size have also colored Western perceptions of China for at least two centuries.

As early as 1798, Thomas Malthus argued that the size of the Chinese population would make it impossible for the country to feed itself.[8] Although China's population had dropped precipitously in the seventeenth century, it had more than doubled between the 1740s and 1790s, the half century before Malthus wrote his famous book.[9] By the middle of the nineteenth century, the population was well over 400 million, putting additional pressure on increasingly scarce arable land. Some observers thought that the population then grew more slowly or even stagnated during the following century, but the first census taken after the founding of the People's Republic of China counted more than 580 million people in 1953.

This population surge did not raise much official alarm in the 1950s for two reasons. First, the enormous enthusiasm and optimism propelled by the successful revolution led Communist leaders to emphasize the advantages of a large population and to be confident about the ability of the new regime to take care of it.[10] Second, Malthusian thinking was associated with the West and Western assumptions about Chinese inferiority (that is, with orientalist thinking). Mao Zedong, China's revolutionary leader and chairman of the Communist Party, rejected the notion of a demographic curse, saying: "It is a very good thing that China has a big population. Even if China's population multiplies many times, she is fully capable of finding a solution; the solution is production."[11]

Between the founding of the People's Republic and the late 1970s, however, China's population had nearly doubled, largely because of a decline in mortality rates. Moreover, the commitment to development led policy-makers to reassess the costs of rapid population growth for the new modernization strategy. Thus China's leaders reached a consensus on the goal of limiting family size to one child per couple. Over the course of two decades, the policies succeeded in substantially lowering the population growth rate.

The success of China's population policies has not been without political controversy or social cost. The controversy results from the use of coercive methods, especially during the 1980s, to control births. Couples needed permission to have a child, the regularity of women's menstrual periods was routinely checked, couples were verbally harassed and were subject to economic penalties (such as loss of housing or food ration cards) if they did not conform to birth control practices, and abortions were common.[12] It is important to note, however, that there have always been regional and ethnic variations—sometimes as a result of central policy directives, but as often the result of inconsistency in local implementation.[13]

One result of the decline in China's fertility rate (combined with increased life expectancy) has been the aging of the country's population. Nationwide, 7 percent of Chinese people are over age 65. This is a much lower percentage than found in Japan and other industrialized countries but also higher than other developing countries: "If ranked as a separate country, China's elderly population alone would make the seventh largest population in the world."[14] In India, for example, only 4 percent of the population is over 65. Moreover, in urban areas, this percentage tends to be much higher, as high as 13.5 percent in Shanghai. Photo 3.2 shows a senior citizen working to stay fit in Shenzhen. From a government perspective, an aging population signals labor shortages in the future, but in the short term there are issues of providing services for the elderly, many of whom have only one child. China, like other Asian countries, thus confronts more than one demographic dilemma (see Focus Box 3).

The next section, which examines the interrelationships of traditional culture, gender, population, and politics, considers the significance of cultural norms for population policies.

PHOTO 3.2 Senior citizen staying fit in Shenzhen. Photo courtesy of Dr. Ping Dou.

FOCUS BOX 3

DEMOGRAPHIC DILEMMAS

A number of Asian countries are preoccupied with both the sex ratio and also the age structure in their countries. Even in countries with large, young populations (such as China), the growing cohort of elderly people concerns governments.

Sex Ratios

The preference for sons is widespread in South and East Asia; it is deeply imbedded in traditional cultural norms and often reflects rational economic concerns, such as the burden imposed by dowry. In addition to India and China, several other Asian countries have unequal sex ratios that disadvantage girls, including Bangladesh and Pakistan. In Southeast Asia, sex ratios are nearly equal in most countries, but Japan experiences a deficit of males—notably in the upper age brackets (see Table 4.2). So in addition to the question of why fewer girls are born in some countries, one should ask why boys don't live as long in many countries.

India and China have made the deficit of girls a public policy issue. The Republic of Korea (South Korea) has also addressed a distortion in the sex ratio that increased abruptly in the 1980s. Traditionally, family law reinforced Confucian norms of son preference. The 1958 Korean civil code stipulated, for example, that families would be headed by the eldest son and that inheritance was through the male line. In 2005, the Korean Supreme Court abolished this legal basis for male dominance.[1] The sex ratio improved from a high of 116 (males to 100 females) in 1990 to 108:100 in 2005, but Korean men already face a shortage of marriage partners. Some men have sought brides in other countries.

Age Structure

One of the demographic results of economic growth in Western Europe is an aging population. As birth and death rates decline, the total population ages. In 2005, approximately 20 percent of Italy's population was age 65 and older; in Germany it was 19 percent and Sweden 17 percent. In Japan, where the speed of aging of the population has been faster than in the West, it was more than 20 percent but is projected to be 32 percent by 2030.[2]

The Japanese government is not the only Asian government to take note of the aging trend. The Republic of Korea is projected to see more than 23 percent

continues

continued

of its population at age 65 and over by 2030; China's will be about 16 percent. Tiny Singapore also has one of Asia's fastest-aging populations, but its efforts at social engineering to increase both the marriage and the birth rate have failed, as they have in Japan.[3]

1. Sidney B. Westley and Minja Kim Choe, "How Does Son Preference Affect Populations in Asia?" *Asia Pacific Issues*, Analysis No. 84 from the East West Center, September 2007, retrieved June 18, 2008, from www.eastwestcenter .org/fileadmin/stored/pdfs/api084.pdf.

2. Data from the Ministry of Internal Affairs and Communications, Statistics Bureau, *Statistical Handbook of Japan 2007*, chapter 2 ("Population"), retrieved September 12, 2008, from www.stat.go.jp/English/data/handbook.

3. See www.singstat.gov.sg/stats; Seth Mydans, "A Different Kind of Homework for Singapore Students: Get a Date," *New York Times*, April 29, 2008.

Gender

A different social cost resulting from the population policies has been their impact on both the quantitative and the qualitative aspects of gender relations. Traditional Chinese culture—like that of most of Asia—has assigned women to subordinate cultural, social, and political status. Even women from rich families traditionally had few life options. Although they might be literate, for example, they were prohibited from taking the state examination, success in which opened up lucrative and prestigious government careers. By contemporary standards, the most repressive practice was foot binding, in which the toes of young girls were forcibly folded under and bound tightly in order to create the tiny feet that were a symbol of feminine beauty and sexuality.

Most scholars believe that the subordinate position of women resulted from one of two factors or from a combination of these. One was the ordering of society according to Confucian norms. The political norms of Confucianism will be discussed further in Chapter 6, but we can note here that central to the Confucian value system is the belief that the ideal society is hierarchically ordered. The first requirement for good government is social harmony, and harmony, in turn, is realized by individuals performing the roles ascribed to them within the family and in the broader society.

One of the most important role relationships in this traditional social system is that of husband and wife. Although in principle this husband-wife relationship is one of mutual respect and reciprocity, it seems clear that the advocacy of a hierarchical social ordering contributed to the development of unequal relationships, in this case between husbands and wives—and between men and women generally.[15] Indeed, some scholars go further and lay most of the blame for women's secondary status and often miserable lives on Confucian values and practices. Even if these values and practices were not advocated by Confucius or cannot be traced to the classic Confucian texts, they came to be accepted as standard by the Confucianized elite that governed China and over time were fostered and mandated (through government policies and laws) for the rest of society.[16]

The importance of having a male heir in every family illustrates these values. Confucianism cultivated families that were both patrilineal (where descent and kinship operate through the male, or father's, line) and patriarchal. Under patriarchy, men controlled property; fathers had great legal authority over women and children, including the right to choose their daughters' marriage partners, sell their daughters, and dispose of their daughters' labor; and women were seen as morally and intellectually less capable than men.[17] Confucianism emphasized the importance of patrilineal ancestor worship, and without a male descendant, the proper rituals could not be carried out. Adoption of a boy or man, if there was no natural male heir, was thus preferable to having only a daughter.

Confucianism is one reason for the traditional inequality between Chinese men and women. In addition to this, scholars point to women's roles in economic production as historically contributing to their secondary status. To understand this factor, we need to distinguish between reproductive activities and productive activities. Reproductive activities are those that assure the survival and well-being of the family and household. These activities include not only biological reproduction but also socioeconomic tasks such as procuring and preparing food, caring for children and elderly parents, cleaning, and health care. This unpaid work is carried out in the household, or private sphere, and is almost always the responsibility of women. Productive labor or production for exchange (usually paid work in industrialized economies) occurs in the public sphere—in fields, factories, and offices. Until recently, this public sphere was regarded in most societies (including China and India) as a male preserve, even when women were involved in agricultural work, for example.

The concepts of the private-public dichotomy and of productive and reproductive work are important because they are linked to the argument that the greater the involvement of women in the public, nondomestic sphere, the greater their status within their culture and in political matters. Women's status, scholars have argued, is lowest when the domestic and public spheres of activity are strongly differentiated and when women are isolated from each other and placed under the authority of a man in the home.[18]

As a general rule, this public-private distinction and the strong differentiation in male and female spheres of activity characterized not only traditional China but also much of post-1949 Communist society, particularly in the rural areas. In the 1980s, after more than three decades of policies designed to destroy old modes of production and campaigns to emancipate women, in part by drawing them into productive activities, the old structures that had been so oppressive to women persisted. The household and kin group relationships were still in place and, as Elizabeth Croll has argued, continued to "reproduce the subordination of women."[19]

With some understanding of the connection between Confucian norms and the importance of productive and reproductive activities, we can return to the issue of the government's population control policy. There are three elements that link gender and population policy. First, women have assumed a disproportionate burden for implementing government birth control objectives. Second, the combination of government policy, cultural norms, and technology contributes to an imbalance in the sex ratio. Third, the link between gender and population policy, when placed in the context of the government's aggressive commitment to modernization, illustrates in ironic and sometimes tragic ways the unintended consequences of government policy.

The differential burden assumed by women and men in implementing birth planning is seen in the means used to control fertility and prevent births. Using intrauterine devices (IUDs) is the dominant contraceptive method, accounting for 40 to 50 percent of cases. This is followed by female sterilization (15 to 20 percent), with male sterilization (vasectomy) at well under 10 percent. Moreover, it appears that induced abortion continues to play a large role in averting births, although the abortion rate has declined dramatically since the mid-1990s.[20] Nonetheless, the physical and psychological burden of population limitation policies has fallen overwhelmingly on women, as it does in most countries.

It will be recalled from the discussion in the previous chapter that the sex ratio is the proportion of females to males in a population: An equal sex ratio would be 100 females to 100 males. Although India and China report their demographic statistics differently, census reports in both countries show an imbalance in the sex ratio such that the proportion of females is lower than would be expected under normal circumstances of birth and death. China's 2000 census found a nationwide sex ratio of 106.6 males for every 100 females of all age groups, but the gap is much higher in some provinces. More striking, however, is the sex ratio for infants and small children: Nationwide, there are about 120 boys for every 100 girls between the ages of 0 and 4, and in some provinces such as Guangdong, it is about 130 (See Table 3.1). These data suggest that China

TABLE 3.1 Selected Regional Sex Ratios in China for Children Aged 0–4 Years

Province	1982 Census	2000 Census
Jiangxi	106.7	132.6
Guangdong	109.2	129.6
Yunnan	104.2	112.9
Tibet	101.9	101.4
Xinjiang	103.7	105.6
National Total	*107.1*	*120.2*

Source: Adapted from *Major Figures on 2000 Population Census of China* (Beijing: China Statistics Press, 2001); and Yong Cai and William Lavely, "Child Sex Ratios and Their Regional Variation," in *Transition and Challenge: China's Population at the Beginning of the 21st Century*, eds. Zhongwei Zhao and Fei Guo (Oxford: Oxford University Press, 2007), 113.

confronts the same troubling trend as India, a persistent preference for sons. Research has implicated the widespread availability of ultrasound screening as an easy and inexpensive method of prenatal sex determination, along with the selective abortion of female fetuses, for the rising sex ratio gap.[21]

Why should there be such enduring disadvantages attached to being female in China, particularly when Communist Party and state policies have long targeted reform of the status of women? Part of the answer lies in the combination of traditional culture and the division of labor that persists, particularly in rural areas. Part of the answer lies also in the gap between rhetoric, policy, and practice that characterizes reform in any political system. Beyond this, however, is the factor of the unintended consequences of public policy: Policies designed to accomplish one goal produce an unanticipated outcome in another policy area. Evidence suggests that the implementation of the one-child policy reinforced the traditional prejudice against girls. Many couples who could have only one child were determined that it be a son (see Photo 3.3). Even though policies have been loosened to permit a second child if the first is a girl, one study found that nine out of ten female fetuses in second pregnancies were aborted if the first child was a girl.[22]

The accelerated push for population limitation occurred in the context of an equally accelerated push for economic modernization; in fact, the latter provided the justification for the former. In the rural areas, however, the reforms often have had contradictory effects. For example, by the mid-1990s, most government restrictions on labor mobility had been lifted, but the new freedom benefited rural men more than women. As husbands migrated to cities for work, wives were left at home, often under the patriarchal authority of his family, and

PHOTO 3.3 Mother and son, Yunnan Province.
Photo courtesy of Martha A. Denney.

always with increased domestic responsibilities. "As is often the case in post-Mao rural China, the mobility and success of the husband was made possible by the back-breaking labor of the wife back home."[23] Despite the necessity of their labor, cultural norms and the lack of viable alternatives have reinforced women's inferior status.

There have been numerous other effects—both intended and not—of population and economic reform policies. Often, these have disadvantaged girls and women, though not always; and it is clear overall that the status of Chinese women has improved dramatically since 1949. For example, female life expectancy has certainly increased, as has women's access to public life. Particularly in urban areas, women have many more choices of lifestyles and employment. To date, the primary political lessons that pertain to gender in the Chinese experience are two: Gender distinctions cut across all socioeconomic arenas and therefore affect and are affected by state policies in every arena, and the entry to public political power is connected to status and well-being in the private sphere.

Thus, it is not surprising that despite the changes in China's political institutions in the first decade of the twenty-first century, there were still only a handful of women present at the highest levels, and women continued to be absent from the single most important political body, the Politburo of the Chinese Communist Party.

Regions, Religion, and Ethnic Minorities

We have already seen how India is fragmented by innumerable differences of language, caste, and religion. There is also great diversity among China's peoples, but the political implications of ethnic diversity in China and the policies that address the status of minorities are different from those in India. This section describes these minorities in terms of their regional distribution and numbers, then summarizes state policy toward them. Special attention is given to Tibet, a region that has both domestic and international significance.

There are fifty-five government-designated minority nationalities in China. The 2000 census put their numbers at 106.4 million, with the largest groups being the Zhuang, Miao, and Yi in the South, the Hui (Muslim), Uighur (Uyghur), and Tibetan in the West and Northwest, and the Mongolian and Manchu in the North. Because of their location, the minorities have political significance disproportional to their numbers: The largest groups are concentrated in the border regions adjacent to Russia, India, and Vietnam, as well the newer republics of Central Asia. Any instability in these regions thus raises security concerns for the central government. In addition, some minority areas possess rich natural resources, including oil, coal, gold, and other minerals.

In India, the majority group is defined by Hinduism, but Hindus are divided by dozens of languages and dialects, as well as by thousands of *jati*. In China, it is the ethnic Chinese, commonly called the Han people, who constitute a unifying majority of more than 90 percent of the country's population.[24] The distinguishing feature of the Han is that their language belongs to the Sinitic language family, which uses the writing system of Chinese characters. Although they *speak* different Chinese languages and dialects, the Han and most Chinese people have been unified by a common written language and its great literary tradition.

It is primarily language and culture (including customs and religion) that distinguish the Han from other ethnic groups. In most cases, the groups recognized as national minorities by the Chinese government speak their own language, but there are exceptions. The Hui, for example, are part of the Han language group; generally they speak *Putongua*, or the Chinese dialect of the region in which they live, and are Muslim.[25] There are also groups that speak a Sinitic sublanguage or dialect and regard themselves (and have been regarded) historically as a distinct people, but for a variety of reasons, they are not recognized as national minorities by the government.[26] An interesting illustration is the Hakka of southern China. The Hakka have long been viewed as a migratory people; they were central to the Taiping Rebellion in the nineteenth century; Hakka women did not bind their feet; and the Hakka are one of the important groups making up the population of the island of Taiwan.[27]

The recognition of the Han-speaking Muslims as an official minority raises questions about the intertwining of religion, ethnicity, and political status in China. The historical experience of Islam is colored by a legacy of Muslim revolts against Chinese rule and conflicts between Muslims and Chinese. In the mid-nineteenth century, for example, both the southern province of Yunnan and the northwest provinces of Gansu and Shaanxi experienced Muslim rebellion, and since the 1990s, there have been Muslim protests over a variety of government policies.[28]

The Cultural Revolution of the 1960s and 1970s (see Chapters 8 and 10) brought direct suppression of religion in China. Religion was ridiculed as superstitious, places of worship or prayer were closed, religious texts and artworks destroyed. Only after the late 1970s did official policy permit renewed religious activity. The 1982 constitution proclaims "freedom of religious belief" (Article 36):

> No state organ, public organization or individual may compel citizens to believe in, or not to believe in, any religion. . . . The state protects normal religious activities. No one may make use of religion to engage in activities that disrupt public order, impair the health of citizens or interfere with the educational system of the state. Religious bodies and religious affairs are not subject to any foreign domination.

In general, religion has not presented the political problems in China that it has in India. However, there are exceptions, notably in cases where religious groups attempt to expand their influence against the interests of the state. Two examples illustrate this point. The first involves transnational Islamic movements and Muslims who, even if not devout, see themselves as different from the Han. The second involves a group that is viewed as religious by some, but has been defined as a "cult" by the Chinese government, namely the Falun Gong.

The growth of Muslim national identity, especially in Western China, has produced political tension. Throughout the centuries, Islamic migrations and religious movements, particularly those coming from Central and West Asia, have influenced the cultures of China's Muslim populations. The dissolution of the

Soviet Union in 1991 and the creation of independent, nominally Muslim states in Central Asia during the 1990s stimulated a new wave of intra-Asian movement. The period of the new Islamic consciousness in Central Asia corresponded with changes in China's policies toward national minorities, changes that initially provided opportunities for expressions of cultural identity and organization. The new openness in policy toward both religion and ethnic minorities, coupled with transnational Islamic movements (including the movement of money), generated a new tide of influence on Chinese Muslims.

Beijing's primary concern, not surprisingly, is the growth of Islamic fundamentalism and the potential for separatist movements. The Uighurs, the Turkic-speaking Muslim population in Xinjiang Province, are viewed with particular concern because they have openly protested Chinese policies on a number of occasions, and have also spawned a small secessionist movement.[29] After the September 2001 terrorist attacks on the United States, government monitoring of the Uighurs increased. The region is geographically sensitive because it borders on Pakistan, as well as three of the post-Soviet Central Asian republics: Tajikistan, Kyrgyzstan, and Kazakhstan. The government restricts the teaching of Arabic to special government schools, limits fasting during Ramadan, and has confiscated passports throughout the province in order to control Hajj pilgrimages. In 2008, restrictions on the practice of Islam and the movement of Muslims were further tightened in response to several attacks on security officers.[30]

The case of the Falun Gong is the second example of the way in which religion becomes contentious in China. A study of the Falun Gong also illustrates the problem of definition and how our understanding of politics is influenced by the lenses we use. The Falun Gong movement shot into world headlines in 1999, when approximately 10,000 of its followers undertook a peaceful protest in Beijing. Since 1999, the Chinese government has vilified the movement, claiming it is an "evil cult," and has systematically tried to stamp it out through arrests and persecution of known practitioners.

Many Westerners, including much of the media, as well as religious and human rights groups, consider the Falun Gong a religion, and they charge that the government's repression is an attack on religious freedom. Adherents say that Falun Gong, which literally means "Dharma wheel practice" and is characterized by exercises and meditation, is a health and spiritual practice linked to traditional Chinese *qigong*. The Falun Gong has generated wide publicity through its websites, handouts, and signs from East Asia, through North America to Europe (see Photo 3.4). From the government's position, however, this "cult" threatens society in much the same way as Aum Shinrikyo presented a threat to Japan in the mid-1990s (see Chapter 4). The government's primary concern has been the

PHOTO 3.4 Falun Gong (Falun Dafa) banner, Japan. Photo courtesy of James W. Boyd.

effectiveness of Falun Gong's organization: "The Communist Party has enough historical memory to know an effective organization when it sees one," and clearly sees that organization, whatever the content of its ideology, as a threat.[31]

Both of these movements show the way in which transnational linkages have come to affect domestic notions of nationality and state security. Beijing's shifting policies toward minority populations reveal the larger dilemma of devising policies that, on the one hand, respond to the different cultures and standards of living that exist among the Han and the minorities and, on the other hand, reflect China's long-standing concerns for security and the need to assure central control over the entire country. The concern with security is itself a reflection of the fact that the Chinese multiethnic state was formed by the territorial expansion of the largest ethnic group, the Han, much as the former Soviet Union was dominated by the Russians. The commitment to centralized control is also consistent with the historical conviction among Han leaders about the superiority of their culture over that of "barbarian" outliers.[32]

By the early twenty-first century, the long-term goal of assimilation of the national minorities could claim notable successes, in large part through the force of economic modernization and its corrosive impact on traditional values and customs. At the same time, the breakup of the Soviet Union and the resurgence of ethnic identity in Central Asia, coupled with a revival of religion in many minority areas, suggested that the role of ethnic minorities in China, if not as contested as in India, would remain a central issue on the government's agenda. Within this broader picture, the case of Tibet illustrates many of the dilemmas still facing China.

Tibet

Tibet is the best known of China's minority areas to outsiders, both because of the PRC's repression of the 1959 Tibetan rebellion and because of the widespread recognition of and admiration for Tibet's traditional spiritual and political leader, the Fourteenth Dalai Lama ("Spiritual Master"). Tibet also demonstrates the difficulty of ensuring cultural integrity for an ethnic minority while guaranteeing national integration and border security in an age of globalization.

The history of Tibet is the history of the intermingling of Asian traditions. Known as one of the most inaccessible lands in the world, Tibet was populated originally by nomadic tribes, whose descendants are still found in the region. Although regular contact with surrounding cultures dates from the seventh century, earlier than that there had been intermittent contact along trade routes that linked China, India, and, further to the west, Persia.

Central to the Tibetan cultural identity is Buddhism, which entered from India in the form that we now know as Mahayana (the "Great Vehicle") Buddhism. By the twelfth century, when Buddhism had disappeared from most of South and Central Asia under Muslim pressure, it flourished in Tibet, with temples, monasteries, elaborate works of art, and an extensive set of sacred books (see Photo 3.5, Potola Palace, in Lhasa). "The Tibetans became in effect the inheritors of the whole Indian Buddhist tradition,"[33] which they then developed in the unique ways that would distinguish the Tibetan culture from that of its Asian neighbors.

Chinese military intervention in the politics of Tibet began in the early eighteenth century when the emperor of the Qing dynasty sought to unify China under Manchu rule. At the height of its power, the dynasty had incorporated areas in eastern Tibet but had never imposed Chinese administrative forms on them. As the dynasty declined, so did its ability to control these areas. By the end of the Qing period in the early twentieth century, a combination of local Tibetan rulers and British maneuvering from North India had reestablished a large measure of Tibetan autonomy.[34] But the Qing dynasty never relinquished its nominal control over the area, thus establishing the basis for the claim made by both the Nationalist and Communist governments that Tibet has always been part of China.

When Chinese Communist armies completed their conquest of Nationalist territory in 1949, the only areas not under their control were Tibet and Taiwan.

PHOTO 3.5 Potola Palace, Lhasa, Tibet. Photo courtesy of James W. Boyd.

The new government repeatedly stated its claim to both areas; in October 1950, Chinese troops entered Tibet, and in 1951, the Lhasa government signed an agreement that proclaimed Tibet an integral part of China but left the region with considerable local autonomy.

Tibet's shifting political status during the first years of the People's Republic was complicated by the early phases of the Cold War and U.S. hostility toward the new government in Beijing, as well as by the outbreak of the Korean War in 1950. Both the Indian and the American governments supported Tibetan resistance against the Chinese, contributing to the mutual suspicion among China, India, and the U.S.[35] External involvement also reinforced Communist China's preoccupation with the security of its territory and government.

Beijing's policy toward Tibet in the 1950s was conciliatory: It emphasized social and economic development, including medical facilities, road building, and the introduction of modern communications. Religion and the Dalai Lama's role as supreme spiritual ruler were left intact. But cultural misunderstandings and mutual distrust increased in proportion to the Chinese presence and the introduction of technological changes. Tibetan resistance grew, particularly after 1955.[36]

In March 1959, protests against the Chinese broke into armed rebellion in Lhasa and the surrounding regions. The Chinese responded with military force, crushing the rebellion and declaring martial law throughout the Tibetan Autonomous Region. Beijing eliminated the surviving remnants of Tibetan autonomy and restructured the administration of the region in order to consolidate its control. The Dalai Lama fled to India, where he was given sanctuary in Dharamsala, Himalchal Pradesh, and where a Tibetan "government-in-exile" was established.

In a portrait of his life and his country, the Dalai Lama, Tenzin Gyatso, stated: "Recently China has begun to take interest in the details of Tibetan history. This is good. Not a single *Tibetan* record states that Tibet has, at any time, been a part of China." [emphasis mine][37] But from Beijing's point of view, Tibetan independence is unthinkable because it would mean breaking up the Chinese state. Therefore, in recent years, talk of compromise has focused on the return of the Dalai Lama and the granting of additional autonomy to Tibet. As the years dragged on, however, the stalemate persisted between the central government and those calling for Tibetan autonomy within the PRC (the Dalai Lama's position). Tensions between Han migrants and ethnic Tibetans continued, and in 2008 and 2009, outbreaks of rioting and attacks on Han Chinese in Lhasa provoked government crackdowns throughout the region.

Compromise along the lines envisaged by the Dalai Lama seems unlikely. Born in 1935, and facing health problems, the Dalai Lama may well see his voice for a "middle way" wane. The Chinese government can afford to wait for his death, and Tibetans outside China—both in India and in the worldwide diaspora—are deeply divided over a strategy for the future.[38] Meanwhile, a rail line linking Lhasa to China's existing rail system began operating in 2006, further undermining Tibet's historic isolation.

Summary

Despite the obvious differences between China and India, there are some important similarities that stand out as we explore their respective political systems. Regional differences are significant, notwithstanding the history of centralization in prerevolutionary and postrevolutionary China. China, like India, has found that economic development has not erased, but has exacerbated, many of these differences. The diversity of peoples living in China and India represents a political challenge for both states as they define the policies and political structures for accommodating or assimilating their minority populations. Both have experimented with preferential policies, for example in higher education admissions, as part of a broader policy of addressing social and economic inequality. An equally obvious and critical difference between the two countries lies in the magnitude of religious and ethnic issues and the way these compete with other political questions on the government agendas. The size and relative cultural dominance of the Han majority in China guarantee that questions of national minorities will normally be subordinated to larger issues.

The special case of Tibet illustrates the convergence of some of our introductory themes. We cannot appreciate the history of Tibetans without recognizing that their homeland has been molded by the confluence of indigenous, intra-Asian, and non-Asian cultural and political forces. The Dalai Lama is powerful both because of his spiritual leadership and because he embodies for many the memory of, and hope for, a Tibetan nation-state. The Tibetan diaspora, as well as hundreds of Tibetan Internet sites—both strengthened by globalization—will help keep his message alive even as the reality of Chinese nationalism undermines regional cultural distinctiveness.

The discussion of China's population here includes an analysis of the role that population policies play in Chinese politics. Like many other policies, those dealing with fertility have gone through different phases that reflect both ideological shifts and changes in state development priorities. The fact that the one-child policy became controversial in the 1980s and 1990s says as much about the lenses that Westerners use to scrutinize Chinese politics as it does about the reception of those policies internally. Increasingly, government preoccupation with the *size* of the country's population has been matched by concerns over the sex ratio and care for the elderly.

Finally, it is clear that an important characteristic shared by China and India is the subordinate place assigned to women. The realization that the philosophical and cultural values of the two countries are so obviously different leads us to ask why there are nonetheless similarities in gender roles. One hypothesis points to the importance of productive and reproductive roles. Whether these roles create cultural norms or primarily reflect them is still debated by scholars. Whatever the case, it is critical for our study of China and India to understand that as a result of all of these factors, politics is predominantly a male vocation.

Exploring Further

Many of Zhang Yimou's earlier films portray traditional gender norms in China, and his 1999 film, *Not One Less*, illustrates urban/rural differences in modern China. Among the many documentaries on China, a National Geographic film, *China Beyond the Clouds* (1994), is recommended for its portrayal of the early impact of modernization in Lijiang, Yunnan Province, and its implications for the Yi ethnic minority.

Notes

1. Statistics are from China's 2000 census, found in *Major Figures on 2000 Population Census of China* (Beijing: China Statistics Press, 2001); and Population Reference Bureau, *2008 World Population Data Sheet*, retrieved from www.prb.org, September 12, 2008.

2. The Worldwatch Institute estimates China's arable land at 13 percent of its territory. Put differently, with approximately 22 percent of the world's population, China has 7 percent of the arable land. Yingling Liu, "Shrinking Arable Lands Jeopardizing China's Food Security," April 18, 2006, accessed December 7, 2008, at www.worldwatch.org/node/3912.

3. Zai Liang, "Internal Migration: Policy Changes, Recent Trends and New Challenges," in *Transition and Challenge: China's Population at the Beginning of the 21st Century*, eds. Zhongwei Zhao and Fei Guo (Oxford: Oxford University Press, 2007), 197–215.

4. Lucian W. Pye, *China: An Introduction*, 4th ed. (New York: HarperCollins, 1991), 19.

5. Frederic E. Wakeman Jr., "The June Fourth Movement in China," *Items* (Social Science Research Council) 43, no. 3 (September 1989), 57–58.

6. Yongshun Cai, "The Resistance of Chinese Laid-Off Workers in the Reform Period," *China Quarterly*, no. 70 (June 2002), 327–344. See also the useful overview by Thomas Lum of the Congressional Research Service, "Social Unrest in China," May 8, 2006, accessed December 8, 2008, at http://www.fas.org/sgp/crs/row/RL33416.pdf.

7. The most controversial period in the history of India's population policy was the Emergency (1975–1977), when the government of Indira Gandhi pursued an aggressive program that included forced sterilization. Opposition to the program helped defeat her government in the 1977 elections.

8. Thomas Malthus's *An Essay on the Principle of Population* was first published in 1798. See his discussion of China in the 1803 edition, ed. Patricia James, for the Royal Economic Society (reprint, Cambridge: Cambridge University Press, 1989, vol. 1, 121–133). Malthus emphasized the role of infanticide in checking population (126, 129–130).

9. Jonathan D. Spence, *The Search for Modern China* (New York: W. W. Norton, 1990), 93–95.

10. H. Yuan Tien, *China's Strategic Demographic Initiative* (New York: Praeger, 1991), 20, 81–82.

11. Mao Tse-tung (Mao Zedong), *On the U.S. White Paper* (Peking: Foreign Languages Press, 1967), 34–35.

12. Tien's work discusses the specific mechanisms of the one-child policy during the 1980s.

13. Weiguo Zhang and Xingshan Cao, "Family Planning During the Economic Reform Era," in Zhao and Guo, *Transition and Challenge*, 18–33; and Wei Chen, "Induced Abortion and Its Demographic Consequences," in Zhao and Guo, *Transition and Challenge*, 87–107.

14. Feng Wang and Andrew Mason, "Population Ageing: Challenges, Opportunities, and Institutions," in Zhao and Guo, *Transition and Challenge*, 177.

15. Wei-ming Tu, *Confucian Thought: Selfhood as Creative Transformation* (Albany: State University of New York Press, 1985), 141–145.

16. Patricia Ebrey, "The Chinese Family and the Spread of Confucian Values," in *The East Asian Region: Confucian Heritage and Its Modern Adaptation*, ed. Gilbert Rozman (Princeton: Princeton University Press, 1991), 50–52; Tu, 144–145; Judith Stacey, *Patriarchy and Socialist Revolution in China* (Berkeley: University of California Press, 1983), chap. 2.

17. Ebrey, 48–49.

18. Michelle Zimbalist Rosaldo, "Woman, Culture, and Society: A Theoretical Overview," in *Woman, Culture, and Society*, eds. Rosaldo Lamphere and Louise Lamphere (Stanford: Stanford University Press, 1974), 36.

19. Elizabeth Croll, *Women and Rural Development in China* (Geneva: International Labour Office, 1985), 65.

20. Weiguo Zhang, "Implementation of State Family Planning Programmes in a Northern Chinese Village," *China Quarterly* 157 (March 1999), 202–230; Yanzhong Huang and Dali L. Yang, "Bureaucratic Capacity and State-Society Relations in China," *Journal of Chinese Political Science* 7, nos. 1 and 2 (2002), 19–46. The highest world abortion ratios (number of abortions divided by number of births) during the mid-1990s were in Eastern Europe, Cuba, and (in Asia) China and Vietnam. Wei, 92.

21. Chu Junhong, "Prenatal Sex Determination and Sex-Selective Abortion in Rural Central China," *Population and Development Review* 27, no. 2 (June 2001), 259–281. As early as 1989, the Chinese Ministry of Public Health acknowledged that sex-selective abortion was a problem and called on medical personnel to stop checking the sex of unborn babies. "Stop Sex Checks of Fetuses," *Beijing Review* 32, no. 28 (July 10–16, 1989), 12–13.

22. The study also found that couples will continue to abort female fetuses until they have the desired son. Chu, 260.

23. Paul G. Pickowicz and Liping Wang, "Village Voices, Urban Activists: Women, Violence, and Gender Inequality in Rural China," in *Popular China: Unofficial Culture in a Globalizing Society*, eds. Perry Link, Richard P. Madsen, and Paul G. Pickowicz (Lanham, Md.: Rowman and Littlefield, 2002), 68.

24. The name Han derives from the Han dynasty (206 B.C.E.–222 C.E.), the period when Chinese imperial rule was consolidated and the territory of the Chinese state was expanded. Confucianism became the state ideology during this period.

25. The Hui presence throughout China is a good example of the intermingling of Asian traditions and thought systems. See the detailed study by Dru C. Gladney, *Muslim Chinese: Ethnic Nationalism in the People's Republic* (Cambridge, Mass.: Harvard University Press, Council on East Asian Studies, 1996). The Hui are one of the ten recognized Muslim national minorities but constitute almost half of Chinese Muslims. Hui has become a catchall category for Muslims not designated as members of one of the other nine groups.

26. On the problem of defining ethnic or "national" minorities in China, see Thomas Heberer, *China and Its National Minorities: Autonomy or Assimilation?* (Armonk, N.Y.: M. E. Sharpe, 1989), chapter 1.

27. Leo J. Moser, *The Chinese Mosaic: The Peoples and Provinces of China* (Boulder: Westview Press, 1985), chapter 15. The Taiping Rebellion (1850–1864) took its name from Taiping Tianguo ("heavenly kingdom of great peace"), a movement that organized economically distressed peasants against the Qing (Manchu) dynasty.

28. Spence, 189–193; and Caroline Blunden and Mark Elvin, *Cultural Atlas of China* (New York: Facts on File, 1983), 40–41.

29. In September 2002, the United States reversed its earlier position and agreed with China that the East Turkestan Islamic Movement should be added to the list of international terrorist movements. Critics of the American policy charged that the U.S. had legitimized Beijing's repression of justifiable protests against Chinese policies.

30. Edward Wong, "Wary of Islam, China Tightens A Vise of Rules," *New York Times*, October 19, 2008.

31. Richard Madsen, "Understanding Falun Gong," *Current History* 99, no. 638 (September 2000), 246. For an overview of the Falun Gong's position, see www.falundafa .org. A helpful summary of the Chinese government's position may be found at "Three Issues Regarding Falun Gong," posted February 21, 2008, at www.chinaembassy.or.th/ eng/ztbd/tj/t408938.htm (Chinese Embassy in Thailand), accessed December 11, 2008.

32. Heberer, 17–18.

33. David Snellgrove and Hugh Richardson, *A Cultural History of Tibet* (Boston: Shambhala, 1986), 72. Today the small country of Bhutan claims to have the remaining authentic heritage of "Tibetan Buddhism" (see Focus Box 13).

34. The British sought to use Tibet as a buffer state between the tsarist Russian Empire and the British Empire in India. Seen from this perspective, Tibet's political history in the late nineteenth to early twentieth centuries was deeply influenced by competing imperial claims among Russia, China, and Britain. See the map entitled "Competing Imperialisms in Eurasia" in Blunden and Elvin, 34–35.

35. India, like Britain before it, was interested in seeing Tibet become a buffer state. But India was one of the first states to recognize the new PRC government in 1949 (and hence, Chinese claims to Tibet).

36. For the period of the 1950s, see Melvyn C. Goldstein, *A History of Modern Tibet*, vol. 2: *The Calm Before the Storm, 1951–1955* (Berkeley: University of California Press, 2007).

37. Dalai Lama of Tibet, with Galen Rowell, *My Tibet* (Berkeley: University of California Press, for Mountain Light Press, 1990), 15.

38. Denis Burke, "The Tibetan Democratic Experiment," *Asia Times*, September 13, 2008, accessed September 13, 2008, at http://www.atimes.com/atimes/China/JI13Ad01.html.

4

Japan

Population Size and Distribution

In contrast to India and China, where the majority of people still live in rural areas, Japan is overwhelmingly urban. As Table 4.1 shows, nearly 80 percent of Japanese citizens live in areas designated as urban, in contrast to 45 percent in China and 28 percent in India.

Japan has a long history of urban centers, but migration to the cities during the twentieth century permanently transformed the nation. As recently as one century ago, Japan was still an agricultural nation whose population was distributed relatively equally across the country. Today, the great population concentrations of Japan lie in the southeastern plains called Kanto (to the east, the greater Tokyo metropolitan area) and Kansai (to the west, centering on the Osaka, Kyoto, and Kobe areas) (see Figure 4.1). The train trip between the two regions is a good introduction both to Japan's population distribution and to the country's

TABLE 4.1 Population Size and Distribution in Japan, China, and India, 2008
Estimate

	Estimated Population (in millions)	Percent Urban	Population Density (per km²)
Japan	127.7	79	343
India	1,149.3	28	350
China	1,324.7	45	139

Source: Adapted from Population Reference Bureau, "2008 World Population Data Sheet," www.prb.org.

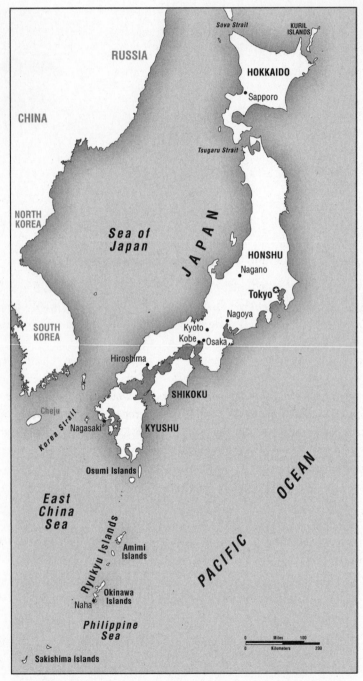

FIGURE 4.1 Map of Japan. The University of Tennessee Carto-graphic Services Laboratory; Will Fontanez, cartographer.

PHOTO 4.1 Mount Fuji. Photo courtesy of James W. Boyd.

topography. At both ends of the trip, cities stretch almost endlessly. In between, one glimpses a few small farms and forests, as well as suburban homes and gardens. The train passes Mt. Fuji to the north, and the coastline of the Pacific Ocean to the south—a reminder of the dominance of sea and mountains in Japan's topography and culture (see Photo 4.1).

Japan is, in fact, a mountainous archipelago with a total land mass of about the same size as the state of Montana. As Table 4.1 shows, the population density is higher than in China; it is comparable to India's and even higher than the average density figure of 343 per square kilometer (0.386 square mile) suggests. More than two-thirds of Japan consists of mountainous terrain, and the population density per unit area under cultivation is the highest in the world. Forty-five percent of the population is concentrated in three urban conglomerations (Tokyo, Osaka, and Nagoya), on six percent of the nation's land mass.[1]

The size and distribution of the Japanese population raise several issues central to the discussions in this book pertaining to demographic changes, development policies, and the linkage between domestic and foreign policies. To begin with, Japan is arguably overpopulated. If we do not hear as much about overpopulation in Japan as in China and India, we may assume that it is due to the country's wealth. But this prosperity is relatively recent and, from a Japanese perspective, rests on a potentially fragile base. The physical vulnerability of the country to earthquakes, tidal waves, typhoons, and volcanic activity is well known. Likewise, the country's limited agricultural base and heavy dependence on imported resources contribute to real and perceived economic vulnerability.

It stands to reason that political leaders must be aware of this vulnerability as they formulate and implement domestic and foreign policies. In order to counteract Japan's increasing reliance on imports, the government began developing nuclear energy in the 1960s. By the twenty-first century, 52 nuclear power units provided about 11 percent of Japan's total energy supply.[2]

This sense of vulnerability, when combined with an understanding of the Liberal Democratic Party's (LDP) traditional political base in rural areas, helps explain the long tradition of government policies of import protection in trade, including restrictions on food imports such as rice. Trade protection and price supports were originally part of the post–World War II agricultural and land reforms designed to modernize farming and increase food production, as well as to foster rural support for democracy. These policies contributed to the creation of a relatively affluent farming population that supported the LDP, which dominated Japanese politics into the twenty-first century.

An Aging Population

The age structure is another aspect of the Japanese population that, like urbanization, is gradually altering the political scene. Japan is not the only Asian country concerned about its aging population (see Focus Box 3), but it is a special case. By 2020, almost 30 percent of the population will be over the age of 65, and the Japanese population will begin to shrink (see Table 4.2). Japan will have the highest old-age dependency ratio of any major industrialized country.[3] This trend reflects a number of demographic changes that reinforce each other: increased longevity, late marriage, low birth rates, and low immigration rates. The increase in average life expectancy is tangible evidence of the improved standard of living of the average Japanese during the past half century. Until the mid-1940s, life expectancy at birth for both men and women was less than fifty years. By 2008, it was eighty-six years for women and seventy-nine years for men.

In the early 1980s, government policy began to shift in order to accommodate the increasing public service burden of a large nonworking population. In 1982, for example, existing provisions for a national system of free health care for the elderly were replaced by a requirement that made elderly persons subject to copayments for medical services. A 1986 amendment further increased the

TABLE 4.2 Population Trends in Japan

	Total Population (1,000)	% 65 and over	% Average Annual Rate Increase	Life Expectancy at Birth		Population Density (per km²)
				Male	Female	
1950	84,115,000	4.9	1.58	60	63	226
1970	104,665,000	7.1	1.08	69	75	281
1990	123,611,000	12.0	0.42	76	82	332
2007	127,771,000	21.5	0.00	79	86	343
Projected 2020	122,735,000	29.2	-0.35	n/a	n/a	329

Source: Adapted from Ministry of Internal Affairs and Communication, *Statistics Bureau, Statistical Handbook of Japan 2008*, http://www.stat.go.jp/english/data/handbook, Chapter 2.

share of costs the elderly and their insurers (rather than the government) would bear for their health care. Even so, by the early 1990s, more than 25 percent of national health care expenditure was devoted to care of the elderly.[4] Soon the government began exploring measures that directly addressed gender roles, for example, by encouraging men to take paternity leave.

The change in the age structure has had other consequences, including a shortage of workers in some areas and an increasing proportion of women in the population as a whole and specifically in the workforce. In the 1950s, for example, rapid economic growth stimulated the exodus of people from rural areas to the cities. The decline of the rural population has led to chronic farm labor shortages, an aging rural labor force, more part-time agricultural workers, and greater numbers of women in farm work—all of this leading to concerns about the impact on Japan's food security.[5]

The combination of labor demands and economic prosperity have made Japan a magnet for immigrants, both legal and illegal, since the 1980s. The largest number of foreign workers came from other Asian countries, notably South Korea, China, and the Philippines. By the late 1990s, an estimated 300,000 foreign workers were illegal immigrants.[6] It was almost a decade later, however, before serious debate began about the desirability of altering traditional Japanese hostility to immigration.[7]

In the mid-1990s and again a dozen years later, recession altered Japan's employment picture. Companies were slower to hire and hired fewer employees. Job competition among college graduates increased, and women, in particular, found it difficult to advance in the workplace despite policy changes in the 1980s and

1990s designed to assure equal opportunity. Some of the reasons for the particular disadvantages women faced are found in many countries; others are unique to Japan.

Gender

As we have seen, the status of Indian and Chinese women has historically been subordinate to that of men in both public and private affairs. The same is true of Japan, although for historical reasons, there are important differences in the evolution of gender relations. Japan's history is marked by extensive borrowing of foreign values and practices at critical junctures. The combination of adopting from abroad and adapting to indigenous conditions has influenced gender patterns, as it has many other areas of Japanese society. Literature, which scholars have used to highlight the impressive cultural achievements of court women in Heian Japan (ca. 794–1185), provides apt early historical examples, the most famous of which is the early-eleventh-century novel *The Tale of Genji*, by Murasaki Shikibu. The status of women changed, however, as the conservative influence of Chinese Confucianism, combined with the government's preoccupation with political and social stability, set the prevailing norms for royalty and commoner alike. The late feudal era, called the Tokugawa, or Edo, period (1600–1868), in particular, was characterized by policies designed to reinforce stability and hierarchy through the application of Confucian norms. Ideal feminine behavior meant obedience and service to men—to father, husband, or son, depending on the woman's stage in life.

From the Tokugawa period through World War II, women were dependents of their male household heads and, by both law and custom, were completely subordinate to them. Even though the Meiji period, beginning in the 1860s, marked a dramatic opening to Western political, social, and cultural influences, there was little in these influences that would overturn earlier patterns, in part because gender segregation, the exclusion of women from public activities, and legal discrimination against women were all characteristic of Western societies themselves in the late nineteenth century. Lower-class women did work outside the home in Japanese fields and factories, but this work was considered an extension of their household positions. When they performed wage labor in mills and manufacturing plants, their wages were less than one-half those of men, and their status was exceedingly low.[8]

Postwar reforms instituted during the American occupation changed conditions for Japanese women. Their new legal status, at least, was comparable to that enjoyed by Western European and North American women in the 1940s. The 1947 constitution affirmed:

All of the people are equal under the law and there shall be no discrimination in political, economic or social relations because of race, creed, sex, social status or family origin. (Article 14)

Marriage shall be based only on the mutual consent of both sexes and it shall be maintained through mutual co-operation with the equal rights of husband and wife as a basis.

With regard to choice of spouse, property rights, inheritance, choice of domicile, divorce and other matters pertaining to marriage and the family, laws shall be enacted from the standpoint of individual dignity and the essential equality of the sexes. (Article 24)

The combination of postwar reform, demographic changes, and the transformation of the Japanese economy brought a freedom to women that would have been unimaginable in earlier decades. But it did not eliminate the traditional cultural assumptions of inequality or revolutionize either politics or public policy. The following discussion examines the degree of change in gender relations by focusing on four factors that help explain the paradoxes in women's status and the ambivalence that many Japanese women feel about changes in gender relations.[9] The four factors are traditional norms, legal precepts, demographic changes, and economic growth.

Formal legal and constitutional norms based on the ideology of democratic equality are important benchmarks of change. But they often conflict with traditional values that emphasize social harmony and hierarchical relations, both in the home and in the workplace. Susan J. Pharr's concept of "status politics" illuminates this tension and its implications for political behavior. In her analysis of the "tea pourers' revolt" of 1963, Pharr showed the persistence of women's secondary status in the workplace and the way in which cultural norms reinforce that status. The tea pourers, employees of the Kyoto municipal bureaucracy, protested job requirements that included custodial duties such as cleaning desktops and pouring tea for male office workers. Symbolically, the most flagrant challenge to the established cultural and bureaucratic order was the refusal of a small group of female civil servants to pour and carry cups of tea to the male employees of their section.[10]

Pharr analyzed the tension that existed in the municipal office and that persists almost a half century later: the tension between the official ideology, which forbids discrimination on the basis of sex, and social norms that determine female work roles and opportunities. "As a ritual engaged in primarily by women, the serving of tea is a potent symbolic act expressing the asymmetry of the sexes. By pouring tea for men, women express their deference and inferiority to them."[11] As much as Japan has changed since Pharr's study, the asymmetrical patterns she described are still clearly visible in many places of work.

The contradictions between official and traditional ideologies continue to affect women's roles in the Japanese workplace, even as the number of women working outside the home has changed dramatically. Fueling the movement of women from households and farms have been several complementary factors: high economic growth from the 1950s to the 1980s in the industrial and service (secondary and tertiary) sectors; changes in consumption patterns and the improvement in household living standards; and demographic changes, such as fewer births and deaths and the longer life spans noted in the previous section. Most directly affected by the demographic changes have been women's life cycles. For example, before World War II, the child-rearing period from the birth of the first child to the youngest child's entrance into primary school was 19.0 years. By the 1980s, the child-rearing period had dropped to less than nine years—reflecting, of course, the decreasing number of children. Even with late marriage and childbearing, many women have forty to fifty years of living after their children enter school, and increasing numbers of women have delayed marriage or chosen not to marry.[12]

Since the 1990s, the Japanese have constructed an elaborate bureaucratic machinery to promote gender equality, partly in response to international and domestic political pressures, and also in recognition that gender equality is linked to the declining birth rate. Despite government policies, Japan still ranks much lower than other industrialized countries on measures of equality and women's empowerment. The United Nations Development Program, for example, compiles a Gender Empowerment Measurement (GEM) that assesses gender equality by the proportion of seats held in parliament by women, the proportion of female professional and technical workers, and the ratio of estimated female to male income. In 2008, Japan ranked a very sorry fifty-four out of more than ninety countries in the data base.[13]

Minority Populations

Minorities in Japan are not only immigrants, as suggested earlier, but indigenous peoples. This section examines both types of minority groups, focusing first on the indigenous Ainu and Burakumin and then on Koreans, who are historically an immigrant population.

The Ainu are the indigenous people of the northern island of Hokkaido. Their history is that of a people and culture confronting rapid erosion over the past 150 years. During much of the Edo, or Tokugawa, period, Ainu peoples were more widely spread through northeastern Asia, ranging across the northern part of Honshu, the southern Kuril Islands, the lower reaches of the Amur River, and southern Kamchatka. The Ainu population in the early nineteenth century was about 24,000 but had dropped to less than 19,000 by midcentury.[14]

The Japanese treated the Ainu as aliens. As their population declined and the base of their traditional lifestyle in hunting, fishing, and gathering disappeared, the Ainu absorbed more and more Japanese cultural characteristics. By the early twentieth century, Ainu-Japanese marriages began to increase, ultimately eliminating a large, culturally distinctive Ainu population. Today, for example, the Ainu language is no longer in daily use.[15] Despite signs of a cultural renaissance and efforts to organize politically in defense of Ainu interests, the Ainu have a contemporary status similar to that of indigenous populations elsewhere whose traditional lifestyle has been destroyed or reduced to a curious reminder of the past for the majority, assimilating population.[16] The dancer at a reconstructed Ainu village in Shiraoi, Hokkaido, illustrates this cultural residue (see Photo 4.2).

In contrast to the plight of the Ainu, issues pertaining to Japan's largest minority populations, the Burakumin and the Koreans, today generate more political

PHOTO 4.2 Ainu dancer, Hokkaido. Photo courtesy of James W. Boyd.

concern. The history, status, and problems of the Burakumin resemble those of the former untouchables in India, with whom they have been compared. Unlike the Burakumin, who are indigenous to Japan, the Koreans are immigrants whose presence in Japan and status were originally a result of twentieth-century Japanese colonialism. There are at least 900,000, and perhaps as many as 3 million, Burakumin and approximately 900,000 Koreans in Japan.[17]

Burakumin

Over the course of a long period, Japan adopted (and adapted) the Chinese Confucian four-tiered class structure that imparted a hierarchical ordering to premodern Japanese society. The samurai (literally, "one who serves"), or warrior-administrators, ranked at the top, above the second level of primary producers or farmers. Artisans ranked third, and merchants were at the bottom. The subclasses of traditional Japanese society, the *hinin* (literally, "nonhumans") and *eta*, or Burakumin, were outside this accepted order. The *hinin* were a heterogeneous group composed of beggars, fugitives from justice, prostitutes, and wanderers. Under the Tokugawa shogunate, they were compelled to undertake the worst jobs, such as caring for victims of contagious diseases, and to dress in specified ways that set them apart from the rest of the population.

The Burakumin were hereditary outcastes originally called *eta*, a word commonly represented by the Chinese characters meaning "much filth." The Burakumin have the same racial and ethnic characteristics as other Japanese, but they were traditionally thought to be subhuman because they performed tasks viewed as ritually polluting, including slaughtering animals and disposing of the dead. Historians and anthropologists are not certain about the origins of *eta* status, but by the fifteenth century, the *eta* were an identified class. Because their pollution might defile others, government edicts during the Tokugawa period forbade intermarriage between *eta* and non-*eta* and required residential segregation in specified hamlets, or buraku—hence the term "hamlet-people," or *buraku-min*. Thus the term *Burakumin* is a relatively modern euphemism for the traditional, more pejorative word, *eta*.

In 1871, the new Meiji government abolished the derogatory terms *eta* and *hinin* and legally emancipated the Burakumin. However, the Burakumin continued with their traditional occupations, and the persistence of the special hamlets, along with an official household-registration system, made them easy to identify. Up to the present time, Burakumin tend to be associated with certain occupations, such as drummaking, shoe repair, meat processing, and garbage collection, and to be concentrated in identifiable neighborhoods in major metropolitan areas such as Osaka. In the late 1990s, it was discovered that private detective agencies in Osaka had investigated job applicants to find out if they were from buraku areas, selling their lists to hundreds of private companies.[18]

In 1906, the novelist Shimazaki Toson movingly portrayed the situation of the Burakumin in *The Broken Commandment*. The central character of the novel is a young Burakumin schoolteacher named Segawa Ushimatsu, who has achieved his position by disguising his background—"passing"—as his father commanded him to do. Finally, friendship with an older Burakumin who is openly campaigning against discrimination, along with the constant tension of keeping his secret, propels the schoolteacher to break his father's commandment and reveal his secret. In the following quoted passages, Ushimatsu wrestles with the consequences of revealing his secret, then does it.

> The deeper his thoughts probed, the darker they grew. Nothing could soften the horror of total rejection: of dismissal from the school, for instance. The humiliation would follow him to the grave. And how, afterwards, could he make a living? . . . Why should he be singled out as less than human, when all he wanted was to live as others lived? . . .
>
> [Later Ushimatsu reveals his secret to his class.] He bowed his head humbly before the class. "When you get home, tell your parents what I have said. Tell them I confessed today, asking your forgiveness . . . *I am an eta, an outcast, an unclean being!*" [italics in original][19]

Ushimatsu's confession in this last scene raises an important question that confronts minorities in any society who do not look or sound different. Is it preferable to "pass" as part of the majority or to "come out" and assert one's identity as a way of calling attention to, and rejecting, patterns of exclusion or discrimination? When *The Broken Commandment* was made into a movie, the Buraku Liberation League (BLL), an organization with roots dating back to the 1920s, called for the wording of Ushimatsu's final confession to be changed to: "I am a Burakumin, but what's wrong with that?" The BLL's secretary-general denied that the organization was practicing censorship and defended both the BLL's position on the wording change for the movie and its demands that Japanese translations of several English-language books be altered to eliminate unacceptable references to *eta* and Burakumin. Those disagreeing with the BLL position included some scholars whose works were changed in translation.[20]

Despite such controversies and the persistence of discrimination in some areas, it is clear that conditions for Burakumin have improved in significant ways since the 1960s, when the government directly addressed discrimination against buraku people. A government report on Burakumin conditions was followed by compensatory legislation, beginning with the Law on Special Measures for Integration (Dowa) Projects in 1969. Government policies have emphasized increasing education and employment rates, confronting human rights violations, and promoting public works projects in buraku neighborhoods. Education statistics illustrate both the progress and the remaining challenges: The disparity between enrollment of Burakumin and non-Burakumin students in high school and public vocational schools dropped from 37 percent in the early 1960s to 4.5 percent in the late 1990s. But Burakumin junior college and university enrollment, although improving, was only 60 percent of the national average.[21]

Koreans

When Japan annexed Korea in 1910, there were approximately 2,500 Koreans in Japan. This number increased dramatically during World War II, when the Japanese government brought Koreans to Japan as forced laborers. Although many of the more than two million Koreans were repatriated at the end of the war, others stayed in Japan and became the parents and grandparents of today's Korean minority. By the late twentieth century, 90 percent of the Koreans in Japan were Japanese-born and had few ties to Korea.[22] Today, most Koreans in Japan do not speak Korean, much as second- and third-generation Japanese-Americans speak no Japanese. However, birth in Japan itself does not give a person legal status as a Japanese citizen, so the majority of Korean-Japanese are noncitizens in the country of their birth.

Discriminated against socially and economically, Koreans have struggled for several decades to improve their conditions. Gradually, their legal status has improved. Nearly 60 percent of Koreans are officially considered legal aliens (permanent residents), not Japanese citizens, and they compose about two-thirds of Japan's registered foreign national population. Between the early 1980s and early 1990s, the Japanese government granted permanent resident status to first-, second-, and third-generation Koreans in Japan. The amendment of Japan's Nationality Law in 1985 made more Korean residents of mixed parentage eligible to become Japanese citizens, and as of 2005 about 285,000 had become citizens.[23]

By the late twentieth century, Koreans were becoming more assimilated into Japanese society through intermarriage, through education in Japanese schools, and by using a Japanese rather than a Korean name. Assimilation, however, creates a different dilemma about identity: Some Koreans, for example, argue that using a Japanese name serves only to legitimize the stigma attached to being Korean.[24] Thus differences of opinion about "passing" and "coming out" exist among Koreans as well as Burakumin. An important distinction between the two communities, however, lies in the international origin of Koreans. Since the 1980s, a new strategy of "living together" while acknowledging difference has gained prominence in some areas.[25]

Still, controversy continues about the status of Koreans in Japan. They are often discriminated against in jobs and education, cannot vote (but pay taxes), and have comparatively little political influence. Their situation has been complicated by the history of conflict between Japan and Korea and the division of Korea into North and South. After World War II, for example, separate organizations were created to address the problems of the Korean-Japanese, one linked to North Korea and one to South Korea. Most Koreans in Japan hold Republic of Korea (ROK/South Korea) nationality, although a substantial minority holds North Korean nationality. The periodic escalation of tensions between North Korea and Japan has been particularly difficult for those Koreans in Japan who claim family lineage in the North.[26]

Another illustration of the connection between domestic and international factors relevant to understanding the situation of Koreans (as well as other immigrant groups) is that of the "comfort women." "Comfort women" is a euphemism for Korean and other Asian women who were forced to provide sex for the Imperial Japanese Army during World War II. The shame of the Korean women imprisoned and exploited during the war had contributed to the lack of public discussion of their history until the 1990s. In 1991, several Korean women brought suit against the Japanese government in a Japanese court, asking for compensation for their wartime ordeal. Only in early 1992, shortly before the visit of Japan's prime minister to Korea, did the Japanese government reverse its long-standing denial of official involvement in abducting women for the army. Previously, the government had claimed that the "comfort stations" were simply private brothels.[27] Later the same year, the issue caught the attention of the Japanese Parliament when a female opposition member accused the government of stalling its investigation of the issue.[28] Ultimately, the government sponsored the creation of a private fund to pay former "comfort women," while continuing to reject making any formal apology or admission of legal responsibility.

The way in which the "comfort women" became part of the political process suggests some parallels for comparison with other countries and with the politicization of other issues in Japan. The issue linked disadvantaged groups—in this instance women and ethnic minorities. A handful of individuals sought (unsuccessfully) redress of their grievances through the courts. Private voluntary and

PHOTO 4.3 Korean women's protest. Photo by the author.

professional organizations played important roles in providing facts and publicizing issues. Opposition Diet members acted as catalysts in prompting government action. The issue then took on international dimensions as nongovernmental organizations (NGOs) in Japan, Korea, and other East Asian countries joined the protest against Japanese government policy. Photo 4.3 shows one such protest staged by Korean women at the NGO Forum on Women at Beijing in 1995. In December 2000, a coalition of these NGOs sponsored a mock "Tokyo war crimes trial" of the Japanese government to publicize the history of military sexual slavery and shame the government.[29]

Religion

It is conventional wisdom among visitors to Japan that the society they are introduced to is secular and materialistic, especially in comparison to a country such as India. Keen observers will also note, however, that there are shrines and temples everywhere. Some are large and celebrated architectural monuments; others are tiny, tucked into back streets and alleys.

Japanese religions coexist in an intricate matrix created by a long and complex history.[30] Until the ancient Japanese came into contact with Chinese civilization and Buddhism, they assumed that the natural world as they knew it was the sacred, original world. The traditional lineage groups, or *uji*, were patriarchal and centered around a world of *kami* (see Chapter 1). Approximately 2,000 years ago, a confederation of *uji* became known as the Yamato kingdom. As Japan and China came into contact, Yamato rulers paid tribute to Chinese courts, from which in turn they received kingly titles. Thus, rulers who were originally responsible for religious ceremonies (as well as for directing the agricultural life of the *uji*) became political rulers.[31]

In the sixth and seventh centuries, Yamato leaders sought to emulate China through political unification and the systemization of the old ceremonial and belief systems. The Sinicized term "Shinto" was adopted to signify "the way of the *kami*," and the Yamato created a legal and administrative structure, the Ritsuryo, that legitimized political rule in accordance with the *kami* belief system.[32] The Ritsuryo was an early predecessor of the imperial edict system that we will encounter again in the context of Japan's nineteenth-century modernization. The Ritsuryo synthesized indigenous and Chinese influences by anchoring the sovereign ruler's claims to legitimacy both in the way of the *kami* and also in monarchical systems of rule found in Chinese philosophies of governing. Japanese rulers were simultaneously the supreme political authority of the nation, the supreme priest, and the living or manifest *kami*, a genealogical descendant of their *uji* ancestor, Amaterasu Omikami, and thus they were entitled to rule the nation. This is the origin of what is commonly known in the West as the myth of the "divine emperor" and the source of "emperor worship," as it was cultivated from the late 1860s to the mid-1940s.

Another important historical theme is the impact of Buddhism and Confucianism on the Japanese court and state. The earliest formal document confirming the significance of Buddhism and Confucianism was the early-seventh-century "constitution" of Prince Shotoku, who endeavored to devise a written code of government for Japan. The prince was influenced by the traditions of both Buddhism and Confucianism, which were part of the strands of Chinese culture imported from the sixth century on. Shotoku's document introduced several principles that are important for understanding the relationship between religion and government later in Japan, such as the importance of obeying the ruler.[33]

The following sections describe those aspects of Shinto and Buddhism that are especially relevant to our study of politics. Christianity is of minor importance in Japan, but its significance is growing elsewhere in East Asia (see Focus Box 4). Confucianism, which was China's paramount ethical and political philosophy and also influenced Japan, is discussed later, in the context of the modern Japanese nation-state.

CHRISTIANITY IN EAST ASIA

The experience of Christianity has been uneven in Asia. From the case of the Philippines, which was colonized by Spain and today is overwhelmingly Christian, to Japan, where the religion claims less than 1 percent of the population as adherents, Christian institutions range from nearly invisible to growing (South Korea and China) or omnipresent, as in the Philippines.

Throughout Asia, Christian organizations have been important in developing educational institutions. Notably, in the late nineteenth and early twentieth centuries, when education was available only in a small number of government institutions or private academies (both limited to boys), Western missionary efforts were central to the expansion of educational opportunity, including for girls and women.

There are notable historical cases of repression of Christians: an early case is from Tokugawa Japan (see Chapter 7); later incidents occurred during post-1949 China, particularly during the Cultural Revolution in the 1960s (Chapter 10). Today, Christian practice is legal in both countries, although formal registration of religious institutions is required. As noted, the number of Christians in Japan is very small, but in 2006 Christian organizations embraced a poll that suggested the percentage was higher than generally reported and is growing.[1]

In China, it is nearly impossible to know the number of Christians. A cursory reading of sources, both print and Internet, reveals reported numbers of adherents ranging from 20 million to more than 100 million. Religious activity is technically illegal outside regular religious buildings, but it does occur elsewhere, including private residences. As noted in Chapter 3, the government is particularly concerned about maintaining national unity; consequently, unauthorized links between Chinese and foreign Christians (including the Vatican) are forbidden and those involved are typically arrested. New "Regulations on Religious Affairs" were adopted by the government in 2005; the regulations permit "normal" religious activities, but the ambiguity in this term leaves room for arbitrary interpretation by the government.

South Korea offers a noteworthy case of the appeal of Christianity and the syncretism that results from the expansion of an institution with Western origins in a cultural context steeped in Buddhism and Confucianism. Christian missions were established in the second half of the nineteenth century in Korea, as in China and Japan, and the appeal of Christianity had spread throughout the nation and through all classes by the time of the Japanese annexation

continues

FOCUS BOX 4

in 1910. From an early period, the faith was associated with progressive ideas seen as part of a national regeneration. Repressed under the Japanese occupation, Christianity became closely associated with national resistance.[2] Today, between 25 and 30 percent of Koreans practice Christianity, and the religion is central to the country's civic culture.

---

1. Audrey Barrick, "More People Claim Christian Faith in Japan," *The Christian Post,* March 19, 2006, accessed December 12, 2008, at www.christianpost.com/article/ 20060319/more-people-claim-christian-faith-in-japan.htm.
2. James H. Grayson, "Christianity and State Shinto in Colonial Korea: A Clash of Nationalisms and Religious Beliefs," *Journal of Religious Studies* 1, no. 2 (1993), 13–30.

Shinto

Because of the close association of Shinto with twentieth-century Japanese militarism, it is important to distinguish between the forms of Shinto that have historically been directly linked to the government and those forms that have broader cultural and religious significance.[34] Imperial House Shinto is observed at imperial institutions and "retains the most archaic styles of Shinto worship."[35] Many rituals of the imperial family are not open to the public, a fact brought home when televised coverage of special events involving the imperial family (such as the 1989 coronation of the present Emperor Akihito and the 1993 marriage of his son, Crown Prince Naruhito) omitted some Shinto rites performed only in the presence of a handful of individuals.

Shrine Shinto is practiced at the approximately 100,000 shrines that cover the Japanese landscape. The shrines are historically linked to a community grouping and today are organized under the Association of Shinto Shrines, which serves as a political pressure group. Rituals and ceremonial festivals, called *matsuri*, emphasize reverence for the various *kami* associated with the shrines and mark important events, as suggested in Photo 4.4.

State Shinto dates from the Meiji period and was a self-conscious government creation that combined Shrine Shinto and Imperial House Shinto. This amalgam was designed to build national identity and unity centering on devotion to the emperor, and it inculcated belief in the uniqueness and superiority of the Japanese people. During the period of State Shinto, which lasted until the end of World War II (1945), Shinto was technically not a religion but a government institution whose priests were government officials (see Chapter 7).

PHOTO 4.4 Small boy prepares for a Shinto ritual. Photo courtesy of James W. Boyd.

Additional forms of Shinto have been identified and categorized, including Sect Shinto. Shinto sects are primarily characterized by their relatively recent origin and linkage to a charismatic personality. The earlier sects were founded in the nineteenth century and in many respects were a response to the massive changes wrought in Japanese society by modernization and urbanization. Scholars increasingly group these sects with Buddhist movements and organizations that are also of more recent origin and are offshoots of the old Buddhist traditions. Together, these "new religions," as they are called, have attracted millions of followers. One of the new religions with Buddhist roots, Soka Gakkai, is both the largest and the most politically significant in Japan. A "new new religion," the Aum Shinrikyo, was held responsible for the 1995 sarin nerve gas attack in a Tokyo subway.[36]

Buddhism

It will be recalled that the earliest Shinto beliefs were institutionalized in the sixth century in response to the Chinese cultural and political influence that entered Japan during this period. Buddhism was one of these foreign imports. Although Buddhism is diffuse, its role in Japanese life since this period can hardly be overstated.

Japan was the geographic terminus in Asia of Buddhism; consequently, the nation inherited a variety of practices and beliefs that would hardly have been recognized in India, where Buddhism was born. In this regard, Buddhism is a prime exemplar of the intermingling and grafting of Asian traditions. Initially, Buddhism, like institutionalized Shinto, was predominantly a religion of the nobility and upper classes. Today, of course, the Buddhist legacy is ubiquitous, from its temples—which often stand next to Shinto shrines—to its death ceremonies, which are practiced by almost every household (see Photo 4.5).

Prince Shotoku's patronage of Buddhism in the seventh century and an eighth-century imperial decision to build state-subsidized temples throughout Japan were testimonies to the early, close association between government and religion. In the centuries after its introduction, numerous schools of Buddhism appeared. For our purposes, the most important were Zen and Nichiren, both dating from the Kamakura period (1185–1333), sometimes referred to as Japan's "medieval" era. Zen, like earlier Buddhism, spread to Japan from China and received official patronage. Soon Zen became associated with the ruling members of the emergent samurai class.[37] As samurai traditions and culture were woven into the fabric of Japanese society, practices originally associated with Zen discipline, such as the tea ceremony, became widely accepted art forms. Today, these are often viewed as synonymous with Japanese culture.

Unlike Zen, Nichiren, so named after its thirteenth-century founder, is indigenous to Japan. Nichiren believed that the social unrest of his day was due to decay in the practice of Buddhism, which he sought to reform. Much later, in the nineteenth century, Nichiren Buddhism fed into Japanese nationalism, in large part because of its emphasis on national revival. Nichiren also contributed to the creation of several new religions, including Soka Gakkai, mentioned earlier. Originally a lay organization affiliated with the Nichiren Shoshu sect, Soka Gakkai dates from the 1930s. In the early 1960s, its members took the lead in creating Komeito (the Clean Government Party) (see Chapter 12).

PHOTO 4.5 Buddhist monk, Kyoto. Photo courtesy
of James W. Boyd.

Summary

The history of religion in Japan clearly reflects the themes that were introduced
in Chapter 1. The indigenous tradition of Shinto—itself incorporating some ancient practices of folk religion—coexists with other Asian traditions that entered
Japan from China and Korea, such as Buddhism and Confucianism. Western religions, notably Christianity, have been introduced to Japan as well, but with
much less impact on the overall social fabric and, therefore, politics. Of all these
traditions, Shinto has been the most closely associated with the modern development process because of the government's use of State Shinto for building and
maintaining national cohesion. The intermingling of different forms of Shinto
and Buddhism, along with ancient folk practices and the philosophical and social imprint of Confucianism, has created a cultural matrix in which it is difficult

to isolate single features. This blending, in turn, helps account for the typically indirect relationship between Japanese religion and modern politics—in contrast to India, where religious communities and priorities are inseparable from the contemporary definition of politics.

The intertwining of religious and cultural traditions also makes it difficult to identify causal links between particular religious tenets and gender differences. In Japan, as in China and India, the history of female subordination is obvious, and it extends into the political realm. But this history is not without its complexities and contradictions. Iwao Sumiko, for example, has argued that women's relative absence from the public sphere, combined with the traditional importance of the family and women's role in the private sphere, gives women freedom and a certain kind of power.[38]

Just as changes in recent decades have altered relations between men and women, the Japanese people have confronted other changes that are directly and indirectly significant for our study of politics: Old minority communities continue to demand redress of grievances, whereas new immigrant groups puncture the homogeneity of Japanese society; rural communities that guaranteed stability and predictability for centuries have been replaced by the urban centers that now dominate the political and economic processes; and an aging population strains the fabric of private lives and public policies. All of these trends suggest comparisons not only with China and India but also with North America and Western Europe.

Exploring Further

For a moving portrayal of the impact an elderly man has on his family, see Ariyoshi Sawako's novel, *The Twilight Years*, trans. Mildred Tahara (Tokyo: Kodansha, 1984). Those interested in contemporary Christianity in Japan are directed to the novels of the well-known writer Endo Shusaku, particularly *Silence*, the story of a seventeenth-century priest in Japan at the height of the persecution of Christians. Itami Juzo's films from the 1980s and 1990s offer wry social comedy (*The Funeral, Tampopo, A Taxing Woman*, and the *Anti-Extortion Woman*).

Notes

1. Japan, Ministry of Internal Affairs and Communication, *Statistical Handbook of Japan 2008*, chap. 2 ("Population"), accessed December 12, 2008, at www.stat.go.jp/English/data/handbook/c02cont/htm. In contrast to the island of Honshu, the population density on the northern island of Hokkaido is 72 people per square kilometer.

2. Government of Japan, "Convention on Nuclear Safety National Report for Japan for the Third Review Meeting," August 2004, accessed September 21, 2008, at www.meti.go.jp/english/report/downloadfiles/NISAreport3e.pdf.

3. *Statistical Handbook of Japan 2008.*

4. James H. Schulz, Allen Borowski, and William H. Crown, *Economics of Population Aging: The "Graying" of Australia, Japan, and the United States* (New York: Auburn House, 1991), 50. The policy changes are analyzed in John Creighton Campbell, *How Policies Change: The Japanese Government and the Aging Society* (Princeton: Princeton University Press, 1992), chap. 9.

5. Kazuhito Yamashita, "The Perilous Decline of Japanese Agriculture," The Tokyo Foundation, n.d. (2008), accessed December 13, 2008, at http://www.tokyo foundation.org/en/articles/the-perilous-decline-of-japanese-agriculture.

6. Other immigrants came from Thailand, as well as South and West Asia, including Iran. Ajay Singh and Murakami Mutsuko, "Japan Is the New Frontier," *Asia Week*, May 9, 1997, online edition.

7. The debate included the criteria for citizenship and dual nationalities. Minoru Matsutani, "The Many Faces of Citizenship: Debate on Multiple Nationalities to Heat Up," *Japan Times Online*, January 1, 2009, http://search.japantimes.co/nn20090101al .html, retrieved January 2, 2009.

8. See the studies in pt. 1 of Gail Lee Bernstein, ed., *Recreating Japanese Women, 1600–1945* (Berkeley: University of California Press, 1991).

9. See the interpretation of Iwao Sumiko, *The Japanese Woman: Traditional Image and Changing Reality* (New York: Free Press, 1993), chap. 10.

10. Susan J. Pharr, *Losing Face: Status Politics in Japan* (Berkeley: University of California Press, 1990), 59–60.

11. Ibid., 67.

12. The marriage rate has declined since the 1970s, despite a bump upward in the 1990s. The divorce rate also increased during this period. Between 1975 and 2005, the average age at which women bore their first child increased from 26 to 29. *Statistical Handbook of Japan 2008.*

13. United Nations Development Program, *Human Development Report 2007– 2008*, accessed September 14, 2008, at http://hdrstats.undp.org/indicators/279 .html.

14. *Japan: An Illustrated Encyclopedia*, vol. 1 (Tokyo: Kodansha, 1993), 21. Hereafter cited as Kodansha, *Encyclopedia.*

15. Ibid., 22.

16. For a moving portrait, see Shigeru Kayano, *Our Land Was a Forest: An Ainu Memoir*, trans. Kyoko Selden and Lili Selden (Boulder: Westview Press, 1994). It is noteworthy that "Ainu" in Japanese is written in katakana characters, which are gen-

erally used for foreign words. Not until 2008 did the Japanese government *officially* recognize the Ainu as an indigenous minority.

17. A 1993 government survey counted nearly 900,000 Burakumin, but the Buraku Liberation League believes that the number is closer to 3 million. The government counted population only in special areas designated for government measures. Yuka Ishikawa, "Rights Activists and Rights Violation: The Burakumin Case in Japan," paper prepared for the Global Conference Against Racism and Caste-Based Discrimination, New Delhi, 2001. Accessed March 24, 2003, at www.imadr.org/tokyo/ishikawareport.html; also the website of the Buraku Liberation and Human Rights Research Institute at http://blhrri.org. See note 23 on Koreans.

18. International Movement Against All Forms of Discrimination and Racism (IMADR), Buraku Liberation League, and Buraku Liberation and Human Rights Research Institute, *Reality of Buraku Discrimination in Japan* (Tokyo: IMADR—Japan Committee, 2001), 49.

19. Toson Shimazaki, *The Broken Commandment*, trans. Kenneth Strong (Tokyo: University of Tokyo Press, 1974), 210, 229–230.

20. Herman W. Smith, *The Myth of Japanese Homogeneity: Social-Ecological Diversity in Education and Socialization* (Commack, N.Y.: Nova Science Publications, 1995), 198.

21. *Reality of Buraku Discrimination in Japan*, 60.

22. Kodansha, *Encyclopedia*, vol. 1, 830.

23. Statistics on Koreans in Japan are reported in a working paper prepared for the visit of former Prime Minister Abe Shinzo to South Korea, Korean Information Service, October 9, 2006, accessed December 12, 2008, at www.korea.net/korea/attach/D/03/123_en.pdf.

24. Jeffry T. Hester, "Kids Between Nations: Ethnic Classes in the Construction of Korean Identities in Japanese Public Schools," in *Koreans in Japan: Critical Voices from the Margin*, ed. Sonia Ryang (London: Routledge, 2000), 182.

25. Jeffry T. Hester, "Repackaging Difference: The Korean 'Theming' of a Shopping Street in Osaka, Japan," in *Urban Ethnic Encounters: The Spatial Consequences*, eds. Aygen Erdentug and Freek Colombijn (London: Routledge, 2002), 177–191.

26. Koreans were shocked, for example, by North Korea's admission in 2002 that it had kidnapped Japanese citizens a quarter century earlier. Tomoko Takemura, "Osaka Residents Struggle to Come to Terms with Abduction Admission," *The Daily Yomiuri*, September 24, 2002.

27. Among the various studies on this topic, Tanaka Toshiyuki's is especially useful for its historical and comparative perspectives. *Japan's Comfort Women: Sexual Slavery and Prostitution During World War II and the U.S. Occupation* (London: Routledge, 2002).

28. *Japan Times Weekly International Edition*, July 20–26 and August 3–9, 1992.

29. The history of the trial is shown in the film *Breaking the History of Silence (The Women's International War Crimes Tribunal for the Trial of Japanese Military Sexual Slavery)* (Tokyo: Video Juku for Violence Against Women in War Network—Japan, 2001).

30. H. Byron Earhart, *Japanese Religion: Unity and Diversity*, 3rd ed. (Belmont, Calif.: Wadsworth, 1982), chaps. 1, 2.

31. See Joseph M. Kitagawa's preface to Donald L. Philippi, *Norito: A Translation of the Ancient Japanese Ritual Prayers* (Princeton: Princeton University Press, 1990), xx–xxii.

32. Ibid., xxii; Kodansha, *Encyclopedia*, vol. 2, 1269–1271.

33. For the text of Shotoku's constitution, see Ian Reader, Esben Andreasen, and Finn Stefansson, *Japanese Religions: Past and Present* (Honolulu: University of Hawaii Press, 1993), 163, 167–169.

34. Various scholars have categorized Shinto forms differently. I have drawn on and synthesized the treatments found in the following: Earhart, chaps. 2–4; Agency for Cultural Affairs, *Japanese Religion: A Survey* (Tokyo: Kodansha, 1972), chaps. 2, 9; Reader, Andreasen, and Stefansson, chap. 4; and Joseph J. Spae, *Shinto Man* (Tokyo: Oriens Institute for Religious Research, 1972), chap. 1.

35. Agency for Cultural Affairs, 29.

36. The definition of "new religions" varies among scholars; Aum Shinrikyo was usually called a "cult" by the press and might better be identified as a "'new' new religion." See Ian Reader, *Religion in Contemporary Japan* (Honolulu: University of Hawaii Press, 1991), 195.

37. H. Paul Varley, *Japanese Culture*, 3rd ed. (Honolulu: University of Hawaii Press, 1984), 94.

38. Iwao, chaps. 1, 3.

PART TWO

The Foundation of Politics

Part One focused on those population characteristics that are especially significant for studying politics in India, China, and Japan. One of the goals of the chapters in Part One is to remind us that a country's population is not undifferentiated. That is, not all Indians or Chinese are ethnically the same, nor do they have the same history, the same socioeconomic status, or—by extension—the same political roles and access to the political process.

Part One also illustrated the book's comparative themes. The endurance of traditional culture and social organization helps account for the unique circumstances and issues in each of the countries, an illustration of this being caste in India. This national uniqueness, however, is muted by the intermingling and grafting of Asian traditions, which is the second broad theme. An obvious case of this grafting is the impact of Buddhism and Confucianism in Japan. An example of the third theme—the influence of Western values and institutions—is the role of Christianity in both South and East Asia.

Part Two builds on these themes and deals more explicitly with the themes of socioeconomic development, state, and nation. Development, which has become a political mandate for Asian governments, is largely a legacy of nineteenth- and twentieth-century political changes that swept Japan, China, and India, as well as other Asian countries. Although the causes of these changes were complex, they cannot be understood apart from Asia's encounter with Western power, ideologies, and technologies. A historical perspective is central to understanding these changes, and the chapters in Part Two emphasize patterns in the interplay between indigenous and external forces. To use one illustration of this interplay that picks up where Chapter 4 left off: The role of Shinto in Japanese politics today can best be understood by seeing it as an indigenous religion that has been molded by its relationship to the Japanese state. This relationship was conditioned by preoccupations

97

with development and national integrity, which, in turn, were deeply influenced by Japan's contacts with the West.

The example of Shinto recalls the fifth and sixth themes introduced in Chapter 1: the relationship between individuals and state institutions, and the formation of national identity. The themes are intertwined, but national identity and the historical movements of nationalism are emphasized in Part Two. Readers should be aware at the outset that this selective focus is an analytical device: It is designed to provide coherence and some insight into rich and extremely complex historical developments. Put differently, the emphasis on nationalism and national identity is a lens that can magnify and clarify—and distort. With this caveat in mind, the remainder of this introduction expands on the significance of national identity and on the way it can help us understand the foundations of Indian, Chinese, and Japanese politics.

The terms "nationalism" and "national identity" as used in this book refer to a modern phenomenon that characterizes the past two centuries of Asian history. Nationalism inspires political movements that seek to foster a sense of identification with a territorially based state. It may reflect a persisting sense of national identity, particularly among intellectuals and government leaders. Typically, nationalism works to create a sense of national belonging among people whose previous political loyalty was owed to family, village, clan, caste, or lord. In its rawest and most negative forms, nationalism is linked to sentiments of ethnic and national superiority such as racism, imperialism, and militarism—all of which are amply illustrated in modern international relations. In its less pernicious forms and even creative aspects, nationalism may lead to liberation (for example, from imperial control), popular sovereignty, economic development, and a sense of self-worth, both individual and collective.

Asian nationalism, like nationalism elsewhere, has been both beneficial and destructive. It has made it possible to defend and enrich indigenous traditions, including the arts, from domination or destruction by foreign imports. It has also produced creative blends of native and foreign, of old and new. The destructive faces of Asian nationalism are equally obvious as subsequent chapters will illustrate.

Part Two uses both the idea of the nation and the process of nation building as it has occurred in the past two centuries to illustrate two sets of interrelationships that are essential for understanding today's politics: the relationships between tradition and modernity and between the indigenous and the imported. Because we are primarily concerned here with the political dimensions of these relationships, the focus on the traditional and indigenous will emphasize political norms or ideologies and institutions. Chapter 5 summarizes the critical periods in Indian political history, including an analysis of the relative strength of classical and modern political ideas in the attempt to forge a common Indian national identity.

India is the only one of our Asian case studies subjected to outright Western colonialism. China's coastal areas felt the direct impact of Western imperialism, but much of its hinterland was left relatively unchanged. Nonetheless, in China, the nationalist reaction to the West was as virulent and (ultimately) as effective, if not more so, than the Indian reaction. It is ironic that in Asia, China stands out both for the endurance of its traditional culture and for the massiveness of its revolutionary experience.

One often-debated question about China is why its response to the "coming of the West" in the nineteenth century was so ineffective in contrast to Japan's. Turning the question around, we might ask: Why and how was Japan able to respond so quickly and effectively to the Western threat? What was the relationship between nationalism and development in this response? These are just some of the questions that the next three chapters will address.

5

Indian National Identity: Secular or Hindu?

Nowhere in Asia is the debate over the meaning of national identity or the effort to create and maintain national unity more vigorous than in India. From the early stirrings of the nationalist movement in the nineteenth century to the end of the twentieth century, there have been deep cleavages over the question of what it means to be "Indian" and how the Indian nation should be defined. At the core of the debate is the issue of Hinduism and the question of whether it is the defining quality of Indianness or whether it is one faith among others in what has been a secular polity.

The roots of the debate are historical and philosophical. It is to the earliest history of India that this chapter first turns in order to understand the traditions of Indian political thought and organization. The chapter then looks at the way in which the Mughal Empire, followed by the British Empire, helped form the modern state of India. The Mughal and British periods are important for three reasons: They affected the political and legal norms that carried over to the twentieth century, they created a precedent for certain institutions of government, and they planted the seeds of modern communalism in India. The term *communalism* is used here in the Indian sense to mean loyalties to and tensions among the communities of faith that characterize the various religious groups, especially Hindus and Muslims.

The third and fourth sections focus on the nationalist movement, which culminated in the partition of British India into India and Pakistan. The chapter closes with a question that, though nearly buried for the first decades of the new republic, reemerged in the 1980s. The question is whether India is, and should be, a secular republic. Two crises, one in Ayodhya and the other in Kashmir, illustrate this dilemma.

Early India: Empire and Village[1]

The Mughal and British Empires were superimposed on a Hindu society that had been evolving for more than two thousand years when the first Muslim invasions in the tenth century began to undermine Hindu rule. Although there were vast differences across the subcontinent during this early period, the pervasiveness of Hindu values and practices, including caste, created a relatively high degree of cultural unity. A variety of political orders came and went, and the richest and most powerful kingdoms created architectural and literary monuments that contributed to the legendary greatness of classical India.

One of the most important of these ancient kingdoms was the Maurya (322–185 B.C.E.), which arose in North India in what is now the state of Bihar. The Mauryan Empire developed extensive civil and military bureaucracies, elaborate irrigation and road systems, and, of course, a taxation system. Although the first Mauryan king, Chandragupta, was the architect of India's greatest ancient empire, today his grandson, Ashoka, is better known as the outstanding ruler of the ancient world (269–232 B.C.E.). Deeply influenced by Buddhism, Ashoka claimed to rule and expand his empire by humane and enlightened government rather than war. Under his missionaries, Buddhism started its long migration outside India, beginning with the island today known as Sri Lanka.

Central to Ashoka's government philosophy was the principle of *dharma*, a word that was explained in Chapter 1. *Dharma* refers simultaneously to the sacred law that governs the universe and to the codes of conduct governing relations between social groups and also between individuals. For individuals, *dharma* denotes a series of duties: personal, social, moral, and religious. It describes the way one is expected to behave in specific situations, and to violate this expectation is to make one liable to various sanctions.[2] Under Ashoka, the Hindu inspiration of dharma was colored by Buddhism and had the effect of relaxing the king's autocratic rule, moderating, for example, the extremes of punishment found under his predecessors. Observing the principle of *ahimsa* (nonviolence to all living things), Ashoka gave up the royal sport of hunting, and his reign helped establish the vegetarianism that today is integral to Indian culture and cuisine. In order to propagate and popularize Buddhist moral principles, Ashoka had pillars erected in different parts of his empire. Proclamations engraved on these pillars preached religious tolerance and warned against envy, impatience, and other human frailties that deviated from Buddhist ideals. The capital, or top, of the pillar at Sarnath, where the Buddha first preached, had four lions, the lion symbolizing royalty. This capital symbolizes the modern Indian state, as it appears on Indian banknotes and serves as a daily reminder of the

PHOTO 5.1 Indian rupee note. Photo by author.

link between the India of 2,300 years ago and today. Photo 5.1 shows the capital of Ashoka's Sarnath pillar (the capital is still in the museum at Sarnath) on a one-hundred-rupee note. (Note also the multiple language scripts.)

One other ancient empire should be mentioned here for its contributions to the history of classical Indian, and specifically Hindu, greatness. The Gupta period (fourth to sixth century C.E.) was India's "golden age," in which the arts and sciences flourished. By the fifth century, Indian surgeons were performing plastic surgery to repair mutilated faces. The decimal and digit systems, which the West learned from the Arabs, originated in India during the Gupta era. Gupta scientists further developed the principles of astronomy learned from the Greeks.

As the West learned the decimal system from India via the Arabs, so it also learned much about the greatness of the Gupta period from Chinese Buddhist monks on pilgrimage to India. According to one of these pilgrims, Fa Xian (Fa-Hsien), the empire was remarkable for its peacefulness, the rarity of serious crime, and the mildness of its administration. "At this time India was perhaps the happiest and most civilized region of the world, for the effete Roman Empire was nearing its destruction, and China was passing through a time of troubles between the two great periods of the Hans and the Tangs."[3]

As is suggested by this description, India was in the crosscurrents of the movement of ideas and peoples for hundreds of years. Invasions from the west brought Persian and Greek influence; Buddhism, born in India, moved south and east, inspiring pilgrims, who, fifteen hundred years ago (as today), returned to the subcontinent for the roots of their faith. Over the course of these same centuries, Hinduism, whose structure and worldview are distinctly Indian, evolved. Although influenced by the movements of Buddhism and Jainism,[4] Hinduism came to dominate India largely in the form in which we see it in the twenty-first century, and the principles, popular deities, and caste system of the Hindu spiritual and social orders consolidated their hold over the worldview of the average Indian.

For these average Indians, the world that mattered was the world of the village, where self-government and caste combined to maintain predictability and order. Contact with law and punishment generally occurred within the context of the caste *pancha*, a traditional council of five or more leaders that heard civil cases and decided outcomes for caste members, and the *panchayat*, an organization of male village elders. In theory, the village was administered by the *panchayat*; it was taxed (in the form of produce, as were villages in China) but generally untouched by changes of rule from one kingdom to another. The principles of *dharma* operated within the village caste system, and acceptance of the obligations of one's caste came to mean the realization and fulfillment of *dharma*. Thus caste, *panchayat*, and *dharma*—all of which survived into the modern period—assured relative peace and social harmony, despite its costs to those most disadvantaged by the system.

Looking back at the premodern period of Indian history, two attributes are noticeable. First, infusions of new peoples and ideas, typically from the northwest, were accommodated in what became a cultural fusion. Second, the centuries saw both imperial centralization and political decentralization; undergirding both was the persistence of Hindu village life and values.[5] The Mughal invasions would terminate formal Hindu rule in the north of the subcontinent, but they never succeeded in incorporating the entire subcontinent in a centralized state. Nor did they erase the memory of Hindu greatness that linked Indians to the period of the early empires.

Creating the Indian State: The Mughal and British Empires

The Mughal Empire

The first Muslim raids and invasions started as early as the eighth century in northwestern India, becoming more persistent and extensive in the tenth and eleventh centuries. The first major Muslim state, the Delhi sultanate, was founded in the early thirteenth century. The most powerful and longest-ruling Muslim state, the Mughal dynasty, was established in 1526 and lasted until 1857, although in reality its control over the subcontinent began to decline after the death of the last great Mughal emperor, Aurangzeb, in 1707. Beginning in the sixteenth century, the first sweep of European expansion into Asia brought English, Dutch,

French, and Portuguese explorers, traders, missionaries, and conquerors. As the Mughal Empire declined in the eighteenth century, the Europeans moved in, taking one territory after another. Gradually, the British, whose effective rule was exercised by the British East India Company, eliminated their competitors, notably the French.

Interpretations of Mughal India have varied, ranging from those characterizing the empires as despotic and centralized to those offering a more nuanced assessment, pointing, for example, to the degree of religious tolerance that existed under Muslim rulers. Political scientist Rajni Kothari has argued that, on balance, four characteristics of Muslim rule are especially relevant to modern politics.[6] First, at the core of Muslim administration lay a strong military emphasis, necessitated by the long periods of fighting accompanying the Muslim incursions, leading to the defeat of indigenous kingdoms, and empire building.

Second, the Muslims confronted Hindus with completely different social and religious systems. Despite important instances of accommodation and periods of harmony, the two communities, with their respective worldviews and social organizations, remained largely separate. The Mughals were initially conquerors, and Islam was a proselytizing faith; thus Muslim mosques often replaced Hindu temples—a point later emphasized by Hindu nationalists. The roots of the Ayodhya crisis examined at the end of this chapter spring from this reality.

The third characteristic of the Mughal state that was significant for India's subsequent political evolution was the creation of a clear center of political authority, located in the northern and the central subcontinent. The Mughal state was backed by an efficient administration responsible for law enforcement and tax collection. The British inherited this administrative structure with a few modifications.

The fourth attribute of Mughal rule was its relative failure to alter local institutions and village affairs.[7] At the local level, public issues continued to be settled through customary channels such as the *panchayat*, and where Muslims came to live next to Hindus in the rural areas, the former typically accommodated to the social (if not the religious) system of the latter. And in one critical way, Muslim and Hindu values reinforced each other: "Among all classes . . . the preference for a son underlined the inferior position of women."[8] Muslim upper-class and court women were kept secluded in purdah (literally, "curtain"), confined to a separate section of the house or palace and veiled when outside. Lower classes and castes aspired to the practice of purdah, and it spread throughout India, complementing the indigenous Hindu norms that confined women to private affairs.

Directly and indirectly, the long periods of Muslim rule established the conditions for twentieth-century communalism. When the Mughal state dissolved, it left a huge Muslim population in North India that was a permanent, integral part of Indian society. Hindus and Muslims learned to live together for the most part, but when political tensions and cleavages rose at the national level—as they did with the nationalist movement—the impact was increasingly felt at the local level. The policies of the British Empire set the context for the nationalist period.

The British Empire in India

The British story in India begins with the founding of the British East India Company in London in 1600. The purpose of the company, a Crown corporation, was to explore and exploit the opportunities for commerce in India, and within a few years, it had secured trading privileges from the Mughals. By the end of the seventeenth century, the company had established commercial enclaves in the coastal cities of Mumbai (Bombay), Chennai (Madras), and Kolkata (Calcutta)—cities that even today are known for their remnants of British architecture. Over the course of the eighteenth century, the company expanded, taking advantage of Mughal weaknesses and playing non-Mughal rulers against each other. By the mid-nineteenth century, the company, which employed both civil and military officials, controlled nearly two-thirds of the Indian subcontinent. This expansion was facilitated by fragmenting tendencies in the Mughal Empire and growing challenges to Mughal rule.[9]

Because the primary objective of the British East India Company was profit, its policies were designed to create the kind of political authority, social and economic order, and physical infrastructure (such as roads and railroads) to make this possible. Until the early nineteenth century, the company interfered little in local affairs or in the religious and social lives of most Indians. But changes in England itself soon made themselves felt in India, when British reformers demanded the elimination of visible and offensive Hindu customs (such as *sati*, the self-immolation of a widow on her husband's funeral pyre) that conflicted with Western, Christian values. Supported by Hindu reformers, the British sponsored limited social change in India. At the same time, the introduction of Western education and the English language as the medium of instruction in Indian high schools and colleges spread British liberal ideas.

Education was to influence profoundly the Indian nationalist movement that developed later in the nineteenth century. For some Hindus, the new learning complemented learning in the Sanskrit tradition, traditionally monopolized by Brahmins. For others, Western education and values largely supplanted the indigenous tradition. By the end of the nineteenth century, a growing class of educated men emerged to form the core of the nationalist movement. It included

PHOTO 5.2 University of Calcutta. Photo courtesy of James W. Boyd.

both Brahmins, who dominated India's religious and literary heritage, and non-Brahmins such as the young Mohandas Gandhi, who at age eighteen sailed to England to study law. The nationalist movement also included those who sought to apply the highest ideals of British liberalism to India, as well as those primarily seeking sinecures in the growing bureaucracy. The bureaucracy was a place where upwardly mobile young Indians could put their English to gain, and it was their stymied access to the bureaucracy that served as a catalyst to the creation of the Indian National Congress in the 1880s.

The collapse of the Mughal Empire and, with it, the replacement of Persian with English as the official language of government contributed to the alienation of Muslims in India. Traditionally educated in their own schools, where classical Arabic (the language of the Qur'an) joined Persian, the Muslims "failed to take advantage of English education and were soon displaced in the civil services by the rising Hindu middle class."[10] Higher education in English continues to this day to be an aspiration for up-and-coming Indian students (see Photo 5.2).

The importance of the new Indian middle class is hard to overestimate, both because it was overwhelmingly Hindu and because through it, the British ruled India:

Through this class new ideas of individualism and constitutionalism gained currency . . . [F]rom this class, political leadership emerged to challenge the might of the British Empire. The overall effect was profound. The new middle class, created by English education and drawn by the concepts of liberty, democracy, and socialism, was indeed the greatest legacy of the British Raj.[11]

To this, one might add that the new leadership ultimately created a predominantly secular vision of independent India. How this came to happen, despite the deep concern for revitalizing Hinduism that motivated important segments of the nationalist leadership, is the subject of the next section.

Defining the Indian Nation-State

The 1840s and 1850s brought growing political and military instability to the Indian subcontinent, largely as a result of British efforts to expand control to the northwest, first into Afghanistan, later into Punjab. India lost 20,000 lives (mostly Indian troops trained and led by British officers) in a futile effort to conquer Afghanistan—foreshadowing a similarly disastrous effort by the Soviet Union 140 years later. In the mid-1840s, British efforts to capture the still-independent Sikh kingdom of Punjab provoked the first of two bloody Sikh wars. Defeated, the Sikhs disbanded their armies and surrendered fertile agricultural lands to the British, along with strategic mountain areas, including Kashmir.

British rule in India combined the ruthlessness and pragmatism of military conquest with the "enlightened" government of educational opportunity and public works projects, both of which were designed to render more effective imperial control and the extraction of wealth. Ironically, it was the combination of these policies that led to the so-called Sepoy Mutiny, the Anglo-Indian War of 1857. Both real and imagined British policy convinced the sepoys, the Indian soldiers who enabled some 38,000 British troops to control 200 million Indians, that their rulers were conspiring to convert them—Hindu and Muslim alike—to Christianity. One policy, for example, required Indian soldiers to accept service "anywhere," and it was rumored that Christian missionaries were conspiring with officials to send high-caste Hindus overseas, where they would be permanently polluted and would be easier targets for conversion.

Finally, in 1857, the British introduced a new breech-loading Enfield rifle, whose cartridges were smeared with cow and pig grease. Soldiers were instructed to bite the tip off the cartridge before inserting it into the breech, an act that violated the sensibilities of both Hindus, to whom the cow was sacred, and Muslims, to whom the pig was unclean. The troops began by refusing to load the rifles, then by rebelling at one post after another. The revolts remained largely isolated, with no leadership sufficiently strong or united to seriously threaten British rule. But the murder of British civilians spread panic. Fear and racial hatred exploded on both sides. The British reasserted military control in 1858, and that same year, the British Parliament in London transferred all rights of the old

East India Company directly to the British Crown. The Raj was now officially a British government affair.

Although the revolt of 1857–1858 has been viewed by some Indian nationalists as an early war of independence, in many ways it was a conservative reaction to the multifaceted changes in early-nineteenth-century Indian society.[12] Ultimately, however, the revolt and the reaction to it contributed to the growth of both nationalism and communalism in India: to nationalism, by widening the gap between ruler and ruled, and to communalism, by deepening the suspicion between Hindus and Muslims as an independence movement began to take shape. To understand how this happened, we turn to the development of the nationalist movement.

Reviving and Reforming the Hindu Tradition

Contact with Western philosophies, literatures, and institutions generated a variety of responses among Indian intellectuals. Central to these responses was the question of the relative merits of Hindu and Western traditions. The introduction of English education expanded familiarity with the West among Indians and broadened the debate to the new middle classes. Ultimately, the debate fused with the political awakening of the 1870s and 1880s.

Called by many the "Father of Modern India," Rammohun Roy (1774–1833) stands out among the early Indian intellectuals. He mastered Persian and Arabic, then Sanskrit, and later English, out of an insatiable curiosity and a desire to read and also in order to qualify for government employment. He rose as high as a non-Britisher could in the Bengal Civil Service, retired early, and devoted his life to educating himself as well as the many Indians and Britishers with whom he came in contact. Deeply interested in Christianity, Rammohun Roy nonetheless defended Hinduism against the attacks of missionaries, whose judgments about Indian traditions were often colored by ignorance and the assumptions of inferiority that characterized orientalist thinking.

Roy is important not only for his individual accomplishments but also because he represents a contributing strain to the development of modern nationalism that insists on the enduring essence of Hindu philosophy while demanding the reform of repressive social practices associated with the status of women and low-caste or outcaste Hindus. Decades later, nationalists such as G. K. Gokhale (1866–1915) and Mohandas K. Gandhi (1869–1948) would seek simultaneously to revive and reform Hinduism as a basis for Indian identity.

In contrast to Roy, a religious reform movement developed in the 1870s that was both less influenced by contact with the West and also more insistent on the uniqueness and superiority of the truth found in the *Vedas*, including the *Rig Veda* mentioned in Chapter 2. The Arya Samaj (Aryan Society), a nationalist group founded in Mumbai in 1875, sought to restore an ideal Hindu Aryan past and criticized the influence of Islam and Christianity in India. The Arya Samaj's proselytizing fundamentalism contributed to the rise of enmity against Muslims in some areas and to a lineage of Hindu nationalism that can be seen today in the Bharatiya Janata Party, the political party most closely identified with the demand for a Hindu India.

Complementing the perspectives of people as diverse as Rammohun Roy, on the one hand, and the leaders of the Arya Samaj, on the other, was a wide variety of views regarding the nature of indigenous Indian traditions, the impact of the West in general, and, more particularly, the nature of British rule and how Indians should respond to it. The growing numbers of the educated elite came from different regions, different economic circumstances, and increasingly from different castes. Their views about their own traditions as well as about the British reflected these different circumstances, and their opinions also shifted as British policy itself shifted. British rule was not static: It responded to political mandates from home as well as to local pressures, such as the views of individual officials, social and economic conditions, and the activities of the Indian nationalists. The intermingling of all of these factors may be seen in the evolution of the Indian National Congress (conventionally called "Congress"), which, after its establishment in 1885, became the driving organization of the nationalist movement. The politics of the Congress reveal the ongoing effort to reformulate an Indian identity in terms of Hinduism, the growing challenge of politically articulate Muslims, and, ultimately, the conviction among key Congress leaders that an independent India must be secular.

The Indian National Congress

Despite the fact that Britain's viceroy (or governor) in India in the early 1880s sought to introduce a measure of self-administration to Indian men, his liberal intentions were largely thwarted by ensconced bureaucrats in the Indian Civil Service (ICS), the administrative "glue" that held British India together. The effective opening of the ICS to Indians, in fact, was one of the primary goals of the seventy-two men who met in Bombay in 1885 to call for a "new India" to respond to the aspirations of these educated Indians, now imbued with the ideals of British liberalism. Most of the representatives to the first annual meeting of the Indian National Congress were high-caste Hindus and Parsis, but several Englishmen also played active roles. Muslims were present at this first meeting, as well as at subsequent meetings, but never in proportion to the strength of their numbers in the Indian population—a factor that contributed to the perception that the Congress was primarily a Hindu organization.

The overarching objective of the Congress during its early years was to persuade the British to establish and expand representative institutions for Indians. Gradually, however, a second generation of Congressmen, impatient with British resistance and desiring more influence within the Congress, advocated more militant policies and extremist tactics. To this newer generation belonged the most successful early efforts to mobilize popular support beyond the educated elite by drawing on Hindu traditions and symbols. Bal Gangadhar Tilak (1856–1920), a Marathi-speaking journalist from western India, is the best known today of these nationalists who called not for reform of British rule but for elimination of it. Tilak became known as a defender of religious customs against both Hindu reformers and the imperial government, when it intervened in social and cultural practices by passing legislation to which conservative Hindus objected. In one such instance, Tilak's popularity soared when he attacked the government's Age of Consent Act, adopted after a young girl died following her husband's intercourse with her. The act raised the age of consent from ten to twelve; any intercourse that took place when the wife was under twelve would subsequently be classified as rape. A storm of protest followed the act, with Orthodox Hindus claiming that it violated the religious injunction that girls marry before puberty. In allying himself with the opposition to the Age of Consent Act, Tilak helped join two political strands that came to dominate important currents of the nationalist movement: direct opposition to government measures and defense of religious values as a way of mobilizing public support.

By the early twentieth century, the Congress was divided between two dominant factions: the "moderates," such as Gokhale, Gandhi's mentor in the Congress, who argued that the British could be persuaded to rule India by liberal political principles and grant Indians greater self-determination; and the "extremists," led by Tilak, who distrusted the British, were impatient, and sought methods that would force the British to leave India. Although some partisans of extremism advocated violence, within the Congress the extremists focused on boycotts as the method that would succeed where argument and negotiation had failed. They thought a political boycott of government institutions with an economic boycott of British goods (*swadeshi*) would force British compliance with Congress demands. From these arguments came the conceptualization that real *swaraj*, or self-rule, meant not just political independence from imperial control but rejection of dependence on the state. This independence could be achieved only by renewed village self-sufficiency.

It would be inaccurate to call Tilak or most of the other extremist leaders Hindu communalists in the modern sense. Nonetheless, the "Hindu tinge" of the boycott movement and other elements of the nationalist movement in the early twentieth century "simultaneously generated unease and apprehension in the minds of the educated and politically conscious Muslims who were suspicious of a movement whose nationalist message was couched in religious terms, and who, therefore, saw the Nationalist Congress as representing a Hindu movement."[13] In 1906, those Muslims who shared this unease and opposition to Congress formed the All-India Muslim League. For many years, the membership of the league remained small and elite. Not until 1913 did Muhammad Ali Jinnah (1876–1948), later the founder of Pakistan, join the league, and not until the 1930s did the league seriously challenge the Congress's view of a united India that would replace the British Raj in the subcontinent. It is to this next phase in the building of the Indian nation-state that we now turn.

Congress and the Politics of Gandhi, Nehru, and Jinnah

Four interrelated developments stand out from the twists and turns of the complex elements of the independence movement that gathered momentum after the turn of the century: (1) British policies of reaction and reform; (2) Gandhi's role in transforming the Congress into a mass movement; (3) the growing Muslim demand for a separate nation-state; and (4) Jawaharlal Nehru's impact on the independence movement and on the newly independent state of India.

As suggested earlier, the British imperial government in India responded to a variety of pressures in devising and implementing its policies. This often meant that those policies bore unforeseen (and unintended) consequences. For example, in 1906, the same year the All-India Muslim League was founded, the British viceroy in India, Lord Minto, agreed to Muslim demands that the interests of the Muslim community be safeguarded in the reforms for India's government initiated in London by the new secretary of state for India, Lord Morley. When the Morley-Minto Reforms became law three years later, they included a provision for separate Muslim electorates in any subsequent elections. "The rights of the Muslims as a distinct community were hence recognized and guaranteed and were in the following decades to prove the major stumbling block between separatist Muslims and the Congress."[14] The British, seeing the utility of blunting the effectiveness of Congress nationalists by calling attention to the distinct needs of the Muslim community, were to resurrect this strategy in the 1930s and again contribute to Muslim-Hindu division.

The year 1919 marked a turning point in the life of the Indian National Congress and imperial rule in India. Mohandas Gandhi had returned to India from South Africa a few years earlier. In South Africa, he had practiced law and also developed his philosophy of *satyagraha*, or nonviolent resistance, which he translated as "soul force." Both law and *satyagraha* became cornerstones of Gandhi's leadership of the nationalist movement. Using law, he reasoned with and confronted the British on their own terms; with *satyagraha*, he mobilized India's masses for the nationalist cause while eschewing the violence found in most independence movements. In one of the earliest tests of his approach, he called for a general strike in protest against new laws extending the emergency powers that the government had assumed during World War I. In several North Indian cities, the strike turned into riots. In the Punjab city of Amritsar, martial law was declared. Defying the ban on meetings, 20,000 people gathered in the central public area of Amritsar, the Jallianwala Bagh, to celebrate a festival. The local British troop commander sealed off the only exit to the Jallianwala Bagh. After a quick order to disperse, he ordered his 150 men to fire on the crowd. Nearly 400 Indians were killed outright, and more than 1,200 were wounded.

Although Gandhi was dismayed by the violence in Punjab and felt that he shared responsibility for the disastrous outcome of the strikes, Amritsar also marked the beginning of Gandhi's leadership in the movement of noncooperation and civil disobedience that became the centerpiece of Congress policy after 1920. In the early 1920s, as it would later, the civil disobedience campaign brought violence, including communal violence, in its wake. In 1924, Gandhi undertook a twenty-one-day fast for Hindu-Muslim solidarity but failed to breach the gap.

Despite his commitment to Muslim-Hindu unity, Gandhi's philosophical roots, his style, and his language carried enough of the "Hindu tinge" that his politics, however secular, raised suspicions among those Muslims already insecure in the Congress. Gandhi worked for improvement in the miserable conditions of untouchables, the *harijans*, but as noted in Chapter 2, he never rejected caste. His belief in *ahimsa* and *satyagraha*, his resort to fasting, and his commitment to village self-reliance—symbolized by the spinning he did at his ashram (a retreat near Ahmedabad in his home state of Gujarat)—all reflected his Hindu inheritance. In the broadest sense, his insistence on obeying moral principles embodied *dharma*. Thus, even though he appealed to people on moral, not religious, grounds, "his political thought was couched in the language of religiosity."[15]

More than Gandhi, Jawaharlal Nehru (1889–1964) stands out as representing the commitment to a secular India. Trained, like Gandhi, with a law degree from London, Nehru returned to India in 1912 to practice law with his father.

The young Nehru also followed his father into politics, where the elder Nehru was a leading moderate in the Indian National Congress. Devoted to Gandhi and seeing him as the inspiration of India's nationalist cause, Nehru nonetheless disagreed with him on many basic questions. Most important, their visions of independent India were poles apart. Gandhi's ideal was embodied in decentralized, agriculturally based, self-sufficient villages where *dharma* and *panchayats* dominated. Nehru's views were influenced by European democratic socialism and emphasized a strong, modernized India with a centralized nation-state and planned industrial economy, a vision that Gandhi rejected.

Despite their differences, mutual respect and affection linked the two men, and they worked with other Congress leaders from the 1920s to the 1940s to end British rule. Another critical turning point in their efforts, comparable to Amritsar and the civil disobedience campaign of the early 1920s, came in the 1930s. By 1930, the Congress had unambiguously established its policy of complete independence, with another civil disobedience campaign declared to force the British to negotiate meaningful steps toward this end. To launch the campaign, Gandhi announced that he would violate the salt tax, which was a continuing burden on all Indians, but especially on the very poor.[16] Gandhi's approach to disobeying the tax law was calculated to mobilize grassroots support for independence by targeting one of the most hated aspects of the Raj and demonstrating that the Congress was not an elitist organization. In slightly more than three weeks, Gandhi and his supporters marched 240 miles from his ashram to the sea, where they took "free" salt. Other acts of civil disobedience, strikes, and mass demonstrations quickly followed throughout India. Within six months, some 60,000 people were arrested, and by 1933, more than 120,000 were imprisoned after another round of the civil disobedience campaign.

The mass arrests, along with indiscriminate beatings of both men and women, were one aspect of the British response. Along with the repression, though, came new efforts to negotiate with Congress leaders. Out of this counterpoint of reaction and reform emerged the 1935 Government of India Act, one of the landmarks of India's political history. The act sought to accommodate Congress demands by increasing responsible and representative government in India, expanding the electorate, and establishing a federal arrangement with a large measure of provincial autonomy. It was not independence, but it continued the movement toward self-rule; although its provisions were criticized by Congress leaders as insufficient, many aspects of the act were carried over to India's Constitution.

The years of the early 1930s left other important political legacies. Through the civil disobedience campaigns, women were drawn into the independence movement for the first time in large numbers. Gandhi is thus credited with this important step in mobilizing women politically and moving them toward emancipation, although only upper-caste and foreign women worked closely with him at his ashram. In retrospect, scholars have analyzed Gandhi's views on gender as intrinsic to his unique conception of India's identity, although he did not support women's political, social, and economic equality in the same manner that women's rights advocates do in contemporary India. Gandhi encouraged women to picket liquor and foreign cloth shops but mainly prized their role as repositories of purity and goodness in the home, the private sphere. Thus, he shared the traditional gender attitude of most Congress leaders. But he went further in creating a national identity that was as androgynous as it was indigenous. Nonviolence and his use of the spinning wheel (a domestic tool), for example, combined Buddhist and Hindu ideals, feminine attributes, and village life. Thus "women appear as a collective representation by means of which the superiority and inviolability of the indigenous social tradition is demonstrated against the modern."[17]

Consolidation of the Hindu-Muslim division also dates from this same period. The constitutional discussions of the early 1930s quickened Muslims' concern to protect their position in the coming devolution of power to Indians. The preoccupation with safeguards led some Muslim leaders, including Muhammad Ali Jinnah, who undertook reorganization of the Muslim League in 1934, to renew their insistence on communal representation. Within a decade, Jinnah would unite Muslim leaders first behind the demand for a separate state within the Indian federation and then for complete independence. As the political stakes grew—as elections were conducted, the power of elected officials became meaningful, and independence loomed—compromise was rejected in favor of dividing the Hindu and Muslim communities into India and Pakistan.

Finally, the 1930s was a turning point for one other group that is critical to our understanding of modern Indian politics: the untouchables, Gandhi's *harijans*, labeled by the British as Scheduled Castes and Tribes in the 1935 Government of India Act. Chapter 2 pointed out the different positions taken by Gandhi and B. R. Ambedkar, leader of the untouchables. Gandhi insisted on the inclusion of *harijans* within the Hindu fold and fought for the abolition of untouchability, whereas Ambedkar maintained that equality was impossible within Hinduism. Ambedkar wanted separate communal electorates for untouchables, but Gandhi protested with a vow to fast to death, arguing that separate electorates premised on the assumption of separate communities violated his principle of reforming Hinduism by admitting untouchables within its fold. A few days into Gandhi's fast, Ambedkar agreed to abandon separate electorates in exchange for reserving larger numbers of seats for untouchables in provincial councils and the central assembly.

The principles established as a result of the controversy carried over to the 1950 constitution and into postindependence politics: schedules (lists) appended to the constitution to identify depressed castes; abolition of untouchability (but not caste) and guaranteed access to wells, water tanks, and other public areas for all Indians; and the initiation of "reservation" policies for the most disadvantaged Indians. Thus, though different in origin, the moral stances of Gandhi and Ambedkar converged to illuminate the untouchables' plight and laid the basis for the political mobilization of the most deprived and despised members of Indian society.

Swaraj and Partition

The years from 1946 to 1948 were years of political promise and tragedy for the new Indian nation-state. At the end of World War II, as part of its new commitment to decolonize in Asia, the British government moved quickly to negotiate independence for India. The chief question was no longer "if" or even "when." The questions were, rather, "what" and "who." What would be the physical boundaries of this new India? Who would be its citizens? By 1946, the Muslim League had developed a following among Muslims that made its vision of separate states in South Asia impossible to ignore. The British government, which earlier had played its part in cultivating communal differences, now sought to preserve a united India, which of course was Gandhi's dream. But the communal lines were drawn: The Congress claimed to represent all of India; the Muslim League claimed to represent all Muslims.

The 1946 elections created an assembly that served two functions: The Constituent Assembly was charged both with drafting India's Constitution and serving as the Provisional Parliament to govern when India actually became independent. Although Muslims had participated in the elections that created the assembly, the Muslim League boycotted its early sessions. Meanwhile, Jinnah had brought the League into India's interim government, headed by Nehru, without abandoning his goal of a separate state of Pakistan. Negotiations over the future lines of independent India reached an impasse; in early 1947, the British government declared that it would quit India and transfer power to "Indian" hands, whatever that might mean. Despite Gandhi's opposition, the majority of the Congress leaders had come to accept the inevitability of two separate states, and a plan for partitioning the subcontinent was drawn up.

Independent Pakistan would include two predominantly Muslim territories, one to the east and one to the west of India. The "vivisection" of the Indian subcontinent[18] may have been politically inevitable, but it had brutal consequences.

India and Pakistan became independent in August 1947, but Partition over-whelmed the promise of the new nation-states. Millions of Hindus were left in Pakistan, millions of Muslims in India. The boundary in Punjab had been drawn in a manner that divided the Sikhs. "Here, in mounting hysteria, violence, and atrocity, Muslims fell upon Sikhs and Hindus in the West, and Sikhs and Hindus upon Muslims in the East. Before the end of the year half a million people had been killed."[19] In the chaos of Partition, four and one half million Hindus and Sikhs left West Pakistan for India, and six million Muslims moved in the other direction. Subsequently Pakistan would follow a different historical path (see Focus Box 5).

| FOCUS BOX 5 |

PAKISTAN: A DIFFERENT HISTORICAL TRAJECTORY

If much of modern Indian history is a search for the role of Hinduism in defining the meaning of being "Indian," Pakistan's history since Partition is imbedded in the search to define the meaning of a "Muslim nation." Although an Islamic religious identity was a central rationale for cleaving the subcontinent, that identity has never been sufficiently coherent to unify all of Pakistan or to create a single vision of the country's future (any more than Hinduism has in India).

Pakistan's estimated population of 173 million people (as of 2008) consists of a number of major ethnic groups that form the basis of strong regional identities and account for many features of Pakistani politics, including its federal structure, some regional political parties, and the difficulty in realizing national unity. Punjabis come from both sides of the 1947 Partition boundary that divided Punjab into two states. Sindhis (the largest group) live further to the south and, like the Punjabis, their homeland abuts the Indian border. The Baloch live primarily in Balochistan to the southwest of the country. The Pakhtuns (Pathans) dominate the North-West Frontier Province, abutting Afghanistan. There are also approximately two million Afghan refugees, most living in the North-West region.[1] Complicating this ethnic mosaic are the descendants of those Indian Muslims who moved to Pakistan at the time of Partition, and those who left the former East Pakistan (Bangladesh) after the 1971 civil war.

Pakistan has had five constitutions, including the original Government of India Act of 1935, which the country inherited at independence. It has also

continues

```
                        ┤ FOCUS BOX 5 ├
```

continued

been governed without a constitution (under martial law) and under a suspended constitution.[2] Throughout these changes, there has been agreement
that Pakistan is an Islamic state, but what that has meant in practice continues
to be contested. For example, since 1979, the legal system has been altered to
reflect the principles of Shari'a as part of a broader process of Islamization.
Some politicians—including former Prime Minister Benazir Bhutto (b. 1953),
who was assassinated in 2007—and women's groups opposed this process,
claiming that it was undemocratic and discriminatory.

Political instability in Pakistan has been characterized not only by constitutional change and identity debates but also by alternating periods of civilian
and military rule, the latter beginning with General Ayub Khan's military
coup in 1958. More recently, General Pervez Musharraf seized power in a
1999 coup. His control of the army seemed to guarantee an early period of
stability, and a 2002 referendum held to affirm his role as president confirmed
what appeared to be overwhelming support. However, increasingly unpopular
due to his collaboration with the United States's "war on terror," and after
months of domestic opposition and conflict, Musharraf resigned as president
in August 2008. In September 2008, Benazir Bhutto's husband, Asif Ali
Zardari, became president, but by spring 2009, he also confronted growing
political instability and a deteriorating military situation in western Pakistan.

---

1. United Nations High Commissioner on Refugees, *2007 Global Trends* (July 2008), accessed December 13, 2008, at www.unhcr.org/statistics/STATISTICS/4852366f2.pdf.
2. Yogendra K. Malik et al. describe the various constitutions and political phases in
Government and Politics in South Asia, 6th ed. (Boulder: Westview Press, 2009), chap. 9.

At the other side of India, Gandhi pledged to fast unto death in order to halt
the viciousness. His dedication to intercommunal harmony partially succeeded,
with the leaders of all the communities pledging to help protect Muslims. But
Gandhi's efforts had alienated many Hindus, and shortly after he had ended his
fast and returned to New Delhi, he was shot to death by a young Hindu associated with the militant Hindu organization, the Rashtriya Swayamsevak Sangh
(RSS, or National Volunteer Organization).[20]

It may be argued that at his death, Gandhi had indeed failed in his vision of a
unified, moral political community. Possibly, India would have received its independence by the postwar period even without Gandhi's mass mobilization
campaigns. But it is certain that he made the Congress a more representative organization by demanding that it address the problems of India's dispossessed. He

provided a model for political leaders that was rooted in Indian tradition rather than in the Western experience. And he left a moral legacy that many years later inspires alternative visions of human fulfillment, community, and development both in India and throughout the world.

With Gandhi's death, Jawaharlal Nehru emerged as the dominant figure in the Congress, now called the Congress Party of independent India. It was Nehru's vision of a secular, modern, centralized India that prevailed in the Constituent Assembly and set the tone for India's constitutional order. And it was Nehru who, as India's first and longest-tenured prime minister, set the new nation-state on its course in the middle of the twentieth century, a course that seemed promising until the 1970s. But the divisions born of empires and the nationalist movement persisted, as the following synopses of the Ayodhya and Kashmir crises illustrate.

A Divided Subcontinent: Ayodhya and Kashmir

The Ayodhya Dispute

Ayodhya is a small town in the eastern part of India's most populous state, Uttar Pradesh, and is the legendary birthplace of the Hindu god Ram (see Figure 2.1). The story of Ram is told in the traditional Indian epic, the *Ramayana*, historically passed down by storytellers and performed in thousands of versions in a multitude of village dramas. In modern times, Hindu revivalists increasingly focused on Ram and the *Ramayana* as vehicles for a renaissance in Hindu identity. Modern technology accelerated this process, as the epic became available on audiocassettes, television, and videocassettes. In 1987, India's state-run television commenced an eighteen-month serial dramatization of the *Ramayana*. The episodes quickly became the most popular program ever shown.[21]

The growth of Ram's popularity, as symbolized by the phenomenal interest in the *Ramayana*, is important to modern Indian politics and especially to the Ayodhya story for several reasons. It illustrates the degree to which popular culture continues to be infused with traditional cultural-religious images, language, and values, hinting at the persistent gap between the secular nation-state ideology of India's postindependence Nehruvian leadership and the worldviews of average Indians—a gap that only Gandhi (temporarily) bridged.[22] The Ram epic also demonstrates the power of modern communication media to create and sustain mass-based ideologies of nationalism. And the "capture" of Ram by Hindu nationalist organizations shows the dynamics of building support in a competitive electoral democracy.

Legend maintains that Ram was born about 1500 B.C.E. at Ayodhya, but not until the eleventh century, according to Hindu nationalists, was a temple in his honor built in the town. Muslim invaders first arrived in the twelfth century, and in the early sixteenth century, the Babri Mosque (Babri Masjid) was built by a nobleman from the court of Babur, the first Mughal emperor. Long before modern nationalism emerged, Hindus claimed that the mosque was built on the earlier Ram temple site, although contemporary historians note that there is no sixteenth-century evidence to verify this.[23] Hindu-Muslim clashes over the site date to the Mughal Empire, and shortly after the 1857–1858 mutiny, the British built a wall to separate the mosque and the adjoining area where Hindus continued to worship. Thus, conflict over the Babri Masjid has deep historical roots.

In the 1980s, the dispute was revived by the Bharatiya Janata Party and the Vishwa Hindu Parishad (VHP, World Hindu Council), the latter linked to the RSS. Dedicated to the establishment of Hindutva, meaning a Hindu India, the VHP announced a fund-raising drive to build a temple to Ram at Ayodhya and called on devout Hindus to make bricks inscribed with Ram's name. Thousands of volunteers joined processions to Ayodhya to deliver bricks, demolish the mosque, and build a temple. By December 1992, after a long period of government indecision over the growing tension, some 300,000 faithful Hindus—overwhelmingly young men—had gathered at Ayodhya. The central government had amassed a large troop force in anticipation of violence but in fact did not intervene when thousands of the volunteers stormed and destroyed the mosque. Within a few days, more than 1,000 Indians lost their lives in the ensuing communal clashes throughout the country.

The legal and political problems associated with Ayodhya continued to rankle Indian politics. Hindu groups pressed the government to permit construction of a new Ram temple, while courts still sorted through the legal dilemmas of conflicting land-use claims at Ayodhya and other mosque–temple sites.[24] More will be said about the implications of Ayodhya in later chapters; meanwhile, the crisis is a good example of the way history (and historical memory) weighs on the contemporary Indian national identity.

The Kashmir Confrontation

Located in India's far north, the state of Jammu and Kashmir symbolizes the costs of Partition. India claims the whole of the state (see Figure 5.1), but large parts of the state are controlled by China (the Aksai Chin plateau in the east, occupied by China in the 1962 Sino-Indian war) and Pakistan (in the west and north). The region reflects the historical confluence of the cultures and religions that have defined the subcontinent. Hindus are concentrated in the southern region of Jammu (bordering Punjab), and Buddhists in the northeastern mountains of Ladakh. Kashmir, includ-

FIGURE 5.1 Map of Kashmir region. The University of Tennessee Cartographic Laboratory Services; Will Fontanez, cartographer.

ing both the central Vale of Kashmir and the area to the north, is largely Muslim, and the state as a whole has a Muslim majority.

Over the centuries, various parts of the region were controlled by a succession of rulers, including all those noted earlier in this chapter, from the Mauryas and Guptas to the Mughals and British, as well as many lesser-known kingdoms.

From the middle of the nineteenth century until 1947, Jammu and Kashmir was ruled by a Hindu Maharajah as a client state of the British Raj. At Partition one might have expected to see the kingdom, with its Muslim majority, join Pakistan. However, the Vale of Kashmir was the traditional home of the Nehru family, and the Congress Party leaders understood the political and strategic importance of the region. The decision about accession rested with the Maharajah, who stalled indecisively until armed Pakistani tribesmen crossed the frontier in October 1947. The ruler promptly declared the accession of Jammu and Kashmir to India, and the arrival of Indian troops led to the first Indo-Pakistani war. The United Nations negotiated a ceasefire in 1948, establishing the Line of Control that still divides Pakistan and India in Kashmir. Two subsequent wars between India and Pakistan in 1965 and 1971 hardened the hostile positions, while Chinese military incursions into Indian-claimed territory in 1962 fueled India's security fears.

The core issues in the conflict remain the same as in 1948: India claims that the documents of accession confirmed Jammu and Kashmir as an Indian state, while Pakistan claims that a Muslim majority would have placed the state with Pakistan if India had held a U.N.-sponsored plebiscite in 1948, as envisaged by the ceasefire agreement. Despite numerous attempts to negotiate a settlement, the conflict has been exacerbated by three factors: the increasing militarization of the region, the inability of the Indian government to find a satisfactory political formula for governing the state (which has alienated many Muslims), and the rise of Islamic fundamentalism supported by militants both in Kashmir and in Pakistan. This last factor was further complicated by U.S. foreign policy in the wake of the September 2001 acts of terrorism. As the U.S. government pressured the Pakistani government of then–President Pervez Musharraf to crack down on Islamic extremists and to permit the United States to pursue the "war on terrorism" on Pakistani soil—both unpopular policies in Pakistan—the Pakistani government pursued a hard line on Kashmir as a way to rally popular support. Although there has been some improvement in the three-way conflict (India, Pakistan, and Kashmiris)—for example by opening a bus route over the Line of Control—the region remains one of the most dangerous in the world. As suggested in Figure 5.2, international politics, as well as national pride and the rise of domestic fundamentalism among both Muslims and Hindus (the latter the central factor in the Ayodhya crisis), have exacerbated the armed standoff over Kashmir.

Summary

The Indian National Congress took the lead in determining a national identity for India in the half century before independence, but the Congress was fre-

PARTITION AND WAR

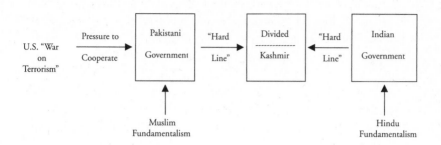

FIGURE 5.2 Diagram of Kashmir conflict.

quently not united and was never the sole "player" in the process of defining an independent India. From the early nineteenth century, Indian intellectual thought was deeply influenced by European ideas and thought systems, including science, law, Christianity, liberalism, and social democracy. It was within the framework of these influences and the realities of British imperialism that Hindu, Muslim, and secular nationalists (such as Nehru) wrestled with the meaning of Indian traditions—historical, spiritual, and cultural—and the strategies that would best serve the goal of pushing the British out of India. The sad irony of *swaraj* was that it happened when and how it did largely as a result of Gandhi's determined moral and political leadership. This leadership, however, contributed to the Hindu tone of Indian nationalism during its formative stages, thus also fueling Muslim anxiety, even as Gandhi risked his life to foster Hindu-Muslim amity. Ultimately, he lost his life to a young Hindu man who believed that Gandhi was pro-Muslim.

Partition was the ultimate tragedy of *swaraj*: It both resulted from and contributed to the spread of communalism in the twentieth century. And as a consequence of Partition, there was less of the subcontinent under the direct control of the Indian state in 1947 than had been controlled by the British Raj at its peak or by the Mauryan Empire of Ashoka more than 2,000 years earlier.

India's politics, both domestic and foreign, remain colored by the issues that were left unresolved at independence. The chief external threat is from Muslim Pakistan, and the regions closest to Pakistan (Punjab and Kashmir) have been badly torn by political and religious strife. Although often isolated, communal violence continues to flare up, with no Gandhi fasting in order to stop it. Ayodhya was a particularly serious crisis, but it has not been the only one. Moreover, the very successes of independent India in introducing and sustaining democratic processes, particularly through elections, have, like the British reforms of the 1930s, increased the political stakes by mobilizing new participants in the political process and thereby sharpening the temptation to appeal to communal loyalties as a way of mustering political support.

Exploring Further

Two films directed by Deepa Mehta (*Earth* and *Water*) address different periods in modern Indian history: *Earth* takes place during Partition and *Water* during the 1930s. The 1982 Richard Attenborough film *Gandhi*—although criticized for its interpretation of both the man Gandhi and the independence movement—offers a broad sweep on the period, with compelling music and photography. Those interested in Gandhi will also find numerous biographies, but his early work, *Hind Swaraj* (*Indian Home Rule*), lays out his philosophy in his own words.

Notes

1. The material in this section was compiled from Sugata Bose and Ayesha Jalal, *Modern South Asia: History, Culture, Political Economy* (London: Routledge, 1998); A. L. Basham, *The Wonder That Was India* (New York: Grove Press, 1959), chap. 3; Romila Thapar, *A History of India*, vol. 1 (Baltimore: Penguin Books, 1966); Stanley Wolpert, *A New History of India*, 2nd ed. (New York: Oxford University Press, 1982); and Deepak Lal, *The Hindu Equilibrium, Vol. 1: Cultural Stability and Economic Stagnation: India 1500 B.C.–A.D. 1980* (Oxford: Clarendon Press, 1988).

2. Rajni Kothari notes that because the principal emphasis is on "duties to" not "rights against," the classical ideal was to limit one's wants, to be content and tolerant of one's lot in life. *Politics in India* (Boston: Little, Brown, 1970), 27.

3. Basham, 66.

4. Both Jainism and Buddhism emerged in the sixth century B.C.E., when their founders sought to reform the rigid Hinduism and tyranny of the Brahmin priests that characterized the period.

5. Bose and Jalal, chap. 4.

6. Kothari, 31–35. Contrast Kothari's emphasis with that of Bose and Jalal, chaps. 3 and 4.

7. Parts of the subcontinent, primarily in the South and West, remained under the Hindu rule of different kingdoms and princely states.

8. Thapar, 301.

9. For the details of British expansion, see Percival Spear, *The Oxford History of Modern India, 1740–1947* (Oxford: Clarendon Press, 1965), chaps. 1–11.

10. Robert L. Hardgrave Jr. and Stanley A. Kochanek, *India: Government and Politics in a Developing Nation*, 5th ed. (Fort Worth, Tex.: Harcourt Brace College Publishers, 1993), 34. See also Bose and Jalal, 85.

11. Kothari, 40. Scholars today argue that colonial influence was even more pervasive than suggested in this quote. Ultimately both the idea and the reality of "India" was largely the result of colonialism. See, for example, Ranajit Guha, *Dominance Without Hegemony: History and Power in Colonial India* (Cambridge, Mass.: Harvard University Press, 1997); and Nicholas B. Dirks, *Caste of Mind: Colonialism and the Making of Modern India* (Princeton: Princeton University Press, 2001).

12. Jim Masselos, *Indian Nationalism: A History*, 2nd ed. (New Delhi: Sterling Publishers, 1991), chap. 2. Bose and Jalal note the mixture of agrarian, religious, racial, and aristocratic dimensions to the rebellion, chap. 9.

13. Bipan Chandra, *Communalism in Modern India* (New Delhi: Vani Educational Books/Vikas Publishing, 1984), 144.

14. Masselos, 134.

15. Chandra, 146.

16. Spear, 261–262, 347. The Raj, like the British East India Company before it, relied on a tax on salt—an essential commodity for all Indians—as a chief source of revenue.

17. Amrit Srinivasan, "Women and Reform of Indian Tradition: Gandhian Alternative to Liberalism," *Economic and Political Weekly*, December 19, 1987, 2226, quoted in Arthur Bonner et al., *Democracy in India: A Hollow Shell* (Washington, D.C.: American University Press, 1994), 200.

18. Granville Austin's term, used in his "The Constitution, Society, and Law," in *India Briefing, 1993*, ed. Philip Oldenburg (Boulder: Westview Press, with the Asia Society, 1993), 111.

19. Hardgrave and Kochanek, 52.

20. The RSS dates from the 1920s; a paramilitary organization, it was opposed to Gandhi's efforts on behalf of Hindu-Muslim unity. The RSS still exists and was implicated in the Ayodhya events of 1992, and the attacks on Muslims in Gujarat in 2002.

21. Susanne Hoeber Rudolph and Lloyd I. Rudolph, "Modern Hate," *New Republic*, March 22, 1993, 26.

22. See the analysis by Sudipta Kaviraj, "On State, Society and Discourse in India," in *Rethinking Third World Politics*, ed. James Manor (London: Longman, 1992), 72–99.

23. Bose and Jalal, 37.

24. Among the cases before different courts were those concerning the rights to worship for both Hindus and Muslims at the disputed site, and another calling for archaeological excavations to determine the truth of the claims regarding a temple to Ram at Ayodhya.

6

Recreating the
Chinese Nation-State

In 2008, the Olympic Games took place in Beijing. The event marked an apex of Chinese confidence and assertiveness after the political and economic instability that had characterized much of the nineteenth and twentieth centuries. Humiliation at the hands of foreign powers; rebellions, civil war, and a revolution that uprooted and impoverished millions of people; uncertainty over both the past and the future of the country—all of this was gone, to be replaced by an obvious sense of national purpose and pride.

To be sure, the Olympics were not without problems. A crackdown in Tibet in May 2008 focused international attention on China's human rights record and the Olympic Torch Relay was dogged by protests in several Western cities. A series of explosions in Xinjiang Province led the government to charges of terrorism and justified another crackdown in that province. Then just as the government might have celebrated an important turning point in contemporary Chinese history in September 2008, it had to focus on a scandal over dairy products tainted with melamine that sickened thousands of children and sent parents across the country into panic.

The overarching political challenge of modern Chinese history has been to establish national unity and, with it, government legitimacy. China has the oldest continuous civilization in the world. Its written language, its traditional system of government, and its ethical norms—to say nothing of Chinese technological and artistic accomplishments—came to define not just the Sinitic world[1] but much of East Asia. Over the course of 3,500 years, the chief features of Chinese civilization developed and with this civilization came a sense of what we would today call national identity. The Chinese defined themselves as the "central country" (the

Middle Kingdom, or *Zhongguo*) and believed they were surrounded by inferior peoples and cultures. The traditions and longevity of the Middle Kingdom bred feelings of confidence, security, and superiority.

Why, with this legacy of a unique, advanced civilization, was China's self-confidence and territorial integrity so badly shaken in the nineteenth century? What has the combination of historical greatness and social, economic, and political demoralization over the course of two centuries meant for the construction of a modern nation-state and a new, or recreated, national identity in the twenty-first century? These are the types of questions this chapter begins to answer by first providing a background in China's traditional system of political and social order, Confucianism. The second major section of the chapter reviews the nineteenth- and twentieth-century challenges to this order, in the form of socioeconomic changes, Western imperialism, and revolution. The chapter then returns to the initial questions posed here and examines two case studies representing the kinds of challenges the Chinese nation-state faces: the reversion of Hong Kong to China and the ambiguous status of Taiwan.

Confucianism: Social Harmony and Virtuous Rule

Approximately 2,500 years ago, there occurred in China a vigorous debate about the nature of government and society. Different philosophical schools proposed alternative answers to questions that are still central to our thinking about politics: the nature of a well-ordered society, the role of force or law in maintaining that order, the desired qualities for rulers, and the ideal relationship between ruler and ruled.

The debate over these questions was generated by the political and social instability marking the decline of one of China's ancient dynasties. Regional kingdoms and their rulers competed for power; the scale and intensity of military conflict grew. But instability and conflict also generated social mobility and intellectual curiosity. Classical Chinese philosophy flourished under these conditions, and not surprisingly, most schools of thought focused more on the problems of this world than on the nature of divinity or deities. As a result, Chinese philosophy took on a predominantly secular and humanistic quality.[2] This secular emphasis is an important source of difference between Chinese and Indian worldviews.

Confucianism, the social and political philosophy that later came to dominate the Chinese government, emerged during this early period. Named after and in honor of the man Confucius ("Master Kung," 551–479 B.C.E.), the doctrines of what we understand today as Confucianism reflect centuries of accretions and reworkings. The disciples of Confucius summarized his life and teachings and, more than Master Kung himself, assured that the master's philosophy would endure. Two centuries after Confucius, for example, Mencius elaborated on Confucius's views regarding human nature, good government, and filial piety.

In addition to the writings of the great teachers and philosophers, government edicts were important in institutionalizing and spreading Confucian ideals, thus transforming Confucius's norms for elite behavior into guidelines and rituals for commoners. In this way, for example, the value placed on patrilineal descent among the ruling houses of early dynasties was embellished by rites for ancestors carried out by sons and grandsons. "Ancestor worship" and filial piety predated Confucius and Mencius, but the emphasis of the scholars on family relationships reinforced preexisting practices. Subsequently, government policies in areas such as population registration, taxation, landownership, and the legal authority of the head of the family (fathers) ensured that these norms would spread across class and geographic lines. After the seventh century, the development of a civil service examination system, which emphasized memorization of the Confucian classics and the concomitant emphasis on education as the road to government success, served also to entrench Confucian ideals and practices.[3]

These Confucian values have played a formative role not just in Chinese civilization but throughout East Asia, as symbolized by Confucian temples (see Photo 6.1). Unlike most Western political philosophy, Confucian thought assumes that individuals exist in a web of social relationships whose maintenance requires conduct characterized by courtesy, proper decorum, compassion, and loyalty. Human beings should strive to perfect their innate qualities of goodness through virtuous and ethical behavior—which means practicing the norms of courtesy, for example, in a manner that sustains and improves social relationships.[4] Thus, there is a logical and inescapable linkage between innate humanness, social context, and public behavior. Social relations ideally mirror family relations, and social (and hence political) order is maintained by the cultivation of proper relationships. Put differently, private and public morality should reflect each other. The goal of the virtuous person—one who reflects both personal and public morality—is government service, a position of great responsibility. In principle, therefore, Confucian norms suggest that modern politicians should be judged as fit or not fit for public roles depending on their personal conduct. Adultery or bad management of family finances or dishonor of one's parents would thus be relevant to the judgments voters make as to a candidate's fitness for public leadership.

As a practical matter, the measure of human perfectibility was best seen in the correct performance of one's social roles. Harmony in family and society alike depended on people knowing what was expected of them in their roles and behaving

PHOTO 6.1 Confucian temple, Taiwan. Photo courtesy of James W. Boyd.

accordingly. This is the origin of the role relationships discussed in Chapter 3 in connection with Chinese patriarchy. In addition to the husband-wife relationship, four others were critical: those between ruler and subject, father and son, brother and brother, and neighbor and neighbor. From the emphasis on social relationships, in turn, came other characteristics of traditional Chinese society: its hierarchical nature, the diminished significance of individual autonomy, and the stress on correct behavior. Both family socialization and formal education would guarantee that people understood their roles and behaved accordingly.

It is worth noting at this point that although there are many important differences between the traditional Confucian and the Hindu worldviews, there are two similarities that are important here: the correct performance of social roles and a ranking of those roles within a social context viewed as naturally hierarchical. Thus, all humans are not "created equal" in the sense commonly understood in North America. This does not mean, however, that individuals do not have intrinsic worth but rather that their worth is defined by social context—whether that context is family, clan, caste, village, or a combination of these.

One of the important differences between these two great traditions is that Confucianism has always been explicitly political in its intent and its consequences. In theory, governing was viewed largely as a matter of ethical conduct, and political power resulted from virtuous conduct. The emperor was the living representative of the natural hierarchical order of the universe and in his person were joined heaven, earth, and humanity, as represented in the Chinese character for "king" (see Figure 6.1). Influential Han dynasty thinkers argued that the emperor occupied the center of heaven but was only "Heaven's agent."[5] This argument contributed to the idea that the emperor's rule reflected the Mandate of Heaven, the loss of which was generally determined after the fact, when a dynasty fell. The Mandate of Heaven and the accompanying theory of dynastic cycles thus injected the potential for dramatic change of rule in an otherwise conservative, increasingly rigid set of governing norms. Dynastic cycles typically reflected the following sequence: Social and political disorder signaled dynastic decline and was followed by military conflict; restored peace brought economic and social well-being; but then growing resource scarcity was followed by repression and exploitation, rebellion, and finally the fall of another dynasty. Dynastic collapse was interpreted as meaning that the ruler had lost his mandate to govern.

Thus, Confucianism contains both conservative and radical elements. Its conceptualization of the good society stresses order, reciprocal relationships, and an ethical hierarchy in which some are more virtuous than others. Confucius and his followers expressed reverence for the past and the study of history, and their system has always been profoundly patriarchal and elitist. At the same time, at its best Confucianism "has been critical philosophy, one that saw a great gap between the possibilities of humanity and the reality of any given era. In this sense it is very radical and progressive."[6] Its emphasis on the educability of human beings offers the potential for both individual and social change. And for all their emphasis on social stability, Confucian philosophers recognized that human misery is incompatible with goodness: Those who are desperate for food or other basic necessities cannot be expected to fulfill human potential.

Despite the emphasis on ethical behavior, law and bureaucracy were hardly absent from traditional Chinese government. Han thinkers, in elaborating Confucian norms, were in large part legitimizing their own dynastic rule against that of

FIGURE 6.1 Chinese character for "king."
Calligraphy courtesy of Kai-Ho Mah.

the preceding Qin dynasty, which had governed briefly and ruthlessly in the third century B.C.E. The Qin rulers were influenced by the so-called Legalist school, one of the numerous philosophies that competed with Confucianism in ancient China. The Legalists' prescription for government exalted state authority, military rule, and absolute, centralized administration, all legitimized through detailed, comprehensive laws. Even though the Qin dynasty was short-lived and Legalist thought gave way to Confucian norms, the emphasis on both bureaucracy and laws would be grafted onto and would coexist with Confucian values in politics. The value placed on proper behavior and virtue, on the one hand, and on centralized, hierarchical institutions, on the other, means that Chinese political philosophy and government practice were both more complex and flexible than is sometimes thought and that in China (as elsewhere) there was often a considerable gap between the ideal society and the political reality.

Opium, Humiliation, and Failed Reform

The Opium War (1839–1842) between China and Britain is central to our story of national identity for two reasons. First, it inaugurated the pattern of foreign imperialism and Chinese weakness that lasted until the twentieth century. Second, because of this pattern, the Opium War became the symbol of Chinese humiliation and prompted a century-long struggle to free China from foreign control and influence.

Western pressure coincided with a period of growing domestic difficulty in China. The late eighteenth and early nineteenth centuries saw the Qing dynasty in economic and political decline, with opposition to Qing rule increasing both at the lowest and highest levels of Chinese society.[7] Although the decline and the corresponding opposition undermined the ability of the Chinese government to resist Western pressure later in the nineteenth century, the government was by no means enfeebled enough to acquiesce in foreign demands at the outset of the century.

The confrontation between Britain and China was caused initially by trade and balance of payments problems. European countries, as well as the United States, found it difficult to balance the cost of their imports of consumer goods from China, notably tea, silk, and porcelain, with sales of Western products. The difference was made up by shipments of silver bullion. By the 1820s, foreigners discovered that opium (produced in British India) commanded high prices in China and that its sale quickly redressed their balance of payments problem (and created one for China). Meanwhile, the conviction that China and the Chinese did not have to be treated as equals and the desire to eliminate all restrictions on foreign trade with China accelerated. Economics and culture—the latter colored by orientalist thinking in Europe—thus merged to produce contempt for Chinese vulnerability. When a Chinese official tried to confiscate all the opium in Guangzhou (Canton), the British, who had been at the forefront of the opium trade and whose efforts to establish diplomatic relations with China had been frustrated for decades, sent warships and troops to the China coast in 1839 and 1840. The fighting that followed was limited, in large part due to China's decidedly inferior military forces.

The Treaty of Nanjing (1842) ended the Opium War and set the standard for the unequal treaties that followed for the rest of the century. China ceded the island of Hong Kong to Britain, and British traders were given the right to reside and conduct business in five cities ("treaty ports") on China's coast. Not to be left out, the United States negotiated a treaty in 1844 that, in addition to securing trading privileges, established the principle of extraterritorial jurisdiction, which meant that foreign residents would be governed by the laws of their own countries, not China's. Belgium, Sweden, Norway, France, Russia, and, ultimately, Germany and Japan followed with more demands and more treaties.

In this fashion, Western imperialism and the unequal treaties provoked a sense in China of national humiliation, which in turn became the focus of a growing nationalist movement. As noted earlier, Western contact coincided with rising discontent within China. The nineteenth century, in fact, was bracketed by two major rebellions, and there was a third in midcentury: the White Lotus Rebellion (1796–1804); the great Taiping Rebellion of the 1850s; and, at the end of the century, the Boxer Uprising (1899–1900).[8] To these were added a growing number of smaller peasant rebellions from the 1840s on, major Muslim revolts in the Northwest and the Southwest, and social disorder sparked by bandit gangs.[9] Both economic and political factors precipitated the revolts. For example, the population pressures that have generated concern in contemporary China had already produced declining standards of living by the beginning of the nineteenth century as arable land, in particular, became scarce.

In retrospect, we know that the decline of the Qing dynasty both reflected and exacerbated the economic problems. The corruption of government officials that accompanied the opium trade undermined the dynasty's effectiveness and legitimacy. As the quality of the government's services waned and the quality of its officials diminished, so did its ability to maintain order. The spiral foreseen in the theory of dynastic cycles was set in motion, with the rebellions of the century punctuating the last phases of the cycle.

Whereas some of the revolts targeted local officials, the Taiping rebels challenged the legitimacy of the Qing dynasty itself. Borrowing extensively from

Taiping beliefs

Western ideas, particularly Christianity, the Taiping resembled the twentieth-century Communists in their rejection of the old order (both Confucianism and Manchu rule), their organizational and ideological discipline, and their missionary zeal.[10] The Taiping were also notable for their apparent commitment to women's rights: Foot binding in areas under Taiping control was forbidden; women received land under the same conditions as men, could sit for government examinations, and could hold official posts. Women even fought in Taiping armies.

The failure of the Taiping Rebellion was complete by the mid-1860s, and by the end of the 1860s, all the other important rebellions that threatened the Qing had been stilled. For a short time thereafter, a reform movement known as the Tongzhi Restoration, so named after the reign title of the young emperor who ascended the throne in 1861, promised revival of Qing rule. Viewed broadly, the Tongzhi Restoration was a conservative restoration whose purpose was to reestablish peace and well-being by using Confucian practices to reverse, at least for a time, the course of dynastic decline. The restoration did not seek massive change legitimized in the name of an emperor "restored" to authority (as in Meiji Japan) but sought rather to restore virtue and stability to public life through the reaffirmation of Confucian values.[11] Hence, the Tongzhi Restoration never became for China what the Meiji Restoration was for Japan during the same period, that is, a period of dramatic modernization and nation building (see Chapter 7). Its failure can be attributed to a variety of factors, including corruption, divided leadership, and the overwhelming nature of the problems China faced in the mid-nineteenth century.

The events of the mid-nineteenth century, including Western encroachment, the Taiping Rebellion, and the Tongzhi Restoration, are all relevant to China's twentieth-century nation building. For late-nineteenth- and early-twentieth-century reformers, the "foreign calamity" of the Opium War and unequal treaties spurred debates about the relative merits of, and relationship between, Chinese culture and Western technology. Many reformers adopted the slogan "Chinese learning for the essence [*ti*]; Western learning for practical use [*yong*]." Putting the *ti-yong* ideology into practice, however, was impossible without undermining the assumptions of the Confucian Chinese worldview.

Although designed to secure social and political stability, Confucian philosophy had always admitted the necessity of change, for change provided the flexibility that ensured maintenance of the overall system. Even the most massive of changes, those in the dynastic cycle, were accommodated by Confucian political theory. The type of change that could hardly be accommodated was that which challenged the universality and the validity of the assumptions undergirding the Confucian worldview. China might learn from the West certain techniques and accept certain kinds of technology, but behind Western technology lay the assumptions and worldview of science, including the primacy of human control over nature and a linear concept of progress. These differed from the core of traditional Confucianism, in which history was viewed as cyclical and thinkers concentrated on the problems of human relationships rather than on human mastery over the material world. To abandon these core assumptions would, in the view of Tongzhi reformers, constitute a refutation of universal truth and a denial of the essence of Chinese greatness.

By the end of the nineteenth century, the gap between Confucian knowledge and institutions, on the one hand, and the reality of the challenge of Western civilization, on the other, was magnified. The temporary vigor instilled by the Tongzhi Restoration had waned. Many of the symptoms that had led to the Taiping Rebellion (overtaxation, high rent, loss of land, lack of protection from corrupt officials) by fueling discontent in rural areas resurfaced. Meanwhile, at the highest levels, lack of direction and corruption in government and the imperial court compounded the crisis. "As a result, there was no real example of honesty and integrity where Confucian theory said they were most essential, at the top."[12]

The nineteenth century ended and the twentieth century began with a series of events that symbolized China's failure to respond to the growing crises besetting the country. The turning point was the Sino-Japanese War of 1894–1895, in which Japan, historically the country that looked up to and borrowed from its more advanced neighbor, now demonstrated the abject weakness of the Chinese state by inflicting military defeat.[13] In 1898, reformers who advocated following Japan's example in the vigorous adoption of foreign knowledge and institutions demanded a constitutional monarchy and for a short time even controlled the government. Ambitious reform, however, provoked a conservative reaction from those who argued that Chinese civilization could not be adapted to Western science and technology, which would inevitably destroy Confucian values.

There was a new element in this late-century debate—nationalism—and it focused attention on a central question: Was it better to try to "save" Confucian culture and Chinese civilization (as traditionally defined) in their mutual dependence or to save the Chinese nation-state even if it meant the (necessary) sacrifice of traditional culture? The reformers argued for the nation-state, the conservatives for cultural integrity.[14] The implications of the question can hardly be overstated. The Chinese had defined themselves for centuries as the Middle Kingdom, superior and central in the scheme of the universe. Now "barbarians" and borrowers (the Japanese had begun their long history of borrowing religion, language, and government institutions from China in the seventh century) alike had gone from imposing unequal treaties to securing territorial concessions along China's coast.[15] The implications for the radical reformers were clear: China's universe no longer existed, having been replaced by a world of cutthroat competition among nation-states.

The Boxer Uprising of 1898–1900 was sparked by a convergence of developments that exemplified the problems China faced at the turn of the century. The Boxers, so-named because of the gestures that accompanied their ritualistic dancing, were centered in Shandong Province, for some years a target of Christian missionaries and the base for German concessions. Beset by prolonged famine, massive flooding, and long-term economic decline, young Chinese men, most of whom faced bleak economic prospects, were drawn to a series of organizations that attacked the growing foreign presence. If the Chinese state would not defend itself against imperialism, gunboat diplomacy, and the expanding power of Christian churches, the Boxers would.[16]

The Boxers attacked churches, missionaries, Chinese Christians, and, ultimately, everything foreign. Support for the Boxers spread throughout Northeast China, and in 1900, they cut rail communications between Beijing and Tianjin and laid siege to foreign legations in Beijing. Originally supporting the Boxers, the government subsequently opposed them as it became clear they were out of control. In the end, it took an international contingent of troops to relieve the legations.

The ignominy of the Boxer Uprising and its repression added to the conviction among many Chinese intellectuals that China's national humiliation was due specifically to the Qing rulers who were, after all, Manchus by origin and therefore foreigners themselves (that is, not part of the Han people). The most important of these reformers was Sun Yat-sen (Sun Zhong-shan, 1866–1925), who, ironically, was a Christian and had been educated at a mission school in Hawaii. Trained as a doctor, Sun practiced medicine in Portuguese Macao; only semi-trained in the Chinese classics, he was never imbued with the full weight of Confucian ideology and this fact, together with his contacts with the Western world and Chinese expatriots, undoubtedly made him more open to ideas of radical change.

In 1905, Sun played a leadership role in founding the Tongmeng Hui[17] in Tokyo, where many Chinese students went to learn from the Japanese experience with modernization. The manifesto of the Tongmeng Hui addressed specifically Chinese concerns while showing the influence of Western republican ideas on Sun's thinking. The manifesto laid out the league's objectives as driving out the "Tartars" (Manchus) and restoring "China of the Chinese," establishing a republic, and equalizing landownership. The manifesto also called for the elimination of "social evils" such as slavery, foot binding, and opium use.[18]

The last major efforts to reform the Qing dynasty came as the revolutionary movement represented by Sun Yat-sen was also building. The government reformers sought to learn both from Japan and from Western nations as they set about abolishing the old examination system (in place since the seventh century); creating new educational programs, a modern army, and legal and financial systems; and exploring the possibilities for constitutional government. Of these changes, the most important was probably education. But in order to have modern education, students had to leave China, which put them in contact with anti-Qing revolutionary groups such as the Tongmeng Hui. "By giving modern education to its prospective official class, the dynasty reared its own executioners, dug its own grave, and signed its own death warrant."[19] It was as the Confucian conservatives had foreseen.

Republican and Communist Revolution

In 1911, the revolutionaries sparked revolts, including troop mutinies, in several cities. The Qing court turned to Yuan Shikai, the general who had overturned the 1898 reforms and had subsequently become one of the most powerful men in China, to crush the rebellion. Yuan had been dismissed from office two years earlier with the fear that he was becoming too powerful. Now he bargained with the court: Manchus were being massacred throughout China; to save the situation, Yuan would become premier of the new Republic of China (ROC). Within a few weeks, on December 25, 1911, Sun Yat-sen returned from Europe and was quickly elected provisional president of the Chinese republic by the delegates of sixteen provincial assemblies, meeting in Nanjing. "China now had both a republican president and a Manchu emperor,"[20] but after frantic negotiations, the last Manchu emperor abdicated in February 1912. Shortly thereafter, in order to consolidate and legitimize the new government, Sun urged the Nanjing assembly to elect Yuan Shikai as provisional president, which it did.

The 1911 Republican revolution was primarily political. It eliminated the imperial system, but in its place were Yuan Shikai, increasingly an autocratic ruler; Sun Yat-sen's fledgling Kuomintang[21] (KMT), or Nationalist Party (the successor to the Tongmeng Hui); and a variety of regional forces whose strength grew as the infrastructure of dynastic rule disintegrated. Within five years after the revolution, China entered a period of warlordism, in which regional military leaders competed for power. Not only did warlordism prevent the development of the strong nation-state that had been a central goal of the revolutionaries, but it contributed to China's economic problems by inhibiting the development of production and commerce.

Juxtaposed against this political confusion and economic dislocation was continued intellectual ferment, especially among the young students exposed to exciting ideas from Europe, the United States, and the newly founded Soviet Union. The appeal of Western liberalism for many of the new intelligentsia turned into disillusionment when the Versailles Conference, which met in 1919 to formally negotiate settlements to end World War I, awarded Shandong to Japan, which had conquered the territory from the Germans in 1914. Japan, like China, had been on the victorious side of the war,[22] but the Chinese assumed that Shandong would be returned to China. When the Chinese delegate to Versailles acquiesced in the Japanese conquest, several thousand Chinese students demonstrated in Beijing at Tiananmen Square on May 4, 1919. The demonstrations set off a nationwide strike, in which the students were joined by members of the new urban working and middle classes. The protesters' themes were anti-imperialism and nationalism; they called for a new society based on science and democracy. Japanese nationals were attacked, and thousands of students were jailed.

The May Fourth Movement that emerged after World War I was first and foremost an intellectual and political movement that attracted significant numbers of young women as well as men. Beijing University had become the preeminent center of nationalism and political activism in China. One can imagine the excitement of the period, with ideas ranging from those of the American pragmatist, John Dewey, to those of Soviet Marxists-Leninists informing the debates about China's future. It was in this atmosphere of the quest for ideas and pragmatic solutions to China's problems, a quest fueled by intense nationalism, that the Chinese Communist Party (CCP) was formed. The first meeting of the party took place in Shanghai in 1921; present were two organizers from the Comintern, or Communist International, the organization established by the Russian Bolsheviks to foster Communist revolutions in Europe and elsewhere. Among the dozen Chinese present was Mao Zedong, who went on to play a central role in the growth of the Communist movement and dominated politics in China from the 1940s until his death in 1976.

Political-Military Conflicts: The Chinese Civil War

In order to provide an overview of the chaotic period from the early 1920s to the Communist victory in 1949, the following discussion is divided into two sections, the first dealing with the general lines of the conflict between the Nationalists and Communist Chinese and the second with the organizational, social, and ideological programs of the Communists that defined their revolution from the 1930s to the early 1950s.

At the time of the creation of the Communist Party, the dominant political force in China was the Kuomintang, and Sun Yat-sen was the most influential political leader, already seen as father of the Republican revolution both in China and elsewhere. Partly because of the legitimacy of Sun and the KMT and partly because Soviet Communists believed that it would be many years before the Communist Party could lead China to the kind of revolution that Russia had experienced, Comintern advisers ordered the handful of Chinese Communists to join the KMT as individuals. While maintaining an individual membership in the Nationalist Party, they would continue their Communist Party membership and discipline and eventually be in a position to shape the KMT into a force to unify the country and lead a socialist revolution. The Comintern position thus established one of the most curious facets of the long and bitter competition between the Communist and Nationalist parties: Both were structured in the early 1920s according to the dictates of Leninist organization in order to create a centralized Chinese government allied to Moscow (see Chapter 10). But from the viewpoint of the Russian Communist advisers in China, in the early 1920s the KMT was far better placed than the Communist Party to serve as a vanguard.

One of the first initiatives of the reorganized KMT was to establish the Whampoa Military Academy in Guangzhou in order to train the military leadership necessary to seize control from China's regional warlords and create a strong, central authority. The head of the Academy was Chiang Kai-shek (Jiang Jieshi, 1887–1978), who assumed leadership of the KMT in 1925, after Sun died. Chiang became the most important non-Communist leader in China during the civil war period and, after 1949, was president of the Republic of China on Taiwan.

Soviet influence was felt not only in the organization of the KMT and the CCP and the mandate for their cooperation but also in the dominant direction of Communist ideology and strategy. Consistent with Marxist-Leninist thought, the Communist Party gave priority to organizing workers in the urban areas. In spite of the fact that this left Communist organizers vulnerable to party opponents, the CCP continued to be urban-based until the late 1920s. The Communists failed in several cities where they organized armed uprisings, but Moscow continued to control organizational and ideological matters at the top level of the CCP.

By the end of the 1920s, the CCP was split between those who still maintained the Moscow ties and gave priority to organizing urban workers, and those who, like Mao Zedong, had retreated to the rural areas to concentrate on organizing the peasantry. By the early 1930s, these rural-based organizers were developing actual governing power in the form of separate "soviets," whose governments were a blend of civilian and military rule, concentrated in the southeastern province of Jiangxi. During this same period, the "Red Army" (which later became the People's Liberation Army, or PLA) was established as the movement's military arm.

The period from the late 1920s to the beginning of China's full-scale war with Japan saw the peak of the Nationalists' power. Chiang succeeded in eliminating or co-opting most of the provincial warlords, establishing a new capital in Nanjing, and undertaking programs of modernization. He also turned his attention to eliminating the Jiangxi soviets through a series of "encirclement campaigns" in which troops were sent to exterminate the Communist bases. Finally, in 1934, this military pressure forced the Communists to abandon their soviets and undertake the Long March, which lasted one year and took the party members, the PLA, and their followers some 6,000 miles to Northwest China. Here the Communists reestablished themselves in Shaanxi Province. During the Long March, in July 1935, the Communist leadership reorganized the party and conclusively ended the old Moscow-inspired line of urban-based revolution. It was during this same period that Mao Zedong became the dominant (though not undisputed) leader of the Communist Party, a position that he was to hold until his death forty-one years later.

Historians continue to debate the accomplishments of the Kuomintang and Chiang Kai-shek during the Nanjing period, when the Communists frequently seemed on the verge of extinction. Whether the KMT might have succeeded in implementing its nationalist revolution is now a moot point, for its efforts were challenged not only by the Chinese Communists, but, more important in the mid-1930s, by the Japanese. In 1931, Japanese militarists provoked a crisis that led to their annexation of resource-rich Manchuria and the creation of a state they called Manchukuo, headed by the last Manchu emperor. In 1937, close to Beijing, Japanese troops attacked Chinese units, an incident that led to all-out war in East Asia. The Japanese moved quickly to control China's principal cities and coastal regions, as well as the railroad system. The brutality of the Japanese, particularly in such incidents as the "rape of Nanjing," discussed in Chapter 1, encouraged national unity for a time between the Communists and the Nationalists, as well as among some remaining regional forces.

In retrospect, it is hard to overestimate the importance of the Japanese invasion and occupation of China. The Japanese skillfully exploited political and regional divisions in China; and their demand for an East Asian "coprosperity sphere" played to the anti-Western strain in Chinese nationalism. But the lingering bitterness in China over Japanese imperialism colors relations between the two countries even today, particularly when issues relevant to the wartime period reemerge (such as the controversy over the way in which Japanese textbooks describe this era).

As the Nationalist government displayed its corruption and its ineffectiveness in dealing with the war effort, the political confusion and self-doubt that were temporarily obscured by the heroism of the early war period began to reemerge. In contrast to the Nationalists, the Communists seemed unified, purposeful, determined, and responsive to the needs of ordinary Chinese. These were the advantages that they brought to the final years of the civil war, after the defeat of Japan in 1945.

Building the Revolution

Those who survived the Long March, approximately 10,000 of the nearly 100,000 who had set out from Jiangxi, settled in the mountainous region of Yan'an. Although the heroism of the Long March became one of the epic stories of the Communist revolution, in late 1935 the potential for revolution looked far from promising. The party had lost its southern bases, massive numbers of troops, and its supporters. For several years, the Communists pursued a "united front" policy with the Nationalists against the Japanese. The Red Army, consisting of more than 30,000 combat troops (including battle-hardened survivors of the Long March), was placed under nominal Kuomintang control, although it was actually commanded by veteran Communist commanders. The CCP leadership worked hard to ensure that, at all levels, its troops did not exploit the local farming communities on which they depended for food and supplies. These practices, along with the education and indoctrination programs of the Communists, gradually widened their base of support.

The united front policy, as well as the need to maximize support in order to secure and expand their bases, encouraged the Communists to pursue moderate strategies during the war period. Their bases utilized a tripartite system of political power: The local governments were composed of one-third Communist Party members, one-third "progressive" (left-wing) elements, and one-third independents. Drawing on Mao Zedong's experience in Hunan Province during the 1920s and the experience of the Jiangxi soviets, the CCP concentrated on building support in rural areas by pursuing a reformist agricultural policy that emphasized reduction of rent and interest rates. In this fashion, both poor and middle-class peasants were attracted to the Communist Party program.

The extent of the Communist revolution as developed at Yan'an (both its promise and its limitations) can be seen in its policy toward women. The area in northern China where the Communist armies settled in the mid-1930s was even more restrictive in terms of the traditional norms governing women's behavior than Jiangxi and certainly more conservative than the urban areas from which some of the revolutionaries came. Foot binding was still practiced and the "big feet" of the women who moved into the region as part of the Communist settlements were strange and

even to some (in the context of the times) shocking. In this atmosphere, issues pertaining to women's rights were avoided by CCP leaders as too sensitive and divisive: "Official policy toward family reform became more conservative. The low-priority support given to implementing women's rights and marriage reforms in Kiangsi [Jiangxi] narrowed further in the wartime base areas and eventually turned to active suppression of those who attempted to raise such issues within the Party."[23]

Despite the low priority accorded social issues such as marriage reform and physical abuse of women, there were periodic efforts to encourage women's political participation and, above all, participation in economic production. The emphasis on production was consistent with the Marxist emphasis on economic revolution as the avenue to sociopolitical revolution and gender equality. Even more important was the desperate economic and political situation in which the Communists found themselves in the early 1940s, when the Japanese accelerated their attacks on Communist areas and cut them off from virtually all outside supplies. Thousands of women were organized (and paid) to produce cloth to meet the army's continuous need for uniforms and blankets. Although the policy was born of necessity, not feminism, one result was to offer women an opportunity to earn some money and to work with other women outside the restrictions of the family.[24]

In retrospect, the Communist experiences of the 1930s and 1940s were important for the post-1949 period because these were years not just of ideological pronouncements but also of practice. Party and army cadres learned both the limits and the possibilities of moderate policies and learned who could be trusted and who not. It was thus a period of organizational consolidation, and it laid the groundwork for the daunting tasks of reconstruction and revolution that confronted the new People's Republic of China (PRC) after 1949.

The Historical Legacy: Hong Kong and Taiwan

In closing, this chapter turns to two contemporary cases of the way in which the history of the past two centuries influences the worldview of China's leaders and sets the context for their thinking about national integrity and state security. These cases also illustrate the dynamic interplay between domestic and international politics. Hong Kong's reversion to China in 1997 (and Macao's in 1999) left only Taiwan outside the Chinese nation-state as it has been defined since the Qing dynasty. The transfer of power over Hong Kong reinforced China's unity, but the ambiguous status of Taiwan was both a mandate for Beijing and a potential threat to East Asian stability.

Hong Kong: "One Country, Two Systems"

The British presence in Hong Kong dates from the late 1830s, when, in the growing tension that preceded the Opium War, the British community in Guangzhou retreated to the island. At that time, the thirty-square-mile island was largely uninhabited, but it would later become the chief port for European ships coming to China. The area between the island of Hong Kong and the Kowloon Peninsula boasts one of the best deep-water harbors in the world, a fact that did not escape the British. The Treaty of Nanjing, signed after the Opium War, provided for the cession of Hong Kong to Britain "in perpetuity." In 1860, the southern part of the Kowloon Peninsula was ceded in perpetuity also, and in 1898, the New Territories were leased to Britain for ninety-nine years. With these acquisitions, the British controlled more than 350 square miles of prime coastal territory by the turn of the century.

It was the impending end of the ninety-nine-year lease on the New Territories that prompted the opening of negotiations between the United Kingdom and the People's Republic of China on the status of all the territories taken in the nineteenth century. After two years of talks, the governments of the two countries issued a joint declaration in 1984 describing a new status for Hong Kong as of July 1, 1997. The most important provision was the PRC's agreement to create a Hong Kong "special administrative region" (SAR) after resuming sovereignty over the area. The SAR would be given the right to maintain its laws and its social and economic systems for a period of fifty years after reunification.[25] In 1988, the Basic Law for the Hong Kong SAR was issued by the National People's Congress of the PRC, and it has served as Hong Kong's Constitution since 1997.[26]

The transfer of power went smoothly, and over the next few years most visitors could see little evidence that reversion had changed life in the former colony. Nonetheless, careful observers—particularly those critical of China's heavy-handed policies after the quashing of the 1989 demonstrations at Tiananmen Square—frequently expressed alarm about the erosion of rights in Hong Kong under the new "one country, two systems" formula. For example, elections to the Legislative Council (LegCo), Hong Kong's legislative body, were structured to guarantee the dominance by representatives deemed loyal to the central government. Representation in the body is split between geographic constituencies, where direct elections determine thirty delegates, and functional constituencies, from which thirty delegates representing professions such as finance, medicine, accountancy, and so on, are indirectly chosen.[27] Democracy activists have pressed for direct elections, believing that under such an arrangement they could win a majority in LegCo. However, talks on universal suffrage and direct elections for both the Hong Kong chief executive and the legislature have been postponed twice.[28]

Five years after reversion, those alarmed by what they saw as Beijing's creeping control focused on language drafted to implement Article 23 of the 1988 Basic Law. Article 23 specifies that:

> The Hong Kong Special Administrative Region shall enact laws on its own to prohibit any act of treason, secession, sedition, subversion against the Central People's Government, or theft of state secrets, to prohibit foreign political organizations or bodies from conducting political activities in the Region, and to prohibit political organizations or bodies of the Region from establishing ties with foreign political organizations or bodies.

The Hong Kong SAR government issued its recommendations for language to implement the provisions of Basic Law 23 in September 2002. Under the proposal, those found guilty of acts of treason or sedition could be imprisoned for life. Those found guilty of inciting violence or public disorder could be jailed for up to seven years. The government stated that it would consider public comments on its proposals before issuing its implementation legislation in 2003, but critics feared that the provisions would severely curtail freedoms such as speech and assembly through broad definitions of offenses in a way to preclude practices that had been legal after 1997, such as reporting on Taiwanese independence movements. The debate over Article 23 came to a head on July 1, 2003, when 500,000 people demonstrated against the proposed legislation. Subsequently, several key members of the Hong Kong administration resigned in response to the controversy. Finally in September, Hong Kong's chief executive, Tung Chee-hwa, announced that he was withdrawing the proposed legislation, presumably with Beijing's acquiescence. In 2005, Tung resigned his post two years before the expiration of his term, citing health problems and stress. He was replaced by Donald Tsang.

There is no guarantee that even when (or if) negotiations for a more democratic electoral system are undertaken, the people of Hong Kong will agree. Changes will require a two-thirds majority of the legislature, and it is possible that in the end, a majority of voters and legislators will succumb to the appeal of maintaining a familiar status quo.

From the outset, the central problem of the "one country, two systems" structure has been the lack of transparency in the administrative interaction between the leadership in Beijing and in Hong Kong, which means that the making and implementation of decisions remains murky. Nominally, the SAR is autonomous: "Yet this autonomy is based on a *noblesse oblige* with Chinese characteristics."[29]

Taiwan: Two Systems, Two Countries?

When China lost the Sino-Japanese War in 1895, it ceded Taiwan to Japan, which controlled the island until the end of World War II in 1945.[30] In the late 1940s, Taiwan was an acknowledged part of China. The ongoing civil war, however, made it impossible for the Chinese government to exercise effective control over all its territory. In October 1949, after the PLA had driven the Nationalists off the mainland, Mao Zedong proclaimed that the formal name of China, including Taiwan, was the People's Republic of China. Taiwan, where the forces of Chiang Kai-shek had fled, kept the name Republic of China. Thereafter, for several decades, the governments of the Republic of China and the People's Republic of China both claimed to be the sole de jure (lawful) government of the State of China. Soon after 1949, most governments recognized the PRC as the legitimate government of China, as the United States was preparing to do until mid-1950. But when North Korean troops invaded South Korea in June 1950, the United States extended its defense perimeter to Taiwan, which quickly became a bulwark to help contain what the American government saw as a "red" (communist) tidal wave sweeping across Asia. Until 1979, when it changed its official policy to recognize the PRC as the sole legitimate government of China, the United States was the primary military and economic supporter of the Republic of China on Taiwan and the Kuomintang, which governed it.

From 1949 until the mid-1980s, Taiwan—however portrayed as part of the "free world"—was, in fact, a single-party dictatorship, ruled by martial law. The KMT, as noted earlier, had benefited from Soviet organizational advice in the early 1920s. Only after the death of Chiang Kai-shek in 1975 did his son, Chiang Ching-kuo (who succeeded his father as president of the ROC), take steps toward liberalizing the political system. Opposition parties became legal only in the mid-1980s, and not until March 2000 was a non-KMT candidate able to win the presidency.[31]

When the new president, Chen Shui-bian, ended a half century of KMT rule, his victory was hailed as an important benchmark in Taiwan's shift toward democratic development. At the same time, his election sent tremors of nervousness throughout East Asia. Chen's party, the Democratic Progressive Party (DPP), had distinguished itself from the KMT as a party supporting Taiwan's independence from China—a position that has always been unacceptable to the PRC. President

Chen was narrowly reelected in 2004, but the DPP lost badly in both the presidential and legislative elections of 2008. Issues such as Taiwan's identity and the often-tense relations with the PRC during the Chen presidency were important, but even more important were the ongoing, widespread charges of government corruption and economic decline under the DPP. Taiwan's new president, Ma Ying-jeou, pledged to maintain the status quo in cross-strait relations, but his party, the Kuomintang, generally favored closer relations with Beijing.

In retrospect, the 2000–2008 period under Chen Shui-bian may prove to have been the high-water mark for a Taiwan independence movement. Chen's pronouncements increased tension with Beijing and often with the United States. For most governments, continuation of Taiwan's legally ambiguous status with its de facto military and political autonomy would be the ideal situation. However, this status has been rejected consistently and forcefully by the PRC, which sees incorporation of its Taiwanese province (like Tibet and Hong Kong) as an essential step toward unifying historic China.

Summary

The reversion of Hong Kong and the status of Taiwan recall themes central to Chinese history that are also critical to understanding contemporary politics. The political and intellectual turmoil generated by the simultaneous decay of the imperial system and Western imperialism convinced reformers and revolutionaries alike that centralized state power, territorial integrity, and socioeconomic change were all essential to recreating Chinese greatness. The Communist Party succeeded where late-nineteenth-century and early-twentieth-century reformers and, later, the Kuomintang failed. Its success was due to a number of factors, the most important of which were the war with Japan, corruption and division within the KMT, and the cohesion and political-military skill, as well as ruthlessness, of the CCP.

The preoccupation with state and nation building, as well as with social revolution, characterized not only the CCP's drive for power in China but its rule after 1949. By the 1960s, it seemed that the Communists had largely succeeded in eradicating "feudal" structures and ways of thinking. In retrospect, we know that to be a hasty judgment: The preference for sons explained in Chapter 3 illustrates just one way in which old social patterns die slowly.

Exploring Further

For background information and annotated links on Taiwan, see the "Taiwan Cross-Strait Directory" at http://apdl.kcc.hawaii.edu/~taiwan/. Among the many historical novels about China, *Snow Flower and the Secret Fan* (2005) provides a compelling portrait of village life in the first half of the nineteenth century, with insights into gender relations, social customs, and economic conditions. The commercial film *The Last Emperor* (1987) offers colorful interpretations of the life of the Emperor Puyi, with good period costumes and views of the Forbidden City.

Notes

1. Technically, the term *Sinitic* refers to a branch of the Sino-Tibetan languages that includes Chinese and its "dialects." As an adjective, Sinitic is also used to mean Chinese.

2. A secular emphasis does not mean that Chinese society (then or now) has been devoid of religious traditions or impulses. Animism, for example, has ancient roots in China, and Confucius, who was profoundly humanistic in his concerns, drew on religious sentiment by linking his proposed good order with Heaven, or the natural order of things.

3. On this historical process, see Patricia Ebrey, "The Chinese Family and the Spread of Confucian Values," in *The East Asian Region: Confucian Heritage and Its Modern Adaptation*, ed. Gilbert Rozman (Princeton: Princeton University Press, 1991), 45–83.

4. Early Confucian scholars debated whether human beings were inherently good. Mencius believed they were, but another third-century B.C.E. philosopher, Xunzi, said that "man was evil" and "goodness is acquired." See his argument in William Theodore de Bary and Irene Bloom, comps., *Sources of Chinese Tradition*, 2nd ed., vol. 1 (New York: Columbia University Press, 1999), 179–183.

5. See, for example, de Bary and Bloom, 300–301.

6. John E. Schrecker, *The Chinese Revolution in Historical Perspective* (N.Y.: Praeger, 1991), 11–12.

7. The Qing (Ch'ing or "Manchu") dynasty lasted from 1644 until the Republican overthrow in 1911. Although the Manchu rulers were foreigners, they did not change the basic structures of Chinese government and society.

8. The White Lotus uprising occurred in the mountainous region of north-central China; it was sparked by growing poverty and resentment against tax collectors and took its name from an old Buddhist-inspired cult, the White Lotus Society. On the Taiping Rebellion, see Chapter 3, n. 27. The Boxer Uprising was specifically antiforeign.

9. For the geographic scope of these revolts, see Caroline Blunden and Mark Elvin, *Cultural Atlas of China* (New York: Facts on File, 1983), 149.

10. Jonathan D. Spence, *The Search for Modern China* (New York: W. W. Norton, 1990), 170–178.

11. Mary Clabaugh Wright, *The Last Stand of Chinese Conservatism, The T'ung-Chih Restoration, 1862–1874* (New York: Atheneum, 1966), 45.

12. Schrecker, 107.

13. The war was fought over Japan's push to dominate Korea, where China claimed historical suzerainty, or political control.

14. In his classic study, *Confucian China and Its Modern Fate: A Trilogy*, vol. 1, Joseph R. Levenson argued that the culture versus nation debate was part of a long tradition: "In large part the intellectual history of modern China has been the process of making *kuo-chia* [a nation-state] of *t'ien-hsia* [a universal empire]" (Berkeley: University of California Press, 1968), 103.

15. As a result of the Sino-Japanese War, China ceded to Japan the island of Formosa (today's Taiwan). In 1896, China signed a defensive alliance with Russia, in turn granting Russia the right to build and operate a railroad across northern Manchuria. In 1897, Germany occupied a port on the Shandong Peninsula, and by 1898, Germany, Great Britain, Russia, France, and Japan had begun the scramble for additional territorial concessions in China.

16. For a detailed study of the Boxers, see Joseph W. Esherick, *The Origins of the Boxer Uprising* (Berkeley: University of California Press, 1987), especially chaps. 1 and 7.

17. The Tongmeng Hui is variously translated as the Alliance Society, Revolutionary Society or Alliance, or League of Common Alliance.

18. For the complete text, see Ssu-Yu Teng and John K. Fairbank, *China's Response to the West: A Documentary Survey, 1839–1923* (New York: Atheneum, 1967), 227–229.

19. Ibid., 196.

20. Spence, 267.

21. In the Pinyin system, Kuomintang is transliterated Guomindang (GMD). I have chosen to use the older spelling, which is still preferred in Taiwan, where the KMT ruled after 1949.

22. China never officially declared war but contributed to the war effort by sending workers to France to work in factories. They were never formally recognized for their efforts. I am grateful to Bernard Olivier for clarifying the history of this period.

23. Kay Ann Johnson, *Women, the Family, and Peasant Revolution in China* (Chicago: University of Chicago Press, 1983), 63.

24. Ibid., 69–72.

25. "A Draft Agreement Between the Government of the United Kingdom of Great Britain and Northern Ireland and the Government of the People's Republic

of China on the Future of Hong Kong" (London: Her Majesty's Stationery Office, September 1984), 11–13.

26. The text of the Basic Law may be found at http:///www.info.gov.hk/basiclaw text/index.html.

27. Detailed information is available on the LegCo website, www.legco.gov.hk/ english/.

28. In 2004, Beijing postponed the talks, originally scheduled for 2007, to 2012, but in 2007, postponed them an additional five years, to 2017. The earliest universal suffrage could be used to elect the chief executive of Hong Kong would be 2017, and 2020 for the Legislative Council.

29. Willy Wo-Lap Lam, "The Powers Behind the Scenes," *South China Morning Post*, June 9, 1999, 17.

30. Prior to 1894, Taiwan (or Formosa, as it was known) had been controlled by both the Dutch and the Portuguese.

31. On the democratic reforms in Taiwan in the late 1980s, see Tun-jen Cheng and Stephan Haggard, eds., *Political Change in Taiwan* (Boulder: Lynne Rienner, 1992), and Peter R. Moody Jr., *Political Change on Taiwan: A Study of Ruling Party Adaptability* (New York: Praeger, 1992).

7

Japan:
Tension in Tradition

By the first decade of the twenty-first century, it was no longer clear whether Japan was an economic superpower in decline, a growing military power, or just another middle power. The debates of the 1990s regarding the use of the Self Defense Forces (SDF) for international peacekeeping missions were largely resolved in favor of their noncombat use. At the same time, the uncertainty over North Korea's military goals and the uneven progress toward normalization of North-South relations on the Korean peninsula supported the arguments of Japanese policymakers who saw the need for strengthening the SDF's capability and mission.

Domestically, the most significant political issue was the state of the economy. In the 1980s, Japan seemed unchallenged as East Asia's economic superpower. In 1990, however, the Nikkei Index plummeted, starting a decline that lasted into the new century. Successive Japanese governments tried to address structural problems in the economy, ranging from the aging of the workforce to a scandal in the multi-billion-dollar public pension fund. Some of the difficulties the country's leadership confronted resulted from the nature of Japan's political parties and coalition governments, political issues that are taken up in a future chapter. The overarching economic reality, however, was China's spectacular economic growth and assertive national pride.

Taken together, these developments contributed to the tensions imbedded in Japan's tradition. What does it mean to be Japanese in the twenty-first century? Neither the tensions nor the debate over Japanese identity is new, as the following sections show.

The Tokugawa Shogunate

The Tokugawa shogunate, or Edo period (1600–1868),[1] is of interest here for its role in setting the stage for the central theme in this chapter: tension in tradition. Through their ideology, institutions, and policies, the Tokugawa rulers sought stability and hierarchy in a country that had been racked by civil war in the sixteenth century. Thus, it is from this period that much of what we today think of as "traditional" in Japan has survived. At the same time, however, the period (unintentionally) laid the foundation for the socioeconomic transformation that occurred during the Meiji period—and hence for tension between modernity and tradition.

The Tokugawa period takes its name from the last of the feudal lords who sought to unify Japan in the late sixteenth century, Tokugawa Ieyasu, who received the title of shogun from the emperor in 1603 (see Photo 7.1).[2] Shoguns

PHOTO 7.1 Statue of Tokugawa Ieyasu. Tomb at Nikko, Japan. Photo courtesy of James W. Boyd.

were the de facto military rulers of Japan between the late twelfth and mid-nineteenth centuries. The origins of their rule lay in military conquest, but all shoguns, including Ieyasu and his successors, stressed the imperial court as the source of legitimacy, prestige, and authority.[3]

From the perspective of modern politics, the most important aspects of the Tokugawa, or Edo, period are those that contributed to the creation of a united, stable state based on Confucian political norms and a clearly delineated social hierarchy. To understand the significance of the nineteenth-century events associated with the Meiji period, it is also important to see the way in which the Tokugawa rulers endeavored to isolate Japan from external, primarily European, influences.

Chapter 4 noted that as early as the sixth century, Japanese rulers had begun a process of borrowing from the Chinese. In addition to Buddhism and the Chinese system of writing, which migrated east from China and Korea, Confucian political and ethical ideas also entered Japan. In Japan, as in China, the Confucian concept of human and social order was fundamentally conservative: It was designed to conserve harmony in society and politics and to provide a set of ethical precepts for social order. It emphasized the obligations of ruler and subject on the basis of rigid relationships of superiority and inferiority. Gradually, the Confucian worldview and political-ethical values were grafted onto Japanese feudal society, both reinforcing and reflecting that feudal order.

A legal and hereditary class system consisting—in theory—of four basic social divisions characterized Tokugawa society. At the apex, of course, were the imperial family and household, the shogun, feudal lords, and priests. Next, the first of the four basic divisions was the samurai class, or *bushi* ("military gentry"), both warriors and administrators. Beneath the samurai ranked classes valued according to their economic contributions: peasants (primary producers), artisans (secondary producers), then merchants. In addition, there were people who, for a variety of reasons, fell outside the system and thus were both degraded and dishonored. The Burakumin were chief among these. It should also be noted that there were gradations within the various social classes, including the samurai. This helps explain how the lower samurai took the initiative in attacking Tokugawa rule in the mid-nineteenth century.

The chief political value of the period was loyalty—loyalty of a particularistic nature. That is, people gave their loyalty primarily to the collectivity to which they belonged: the family, the village, the feudal realm (*han*), and, ultimately, Japan itself. The head of the collectivity held enormous symbolic importance, for he embodied the group and loyalty to it. Whether he was the family head, feudal lord, or emperor, he commanded and received absolute loyalty. Loyalty meant more than passive devotion; it meant active service and performance.[4] In large part because Tokugawa Japan was still feudal, loyalty was not, therefore, focused solely on the national government or its representatives. But the norm of compliance with higher authority, which characterized both the political and social systems, was entrenched in the behavior of every individual. This accounted for the high degree of public order, as well as for individual acts such as the willingness of samurai to commit *seppuku* (ritual suicide, or hara-kiri).

In these values and structures of loyalty are rooted two seemingly contradictory features of twentieth-century Japanese politics. On the one hand, the norms and practices of hierarchical loyalty could be, and were, transformed into a cohesive movement of nationalism. On the other hand, Japanese politics from the eighteenth century into the contemporary period have been filled with factionalism, reflecting the reality that loyalty was historically identified first and foremost with a specific subnational group (before there was any "nation" in the modern sense) and with the head of that group. Thus, identification with subgroups often superseded loyalty to the larger organization (such as a political party) or to the wider society.

Another important dimension of Tokugawa rule was the policy of deliberate isolation after 1600. The policy was facilitated by relative geographic isolation and by Japan's having escaped Chinese military and political domination (unlike Korea). Myths of divine protection linked isolation with a strong belief in Japan's invulnerability. In the thirteenth century, for example, the Mongols had attempted two invasions of Japan, the second one amassing about 140,000 men. The invaders were held at bay for almost two months until a typhoon struck, destroying much of the invading fleet. Those who survived returned home in defeat. The Japanese success was attributed to the country's uniqueness, manifest in the kamikaze ("divine wind") that had helped to destroy the enemy. The kamikaze was seen as intervention by the gods of Ise Shrine, one of Japan's most important Shinto centers, and thus reinforced the Japanese belief that their land was protected by the gods.[5]

Part of the policy of isolation was the elimination of Christianity. Another element was restricting contacts with Europeans only to the Dutch at the port of Nagasaki. The persecution of Christians and the restriction of trade were also signs of the hardening of the feudal system, which was based on agriculture, and the diminished importance of international trade as part of Japan's economic system. The primary source of revenue for the government was taxes on agricultural production rather than, for example, manufacturing. The priority given to agriculture in both fiscal and social matters and the downgrading of commercial activities contributed to the prosperity merchants enjoyed by the eighteenth century because they were left largely unregulated and untaxed. The growth of the commercial classes, urban centers, internal trade, and a monetary system led to a unified national market—even though all of these trends violated the theory of an agrarian-based, feudal, rigid socioeconomic structure.

The last feature of the Edo period to examine here is the development of the idea of *kokutai*, usually translated as "national polity," "national essence," or "essence of the state." *Kokutai* was a new theory in which familial, political, and religious ideas were merged and the state was conceptualized as a large family. The hierarchical loyalties mentioned earlier were gradually fused into a system of thought in which the emperor became the center of national unity. The relationship between the emperor and his subjects was like that between a father and his children, and the obligations of loyalty and service to the emperor would take precedence over all other obligations. This family concept of the state rested in turn on the belief that Japan's uniqueness lay in the direct descent of the imperial line from Amaterasu Omikami, the Sun Goddess. This myth, it may be recalled, had its origins in the Ritsuryo, which predated the Edo period by nearly one thousand years (see Chapter 4).

The ideas that characterized *kokutai* developed from a variety of writings that were part of the intellectual debates of the Edo period. *Kokutai* was also part of the reaction against foreign influence, but in this instance, the antiforeign sentiment was directed against China, not Europe. The best-known representative of *kokutai* was Motori Norinaga (1730–1801), who devoted his life to identifying, studying, and publicizing Japanese classics, including *The Tale of Genji*. Rejecting both Confucianism and Buddhism because of their Chinese origins, Motori drew on Shinto tradition to define Japanese uniqueness and in doing so helped to consolidate the underlying rationale of *kokutai*: the role of Amaterasu Omikami, the "Heaven-Shining Goddess." One of Motori's central themes was the way in which China had lost sight of the truth of the Sun Goddess, and he noted that only in "our Imperial Land" had the tradition been correctly and clearly transmitted. "Thus our country is the source and fountainhead of all other countries, and in all matters it excels all the others."[6]

In Motori's writings, one sees the core ideas that defined Japanese nationalism one century later. The clearest legacy of the *kokutai* scholars was to resurrect Shinto, recraft its political meanings, and thus define a unique Japan connected to its literature, history, and the Imperial Way (the special role of the emperor in the country's history and culture). In this manner it was an indispensable link in the chain of ideas and events that created a modernizing Japan in the nineteenth century.

The Meiji Period

The Meiji period dates from 1868, when the young emperor Mutsuhito chose the name Meiji, or "Enlightened Rule," for his reign. It lasted until his death in 1912, and the emperor himself is known posthumously as Meiji. The era is sometimes referred to as the Meiji Restoration because early in 1868, samurai opposed to Tokugawa rule undertook what was in effect a coup d'état. They seized the Imperial Palace in Kyoto and announced that political power would revert to, hence be restored to, the emperor. The emperor had never been deposed, of course; but after eight centuries of military, or shogunal, rule, the idea of restoring the emperor signaled fundamental changes in norms of authority and legitimacy, as well as changes in domestic and foreign policies.

There were two general reasons for the collapse of Tokugawa rule: domestic economic and social problems and the growing threat from Western powers in East Asia. Despite the fact that the lives of peasants were minutely regulated, worsening economic conditions resulted in increasing numbers of revolts. In the mid-1830s, for example, a major famine led to the deaths of hundreds of thousands of people; destitute peasants flocked to the cities, and there were uprisings throughout Japan.[7] Nor were the peasants alone in protesting their declining living conditions. As both the government and feudal lords ran short of money, the stipends of samurai were often reduced. Hard-pressed even to support their families, some samurai actually crossed classes in order to be free to pursue commercial pursuits. Indigence brewed discontent among many samurai, as it did among the peasants.

The shogunate responded with a variety of reforms, although these did little to stop the decline. Some reforms, notably attempts to improve the efficiency of government activities (such as taxation) did, however, strengthen the central authority of the national government over feudal domains. These efforts later received the full attention of the Meiji reformers.

The external threat was even less successfully resolved. The news of China's defeat by Britain in the Opium War brought home to the shogunate's rulers the truth about Western power *and* intentions. One decade after the British victory, the arrival of the American flotilla under Commodore Matthew C. Perry set off a chain of events that culminated in the Meiji Restoration. In the course of Perry's visits in 1853 and 1854, negotiations produced a treaty that opened two ports to American trade and provided for American consular representation in Japan. The shogunate's concessions divided both the feudal lords and the imperial court. By the end of the 1850s, the influx of foreigners sparked latent xenophobia, exemplified by the slogan *sonno joi*: "Revere (or honor) the emperor; expel the barbarians." Not surprisingly, the concepts of both *sonno* (imperial rule) and *joi* (repelling foreigners) had been developed by the *kokutai* schools of thought.

This background to the Meiji period helps us understand the various policies pursued after 1868, policies that otherwise seem contradictory. For example, Meiji rulers disestablished both the feudal domains and the traditional role of the samurai, while extolling the virtues represented by the old order, such as veneration of the martial arts and absolute loyalty to one's superior. The emperor was carefully cultivated as a figurehead for national unity.[8] Out of the Meiji period would come both nascent democratic institutions and the trappings of modern authoritarianism, both aggressive borrowing from other countries and aggressive xenophobia.

The restoration events of 1868 were followed by a brief civil war between supporters of the new Meiji government and defenders of the old Tokugawa rule. During this period, Edo was renamed Tokyo and designated as the national capital. The new government was composed of samurai from the southwestern domains that had led the assault on the shogunate. It moved immediately to reunify the country and establish a strong central administration. Inspired by Western models, the government also drew up a Charter Oath to placate (or co-opt) potential opposition to the new regime. Issued by the emperor, the oath introduced ideas of assemblies, national unity, rejecting the past, and embracing the new. The assemblies and public discussion promised in the Charter Oath came to very little in the early years of the Meiji period, as the reformers emphasized the norm of unity. The restoration leaders, increasingly younger samurai who had replaced the older, high-ranking nobles in imperial offices, moved quickly to abolish feudal structures and to launch Japan on a rapid course of modernization that touched every aspect of the country, including finances, government bureaucracy, industrial technology, culture, and even dress and food.

The restoration successes do not mean that there were no divisions among the government leaders or that there were no crises. There were both: One of the most important crises was in fact an armed rebellion against the government in 1877 by impoverished and disestablished samurai; the problems of the samurai were linked also to divisions among the ruling oligarchy. Some government leaders sought an expedition to Korea to re-create the old martial role for the samurai. The debate about Korea divided the Meiji oligarchs and led to the resignation of the militant faction that demanded action in Korea; the leader of this faction eventually headed the rebellion against the government in 1877.

The unity of the restoration leaders was broken, and factionalism soon became an acknowledged feature of national politics. Although the 1877 rebellion was the last military challenge to the Meiji government, members of the oligarchy began to reach beyond the government for support of their views. The political societies they created to build support were the precursors of today's political parties. One of the most notable leaders of the period, Itagaki Taisuke, created the Society of Patriots, whose original aim was to help the samurai. Support for Itagaki's society spread from samurai to rural aristocracy and, ultimately, to lower rural classes—all those hurt by the government's heavy reliance on rural taxation.

Itagaki had been a member of the restoration oligarchy, and his initiatives to pressure the government by creating nongovernmental associations illustrated the early, tentative roots of democracy in Japan, as well as the persistence of factionalism in a ruling coalition. In 1881, Itagaki reorganized his forces into the Liberal Party (*Jiyuto*), Japan's first political party. The *Jiyuto* went through several major reorganizations over the course of subsequent decades, but it re-emerged after World War II and became one of the two core parties that merged to establish the Liberal Democratic Party (LDP).[9]

Neither *Jiyuto* nor the other political parties established in the 1880s were mass-based or tightly organized. Typically, they reflected personalism or a leader-follower relationship, and they were often permeated by cliques, a pattern that has persisted into the contemporary period, especially in the LDP. Likewise, none of the parties represented the growing classes of urban workers, the poor, or women. In this regard, they were not unlike parties that emerged in Europe during the nineteenth century, from which Japan's restoration leaders took much of their inspiration.

Perhaps inevitably, the movement for people's rights that Itagaki represented and the rapid permeation of Japanese society and politics by Western influences provoked a conservative reaction as the century drew to a close. The combination of rural outbreaks—a sign of persistent economic problems and social instability—and the increasing demands for political rights led the government to restrain political activity in the mid-1880s through laws that regulated the press and freedom of assembly. The government also sought to institutionalize Japan's new political system, while co-opting dissidents through the creation of a parliamentary assembly, the Diet. The Meiji Constitution of 1889 thus represented the two political traditions that were in tension as a result of the changes of the Meiji period: liberalization and conservative reaction. The creation of a bicameral Diet formally recognized the principle of popular participation in government. The electorate responsible for choosing the members of the lower house, the House of Representatives, was relatively small (it excluded all women, as well as men who did not meet certain tax qualifications), and the upper House of Peers (patterned after the

British House of Lords) was not elected. But the Diet did have some real power; for example, its approval was necessary to pass the government budget.

The Meiji Constitution also created the institutions of prime minister and cabinet. The key element of parliamentary responsibility of the cabinet to the Diet—which characterized true parliamentary systems in Europe—was not present, but the constitution did set the precedent for the parliamentary structures that were incorporated in Japan's post–World War II constitution.

The ultimate source of sovereignty under the 1889 Constitution was the emperor, whose authority was "sacred and inviolable." The constitution, in fact, had been presented to the people as a gift from the emperor. In no way were any of the new government institutions structured so as to interfere, or appear to conflict, with imperial prerogative. Thus, the core norm of the constitution was compatible with the *kokutai* theory of the state.

Despite the affirmation of imperial sovereignty, the emperor continued to reign rather than rule. The cabinet and the Diet shared power with the Imperial Household Ministry (responsible for the personal and official affairs of the emperor and his family), the bureaucracy of the various ministries (which in effect prepared most of the legislation passed by the Diet), and the general staffs of the army and navy, which had direct access to the emperor. These institutions would assure the continuation and, ultimately, the supremacy, of the most conservative elements of Japanese political values well into the twentieth century.

In 1890, the conservative backlash found one of its most eloquent and effective embodiments in the Imperial Rescript on Education. More than any other document of the Meiji period, the rescript illustrated the fusion of the *kokutai* principles with Confucianism, whose supporters had successfully argued that the rapid pace of modernization needed to be counteracted by reaffirming the legitimacy of the imperial order.[10] The rescript remained in place until the end of World War II and was a critical source of political indoctrination, as this extracted passage illustrates:

Know ye, Our subjects:

Our Imperial Ancestors have founded Our Empire on a basis broad and everlasting, and have deeply and firmly implanted virtue; Our subjects ever united in loyalty and filial piety have from generation to generation illustrated the beauty thereof. This is the glory of the fundamental character of Our Empire, and herein also lies the source of Our education. Ye, Our subjects, be filial to your parents, affectionate to your brothers and sisters; as husbands and wives be harmonious, as friends true; . . . should emergency arise, offer yourselves courageously to the State; and thus guard and maintain the prosperity of Our Imperial Throne coeval with heaven and earth. . . .

The Way here set forth is indeed the teaching bequeathed by Our Imperial Ancestors, to be observed alike by Their Descendants and the subjects, infallible for all ages and true in all places.[11]

Copies of the Imperial Rescript on Education were distributed to every school in Japan, and all students were required to memorize the text as part of their moral education. Ceremonial readings of the rescript developed into elaborate rituals, and Shinto priests were mobilized to distribute the document; they in turn standardized the rites conducted around it.[12] This intertwining of public education and Shinto ritual helps to explain the importance of State Shinto during the formative period of modern Japanese nationalism.

Readers may recall from Chapter 4 that State Shinto was a government-fostered ideology that combined the stories and myths of the origin of the imperial house with a belief in the superiority and uniqueness of the Japanese people. Shinto shrines and priests served to transmit the Imperial Way and to invoke loyalty to state and emperor alike. Viewed in this way, the rites of the shrines helped popularize the doctrine of *kokutai*, the special concept of the national polity. It was for these reasons that disestablishment of Shinto as a state doctrine was a high priority for American reformers during the post–World War II occupation of Japan.

The Meiji period ended in 1912, with the death of the emperor. By this time—that is, after less than a half century—Japan had undergone a massive economic transformation, catapulting itself to the threshold of the industrial age. The international implications of this transformation were perhaps inescapable, given the Meiji emphasis on national unity, securing Japan from aggression, and winning equality with the West. Two external wars in the space of ten years showed just how quickly economic prowess had been translated into military prowess. The first war, between China and Japan (the Sino-Japanese War), was fought over control of Korea, where China claimed suzerainty. The Japanese victory in 1895 was quick and decisive, and as a consequence, China ceded Formosa (today's Taiwan) and some other territories to Japan.[13] The Chinese government was also forced to recognize Korea's independence and negotiate a commercial treaty that gave Japan the privileges in China that the Western powers had secured. Thus, Japan began its long march to domination of East Asia, and the seeds of political discord between China, Japan, and Korea were further spread.

It was during this same period that Japan secured revision of its unequal treaties with Western nations, thus realizing a foreign policy goal that had become "a

KOREA AT THE CROSSROADS

The title of this focus box points to the role of Korea in the long history of East Asia, as well as the contemporary period. Historically, Korea is significant both for its own culture and also as a bridge for cultural transmission from China to Japan. For example, in the seventh century, Buddhism came to Japan from China *through* Korea, and for the next seven centuries Korea and Japan shared the Buddhist tradition. The long-ruling Choson dynasty (1392–1912), however, suppressed Buddhism while privileging Confucianism to enhance its legitimacy. In contrast, Japanese rulers used both traditions.

Twentieth-century Japanese colonialism in Korea ruptured any sense of shared bonds between the two countries that might have survived their different historical trajectories. World War II and the Korean War further shattered the integrity of the Korean nation: after Japan's defeat in 1945, the Soviet Union occupied the north and the United States the south, and the Korean War (1950–1953) terminated any hopes of reunifying the peninsula for the foreseeable future. The Democratic People's Republic of Korea (DPRK, North) is one of the few remaining self-styled communist states left in the world, relying on China as its single regional supporter and remaining closed to most outsiders. The Republic of Korea (ROK, South) carved out a different future, relying heavily on American military support during the second half of the twentieth century and building one of the most dynamic economies in the world.

North Korean politics have been identified primarily by the country's two preeminent leaders, Kim Il Sung (in power 1948–1994) and his son, Kim Jung Il (in power 1994–). North Korea is a party-state system on the Leninist model (see chapter 10), on the surface resembling China and Vietnam but in reality more authoritarian, closed, and certainly poorer. South Korea, in contrast, developed political parties in the 1940s, and its new constitution called for a presidential form of government, although in reality politics were heavily influenced by the armed forces. A military coup in 1961 led to a long period of authoritarian rule, and not until the 1980s did the country undertake the transition to democracy. In 1987, the ROK adopted its sixth constitution, permitting direct election of the president and strengthening powers for the National Assembly, whose members are elected for four-year terms. South Korea has a multiparty system, with two parties dominating in recent years: the Grand National Party, which won the 2008 elections, and the Democratic Party.

Contributing to interest in South Korean politics is the role of Christianity, with which more than one-third of Koreans identify (see Focus Box 4.1).

continues

FOCUS BOX 7

continued

Lee Myung-bak, elected president in 2008, is a Christian, as are many of his cabinet officials—prompting thousands of Buddhists to march in Seoul in August 2008 to protest what they claimed was discrimination by the government. Equally significant is the role of nongovernmental organizations, which have grown dramatically in the past thirty years and mark a vibrant civil society. Civil activism is now considered more important in South Korea, for example, than in Japan. This activism has occasionally been directed against the United States and further complicates efforts to resolve military tension in the region (see Focus Box 14).

national obsession."[14] As has so often happened in modern history, once the liberal goals of nationalism, such as freedom and equality, are secured, nationalism moves into an aggressive, even xenophobic, phase. So it was with Japan. One of the immediate consequences of the Sino-Japanese War was to exacerbate the international competition for land and influence in Northeast Asia. One of the implications of this competition was the near-destruction of China's territorial integrity, as was discussed in the previous chapter. Another consequence was the growing tension between Russia and Japan: Japan was now the dominant power in Korea and was challenging Russia's economic and military presence in Manchuria. War broke out when the Japanese surprised the Russian fleet at Port Arthur with a night attack in 1904. The ensuing military battles confirmed Japan's stature as a modern nation, and the 1905 treaty that marked the end of the Russo-Japanese War confirmed Japan's paramount role in Korea and its expanding interests in Manchuria. It is perhaps a sad irony that just at the point that Korea itself was enjoying a nationalist awakening, the country was annexed outright (in 1910) by Japan.[15] Japan's colonization of Korea produced the Japanese-Korean minority discussed in Chapter 4. Control over Korea was also viewed by many Japanese as further evidence of their country's cultural and historical superiority (see Focus Box 7).

The Twentieth Century:
Pluralistic and Authoritarian Legacies

The key political issue after the death of the Meiji emperor in 1912 was the competition between authoritarian and liberal democratic political forces in defining the meaning of modern Japan. Was the surge of militarism in the 1930s and 1940s a logical consequence of the process of nation building as it occurred in Japan? Central to the conditions that led to militarism were the social and economic changes resulting from the policies of the Meiji leaders. These changes brought new groups into the political process, and at the same time, the old consensus about the basic goals of modernization was replaced by deep political cleavages among the leaders who gradually supplanted the nineteenth-century Meiji oligarchs. Ultimately, those who adhered to the interpretation of *kokutai*, State Shinto, and emperor worship, which represented the most conservative vision of Japan, prevailed.

The most important social and economic changes of the early twentieth century were the increasing integration of the Japanese economy into the world economy and uneven modernization throughout the country. Internationalization made the Japanese economy more susceptible to the business and financial cycles that affected other industrializing countries. Trade came to play a larger role in the structure of economic production, both in terms of defining markets and assuring raw materials. Industrial output rose, so it became necessary to import more raw materials, which in turn had to be paid for by selling exports. This resulted in the preoccupation with dependence on external resources that spurred Japanese territorial expansion in the 1930s and 1940s.

Both inflation and deflation accompanied the growth of the Japanese economy during the first three decades of the twentieth century, and not all sectors benefited equally from the economic changes. Silk, for example, was the chief export from Japan in the 1920s, and although the industry enjoyed price increases during the early part of the decade, the price of silk fell by more than two-thirds between 1925 and 1929.[16] By the end of World War I, more than 300,000 workers, mostly girls, were employed in silk filatures, the establishments where silk from cocoons was spun into threads. Most of the workers came from impoverished rural families, and their wages, although very low, helped sustain those families.[17] But declining prices, increased competition from synthetic fabrics, and the Great Depression of 1929 meant falling wages and unemployment. Industrialization thus provided opportunities but also left some social groups especially vulnerable to the economic cycles that were exacerbated by the opening of Japan's economy to international influences. Women in particular assumed the role that would later define much of their economic participation after World War II—as a flexible source of labor moving in and out of the formal workforce, fueling economic growth with low wages and yielding jobs to male workers in times of economic downturn.

Industries such as silk and, later, cotton slowly changed the traditional social structures. The migration of young women to work in urban textile mills, for example, stimulated the urbanization process and linked the urban and rural areas in an era of rapid economic change.[18] An urban proletariat gradually developed, spawning labor unions, workers' strikes, and the establishment of leftist parties. Small socialist "parties," drawing on the ideas of both Christian socialists and early Marxists, were created (and banned) before World War I. The greatest surge of interest came during the 1920s, when leftists of various stripes gained followers in parts of the labor movement and especially in universities. The Japan Communist Party, formally organized in 1922, dates from this period.

For one dozen years, from the end of World War I to the early 1930s, political parties enjoyed considerable growth in their popular following and in their government influence. Taisho democracy, as the period of the 1920s came to be called,[19] was tentative and fragile, at best. The parties that existed had roots that were neither deep nor wide. The structure of political leadership was still oligarchic, not pluralistic. Traditional social structures and loyalties were only partially eroded, and the erosion that had occurred made militant nationalism appealing for those who were especially vulnerable to socioeconomic changes. At the same time, state institutions, including the military and police bureaucracies, had become larger, centralized, and more efficient, their efficiency enhanced by the development of mass transportation and communication. By the early 1930s, state-created and state-administered mass organizations, which sought to organize people by social category, were more important than political parties.

In the late 1920s, a combination of international and domestic developments stimulated demands for a new phase of national reconstruction. The rise of Chinese nationalism threatened Japanese interests in Manchuria, and depression at home raised calls from a variety of right-wing groups, both inside and outside the military, for new leadership. In 1931, Japanese army officers stationed in Manchuria plotted a complete takeover of Manchuria. Japanese railway tracks near the city of Mukden were bombed; army leaders blamed the Chinese and launched an attack against Chinese troops in Mukden. In Tokyo, the civilian government, divided over how to respond, was unable to stop the Japanese aggression in Manchuria. The following year, a new prime minister sought to terminate the conflict and reassert civilian control over the army. His assassination in 1932 ended these efforts and also ended the last party-led government until the end of World War II.

The historical line between the events of 1931–1932 and the full outbreak of war with China in 1937 was not without twists and turns. But the cumulative effect of the period was to consolidate the military's hold (in cooperation with high-ranking civilian bureaucrats) on the government, to "clarify" a nationalist line, and to silence all political and intellectual voices opposed to that line. Much like the Imperial Rescript on Education before it, the 1937 Fundamentals of Our National Polity, published by the Education Ministry, was distributed throughout

Japan as a guide for national unity. The text criticized the assumptions and impact of imported Western ideologies that, by emphasizing individualism and human beings more generally, lacked "historical views." The text also stated that these ideologies had led to social confusion and were antithetical to Japan's history, which was grounded in the lineage running between Amaterasu Omikami and the emperor: "To serve the emperor and to receive the emperor's great august Will as one's own is the rationale of making our historical 'life' live in the present; and on this is based the morality of the people." From this restatement of the core doctrine of *kokutai*, the Fundamentals asserted the importance of "Oriental morals," including loyalty, patriotism, filial piety, the martial spirit as exemplified in *bushido* (the "way of the warrior"), and national harmony. The concluding section of the text contrasted the Imperial Way with occidental theories of the state that stressed the state as existing for the benefit of individuals. Japanese uniqueness lay in its history of assimilating imported ideologies and producing a new, original synthesis, including a view of the state as the "nuclear existence that gives birth to individual beings, which it transcends."[20]

Whereas the notion of the superhuman quality of the Japanese emperor disappeared with the postwar occupation and the new constitution, other themes found in the Fundamentals of Our National Polity have periodically reappeared: the importance of distinguishing between Western and Eastern views of humans and society, the special assimilative qualities of Japanese culture, the enduring value of "Oriental" (Confucian) mores, and the transcendent nature of the state.

A New Constitutional Order

In the wake of the American nuclear bombings at Hiroshima and Nagasaki, World War II ended disastrously for Japan. The revulsion most Japanese felt against the war and the old leadership opened the way to radical changes. In the words of historian Edwin Reischauer:

> In the early postwar months, most Japanese were absorbed in the struggle to keep body and soul together, but underneath these immediate concerns there was a great longing for peace and a determination to avoid any repetition of this great catastrophe. People wanted something new and better than the old Japan that had come to grief. They were confused but open to change in a way they had never been before.[21]

Responsibility for the occupation (1945–1952) was nominally shared by the victorious allies of World War II, but in reality it was largely an American affair, conducted under the determined leadership of General Douglas MacArthur, Supreme Commander for the Allied Powers, or SCAP (as both MacArthur and his headquarters were known). SCAP policies set the tone for an occupation that would be both radical and conservative: radical in the scope of some of the changes demanded of Japanese society, conservative in the preservation of important institutions such as the emperor and the bureaucracy. The continuity provided by the bureaucracy accounted for much of the smoothness of the occupation, while also diluting its impact, because all occupation orders were issued to and executed by the Japanese government. The occupation sought wide-ranging changes, from demilitarization and purging those deemed responsible for the war to social, economic, and political reforms designed to prevent a recurrence of Japanese militarism.[22] Land reform resulted in a dramatic decrease of tenant farmers and a concomitant increase in small landowners. Labor unions were legalized, women were enfranchised, and compulsory education for girls and boys was extended.

Some reforms had less success than others. For example, American authorities blamed the *zaibatsu*, industrial and financial conglomerates, for much of the drive behind Japanese economic and military expansion. Reformers also believed that breaking up the *zaibatsu* would, like land reform, further the goal of distributing wealth throughout Japanese society. The great clan-based *zaibatsu* were broken up, but the old economic elites survived (along with their personal ties), as did the names of their concerns, such as Mitsubishi and Sumitomo.

After the occupation, the *zaibatsu* were succeeded by *keiretsu*, company networks joined by common links to banks and trading companies. None of Japan's top business barons figured in the war crimes trials, and within four years after the end of the war, the policies aimed at deconcentration of the economy were shelved. An important reason for the ease with which the combines were reconstituted was a shift in American occupation policies in the late 1940s, during the early phases of the Cold War. Events in Europe and Asia, including the successes of the Communist movement in China, led to a "reverse course" in American policy that emphasized rapid economic reconstruction of Japan as part of a broader strategy to build an anticommunist presence in East Asia.[23]

The political basis for a postwar democratic Japan was to rest on a new constitution that would replace the Meiji Constitution. As noted earlier, the 1889 Constitution had been drafted as part of the conservative reaction against Japan's lavish borrowing of Western practices. But that constitution had also introduced institutions that, especially during the 1920s, laid a foundation for parliamentary democracy. Japan at the end of World War II thus had a democratic as well as an authoritarian constitutional heritage, albeit the latter had dominated for a generation. The SCAP authorities were determined to strengthen the former, and the constitution of 1947, which is discussed further in Chapter 8, established a new concept of state power, replacing the *kokutai* theory with norms of popular sovereignty and parliamentary democracy. At the same time, SCAP made the decision to retain the emperor, the most important symbol of the old order, of hereditary privilege, patriarchy, and racial identity.[24]

Despite the widespread acceptance of the changes wrought through the occupation, the cataclysmic events of the 1940s left questions about Japan's national identity. By the early twenty-first century, a combination of factors set the stage once again for a rethinking of Japanese history. A decade of economic and political stagnation after the collapse of the Tokyo stock market in 1990[25] and a series of political scandals fostered public uncertainty about basic institutions; tensions over North Korea prompted consideration of Japan's acquisition of nuclear weapons; and ultranationalists pushed their agenda openly. The persistent debate about Japanese identity, known as *nihonjinron*, illustrates the lingering effects of the historical tensions, just as the physical presence of Yasukuni Shrine symbolizes unresolved political conflicts.

Nihonjinron

Properly speaking, the term *nihonjinron* refers to the broad discussion about what it means to be Japanese; it is, therefore, inextricably linked to the question of national identity. The identity debate has been central to modern Japanese history, but since 1945, it has taken on new implications, becoming, in the words of one scholar, "a minor national pastime."[26] One might ask why Japan is any more prone to this debate than other countries, including India and China, which have confronted the challenges of nation building. Many Japanese scholars argue that it is precisely the homogeneity of Japanese society that makes Japan unique, although they focus on different aspects of this uniqueness, ranging from ecology to social structure to racial origins and language.[27]

Examples of the various schools of thought in the *nihonjinron* discourse include Mishima Yukio, the novelist who committed *seppuku* in 1970; the founders of the revisionist Japanese Society for History Textbook Reform; and the contemporary anime filmmaker, Miyazaki Hayao. Mishima yearned for the patriotism and samurai spirit of the past. The Society for Textbook Reform, founded in the mid-1990s, has sought revision of school texts to minimize or recast Japan's role in World War II. In contrast, Miyazaki's films criticize many elements of contemporary Japan, including environmental degradation, and suggest nostalgia for the past. "Authentic" Japanese values, such as *kokoro* (heart-mind), are emphasized in his films.

Nihonjinron clearly has been a response to the major changes confronting Japan since World War II. Militarism and war, followed by the devastation of 1945, led to a reconceptualization of Japan as a peace-loving nation. Old values do not disappear suddenly, however, and many traditional norms in Japan— such as unity, ethnic pride, and hierarchy—periodically reappear in political debates as well as popular culture and, as noted above, have led to a demand for revising standard accounts of Japanese history. The country's economic prowess, particularly during the 1980s, sparked an assertion that the rapid rebuilding of the postwar economy proved that the Japanese spirit was special. Similarly, both the economic downturn of the 1990s and the growing impact of globalization challenged these notions of uniqueness. Despite the variety of strains in the *nihonjinron* discourse, there is an underlying continuity.

Yasukuni Shrine

Yasukuni Shrine, a large, imposing structure in central Tokyo, was founded in 1869 to enshrine the spirits of those who had died fighting for the country, including more than a dozen convicted World War II Class A war criminals. It is historically and emotionally linked to the most patriotic aspects of Japanese nationalism. Since 1945, there have been numerous attempts by conservatives both inside and outside the Diet to legalize government funds for the shrine's support; they argue that it is a war memorial like those found in other countries and as such deserves official public support.[28] Opponents to state support see moves toward subsidies or any official recognition as a step toward reviving the negative elements of Japanese nationalism, and they are also sensitive to the controversy that the shrine generates in East Asian countries that were victims of Japan's World War II expansion. To support their position, they invoke Articles 20 and 89 of the constitution, which state:

> No religious organization shall receive any privileges from the State, nor exercise any political authority. . . . The State and its organs shall refrain from religious education or any other religious activity. (Article 20)
>
> No public money or other property shall be expended or appropriated for the use, benefit or maintenance of any religious institution or association, or for any charitable, educational or benevolent enterprises not under the control of public authority. (Article 89)

The controversy over Yasukuni reflects elements of the *nihonjinron* debate and the ambiguous role of Shinto in Japanese society (see Photo 7.2). Is Shinto a

PHOTO 7.2 Contemporary Shinto priest. Photo courtesy of James W. Boyd.

religion, a folkway, or a traditional "civil religion" that is less religion than a facet of the country's culture?[29] If U.S. politicians can invoke God and important political institutions like the U.S. Congress open with prayers, why not accept Shinto—and Yasukuni Shrine—as a similar reflection of widespread patriotism? Critics in Japan (as in the United States) charge that the idea of a beneficent and widely accepted civil religion is misleading, if not dangerous, because it assumes (or enforces) a conformity of religious and political beliefs that masks real and legitimate diversity. Moreover, Shinto, and especially Yasukuni, cannot escape its historical link with State Shinto, Japanese militarism, and the notion of primordial ethnic identity.

The Yasukuni Shrine debate has been a lingering irritant in Japan's relations with its neighboring countries. In 1983, Prime Minister Nakasone Yasuhiro reignited controversy over a bill to establish government support for Yasukuni when he visited the shrine and signed the registry with his official title. His gesture created an uproar among both supporters and opponents of shrine recognition. Since the 1980s, the battle has continued in the press, parliament, and the courts, engaging interest groups on both sides of the issue, as well as voices throughout East Asia. Court decisions at all levels have left the matter unresolved, with some suggesting that a shrine visit simply means paying tribute to those who lost their lives in war, and others finding that official visits by politicians violate the constitutional distinction between religion and the state.

Summary

In modern centuries, Japan has never—not even at the height of Tokugawa isolation—been completely cut off from foreign influence. Yet ideas and institutions from elsewhere in Asia and from Europe and North America have often been in tension with indigenous traditions and values. Both rejection of the foreign and assimilation of it have marked Japanese national identity at various periods. Stated differently, the development of national identity contains uniquely Japanese elements, such as *kokutai* and Shinto, as well as adapted nonindigenous traditions, such as Confucianism and democratic parliamentarianism. All of these elements find their way into the *nihonjinron* discourse, as well as the controversy over Yasukuni Shrine.

The tension in the evolution of Japanese nationalism provoked by the juxtaposition of indigenous and foreign has been reinforced by ambivalent attitudes toward the countries that have most directly influenced Japan: China and the United States. In the eighteenth century, for example, some intellectuals of the *kokutai* school sought to develop national learning through explicit rejection of Chinese influence. For others, admiration of Chinese civilization crumbled as China itself seemed to crumble before the West in the nineteenth century. By the 1930s, there were those who argued that efforts to establish Pan-Asianism or associations dubbed "Greater Asia" or the "New Order in East Asia"—all to be led by Japan—would serve to rescue China from the pervasive Western threat.[30] Thus, a period viewed as unbridled Japanese aggression by most Chinese (and Americans) was (and is) seen by many Japanese nationalists as a necessary response to a much longer historical problem of East Asian regeneration and redefinition vis-à-vis the Western challenge.

Just as modern Japan cannot be understood in isolation from East Asia, neither can it be understood without reference to the occupation and subsequent relations with the United States. Although many Americans view Japan with ambivalence, few of us understand the ways in which, grappling with their own history, many Japanese carry the same attitudes toward the United States and the West in general. These attitudes emerge in a variety of contexts, ranging from Japanese perceptions of their country's policies in the 1930s and 1940s to views about the social and cultural costs of economic modernization to the legitimacy of the 1947 constitution.

Exploring Further

Natsume Soseki's novel, *Kokoro*, is a moving portrait of changes at the end of the Meiji Era. Gail Tsukiyama's novel, *The Samurai's Garden*, is a beautifully written portrayal of a young Chinese man living in Japan in the late 1930s, when the war in China was escalating. *Hiroshima*, by John Hershey (expanded edition, 1985), remains one of the best accounts of the effects of the 1945 atomic attack on Hiroshima. Miyazaki Hayao's anime films are popular both in Japan and abroad. *Howl's Moving Castle* illustrates Miyazaki's position in the *nihonjinron* discourse.

Notes

1. Edo, modern Tokyo, was a coastal village in the late sixteenth to early seventeenth centuries. It became the capital of the shogunate and hence its name is used for the historical period.

2. Ieyasu overcame his chief rival in battle in 1600, so his rule is sometimes dated from that year, though he did not receive the title of shogun until 1603.

3. The shogunate is also referred to as the *bakufu* (literally, "tent government"), which recalls the military origins of the rule. The castle built by Ieyasu and his successors for the capital of the shogunate became the Imperial Palace in the nineteenth century.

4. Robert N. Bellah, *Tokugawa Religion: The Values of Pre-Industrial Japan* (Boston: Beacon Press, 1957), 13–14.

5. *Japan: An Illustrated Encyclopedia* (Tokyo: Kodansha, 1993), vol. 1, 727–728. During World War II, the word "kamikaze" was applied to pilots who flew suicide attacks on Allied ships.

6. Ryusaku Tsunoda, William Theodore de Bary, and Donald Keene, comps., *Sources of Japanese Tradition* (New York: Columbia University Press, 1958), 523.

7. Hundreds of thousands also died in the famine of the 1780s. In addition to causing starvation, famines forced peasant families to practice infanticide; many also sold daughters to brothels. Mikiso Hane, *Peasants, Rebels, and Outcastes: The Underside of Modern Japan* (New York: Pantheon Books, 1982), 3–8.

8. Takashi Fujitani, *Splendid Monarchy: Power and Pageantry in Modern Japan* (Berkeley: University of California Press, 1996).

9. The other major constituent party of the LDP was the Japan Democratic Party, whose roots can be traced to another party formed in the 1880s, the Constitutional Reform Party (*Rikken Kaishinto*).

10. Carol Gluck notes that the precise meaning of *kokutai* changed in the course of the nineteenth century, depending on the political goals of those invoking the supremacy of the national polity. *Japan's Modern Myths: Ideology in the Late Meiji Period* (Princeton: Princeton University Press, 1985), 143–146. See also her discussion of the drafting of the rescript, 120–124.

11. Tsunoda, de Bary, and Keene, 646.

12. Helen Hardacre, *Shinto and the State, 1868–1988* (Princeton: Princeton University Press, 1989), 108–109, 122–123.

13. Also ceded were the Pescadores Islands and the Liaotung (South Manchuria) Peninsula. Under Russian-German-French diplomatic pressure, Japan then gave up Liaotung for an additional indemnity from China.

14. H. Paul Varley, *Japanese Culture*, 3rd ed. (Honolulu: University of Hawaii Press, 1984), 238.

15. One sign of growing nationalism in Korea was a virtual rebellion against Japanese control in 1908–1910. The Japanese governor in Korea was assassinated in 1909 by a Korean patriot, and annexation followed the next year.

16. John K. Fairbank, Edwin O. Reischauer, and Albert M. Craig, *East Asia: The Modern Transformation*, vol. 2 (Boston: Houghton Mifflin Co., 1965), 498.

17. Hane, 172–204.

18. By the 1930s, cotton-spinning firms employed more than one-half of all industrial workers and more than 80 percent of all female industrial workers. Barbara Molony, "Activism Among Women in the Taisho Cotton Textile Industry," in *Recreating Japanese Women, 1600–1945*, ed. Gail Lee Bernstein (Berkeley: University of California Press, 1991), 219–220, nn. 9, 14.

19. The Taisho (literally, "Great Righteousness") emperor, Meiji's son, reigned from 1912 to 1926, when he died. He was replaced by his son, Hirohito.

20. For excerpts from the text, see Tsunoda, de Bary, and Keene, 785–794. The complete text, with introduction, is in Robert King Hall, ed., and John Owen Gauntlett, trans., *Kokutai no hongi (Cardinal Principles of the National Entity of Japan)* (Newton, Mass.: Crofton, 1974).

21. Edwin O. Reischauer, *The Japanese* (Cambridge, Mass.: Harvard University Press, 1978), 104.

22. Among the most useful of the many sources on the occupation are Howard B. Schonberger, *Aftermath of War: Americans and the Remaking of Japan, 1945–1952*

(Kent, Ohio: Kent State University Press, 1989); Richard B. Finn, *Winners in Peace: MacArthur, Yoshida, and Postwar Japan* (Berkeley: University of California Press, 1992); and John W. Dower, *Embracing Defeat: Japan in the Wake of World War II* (New York: W. W. Norton, 1999). In emphasizing the role of Yoshida Shigeru, Japan's prime minister for two-thirds of the occupation, Finn's study explains the way in which SCAP policies were tempered and filtered by the Japanese upon whom the occupation depended.

23. Schonberger, chap. 6; Michael Schaller, *The American Occupation of Japan: The Origins of the Cold War in Asia* (Oxford: Oxford University Press, 1985).

24. Dower, chaps. 12 and 13; and Kathleen Krauth and Lynn Parisi, "Teaching from Embracing Defeat: An Interview with John Dower," *Education About Asia* 5, no. 3 (Winter 2000), 25–36.

25. In 1990, the Nikkei Stock Market Index fell 39 percent, sparking a sudden real estate deflation and a decade-long recession. In December 2008, the Index plummeted 42 percent on the year.

26. Harumi Befu, *Hegemony of Homogeneity: An Anthropological Analysis of Nihonjinron* (Melbourne: Trans Pacific Press, 2001), 3.

27. Ibid., chap. 2. For a comparison with Korea's identity debate, or *hanguginnon*, see Kyung-Koo Han, "The Anthropology of the Discourse on the Koreanness of Korea," *Korea Journal* 43, no. 1 (2003), 5–31.

28. There has, in fact, been some "covert" patronage, particularly by the Ministry of Welfare, which has assisted Shrine officials in their efforts to apotheosize or glorify war dead. Hardacre, 149.

29. See Bellah on the concept of civil religion in both Japan and the United States. David M. O'Brien notes the problems with Bellah's interpretation; with Yasuo Ohkoshi, *To Dream of Dreams: Religious Freedom and Constitutional Politics in Postwar Japan* (Honolulu: University of Hawaii Press, 1996), 61–62.

30. Miwa Kimitada, "Japanese Policies and Concepts for a Regional Order in Asia, 1938–1940," in *The Ambivalence of Nationalism: Modern Japan Between East and West*, eds. James W. White, Michio Umegaki, and Thomas R. H. Havens (Lanham, Md.: University Press of America, 1990), 133–156.

PART THREE

Government Structures:
Form and Substance

Part One described the demographic and cultural realities that underlie politics in India, China, and Japan. Part Two provided historical background, emphasizing the growth of nationalism and the building of modern nation-states. Chapters 1–7 also introduced some public policy issues that illustrate the significance of history and culture in contemporary politics, such as the Kashmir crisis in South Asia, demographic pressures, Tibet, and the Yasukuni Shrine controversy in Japan.

Part Three describes government structures, the formal decision-making framework within which public policy unfolds. Chapter 8 provides a constitutional overview of the three countries, and a Focus Box looks at four cases of contemporary constitutional change. Chapter 9 then compares the parliamentary systems of India and Japan. A Focus Box illustrates the variety of presidential systems in Asia. Chapter 10 focuses on the distinctive governing system China. Both Chapters 9 and 10 concentrate on national structures, whereas Chapter 11 examines the role of regions and regionalism. India, China, and Japan all face pressures for greater government decentralization, although the pressures come in different forms.

Throughout the continent, the dynamics of politics are changing rapidly, in large part as a result of socioeconomic changes that challenge governments at every level. Development has stimulated greater political participation, raising both old and new questions about the endurance of traditional cultures. The preceding chapters have already shown some of the ways in which indigenous cultural values are reshaped or reinforced in the contemporary era. The Bharatiya Janata Party has emphasized Hinduism in its nationalist ideology. China's development policy unintentionally reinforced the centuries-old preference for male offspring. The fate of other norms is more complex. In India are the strictures of caste dead as a consequence of urbanization and new forms of grassroots political participation, or has democracy reinforced caste identity? To what extent do new currents of Japanese nationalism draw on traditional values or symbols? The remainder of the book is intended to provide additional insight into these questions by examining the substance as well as the form of government institutions.

8

Constitutions

Constitutions provide a useful starting point for understanding government structures and procedures, and the evolution of constitutions over time tells us much about political values and behavior. In contrast to the stability of the U.S. Constitution, it is not unusual for constitutions to undergo frequent amendment or to be replaced completely by a new constitution. Although these changes do not necessarily indicate political instability, they often signal shifts of power. The new constitution inaugurating France's Fifth Republic in 1958, for example, marked the end of a system dominated by parliament in favor of one with a strong president. Some changes are more dramatic: In the space of a two-year period, Nepal and Bhutan made major changes in their constitutional orders (see Focus Box 8).

The classical liberal conception of a constitution is that it *restricts* state power, but constitutions may also be used as a mandate to *expand* state prerogative. At the extreme, a constitution may simply be a tool to legitimize authoritarianism, as is the case of the 2008 Myanmar constitution, which guarantees military dominance in government bodies.

The following sections explain the background of the Indian, Chinese, and Japanese Constitutions, then investigate the relationship between the constitutions and politics in the three countries. Each section places the constitution within the historical framework introduced in earlier chapters and summarizes the structure of the document. Short cases illustrate the relevance of the documents to contemporary politics, for it is the political context that over time gives meaning to a constitution.

India

The drafting of the Indian Constitution was heavily influenced by the experience of British colonialism and by the nationalist movement, particularly the Indian

---

CHANGING CONSTITUTIONS

Asia's recent experience with constitutions reveals a variety of patterns in drafting, altering, and scrapping national constitutions. Four examples illustrate the diversity of these patterns: Indonesia has kept its first postcolonial constitution, but with substantial amendments; Thailand has had numerous constitutions, the most recent in 2007; Nepal adopted an interim constitution in 2007, then in 2008 abolished its monarchy and elected a constituent assembly to draft a new constitution; and between 2005 and 2008, Bhutan drafted, revised, and adopted a new constitution, its first ever, to frame the country's transition to a constitutional democracy.

Japan's surrender in 1945 ended its occupation of Indonesia, then still a colony of the Netherlands; immediately after, Indonesian nationalist rebels declared the country's independence. Although the anticolonial struggle lasted until 1949, when the Dutch government recognized the country's independence, a constitution was hastily issued in 1945 and, despite numerous efforts to replace it over the ensuing years, has survived as the basic government framework for the country. After the Suharto dictatorship ended in 1998, the People's Consultative Assembly, empowered under the original constitution to amend the document, passed four major amendments between 1999 and 2002. The amendments sought to strengthen the transition to democratic rule by emphasizing civilian rule, decentralizing power to the regions, and enhancing basic rights for citizens. Debate over further changes continued, however, with regional representatives demanding changes in the governance structures to enhance their power.

Thailand also has found itself embroiled in constitutional debate over the past decade. Since the 1930s, when the country's first constitutional monarchy was established, cycles of political instability have manifested themselves in constitutional changes. Constitutions have come and gone, some emphasizing military rule, others civilian rule, with institutions created, then abandoned. The only consistent feature has been preservation of the monarchy. After a coup that deposed Prime Minister Thaksin Shinawatra in 2006, the new military rulers abrogated the 1997 constitution, issued an interim charter, and established a panel which drafted the 2007 constitution. But when a civilian government was elected in late 2007, protestors—who associated the new prime minister with the discredited Thaksin—took to the streets in

continues

Bangkok, with protests that lasted for months. By late 2008, political leaders suggested that only a new constitution would end the crisis. Thus the long-standing Thai linkage between political and constitutional instability was again affirmed.

After a decade of civil war and antigovernment protests in Nepal, a cease-fire was signed between the government and the Maoist rebels. In 2007, an interim constitution (Nepal's fourth) was issued to govern the country until a new, permanent constitution could be drafted. In 2008, elections were held to a new constituent assembly to draft this permanent constitution and simultaneously serve as the legislature. The Communist Party of Nepal emerged as the largest party in the legislature, with almost 40 percent of the seats. At its first meeting, the legislature voted formally to abolish the monarchy and declare Nepal a republic.

The initiative for drafting Bhutan's first constitution came in 2001 from the Druk Gyalpo, Jigme Singye Wangchuk, the country's fourth "Dragon King," who saw a written constitution as the preliminary step in transforming Bhutan into a modern democracy. The approximately forty members of the drafting committee represented the chief government departments and the country's administrative regions. The final draft was published in 2007 and was formally adopted by Bhutan's first elected parliament in 2008. The constitutional drafting effort was distinctive in having been implemented by political elites at the direction of the monarch. The constitution itself is unusual in several respects: It reaffirms the centrality of Buddhism as Bhutan's national heritage; it shows the influence of India's constitution in enumerating Fundamental Duties and also Principles of State Policy; it outlines in detail requirements for political parties; and it provides for the mandatory retirement of the monarch at the age of sixty-five years.

National Congress, as well as by the interests and background of the delegates to the Constituent Assembly. The assembly served simultaneously as a provisional parliament and as a constitutional drafting body. Elected in summer 1946, its members met from December 1946 to December 1949. The Indian National Congress won the overwhelming majority of assembly seats, with the result that the constitutional debates were dominated by Congress values and leaders, particularly Jawaharlal Nehru.

Building Constitutionalism in India[1]

Two characteristics of the Constituent Assembly's deliberations explain both the nature of the document that emerged in 1949 and its evolution since. First, the deliberations were generally noncontroversial, largely because much of the constitutional development begun under British rule was continued after independence. Second, Congress's domination of the assembly insured that when potentially controversial issues did arise, the Congress position would usually prevail. But as the period of postindependence unity waned, new political forces brought pressures for constitutional amendments. At its drafting, the Indian Constitution was already one of the longest and most complicated constitutions in the world, and these changes made it even more complex.

By the early twenty-first century, the official version of the Indian Constitution was roughly two hundred pages long and contained approximately four hundred articles, twelve schedules, and several appendixes. It had been amended nearly one hundred times, under a procedure that requires only a two-thirds majority of members present and voting in both houses of Parliament to alter most provisions.[2] More than half of the articles, most dealing with India's administrative framework, were taken with generally minor changes from the 1935 Government of India Act passed by the British Parliament. Thus, the continuity of a parliamentary form of government was guaranteed for independent India.

For students of Indian politics, the most interesting—and typically the most controversial—sections of the constitution are those pertaining to fundamental rights and directive principles, government emergency powers, and relations between the central and state governments. Part Three of the constitution contains an extensive list of fundamental rights that define constitutional government in democracies, including the right to freedom of speech, assembly and association, and religion. Also included are social provisions, such as the "right against exploitation," which prohibits traffic in human beings, forced labor, and child labor. In general, the political rights have been both more controversial and more honored than the social guarantees, reflecting the difficulties of changing long-entrenched widespread practices.

Part Four of the constitution, entitled "Directive Principles of State Policy," is the counterpart to Part Three. The directive principles are not enforceable by any court but were viewed by the framers as principles to be followed in developing and implementing government policy. Whereas Part Three details provisions essential to the spirit of democracy and is designed to restrict state power, Part Four contains the vision of social revolution. For example, Article 39 lists "certain principles of policy to be followed by the State," to secure

A. that the citizen[s], men and women equally, have the right to an adequate means of livelihood;

B. that the ownership and control of the material resources of the community are so distributed as best to subserve the common good;

C. that the operation of the economic system does not result in the concentration of wealth and means of production to the common detriment;

D. that there is equal pay for equal work for both men and women.

Part Four also calls on the state in Article 46 to promote the "educational and economic interests of Scheduled Castes, Scheduled Tribes and other weaker sections" to protect them from social injustice and all forms of exploitation. This and related constitutional provisions giving the state a policy mandate to act on behalf of "weaker sections" undergird some of the most controversial government policies undertaken since independence.

The following discussion briefly reviews the debate over the role of religion in India, a debate accentuated by the Ayodhya crisis (see Chapter 5). The provisions regarding religion reveal some of the ambiguities and contradictions of the Indian Constitution, especially in the sections called Fundamental Rights and Directive Principles of State Policy. Discussion of other controversial areas in the constitution, notably emergency powers and relations between the Union and state governments, is deferred to later chapters.

Religion and "Secularism" in the Indian Constitution

Chapter 2 explained the way in which the diversity of the Indian population is grounded in religion, caste, gender, and language. Because religion and caste are historically intertwined in India, the constitutional provisions regarding religion are found both in the elaboration of the fundamental rights that are central to Indian democracy and in articles furthering the goal of social revolution. Part Three established freedom of religion as a fundamental right of Indian citizens. Article 25 (1) states: "Subject to public order, morality and health . . . all persons are equally entitled to freedom of conscience and the right freely to profess, practice and propagate religion." But Article 25 (2) qualifies this further by adding that the state may regulate any secular activity (economic, financial, political) associated with religious practice, and the state may also provide "for social welfare and reform or the throwing open of Hindu religious institutions of a public character to all classes and sections of Hindus." This last provision has the effect of removing, in principle, caste restrictions on access to Hindu institutions such as temples. Similarly, although the completely free exercise of Hindu traditions would continue the practice of untouchability, Article 17 abolishes "Untouchability" (but not caste) and forbids its practice "in any form."

Largely through the campaigns of the Bharatiya Janata Party, the question of whether India is and should be a secular democracy reemerged in the political debates of the late twentieth century. Acutely aware of the implications of religion for national unity, India's independence leaders were committed to establishing a secular, democratic republic. For a variety of reasons, the word "secular" was not included in the constitution until 1976, when it was added by amendment to the preamble (it is not found elsewhere in the document). Yet it is clear that the Constituent Assembly presumed that India would have a secular democracy without, obviously, being a secular society. This distinction between a secular polity and secular society is worth emphasizing as an important part of the puzzle of contemporary Indian politics. Stated simply: Can—and should—a society in which the overwhelming majority of people share the fundamentals of a Hindu worldview and make no distinction between secular and sacred aspire to a government that does not reflect this *Hindu* reality? The answers are multiple, as we will see throughout this book, and they all bear on the continued viability of the constitution and the goal of national unity.

Scholars point out the inherent problems in using the English word "secular" for India, and they imply that these difficulties help account for the word's absence from the original version of the constitution. Secularism is inextricably linked to the European experience of conflict and distinction between church and state. Thus imbued with historical and cultural meaning, secularism implies a distancing from religion that is ill-suited to the Indian context. In contrast, the Indian Constitution assumes state neutrality and evenhandedness toward different religions, modified by the social goals noted earlier.[3] Executing the principle of evenhandedness, however, has been extremely difficult. Nowhere is this better illustrated than in the widely publicized Shah Bano case, which inflamed political passions and raised questions about constitutional principle and legal intent. The broader philosophical issue raised by the case is how minority rights are to be protected in a liberal democracy.

Shah Bano. The Shah Bano case began in the late 1970s, when Shah Bano's husband of forty-three years divorced her. He returned her *mehr*, or marriage settlement, a sum of about US$300, as required by Islamic law. She then sued for maintenance under the Criminal Procedure Code of India. A regional court awarded her maintenance, but her former husband appealed the judgment to the Supreme Court of India on the grounds that as a Muslim he had to obey the Shari'a, (the body of Islamic law), which required that he pay maintenance for three months only. The Supreme Court ruled in 1985 that under the criminal code, a husband was required to pay maintenance to a wife without means of support. In his written opinion, however, the chief justice went further in his comments to call for a common civil code for all Indians.

The justice's argument epitomized a secular definition of the ideal nation-state, but it was viewed as an imminent threat to Muslims whose rights to community identity have been protected by the Indian legal system, which provides for state guarantees of Muslim and Christian (but not Hindu) laws in "private" matters of marriage, divorce, and inheritance. Although there have been many demands over the years for a common civil code,[4] communal tensions between Muslims and Hindus have generally guaranteed that Muslims who feel threatened by the Hindu majority will resist any policies seen as encroachments on their community laws and practices.

The Supreme Court ruling, combined with the chief justice's statements, generated more Muslim-Hindu conflict throughout India. Muslim religious leaders denounced the decision as interference in the rights of the Muslim community, and thousands of Muslims protested in the streets. Initially, the government, headed by Prime Minister Rajiv Gandhi, defended the court ruling and the secular authority of the state. Ultimately, however, the government backed down over fear of the political implications of its position: In dozens of hotly contested parliamentary constituencies, Gandhi's Congress Party depended on Muslim votes. Even though the overwhelming majority of Hindus—many of whom doubtless viewed Muslims as a legally privileged community—supported the court ruling, the government proposed legislation exempting Muslims from the provisions of the criminal procedure code that required husbands to support divorced wives. The 1986 Muslim Women (Protection of Rights on Divorce) Bill (which actually reaffirmed the control of the Muslim community over divorced women) was passed despite widespread opposition, leaving unresolved the meaning of religious freedom in the constitution.

The Shah Bano case is important because it highlighted tensions in the relationship between individual and group rights. Is the purpose of religious freedom to protect the individual against state intervention, or does it mean that the government is obliged to support customs that the *leaders* of a religious community claim are basic to their identity? Complicating this question is the reality that Shah Bano, like many Muslim and Hindu women, was illiterate, and like most other women was excluded from the central tasks of public religious life. Her fate was ultimately determined by men—both her sons, who advocated her case—and ultimately the male leaders of her community and Indian politicians in New Delhi. "Underlying the entire affair . . . was the desperate attempt by conservative factions to preserve patriarchal domination among Muslims—an interest shared by many Hindus as well."[5]

The Shah Bano case was unusual in the way it catapulted the role of the Supreme Court into public attention, but it highlighted the way in which Court decisions, especially those that touch on basic constitutional provisions and the principles of democracy, are part of the political process in India.

Judicial Review

Under the Indian Constitution, the principle of judicial review is the same as in the United States and Japan: Any act passed by the legislature must be in conformity with the constitution and the Supreme Court is the court of last resort in determining constitutionality. Judicial review in India has occasionally been controversial, much as it has also been in the United States. The controversy in India results from inherent conflicts between the principles of parliamentary sovereignty and judicial review and also between the fundamental rights and the goals of social revolution enumerated in the Indian Constitution. The conflict over judicial review and, ultimately, the independence of the courts, came to a head when Indira Gandhi was prime minister. In particular, the period of the 1975–1977 Emergency (see Chapter 9) demonstrated the vulnerability of judicial review and judicial independence in India. A 1975 high court finding that Mrs. Gandhi was guilty of corrupt electoral practices in the 1971 election catapulted the court into political controversy and precipitated the chain of events leading to the Emergency. The Supreme Court, under enormous political pressure and led by a chief justice who owed his position to the prime minister, failed to defend the basic right of habeas corpus for people detained during the Emergency. This capitulation badly eroded the credibility of the court, although subsequent decisions sought both to reinforce citizen rights and to reassert judicial authority.

Despite the unhappy history of the Emergency, the Indian Supreme Court continues to play an important role in judicial review and, more broadly, in Indian politics. As noted in Chapter 5, there are a number of cases generated by the Ayodhya dispute that have come before the court. The court has also issued important decisions regarding reservations quotas for disadvantaged groups and in environmental matters.

Japan

Chapter 7 concluded with a summary of the 1947 Japanese Constitution, which was adopted early in the postwar occupation of Japan. As explained below, the status and role of the Self Defense Forces illustrate the way in which a constitutional question may become the focus of public debate. More than any other section of the constitution, Article 9 raises the broader issue of the legitimacy of the entire document. To what extent can one expect that a constitution adopted under foreign tutelage, a document that deliberately curtailed a critical attribute of national sovereignty, would be accepted as legitimate by Japanese citizens? The answer to this question lies both in the origins of the Japanese Constitution and in its political and legal life since 1947.

The Occupation and the Japanese Constitution[6]

Within two weeks of his arrival in Japan, General Douglas MacArthur stated that Japan's Constitution should be revised, and the following month, he issued a "bill of rights" directive ordering the Japanese government to free all political prisoners and remove all restrictions on political, civil, and religious liberties. The Japanese government was already working on election reform and by mid-December 1945 had passed a law giving all citizens over the age of twenty the right to vote. Meanwhile, three dozen political parties had formed (or reformed), and the forces that would come to dominate postwar Japanese politics were taking shape.

The importance of these activities is that in the space of four months, the movement for major political reform was well under way on both the Japanese and the occupation sides. SCAP was not operating in a vacuum or without the knowledge of Japanese leaders. The rebirth of Japan's political parties, in turn, brought a surge of debate about reform, particularly among those on the Left whose voices had been silenced by political repression in the 1930s and early 1940s. The tone of this momentous period was set at the end of 1945, when the emperor issued a New Year's rescript restating the Charter Oath of 1868 and renouncing the beliefs that the emperor was "divine"[7] and that the Japanese people were superior. With this rescript and the other changes of the early occupation, essential constitutional principles were in place before any new document was drawn up.

In early 1946, MacArthur made the decision to draft a new constitution without consulting either U.S. allies, the U.S. government in Washington, D.C., or the Japanese government. By moving so quickly, he planned to affirm the new position of the emperor (thus stilling demands for elimination of the imperial institution) and to link Japan's future to pacifism. SCAP officials, who took barely one week to produce a draft in February 1946, became, in effect, Japan's "constitutional convention."

When the American draft was presented to Japanese leaders responsible for implementing occupation policy, the officials were shocked by the Americans' sudden and direct pressure. MacArthur's argument that the SCAP Constitution offered the best way to preserve the imperial institution, however truncated, ultimately persuaded the Japanese government, but not without opposition in the cabinet, and not without the emperor's intervention.[8] Even at this point, Japanese leaders were concerned about the implications of the no-war clause demanded by the Americans. Japanese negotiators subsequently succeeded in making some changes in the draft, but its essence was not altered, and on March 6, 1946, an imperial rescript approved the constitutional proposal.

From late spring to early fall 1946, the draft constitution was debated in the wider political arena. Elections for the first postwar House of Representatives, the lower house of the Diet, were held in April 1946. Over the course of the late spring and summer, special Diet committees examined the proposed constitution, and the Diet amended the draft numerous times. Some of the amendments were minor and others were relatively significant, but none altered the basic structure or intent of the original SCAP draft.

Not surprisingly, the no-war clause was again scrutinized, with numerous questions raised about Japan's eventual ability to defend itself. One of the Diet committees studying the draft proposed a wording change to Article 9 that, however subtle, was significant because it established the basis for justifying the Self Defense Forces. The change (shown here in italics) was the addition of introductory phrases to each of the two paragraphs in the article: "*Aspiring sincerely to an international peace based on justice and order,* the Japanese people forever renounce war as a sovereign right"; and "*In order to accomplish the aim of the preceding paragraph,* land, sea, and air forces . . . will never be maintained." As interpreted by successive Japanese governments, this wording linked the "renunciation of war" to the existence of a peaceful international order and rejected the maintenance of war potential for the purpose of settling disputes but did not exclude self-defense.[9]

Both houses of the Diet overwhelmingly approved the new constitution in October 1946, technically as an amendment to the 1889 constitution. The emperor promulgated the constitution in November, and it went into effect in May 1947.

Constitutional Evolution and Legitimacy

The Japanese Constitution is much shorter than its Indian and Chinese counterparts. Approximately one dozen pages long, it begins with a lengthy preamble that introduces popular sovereignty in language in which the American imprint is unmistakable.

> We, the Japanese people, acting through our duly elected representatives . . . do proclaim that sovereign power resides with the people and do firmly establish this Constitution. Government is a sacred trust of the people, the authority for which is derived from the people, the powers of which are exercised by the representatives of the people, and the benefits of which are enjoyed by the people. This is a universal principle of mankind upon which this Constitution is founded.

The constitution contains 103 articles divided into 21 chapters, including Chapter 2 (Article 9), "Renunciation of War." In sequence, the document defines the role of the emperor, the rights and duties of the people, and the functions of the Diet, cabinet, and judiciary. Additional chapters address finance, local government, and the amending process. Chapter 10 reiterates the underlying philosophy of American constitutionalism that basic rights are not created by a constitutional document (where they might be removed through amendment or legislation) but are recognized and safeguarded by the constitution. This is an important distinction for any constitutional order, but especially so for Japan, which historically had a different legal tradition than the United States. The 1889 constitution had defined subjects' rights and duties but had qualified them with the statement that they existed "within the limits of the law." It was, in fact, the Diet that had passed the laws suppressing freedom from the end of the nineteenth century through World War II.

Chapter 3, "Rights and Duties of the People," is the longest chapter, with 31 articles addressing a wide range of civil and social rights. Some provisions recall familiar civil rights and liberties, such as the "right to life, liberty, and the pursuit of happiness," freedom of religion, freedom of assembly and association, and the right to be secure in the home against unwarranted searches and seizures. Other provisions reflect twentieth-century thinking about social and economic concerns on the list of citizen rights. Article 14, providing for equality under the law and specifying no discrimination in political, economic, or social relations "because of race, creed, sex, social status or family origin" is one example. The constitution also states that "children shall not be exploited" (Article 27) and guarantees the availability of compulsory and free education to both boys and girls.

Unlike the Indian Constitution, the Japanese Constitution has never been amended, despite the contradictions of Article 9 and the long-standing desire of conservative politicians for change. In January 2000, however, the Diet formed a Research Commission on the Constitution to examine issues of revision. In April

2005, the commission issued its report, in which it identified subjects on which a consensus had been reached and those where there existed a "dominant view," and "major issues with separate views." The issues with conflicting views are listed in question format, for example: "The current Constitution is interpreted as allowing the SDFs and the right of self-defense. Should they be specified in the Constitution?"[10]

Formal constitutional revision is a long process. Article 96 of the constitution requires that amendments receive the support of two-thirds or more of the members of each house of the Diet, and the majority of voters must also approve any amendments in a referendum or election. The publication of the commission report was followed by several years in which no proposals for revision were presented to the legislature. The lack of activity may have been partly the result of disarray in the LDP leadership (see Chapters 9 and 11), but an equally plausible explanation is what Helen Hardacre has called a "stealth approach" to constitutional revision. For example, the 1947 Education Law was revised under the conservative tenure of LDP Prime Minister Abe Shinzo in 2007. The new law mandates the teaching of patriotism in the classroom and makes education the responsibility of the family, not a right. Revisions in the area of administrative law may thus smooth the way for altering the constitution.[11]

Judicial Review

The principle of judicial review is the same as in India, but the implementation of this principle over the past half century is different. In contrast to India, both judicial review and the Supreme Court in Japan have been largely noncontroversial. Japanese courts are generally conservative and have established a pattern of frequent support for government positions. The reasons for this are both political and cultural, and they explain the wide-ranging acceptance of, but relative lack of interest in, the constitution as a whole. The courts have played an important role in some political and social conflicts, but their history is one of privileging government bureaucrats in their findings.[12] This pattern is consistent with a history of government initiative and leadership in socioeconomic matters that dates to the Tokugawa period and helps explain why Japanese courts often defer to administrators or politicians for dispute resolution and, more particularly, explains why the Supreme Court has not been more active in asserting its constitutional prerogatives in judicial review.

Article 9 of the Japanese Constitution has generated cases for judicial review of the SDF's constitutionality, but both the lower courts and the Supreme Court have resolved the technical questions in the cases without ruling on the constitutional question of the SDF's status, viewing the issue as outside the scope of their jurisdiction.[13] Although from one perspective this response seems like an excessively narrow definition of judicial prerogative, from another, it is true that the SDF is only one part of a much broader debate about Japanese foreign policy, relations with other countries (especially the United States), and, therefore, national identity and self-determination.

Despite this generally conservative stance, the Supreme Court *has* exercised judicial review in some important instances, and the courts in general appear to be playing a growing role in protecting citizen rights. An early example of this role appeared in 1973, when the Supreme Court ruled unconstitutional an article in the penal code that specified heavier penalties for the crime of patricide than for homicide, on the ground that the penal code provision violated Article 14 of the constitution, which stipulates that "all of the people are equal under the law." The treatment of patricide as a worse crime, of course, stemmed from the Confucian tradition of respect for the father as the head of the family.[14] In a more recent case, the court found in favor of the plaintiffs in a sexual discrimination suit filed by thirteen female bank employees who charged that their employer had discriminated in salary and promotion policies.[15]

China

China's history of constitutionalism is both checkered and disjointed. The essence of European and American constitutions—that the power of the state is defined and restrained by basic law—is absent from the Chinese political tradition. Rather, law has traditionally been viewed as a tool at the service of the state; it never evolved as part of a broader constitutional philosophy of limiting the scope or powers of government for the benefit of the individual.

The Search for Constitutional Government

Modern ideas of constitutionalism were introduced into China in the early twentieth century. It will be recalled from Chapter 6 that by the nineteenth century, the Qing dynasty was disintegrating. Qing rule ended shortly after the first decade of the twentieth century, a period of rapid political change and government reform efforts. Japan's successful modernization inspired Chinese reformers to look to constitutionalism as one way to unite rulers and ruled in the new era of the nation-state. In 1908, the empress dowager proclaimed a set of principles for a nine-year program to prepare China for constitutional self-government. But she died before the year was over, and political turmoil soon derailed the program.

As leader of the Republican movement, Sun Yat-sen also proposed a nine-year transition to constitutional government, but his plans were overtaken by the events of the early Republican period. China's first constitution, drafted and promulgated in 1912, was never implemented. A second provisional constitution was written in the early 1930s, but it too fell victim to political chaos, and not until 1947 was another constitution promulgated. This constitution had a short life in mainland China, but when the Nationalists moved their government to Taiwan in 1949, they took with them the constitution that is still found in the Republic of China.[16]

Constitutional Change in the PRC

The People's Republic of China (PRC) has had four different state constitutions since it came to power in 1949, each indicating a different phase of China's political evolution. The 1954 constitution signaled the consolidation of the new revolutionary regime that came to power in late 1949; the 1975 constitution marked the transition from the Cultural Revolution to a period of normalization but was followed by a new document in 1978 that reflected the priorities of the leaders who rose to prominence after the death of Mao Zedong in 1976. The 1982 constitution, which is still in force, signaled the ascendancy of Deng Xiaoping. In addition to these four documents, the Chinese Communist Party (CCP) adopted five different constitutions during this same period. The first was in 1956, two years after the state constitution, and the last was adopted in 1982, the same year in which the most recent state constitution was adopted. In view of the preeminent role of the CCP, studying the role of constitutions in Chinese politics necessarily includes both the state and the party documents—a total of nine between 1954 and 1982.

The procedures for drafting and issuing both state and party constitutions have been similar: deliberation and writing by a committee of high-ranking leaders under the direction of preeminent leaders such as Mao Zedong, Deng Xiaoping, or Hu Jintao, and approval by either the National People's Congress (state) or the CCP National Party Congress. This ratification process has helped legitimize both the constitutional document and the political changes it marked. The following historical overview shows the rhythm of constitutional change and the role of constitutions in reestablishing legitimacy after major political shifts.

The Early Constitutions

Between 1949 and 1954, the PRC operated under the legitimacy and authority created by the revolutionary leadership of the Communist Party and a series of basic laws that established the structure of the central government and outlined programmatic goals. These early years were characterized by efforts to build support for the new government among other "democratic" (non-Communist, anti-Kuomintang) groups. Coalition building and legitimizing the regime were made all the more urgent by China's engagement in the Korean War in late 1950. The combination of external threats and domestic consolidation delayed drafting of a state constitution until 1953.

When the new leaders were confident that the revolution was secure, they submitted a constitutional draft, prepared by a government committee chaired by Mao Zedong, to public discussion. This exercise was less important for the content of proposed or actual changes than for the way in which it contributed to the legitimacy of the new regime.

Both consolidation and experimentation prompted the adoption of a constitution in 1956 for the Communist Party as well. This party constitution remained in force until 1969, when the radical phase of the Cultural Revolution subsided. The events of the Cultural Revolution, however, had rendered both the party and state constitutions irrelevant to the dynamics of politics.

From 1969 to 1978, three party and two state constitutions were issued. Taken together, they reflected the turbulence of the Cultural Revolution and the struggle over succession to Mao Zedong that are described in Chapter 10. One of the Cultural Revolution's immediate effects was to elevate the military's role in politics when the People's Liberation Army became the only institution capable of restoring public order. The CCP's Ninth Party Congress in 1969 signaled the phase of stabilization after the Cultural Revolution. A newly adopted Communist Party Constitution identified Lin Biao, China's defense minister, as the "heir apparent" to Mao Zedong. The following year, party leaders secretly drafted a new state constitution, but the looming succession struggle intercepted its publication and ratification.[17]

The elevation of Lin Biao as constitutionally designated successor to Mao heralded the expanded power of the military in China's politics. But the growth of military influence produced a counter-reaction among civilian leaders of the party. A new party constitution in 1973 and a state constitution in 1975 marked another shift in power. Premier Zhou Enlai, China's number-two leader, and Mao Zedong both died in 1976. Immediately after Mao's death, maneuvering to replace him reached a peak. The Central Committee of the Communist Party announced in October 1976 that Hua Guofeng would succeed Mao as party chairman. A new CCP Constitution in 1977, followed by a third state constitution in 1978, legitimized the new coalition that emerged after Mao's death and presumably marked the end of nearly two decades of struggle over leadership.

In fact, however, Hua Guofeng himself turned out to be a transition leader. Deng Xiaoping, twice purged in earlier conflicts among leadership factions, skillfully rebuilt his party support in the late 1970s. His supporters came to control the Central Committee and Politburo, the top CCP organs, and by 1980 were secure enough to begin the process of drafting new constitutions for the party and the state. Two years later, the CCP and the PRC both had new constitutions, documents that have remained in place to the present. Table 8.1 summarizes these key events in China's post-1949 political history and shows the dates of the nine state and party constitutions adopted from the 1950s to the 1980s, as well as the pattern of amendments since 1982.

This checkered history of constitutional change illustrates the different roles that Chinese constitutions play, in contrast to the role of the constitution in India and Japan. Constitutions become fictive when they are overtaken by events that leave them outdated. Nonetheless, Chinese leaders obviously have viewed these documents as an important way to enhance political legitimacy, and it is noteworthy that the earlier pattern of changing constitutions has been replaced by an amending process that reflects broader stability in the political system.

The 1982 Constitutions and Amendments

One of the distinguishing features of both state and party Chinese Constitutions is a lengthy introduction or preamble that seeks to legitimize the political system through reminders of China's historical greatness and the revolutionary missions of the PRC and the CCP. Statements of broad policy goals are also woven into the preambles. In general, these preambles serve the same purpose as the much shorter introductions to the Japanese and American Constitutions: They link the past, present, and future through idealistic visions and ideological assertions. The following excerpts from the 1982 state constitution of the PRC illustrate this linkage.

> China is one of the countries with the longest histories in the world. The people of all of nationalities in China have jointly created a splendid culture and have a glorious revolutionary tradition. Feudal China was gradually reduced after 1840 to a semi-colonial and semi-feudal country. The Chinese people waged wave upon wave of historic struggles for national independence and liberation and for democracy and freedom. . . . After waging hard, protracted and tortuous struggles, armed and otherwise, the Chinese people of all nationalities led by the Communist Party of China with Chairman Mao Zedong as its leader ultimately, in 1949, overthrew the rule of imperialism, feudalism and bureaucratic capitalism . . . and founded the People's Republic of China.

TABLE 8.1 State and Party Constitutions in the People's Republic of China

Year	Political Event	PRC Constitutions	CCP Constitutions
1949	PRC founded	—	—
1950–1953	Korean War	—	—
1954		new	—
1956		—	new
1966	Cultural Revolution begins	—	—
1969	Ninth CCP Congress	—	new
1971	Lin Biao dies	—	—
1973		—	new
1975		new	—
1976	Mao Zedong dies; Hua Guofeng new leader	—	—
1977		—	new
1978		new	—
1979–1980	Rise of Deng Xiaoping	—	—
1982	Twelfth CCP Congress	new	new
1987		—	amended
1988		amended	—
1989	Tiananmen Square movement; Jiang Zemin becomes CCP head	—	—
1992		—	amended
1993		amended	—
1997	Deng Xiaoping dies	—	—
1999		amended	—
2002–2003	Transition from Jiang to Hu Jintao	—	—
2004		amended	amended
2007	Seventeenth CCP Congress	—	amended
2008	Eleventh NPC opens	amended	—

Comparing the introductions with specific constitutional provisions further illuminates the rationale for important Chinese policies, both domestic and foreign. For example, the preamble and various articles of the PRC Constitution state the official policy on national minorities discussed earlier in Chapter 3. The section quoted above refers to "the Chinese people of all nationalities," acknowledging the diversity that is reemphasized in a later paragraph that warns against "Han chauvinism." This same paragraph, however, affirms that the People's Republic of China is a "*unitary* multinational state" [emphasis added] and cautions that it is also necessary to "combat local-national chauvinism." Local-national chauvinism would include activities by any ethnic groups seen as a threat to national unity. Article 4 of the constitution suggests both the supportive and the limiting nature of the policies toward minorities:

> All nationalities in the People's Republic of China are equal. . . . The state helps the areas inhabited by minority nationalities speed up their economic and cultural development in accordance with the peculiarities and needs of the different minority nationalities. Regional autonomy is practiced in areas where people of minority nationalities live in compact communities. . . . All the national autonomous areas are inalienable parts of the People's Republic of China.

By extending the logic of the central historical goal of modern China—national unity and independence—the constitution also signals the official policy toward Taiwan: "Taiwan is part of the sacred territory of the People's Republic of China. It is the lofty duty of the entire Chinese people, including our compatriots in Taiwan, to accomplish the great task of reunifying the motherland."

The CCP Constitution includes the same themes found in the state constitution. Its introduction discusses at greater length the nature of "socialist democracy" in China, as well as the role of the Communist Party in nation building and economic development. Whereas the PRC Constitution explains the organization of the state, including the role of the National People's Congress, the president, and the State Council, the CCP Constitution lays out the criteria for party membership and describes party organization.

Taken together, China's constitutions serve as a guide to the chief ideological tenets that drive Chinese politics. They also explain, in broad terms, the organizational framework for both the state and the Communist Party. They are not reliable guides to the daily operations of the government, party, or other important political organs, such as the military—but of course this is true of constitutions in general. However, they are guides to what the leadership views as important changes, as the evolution of the 1982 constitutions illustrates.

Both the party and the state constitutions have been frequently amended since their adoption in 1982. The fact that they have been amended, rather than replaced by new constitutions, suggests two important developments in Chinese politics that are explained in future chapters: regularization of the process of leadership transition, and consensus among China's leaders on the fundamental goal of economic modernization.

An illustration of the nature and significance of constitutional change in China is found in the 2002 and 2007 amendments to the party constitution ratified by the Sixteenth and Seventeenth Party Congresses, which marked the transition from Jiang Zemin to Hu Jintao and the beginning of Hu's second term as party leader. The 2002 amendments added references to the "Three Represents," to acknowledge Jiang Zemin's party leadership. The phrase "Three Represents" remind us of the massive changes that have taken place since the original constitution was adopted: The party must represent the most advanced forces of production (including the private sector), the most advanced forces of culture, and the fundamental interests of the broadest number of people. This last commitment is linked to an important change in the party's definition of eligible members, which was expanded to include "any advanced element" of society (Article 1), thus opening the door to recruiting members from China's most dynamic private business sector.[18] The 2007 amendments further emphasize the consensus on modernizing China by inscribing in the constitution the phrase, "Scientific Outlook on Development," to symbolize Hu Jintao's role in leading the party.

Summary

For all three countries, the idea of constitutionalism was a late-nineteenth-century import from the West, and one of the outstanding characteristics of the Indian and Japanese Constitutions is the degree to which they still bear the imprint of Great Britain and the United States, respectively. In contrast to China, India and Japan continue to operate under the norms and institutions laid out in their post–World War II constitutions, documents that have established, in large part, the fundamental legitimacy of the two democracies. In China, legitimacy still derives largely from the role of the Communist party, but the evolution of both the state and party constitutions over the past thirty years suggests that their role in fortifying political legitimacy has become more relevant to Chinese politics.

In all three countries, as in most countries, constitutional provisions may be ignored or bypassed. This has long been an issue in China, and is becoming a greater problem in India. One may speculate that if the Indian Constitution is becoming more fictive, it is due to the weight of the political problems and conflicts confronting the country. These conflicts, in turn, guarantee that constitutional issues play a greater role in the vigorous debate about India's future than they do for either Japan or China.

Exploring Further

The constitutions discussed in this chapter are accessible online, and each of the three countries also has an online site for supreme and high courts (India and Japan) and the Supreme People's Court (China); all are worth exploring. Additional perspectives on the process of drafting and amending the Japanese constitution may be traced through the research project of the Edwin O. Reischauer Institute of Japanese Studies, "Constitutional Revision in Japan," online at www.fas.harvard.edu/~rijs/crrp.

Notes

1. On the origin and structure of the Constitution, see Granville Austin, *The Indian Constitution: Cornerstone of a Nation* (Oxford: Clarendon Press, 1966); and Zoya Hasan, E. Sridharan, and R. Sudarshan, eds., *India's Living Constitution: Ideas, Practices, Controversies* (Delhi: Permanent Black, 2002).

2. The exceptions are provisions pertaining to the election of the president, the structure and functions of the Supreme Court, the high courts in the states, legislative relations between the Union and state governments, and the distribution of functions between the Union and state governments as found in the Seventh Schedule. Amendments to these provisions require that at least one-half of the state legislatures also approve the change.

3. For a discussion of these and related issues, see the essays in M. M. Sankhdher, ed., *Secularism in India: Dilemmas and Challenges* (New Delhi: Deep and Deep, 1992); and Rajeev Bhargava, "India's Secular Constitution," in Hasan, Sridharan, and Sudarshan, 105–133.

4. Article 44 of the Constitution (in Part Four, Directive Principles of State Policy) says that "the State shall endeavor to secure for the citizens a uniform civil code throughout the territory of India." In the nineteenth century, the British adopted a policy of permitting Hindus to be governed by Hindu laws and Muslims by Muslim laws in family matters, and this policy was carried over after independence, despite Article 44. The result is a patchwork of laws, practices, and state and Supreme Court decisions concerning such matters as marriage, divorce, maintenance, inheritance, and adoption throughout India.

5. William Johnson Everett, *Religion, Federalism and the Struggle for Public Life: Cases from Germany, India, and America* (Oxford: Oxford University Press, 1997), 90.

6. The information in this section relies primarily on the following sources: Richard B. Finn, *Winners in Peace: MacArthur, Yoshida, and Postwar Japan* (Berkeley: University of California Press, 1992); Robert E. Ward, "Presurrender Planning: Treat-

ment of the Emperor and Constitutional Changes" and Theodore H. McNelly, "'Induced Revolution': The Policy and Process of Constitutional Reform in Occupied Japan," both to be found in *Democratizing Japan: The Allied Occupation*, eds. Robert E. Ward and Sakamoto Yoshikazu (Honolulu: University of Hawaii Press, 1987), 1–41 and 76–106, respectively; and Yoshida Shigeru, *The Yoshida Memoirs: The Story of Japan in Crisis* (Boston: Houghton Mifflin and Cambridge: Riverside Press, 1962), chap. 13.

7. See the discussion of *kami* in Chapter 1.

8. Finn, 99–100; Yoshida, 135.

9. Key SCAP officials also apparently understood the modifications as permitting defense forces. McNelly, 92–93.

10. The record of proceedings and the text of the report may be found at www.sangiin.go.jp/eng/report/ehb/ehb_index.htm. Leftists, including the Socialist and Communist Parties, as well as a number of prominent intellectuals, have continued to oppose constitutional amendments. But with half of the commission members coming from the Liberal Democratic Party, and more than 90 percent of legislators in the governing coalition reportedly favoring revision (*The Japan Times*, October 29, 2002), recommendation of changes was certain.

11. Hardacre's comments were made at a symposium organized by the Edwin O. Reischauer Institute of Japanese Studies at Harvard University, November 21, 2008. Ruth Walker, "Revising Japan's Constitution: History, Headlines, and Prospects," *Harvard University Gazette Online*, accessed December 5, 2008, at http://www.news .harvard.edu/gazette/2008/12.04/11-japan.html.

12. Frank K. Upham, *Law and Social Change in Postwar Japan* (Cambridge, Mass.: Harvard University Press, 1987).

13. James E. Auer, "Article Nine: Renunciation of War," in *Japanese Constitutional Law*, eds. Percy R. Luney Jr., and Kazuyuki Takahashi (Tokyo: University of Tokyo Press, 1993), 80–81. From the court's perspective, the Diet is the "highest organ of state power" and is responsible for important policy decisions.

14. Hidenoru Tomatsu, "Equal Protection of the Law," in Luney and Takahashi, 188–192.

15. Increasingly, women are using both Japanese courts and international organizations to press their claims of sex discrimination in the work place. Suvendrini Kakuchi, "Japanese Women Attack Discrimination," *Asia Times*, April 27, 2002 (online edition).

16. The ROC Constitution was extensively amended in the 1990s to reflect changing circumstances.

17. For the text, see Winberg Chai, introduction and "Text of the 1970 Draft of the Revised Constitution of the People's Republic of China," *Studies in Comparative Communism* 4, no. 1 (January 1971), 97–106.

18. Party leaders still tightly control the process of amending the constitution. Key changes to the CCP Constitution, for example, were determined a year earlier and were confirmed at a summer retreat of party leaders prior to the Sixteenth Congress in November 2002. Guoguang Wu, "From the July 1 Speech to the Sixteenth Party Congress: Ideology, Party Construction, and Leadership Transition," in *Chinese Leadership in the 21st Century: The Rise of the Fourth Generation*, eds. David M. Finkelstein and Maryanne Kivlehan (Armonk, N.Y.: M. E. Sharpe, 2003), 179.

9

The Parliamentary System in India and Japan

Introduction:
Structuring Power at the National Level

There are multiple ways to structure national power in both democratic and authoritarian states. Power may be deliberately fragmented with "checks and balances," as in the American presidential system. The president is simultaneously head of state and head of government and has considerable authority, but that authority must be shared with a strong legislature (Congress) and judiciary. Presidential systems in Asia, such as those found in South Korea, Taiwan, Indonesia, or the Philippines, illustrate the variations in how real power is diffused or concentrated, depending on historical context and political dynamics (see Focus Box 9).

In contrast to the presidential model, the parliamentary model divides the role of the executive into two positions: a ceremonial executive (the head of state) and a political executive (the head of government). The head of government, generally called the prime minister, is the leader of the largest party in the legislature, and this party may hold a majority of seats by itself or, alternatively, may be the largest of several parties in a coalition government. Both situations have occurred in India and Japan, as explained later in this chapter. The members of the legislature (or parliament) are directly elected by the voters; government cabinet ministers are usually elected legislators and retain their seats while they serve in the government. In this manner, there is a fusion of powers in parliamentary systems that contrasts with the separation of powers found in presidential systems such as that of the United States.

PRESIDENTIAL SYSTEMS IN ASIA

Presidential systems come in various forms. As a general guideline, we assume that a presidential *system*—as opposed to the existence of a president in a parliamentary structure such as India's—implies the separation of powers between the executive, legislative, and judicial branches of government. In this structure, the president, as head of the executive branch, serves as both head of state and head of government, in contrast to a parliamentary system where these roles are divided. In its clearest form, the chief executive is directly elected by the voters. However, there may be alternative arrangements for electing the chief executive, such as funneling the popular vote through an electoral college (as is found in the United States).

In addition, there are quasi-presidential systems, in which the president has considerable power and may even be directly elected, but there is also a prime minister who serves some of the same functions as the prime minister in a parliamentary system. The best known case of this arrangement is France under the Fifth Republic, where the president is directly elected by the voters. The president then appoints a prime minister who must secure the support of parliament.

Asia illustrates these variations on presidential systems. For example, the Philippines resembles the United States. The president is both head of state and government, as well as serving as commander in chief. She or he, along with a vice-president, is directly elected by the voters for a six-year term and has the authority to make cabinet appointments. Indonesian presidents are also directly elected and serve five-year terms.

South Korea, Taiwan, Sri Lanka, and Pakistan are all mixed systems, with both a president and a prime minister or premier. But the allocation of powers and responsibilities varies among these nations. For example, the South Korean president is elected for a term of five years by direct popular vote and chooses a prime minister. Cabinet members are appointed by the president on the advice of the prime minister and with the approval of the country's unicameral legislature. In Taiwan, the president is directly elected for a four-year term; he selects a premier, who does not need the confidence of the legislature. The premier heads the Executive Yuan, or cabinet. The president is generally more powerful than the premier in this system, although because of some limits on the president's power, deadlock between the executive and the Legislative Yuan occasionally occurs.

continues

FOCUS BOX 9

The Sri Lankan system is modeled after the French system and has a directly elected president for a term of six years. The president appoints the prime minister and may summon or dissolve the unicameral legislature. Finally, Pakistan offers another variation. The president is elected for a five-year term by an electoral college consisting of members of the Senate, National Assembly, and provincial legislatures, whereas the prime minister is elected by the assembly alone. In principle, the president acts on the advice of the prime minister, but in fact he or she has important residual powers, such as the right to dissolve the assembly.

In addition to the prime minister, parliamentary systems also have a symbolic executive or head of state. The head of state represents the historical continuity, dignity, and ongoing legal authority of the nation-state that transcends the political majorities resulting from periodic elections. Although the head of state may be called the president (as in India), the coexistence of this position with a prime minister distinguishes the system as parliamentary, not presidential. The head of state formally appoints a prime minister, accepts the resignation of a government, and calls elections, but these functions are exercised only on the advice of the prime minister and under defined constitutional limits.

There are numerous variations on this basic parliamentary pattern. By way of illustration, heads of state may differ: Some inherit their positions (monarchs), whereas others are indirectly elected, for example by an electoral college; legislatures may be bicameral or unicameral; and the ways in which the prime minister and cabinet secure legislative support or confidence also vary.

On paper, authoritarian states may be either presidential or parliamentary in form. Several military-dominated governments in Asia have formally been presidential, with the president enjoying effective power through ties to the military, not as the result of popular election. President Musharraf of Pakistan (1999–2008) and President Suharto in Indonesia (1967–1998) are examples of military-backed presidents. In contrast, the Chinese government structure resembles a parliamentary system, although the role of the Communist Party means that the political reality is very different from that found in India or Japan (see Chapter 10).

India and Japan are both parliamentary systems, and the governments of both countries follow basic conventions that are characteristic of the parliamentary systems of Europe. In both countries the constitutional structure of power is largely inspired by the British (or "Westminster") model. Yet the way each operates is distinguished by dynamics as varied as the countries themselves, including regional diversity in India and World War II legacies in Japan.

Legislative Frameworks

India and Japan have bicameral legislatures, with the lower house in each case being the more powerful of the two bodies. The lower houses are directly elected by the voters and have greater legislative power (especially in money matters), and the government is responsible to and must have the confidence of the lower house. It is in this relationship between the government and the lower house that the British model has left its stamp on the political institutions of the two countries (see Figures 9.1 and 9.2).

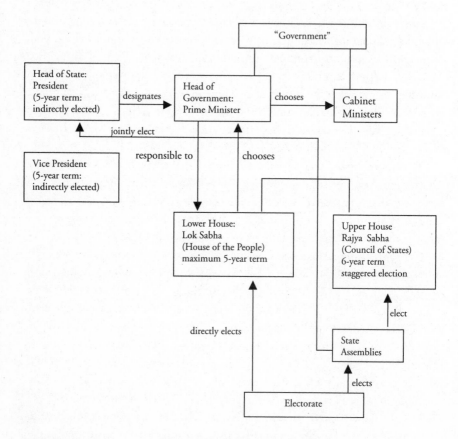

FIGURE 9.1 Major institutions of the government of India

The Indian Parliament

The Indian national Parliament consists of the lower house, the Lok Sabha (House of the People); the upper house, the Rajya Sabha (Council of States); and the president of India.[1] All but two of the 552 Lok Sabha members are elected from single-member constituencies throughout India's states and Union Territories; two representatives of the Anglo-Indian community may be appointed by the president if, in the words of the constitution, "he is of the opinion that the Anglo-Indian community is not adequately represented" (Article 331). The term of the Lok Sabha, like that of the British House of Commons, is five years, unless it is dissolved sooner. Under a proclamation of emergency, however, the president of India may extend the life of the Lok Sabha by one year at a time, although not for longer than six months after the term of the emergency proclamation expires.

The Rajya Sabha is about half the size of the Lok Sabha; the constitution limits it to 250 members, twelve of whom are nominated by the president in recognition

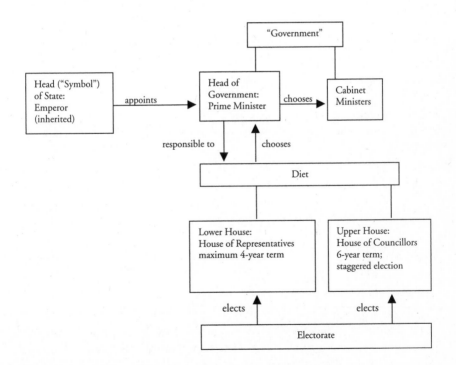

FIGURE 9.2 **Major institutions of the government of Japan**

of their "special knowledge or practical experience" in literature, science, art, or so-cial service (Article 80). The remaining members are elected by the state legislative assemblies according to a formula that allocates seats to the states in approximate proportion to the size of their population. The primary purpose of the Rajya Sabha, as this system of indirect election suggests, is to emphasize the role of the states in India's federal system (see Chapter 11). Unlike the Lok Sabha, the Rajya Sabha may not be dissolved. Its terms are staggered so that (as in the case of the U.S. Senate), one-third of the membership is elected every two years.

With the exception of "money bills" dealing with taxation, borrowing, or spending, legislation may be introduced in either house. Not only must money bills originate in the Lok Sabha, but the Rajya Sabha may only delay—not stop—passage of a money bill approved by the Lok Sabha. Other legislation, however, must be approved by both houses.

The Japanese Diet

There are numerous similarities between the houses of the Japanese Diet[2] and those of the Indian Parliament (see Figures 9.1 and 9.2). The lower house, the larger of the two, is the House of Representatives. Its 480 members are all elected for four-year terms, although the house (like the Lok Sabha) may be dissolved sooner if the cabinet so decides.[3] Early dissolution in Japan, like India, Britain, and other parliamentary systems, may occur either when the government loses the confidence of the lower house or when the prime minister seeks to increase his or her party's strength in parliament. Although the Japanese Constitution makes it clear that the cabinet must maintain the confidence of the House of Represen-tatives in order to govern, the constitution also states that the cabinet is collec-tively responsible "to the Diet," meaning both the upper and lower houses, for its policies. In contrast, the Indian cabinet is responsible only to the Lok Sabha.

The powers of the House of Representatives are superior to those of Japan's upper house, the House of Councillors, in two important areas. The constitu-tion directs that the prime minister must be chosen from the members of the Diet and that a majority of the cabinet ministers must also be Diet members. However, should the two houses of the Diet disagree on the choice of the prime minister and no agreement be reached through a joint committee, "the decision of the House of Representatives shall be the decision of the Diet" (Article 67).

The House of Representatives also has superior legislative authority, not just in budgetary matters but in all cases where there is disagreement between the two houses. A bill passed by the House of Representatives and on which the House of Councillors makes a different decision becomes a law when passed a second time by a two-thirds majority of the House of Representatives. This occurred in early 2008 when, for the first time in over a half century, the prime minister, Fukuda Yasuo, pushed through a bill to permit the Self Defense Forces to resume fueling in the Indian Ocean in support of U.S. operations in Afghanistan, a bill that had been defeated by the upper house. Finally, as in India, the budget must first be submitted to the lower house, and in case of disagreement between the two houses, the decision of the House of Representatives stands as the decision for the Diet as a whole.

The House of Councillors has 242 members chosen through an electoral formula designed to balance local and national constituencies. Approximately 60 percent of the councillors are elected from constituencies that are coterminous with the prefectures, the basic unit of local government in Japan. The remaining councillors are chosen from a single national constituency, using a system of proportional representation. Thus, the upper house is structured to represent voters in a different way from the lower house, which is also the case in India. Another similarity with India is that councillors' terms are staggered: The term of office for members of the House of Councillors is six years, with half elected every three years. Finally, like the Rajya Sabha, the House of Councillors may not be dissolved.

As this sketch of the Japanese and Indian legislatures suggests, the rationale behind the structures and functions of the two parliaments is the same. The differences that stand out—such as the fact that the Japanese cabinet is collectively responsible to the Diet as a whole, not just the lower house—are less significant than the similarities. Ultimately, what distinguishes both systems as parliamentary is the fusion of legislative and executive roles and the constitutional requirement that the cabinet (or Council of Ministers) maintain the confidence of the lower house of Parliament. This observation is not to diminish the differences that result from variations in culture, political party dynamics, and the internal rules of operation of the legislatures but rather serves to demonstrate that undergirding these variations is a fundamental logic about how government authority should be structured.

Dual Executives: Political and Symbolic Roles

Prime Minister and Cabinet: The "Government"

The political executives (prime ministers) of the two countries bear more similarity to each other than do the heads of state. The constitutional provisions regarding the designation of the prime minister and cabinet in both countries are characteristic of other parliamentary systems, and the differences between the two countries are consistent with variations in other parliamentary systems. The prime ministers are leaders of the largest party in their respective legislatures; if their parties do not have an absolute majority, then they are the leaders of the dominant party in a coalition government. As government heads, they choose cabinet ministers to reflect the diversity of their parties or coalitions. The ministers are expected to observe the norms of collective responsibility for government policy, as well as individual responsibility for their cabinet portfolios. If, for example, they oppose a government position, they are expected to resign. They are also expected to resign to take blame for a major failure or scandal in their ministry—as the Indian home minister did in the wake of the terrorist attacks on Mumbai in November 2008. In the event of a defeat of government policy that entails a loss of confidence, all cabinet ministers, including the prime minister, are expected to resign. This resignation is followed either by the reconstitution of a government that can secure majority legislative support or, failing that, new legislative elections.

In Japan the emperor formally appoints as prime minister the person previously chosen by the Diet. The prime minister then appoints cabinet ministers, who must be civilians and a majority of whom must be Diet members. The prime minister may also remove ministers "as he chooses" (Article 68). Although ministers may be chosen from either house of the Diet, in practice, the great majority, as well as all of the prime ministers, have come from the lower house.

In India, the president chooses the prime minister, who in turn selects the members of the Council of Ministers to be officially appointed by the president. All ministers must be members of either the upper or the lower house of Parliament, and following the British custom, it is customary that the prime minister come from the Lok Sabha. However, there are exceptions: Manmohan Singh, prime minister from 2004 to 2009, was a member of the Rajya Sabha.

Symbolic Executives

Although the Indian president and the Japanese emperor share important constitutional similarities, there are also significant differences that can be traced to the countries' varied histories. Earlier chapters provided historical perspective on the decisions that led to one of the most obvious distinctions. Nationalist leaders in India emphasized their liberation from British colonialism by rejecting any continued role, however symbolic, for the British monarch in Indian politics. The framers of the Japanese Constitution, in contrast, chose to maintain an emperor, however apolitical, for symbolic continuity. Thus, India and Japan offer different models of parliamentary democracy: One is a republic, the other a constitutional monarchy. Both in terms of constitutional delegation of authority and political reality, the Indian president is more powerful than the Japanese emperor as head of state, but even the Indian president is clearly subordinate to the prime minister.

The Indian President. India has a president and a vice president, with the vice president charged primarily with executing the functions of the presidency during the president's illness or absence. The vice president becomes acting president in the event of the latter's death, resignation, or removal. He is also the ex-officio chairman of the Rajya Sabha.

Both the president and the vice president are indirectly elected. The procedure for presidential election is the more complicated of the two, involving an electoral college composed of all elected members of the state legislative assemblies and the national Parliament. In contrast, the vice president is elected by the members of both houses of Parliament sitting in joint session.

The president and the vice president are elected for five-year terms and may be reelected. In the earliest years of the republic, men of great stature who might be considered above the political fray were chosen as president, but in recent decades the most important criterion has been the presidential candidate's acceptability to the prime minister. In 2007, India's first female president, Pratibha Patil, was chosen largely because she was viewed as acceptable to the leadership of the Congress Party, which headed the government coalition. For the past thirty years, the pattern has also been to use the presidential office to reflect the diversity of India's population (see Table 9.1). In 2002, A. P. J. Abdul Kalam, a nuclear scientist, became India's third Muslim president; his predecessor from 1997 to 2002 was the first Dalit president.

TABLE 9.1 Indian Presidents, 1974–2007

President	Dates in Office	Profession	Community
P. D. Patil	2007–	Politics	Hindu; Female (Rajasthan)
A. P. J. Kalam	2002–2007	Nuclear Engineering	Muslim (Tamil Nadu)
K. R. Narayanan	1997–2002	Diplomacy; Politics	Hindu; Dalit (Kerala)
S. D. Sharma	1992–1997	Legal Scholarship	Hindu (Uttar Pradesh)
R. Venkataraman	1987–1992	Law; Politics	Hindu (Tamil Nadu)
Giani Zail Singh	1982–1987	Politics	Sikh (Punjab)
N. S. Reddy	1977–1982	Politics	Hindu (Andhra Pradesh)
F. A. Ahmed	1974–1977	Politics	Muslim (Delhi)

Source: Compiled from the official website of the President of India at http://presidentofindia.nic.in.

As in most parliamentary systems, the president as head of state nominally has formidable powers that, however, are exercised on the advice of the Council of Ministers, or cabinet. Since the Council of Ministers is dominated by the prime minister, it is the prime minister in effect who provides the advice on which the president acts. All executive actions of the government of India are expressed in the name of the president (Article 77). He or she summons both houses of Parliament and dissolves the lower house when necessary; the president assents to legislation, appoints the governors of the states, the justices of the Supreme Court and state high courts, the attorney general, and the auditor general of India; and he or she is the commander in chief of the armed forces and also has the power of pardon.

In the 1950s, when Rajendra Prasad was India's first president, the issue of presidential discretion emerged on several occasions. As early as 1951, Prasad expressed the desire to act solely on his own judgment, independently of the Council of Ministers, when assenting to parliamentary legislation and when sending messages to Parliament. Had Prasad's position prevailed, it would have undermined the conventions of cabinet government as they had developed in Britain and as had been intended by the Constituent Assembly.[4]

The Forty-Second Amendment to the constitution, passed in 1976, was designed to eliminate ambiguity by clearly articulating the convention inherited from the British and reinforced in the 1950s. Article 74 states that there shall be a Council of Ministers headed by the prime minister "to aid and advise the President who *shall*, in the exercise of his functions, act in accordance with such advice" [emphasis added]. Under normal circumstances, the president thus represents and reflects the political will of the prime minister and cabinet. In time of political instability, however, presidential discretion may come into play—as, indeed, the British monarch may have greater discretion when there is no parliamentary majority. The discussion of coalition governments in the last section of the chapter looks more closely at this question.

The Japanese Emperor. We have already been introduced to the *kokutai* theory of state found in the Meiji Constitution of 1889. Under that constitution, the emperor, who was "sacred and inviolable," possessed supreme authority. But the constitution also provided that the emperor exercise his powers with the guidance of advisory bodies. The ambiguity here is that in principle the monarch was not answerable to any other source of authority or political institution, yet it was acknowledged simultaneously that the emperor did not act alone and that advisers shared responsibility.[5] Thus, the 1889 Constitution continued the traditional separation of power and authority with an emperor who reigned but did not rule—at least not in the meaningful day-to-day sense of a political executive. This ambiguity, in turn, helped explain how, in the 1940s, both those who blamed the emperor for the war and those who viewed him as buffeted by (if not captive to) his advisers, could claim historical support for their positions.[6]

The 1947 constitution eliminated any ambiguity about the emperor's role at the outset. Rejecting the doctrine of *kokutai*, Article 1 states: "The Emperor shall be the symbol of the State and of the unity of the people, *deriving his position from the will of the people with whom resides sovereign power*" [emphasis added]. Article 3 states that the advice and approval of the cabinet is required for all acts of the emperor "in matters of state," and Article 4 adds that the emperor shall not have any powers related to government. Nonetheless, the emperor's powers as described in the constitution are typical of those accorded most heads of state. He appoints the prime minister ("as designated by the Diet") and also the chief judge of the Supreme Court ("as designated by the Cabinet"). He convokes and dissolves the Diet, with the advice and approval of the cabinet and "on behalf of the people." To these essential functions are added other symbolic activities, such as receiving foreign ambassadors. All of these activities are carried out under the authority of the cabinet, however. Despite his truncated role in modern Japan, the Emperor—and more broadly the Imperial House—has not escaped controversy, as the next section explains.

Tensions and Controversies

Constitutional stipulations may be clear, but this clarity does not preclude the tension or even controversy that emerges with the dynamics that characterize any political system. To illustrate the reality of the political dynamics in the Japanese and Indian systems, three issues are described here: the Imperial system and secondly the weakness of most prime ministers and in India, the use of "President's Rule" and emergency constitutional provisions.

Imperial Dilemmas

To many Japanese citizens, the Imperial House is either archaic or boring, or both. But to other Japanese, the Emperor, as the inheritor of the oldest imperial line, symbolizes the essence of Japanese tradition. This tradition, in turn, may be celebrated or viewed as cause for concern because of its links to Shinto.

It is worth recalling here some historical features of Japan's imperial institution. The Japanese term for the emperor, *tenno*, literally means "heavenly sovereign." The ceremony of imperial accession is followed by a complex and ancient ritual called *daijosai*, in which the emperor offers specially prepared foods to the "Sun Goddess," Amaterasu Omikami, and then enters a ceremony of spiritual communion with the Shinto *kami*.[7] These rituals, preserved as part of Imperial House Shinto, last served to remind the Japanese people of their imperial traditions when Emperor Akihito succeeded his father, the Emperor Showa (Emperor Hirohito) in 1989.

The various ceremonies, both private and public, that marked the 1989–1990 imperial transition were surrounded by renewed controversy over the imperial system and the constitutionality of using public funds for religious rituals. The preparations for Emperor Akihito's *daijosai* in fall 1990 were carried out in secrecy because of threats of terrorism by those opposed to the imperial system. Earlier, funeral preparations for Akihito's father, Hirohito, were complicated by the fact that so many of the traditional rites spring from Imperial House Shinto and are associated with State Shinto. Consequently, two funerals were held: Private Shinto rites were conducted by the Imperial Household Agency, whereas the public state funeral was secular but preceded by a ninety-minute Shinto ritual. Although the ritual was not technically part of the state funeral, it was held at the same place as the funeral and was observed by the official guests assembled for the state ceremony. In protest, members of leftist parties critical of Japan's history of aggression arrived late in order to avoid the Shinto rites or boycotted both the Shinto and state ceremonies.

In contrast to this, rightists protested against anyone who criticized their ultranationalist interpretation of the historical and symbolic roles of the emperor. Perhaps the most notorious case involved the mayor of Nagasaki, who was divested of his honorary functions in the local branch of the Liberal Democratic Party after he stated that Emperor Hirohito bore responsibility for the events of World War II. Then, in January 1990, as he left his office, the mayor was shot and wounded by a member of a right-wing group.[8] Ironically, the new Emperor Akihito visited the mayor and conveyed his sympathy.[9]

In the early twenty-first century, the subject of the Imperial House returned to public debate over the issue of imperial succession. Under a law passed initially during the Meiji period, only a male may succeed to the Japanese throne; the convention of patrilineal inheritance was reaffirmed in the 1947 Imperial House Law. For a brief period, the Japanese government considered amending the 1947 legislation in order to permit equal succession rights because no boys had been born to the Imperial family for decades. Although Japan has seen eight empresses, there have been none since the eighteenth century. However, in 2006, the birth of a boy to the wife of Prince Akishino, the younger brother of the current crown prince, derailed any plans for immediate change.

Although polls have shown that a majority of Japanese favor amending the succession law—seemingly an obvious way to handle the problem of succession—some conservatives have balked at any change, arguing that female succession would violate Japanese tradition. In the words of Takeda Tsuneyasu: "The Emperor is not valued because he is intelligent or handsome. It is because he is the inheritor of the blood that has been preserved for 2,000 years."[10]

Japanese Prime Ministers

While prime minister, Koizumi Junichiro had proposed revising the Imperial succession law, and had he continued as prime minister for a few more years, it is possible that the legislation might have passed the Diet. However, Koizumi was succeeded by several weak prime ministers, none of whom was interested in or strong enough to undertake the reform. In this respect, they were typical of most Japanese prime ministers.

Why should the prime minister of Japan be weaker than the British prime minister, for example? The primary reason may be found in the country's political parties, particularly the LDP, from which the overwhelming majority of Japan's prime ministers have come. The number, kind, and relative strength of political parties affect the degree of freedom any political leader has to formulate and implement policy. A prime minister at the head of a party that is internally unified and has a strong parliamentary majority, especially in the lower house, is able to form a government with concentrated power rarely found in a presidential system, with its separation of powers. In contrast, a prime minister confronted with intraparty factionalism or indiscipline and perhaps a coalition government is constrained by his or her own party organization, along with the need to negotiate with other parties.[11] Japan, both under Liberal Democratic Party (LDP) rule and under coalition governments, provides numerous illustrations of these constraints.

Between 1945 and 2008, Japan had thirty-one prime ministers (India had fourteen during the same period), most of whose names have been forgotten by all but the specialist in Japanese politics. In contrast to the United States, Britain, or India, where political eras are marked by the name of a president ("the Bush administration") or prime minister (politics "under Tony Blair" or "under Manmohan Singh"), Japanese prime ministers seldom see their names used as the benchmark of an era. One obvious reason for this difference is the relatively high rate of turnover in Japanese prime ministers. However, unlike those European countries that also experience frequent turnover of heads of government, between 1955 and 2008, Japan was essentially ruled by one party—the LDP—despite several periods of coalition governments. The explanation for the lower profile of the

Japanese prime minister during this period lies not in interparty politics but rather in intraparty politics, that is, the political nature of the LDP itself.

The LDP has always been structured around formal factions, and with rare exceptions, all LDP presidents have been faction heads (see Chapter 12). Some years ago, Kenji Hayao's study of Japanese prime ministers found that in order to become a faction leader, party leader, and likely prime minister, a potential candidate had to meet a number of criteria, including membership in the lower house, seniority (having served five or six terms), and relative youth.[12] Hayao does not list gender as a criterion because it is assumed that successful candidates will be male, even though in recent years a few women have been nominal candidates for the post.

These criteria, in turn, imply a number of others. Seniority, for example, requires a safe seat. Long tenure also means that candidates win their first races as young men and are career politicians.[13] During the years that it takes to move up the ranks, the would-be party presidents will become experts not only in policy matters and legislative politics but also (and perhaps more important) in factional and party affairs. And to do well within one's faction and party means helping others gain government and party appointments and raising money for election campaigns. Some of these qualities, such as fund-raising and organizational ability, characterize successful politicians nearly everywhere. In the LDP, the ability to rise both within a faction and across faction lines also requires a collaborative, even self-effacing, style of leadership. LDP prime ministers have long practiced the art of managing intraparty coalitions. Nevertheless, they have never been able to take party support for granted; LDP presidents are elected for a two-year term with a maximum of two consecutive terms allowable, and a one-year extension is permissible only with the support of two-thirds of the LDP Diet members.

The consequence of these factors is that LDP prime ministers traditionally have been inclined more toward a reactive than a proactive leadership role in policy matters. However, in 2001, a newly elected prime minister, Koizumi Junichiro, challenged this traditional pattern. Comparatively young (59) at his election, unmarried, with an unconventional personality (and haircut), Prime Minister Koizumi enjoyed huge public popularity as he challenged Japan's traditional political practices.[14] (See Photo 9.1.) Launching a populist, top-down leadership style, Koizumi pushed for a wide variety of structural reforms in both economics and politics. He broke with party practice by choosing his own cabinet ministers, "in total disregard of wishes of the faction leaders."[15] His goal was to exercise greater control over public policy formation by making policy initiatives less subject to dilution by factions or bureaucrats.

PHOTO 9.1 Former Prime Minister Koizumi Junichiro. Photo courtesy of James W. Boyd.

As noted above, under LDP rules, the party's president may serve a maximum of five years. When Koizumi's presidency ended, no strong leaders emerged to replace him. A combination of political gaffes, intraparty disorganization, and the success of the opposition Democratic Party in the 2007 House of Councillors election weakened successive governments. It seemed likely that Japan's prime ministers would return to a reactive, mediating style of leadership. Elected LDP president in 2008, Aso Taro became Japan's fourth prime minister since 2006, and his success was due largely to his ability to cross factional lines.[16]

Emergency Powers in India

The most important political controversies that have engaged the Indian presidents and prime ministers are strikingly different from those in Japan. Certainly there is no parallel to the debates over the symbolism of the Imperial throne. Although there are debates about the weakness of the prime minister and central government, there have been as many over the misuse of power at the Centre, particularly in implementing the emergency provisions found in the Indian constitution.

National and regional emergencies were foreseen by the drafters of the constitution who, it is recalled, were working in the shadow of the 1947 Partition of the subcontinent and conflict with Pakistan. Articles 352 to 360 of the Constitution anticipate three types of emergency: (1) a threat to India's security by war, external aggression, or internal disturbance; (2) a breakdown in the government of a state; or (3) a threat to financial stability. The first of these justifies a declaration of national emergency, a case that is so rare that it is associated in Indian political history with "the Emergency," the period from 1975–1977, when Indira Gandhi was prime minister.

The Emergency. The origins of the Emergency lay in a combination of political and economic developments in the late 1960s and early 1970s. The ruling Congress Party had weakened and was split by factions. Indira Gandhi, prime minister since 1966, sought to free herself from the control of the party machine and a small group of powerful state leaders. Determined to build a broad base of support, she established a separate political party called the Congress (I) [for Indira] Party. Her strategy was one used by other leaders confronting resistance from entrenched interests, whether in party or government: appeal directly to the people with populist images and policies, bypassing or undermining intermediary structures.[17]

In March 1971, Mrs. Gandhi dissolved the Lok Sabha and called new elections, in which the Congress (I) won more than two-thirds of the seats. But by 1973, severe economic problems, including food shortages, encouraged widespread rioting and strikes. The antigovernment opposition gathered support in one state after another, and by 1975, demands for the prime minister's resignation were widespread. Finally, in mid-June, a state high court found that the prime minister had violated the election code in her constituency during the 1971 Lok Sabha election. The court finding meant that she would lose her parliamentary seat, forcing her resignation as prime minister. When a mass rally in New Delhi called for the government to resign, Indira Gandhi asked the president to proclaim a state of emergency as provided for by Article 352 of the constitution.

Before most Indians knew of the proclamation, the principal opposition leaders had been arrested and a news blackout imposed on New Delhi. During the twenty-one months that the proclamation was in force, more than 100,000 people were detained without trial, 2 dozen organizations were banned, and rigorous press censorship was imposed. Parliament—dominated by Indira Gandhi and the Congress (I) since 1971—approved these measures as it had the original emergency proclamation. Even more important for the evolution of the Indian Constitution and Indian politics, the Parliament approved wide-reaching changes to the constitution. The primary effect of these changes was to secure parliamentary (and prime ministerial) supremacy and to diminish the power of the courts and the constitutional guarantees to fundamental rights.

The Emergency ended in early 1977, when Prime Minister Gandhi, in anticipation that her party would win, called for new Lok Sabha elections. The newly formed Janata Party, however, won a majority of seats, sweeping the Congress (I) government out of power and officially ending the Emergency.

The significance of this dramatic period for our discussion lies in the way it illustrates the interplay of history and personality in defining the role of the prime minister and executive-legislative relations in a parliamentary system. Would other Indian prime ministers have reacted the way that Indira Gandhi did under the same circumstances? Although this question is rhetorical, we can use it to explore two related factors relevant to understanding executive power. It is clear that Mrs. Gandhi viewed herself and her political survival as indispensable to India under the threatening conditions the country faced in the early 1970s, including a hostile international environment and domestic poverty. "Her experiences in childhood [as the daughter of independence leader Jawaharlal Nehru] and as a young adult revolved almost completely around duty to the nation. . . . No wonder the boundaries between her own interests and those of the nation were so blurred."[18] In this respect, her autocratic leadership recalls the style of many nationalist leaders, especially in countries emerging from colonial rule and confronting seemingly overwhelming problems (see Photo 9.2).

In retrospect, the Emergency highlights a central dilemma in Indian politics. In view of both the actual and anticipated threats to the Indian republic in the 1940s and since, wasn't it appropriate that the Constituent Assembly provide constitutionally sanctioned states of emergency? But is there not also an inherent danger in the combination of sanctioned emergency procedures and a parliamentary system that, by definition, admits to the possibility of concentrated executive power, a danger exacerbated by competitive elections that mobilize people for political participation and thus increase pressures on the government

"NATIONAL INTEGRATION IS THE VERY CONDITIO
OF OUR NATIONAL SURVIVAL

Smt. INDIRA GAND

PHOTO 9.2 Indira Gandhi billboard. Photo courtesy of James W. Boyd.

to take decisive action? Although the term "President's Rule" refers to the second type of emergency envisaged by the Constitution, one confined to a single state within India, it raises similar questions.

President's Rule. On the receipt of a report from the governor of a state that a situation has arisen in which state governance cannot be carried on in accordance with the provisions of the constitution, the president may then (1) assume all or any of the state government's functions or vest these in any authority (such as the governor) in the state other than the state legislature; (2) declare that the powers normally exercised by the state legislature will be exercised by the national Parliament; or (3) make other provisions necessary to carry out the proclamation, including suspending the operation of the Indian Constitution or any body (*except* the judiciary) in the state.

Invoked infrequently until the late 1960s, President's Rule soon became a tool in the hands of the ruling Congress Party and was used both to deal with regional instability (as intended by the constitution) and to eliminate state governments headed by opposition parties. Between 1966 and 1977 alone, India's presidents acquiesced in Prime Minister Indira Gandhi's demands to invoke President's Rule in thirty-nine instances. By the end of the twentieth century, President's Rule had been declared in approximately one hundred cases.

The increased use of President's Rule reflects a number of long-term developments in Indian politics: the preoccupation with threats to national unity, the efforts of a declining Congress Party to maintain control over both the national and state governments, and the erosion of the federal system established by the constitution. In Punjab, for example, President's Rule was declared first in 1951, and subsequently in 1968, 1971, 1983, and 1987. Finally, in the early 1990s, the constitution was amended to exempt Punjab from the three-year limit for successive proclamations of emergency (each of which is in effect for a maximum of six months if approved by Parliament). Supporters of invoking President's Rule in Punjab insisted on the central government's legitimate concerns with national security in a highly volatile political climate on the border with Pakistan. Thoughtful critics, however, made an equally plausible case that excessive use of President's Rule exacerbated an already difficult political situation by undermining the normal development of state government and regional political parties.[19]

At the core of the debate over President's Rule is its use for partisan purposes—that is, to suspend state executives (the chief minister and Council of Ministers) and legislative assemblies that, though popularly elected, contravene the political wishes and priorities of the prime minister and Council of Ministers at the Union level. Prime Minister Indira Gandhi was especially criticized for expanding the partisan use of President's Rule, but even her father, Jawaharlal Nehru, recommended the imposition of President's Rule to eliminate non–Congress Party governments in some states.[20] The decision *not* to invoke President's Rule may be equally partisan: In 2002, the national BJP-led government declined to use President's Rule in Gujarat after widespread attacks on Muslims by Hindus (see Chapter 11) arguably justified its imposition. The state government at the time was headed by the BJP.

Is the use of emergency powers a case in which the head of state should exercise leadership and discretion? The president is clearly charged by the constitution to act on the advice of the Council of Ministers and the prime minister. But some presidents have weakened the stature of their office by acquiescing in the erosion of the constitution's civil rights protections through excessive declarations of both President's Rule and national emergency.[21]

Despite these concerns, a weak president is consistent with constitutional intent, and a strong president might well provoke both a political and a constitutional crisis. One scenario in coming years is an incremental enlargement of presidential discretion in an era of divided parties and unstable parliamentary majorities, a scenario that might encourage a more assertive presidency. This scenario, however, is juxtaposed with the alternative of general weakness of the central government in India, as in Japan, in part due to increased political splintering. Coalition governments are both a cause and an effect of this.

Coalition Governments

In the absence of a single-party majority in the lower house of parliament, governments are formed by negotiating coalitions between parties. The coalition may include parties in the legislature that agree to support the government for a vote of confidence, but which do not actually join the government. Most often, pro-government parties will be incorporated into the government; that is, the prime minister will designate at least one cabinet minister from the parties in the coalition. Parties supporting the government, in fact, generally demand cabinet representation as part of the bargain for helping to form a government.

Coalition governments may combine as few as two and as many as a dozen or more parties. In some instances, two dominant parties may choose to form a "grand coalition," either to demonstrate national unity in time of crisis (for example, the United Kingdom during World Wars I and II) or when one of the parties is unable to secure a majority to form a government. In Germany, the Social Democrats and Christian Democrats formed such a coalition in 2005 after the inconclusive elections to the lower house (Bundestag) of parliament. In fall 2007, there were unsuccessful efforts in Japan to form a grand coalition between the LDP and the Democratic Party of Japan after the latter won a major victory in the House of Councillors elections.

The typical coalition in Japan since the 1990s has been between the LDP and the small New Komeito Party (see Chapter 12), although earlier in the 1990s, the Socialist Party of Japan headed a coalition government for a short period. In contrast, coalition governments in India have become increasingly complicated, in proportion to the proliferation of political parties. The reasons for the increased number of parties are explored in Chapter 12, but one of the consequences of this development has been a political situation in which negotiations to form governments involve numerous trade-offs between parties with different policy agendas. The Bharatiya Janata Party (BJP) took the lead in forming a coalition government after the 1999 Lok Sabha elections. The party headed the National Democratic Alliance, which included twenty-one other parties. In 2004, the Congress Party, headed by the prime minister–designate, Manmohan Singh, was able to form a government only with the support of almost twenty small parties, including the Communist Party of India (Marxist). The United Progressive Alliance (UPA), as the coalition was called, was predictably fragile due to the large number of parties involved and their differences over key policy issues. In 2008, the Marxists withdrew support from the government in opposition to a U.S.-India nuclear agreement (see Focus Box 14). This act set off a frenzy of bargaining, as Prime Minister Singh looked for votes from other parties to survive a vote of confidence. He was successful, but the cost was to further hamstring government initiatives opposed by key parties whose support was critical to the government's survival.

The realities of coalition arithmetic in India recall the issue of presidential discretion. As the political landscape in the Lok Sabha continues to fragment, the president is positioned to exercise some discretion in calling on parties to form a government. For example, after the 1996 elections, President S. D. Sharma called on the largest party, the BJP, to form a government, even though it was more than seventy seats short of a majority, and there was no guarantee of support from smaller parties. When, thirteen days later, the new prime minister–designate resigned after an unsuccessful effort to build a majority, the president turned to a multiparty opposition coalition that, had it been faster to organize itself, might have been the president's first choice.[22] Criticized for not insisting that his first prime minister–designate show that the BJP had sufficient support to form a government, President Sharma subsequently required letters of support from potential coalition parties before inviting another party to take the lead in forming a government, and his successors continued the practice.[23]

Summary

The parliamentary systems of India and Japan are very similar in terms of their key features: bicameral legislatures, with a more powerful lower house; fusion of powers between the legislative and executive branches; and a dual executive with authority concentrated in the prime minister and secondarily in the cabinet. In both countries, a shifting political landscape has made coalition governments increasingly common. Differences can be traced to historical and constitutional factors, which have, for example, shaped the discretion of the Indian president and set the context for the political debates linked to the Japanese emperor.

Exploring Further

Official government websites are maintained for all of the government institutions mentioned in this chapter, and blogs that address government issues multiply rapidly. The website for *Japan Echo* (http://www.japanecho.co.jp/resources.html) offers numerous useful links to government branches, political parties, and related sites. For a sample of the debate among bloggers over Imperial succession, see Scilla Alecci, "Japan: Controversy over Imperial Succession," *Global Voices*, December 14, 2008, accessed December 28, 2008, at: http://globalvoicesonline.org/2008/12/14/japan-controversy-over-imperial-succession. One place to start for the flavor of India's "blogosphere" is www.indiablogwatch.com.

Notes

1. It is unusual for the head of state in a parliamentary system to also be designated as part of Parliament (the head of government almost always is). India's Constituent Assembly chose to emphasize the interdependence of the legislative and executive branches in this fashion and may also have seen the provision as further assurance against uncontrolled executive authority. Granville Austin, *The Indian Constitution: Cornerstone of a Nation* (Oxford: Clarendon Press, 1966), 126–128.

2. The Japanese name of the legislature is *Kokkai*, more literally translated as national "assembly" than "Diet." However, its official English name is Diet or National Diet, which is also by convention more familiar.

3. The number of house seats varies with redistricting, as in other parliamentary systems. For example, there were 512 seats at stake in the 1990 election, and 511 in 1993. Under a new election system adopted in 1996, the number was reduced to 500, and reduced again in 2000 to 480.

4. Austin, 135–143. Prasad was opposed to a piece of legislation, the Hindu Code bill, which, as a conservative Hindu, he found distasteful. James Manor, "The Prime Minister and President," in *Nehru to the Nineties: The Changing Office of Prime Minister in India*, ed. James Manor (Vancouver: University of British Columbia Press, 1994), 120.

5. Koichi Kishimoto, *Politics in Modern Japan: Development and Organization*, 3rd ed. (Tokyo: Japan Echo, 1988), 28.

6. Controversy over the emperor's role during the war influenced the debate over the role he should play in the postwar order. Robert E. Ward, "Presurrender Planning: Treatment of the Emperor and Constitutional Changes," in *Democratizing Japan: The Allied Occupation*, eds. Robert E. Ward and Sakamoto Yoshikazu (Honolulu: University of Hawaii Press, 1987), 1–41.

7. On the imperial regalia and *daijosai*, see *Japan: An Illustrated Encyclopedia*, vol. 1 (Tokyo: Kodansha, 1993), 80 (Atsuta Shrine), 262–263, 596, 627–628 (Ise Shrine).

8. For a discussion of this and related incidents, see Yoichi Higuchi, "The Constitution and the Emperor System: Is Revisionism Alive?" in *Japanese Constitutional*

Law, eds. Percy R. Luney Jr., and Kazuyuki Takahashi (Tokyo: University of Tokyo Press, 1993), 65–67.

9. Akihito has also been credited with deepening public remorse over Okinawa's wartime devastation and Japan's World War II attacks on China. He is the first Japanese emperor ever to visit China, which he did in 1992.

10. Quoted by Adrienne McPhail, "The X Versus Y Chromosome," *Japan Today*, January 4, 2006, accessed December 27, 2008, at http://archive.japantoday.com/jp/comment/882. Takeda is not a disinterested observer. He is a member of a collateral branch of royalty disestablished by the occupation authorities, and one of his recommendations is to restore succession rights to the former royalty branches. Takeda and others have also observed that a woman would not be able to execute Shinto rites during menstruation and after childbirth—an acknowledgment of the close relationship between Shinto and notions of purity. The debate about succession was rumored to cause tensions within the royal family and between the family and the Imperial Household Agency. "Ailing Emperor Mirrors Japan's Sharp Decline," *The Sunday Times*, December 28, 2008, retrieved March 20, 2009, at http://www.timesonline.co.uk/tol/news/world/asia/article5404140.ece.

11. Patrick Weller noted: "The structure of the party outside parliament determines the number of independent centres of power that exist within the party and therefore the number of bodies with whom the prime minister may need to maintain a direct relationship." *First Among Equals: Prime Ministers in Westminster Systems* (Sydney: George Allen and Unwin, 1985), 19.

12. Kenji Hayao, *The Japanese Prime Minister and Public Policy* (Pittsburgh: University of Pittsburgh Press, 1993), 97–105. The average age at which prime ministers assumed power through 1991 was 65, but in 2006, Abe Shinzo became Japan's youngest prime minister at the age of 42. His successor, Fukuda Yasuo, was 71 when he assumed office.

13. They often come from political families and inherit their seats from their fathers or fathers-in-law. Hayao, 105. A somewhat different case is that of Aso Taro, who became prime minister in 2008. His maternal grandfather was Yoshida Shigeru, the most important prime minister during the occupation era (1946–1947 and 1948–1954).

14. Despite Koizumi's maverick reputation, in many ways he followed the LDP pattern: he inherited his father's electoral constituency, was reelected ten times before becoming prime minister, and had been loyal to his faction. Jonathan Watts, "Lion King and the Politics of Pain," *The Guardian*, September 1, 2001, accessed December 29, 2008, at http://www.guardian.co.uk/world/2001/sep/01/japan.jonathanwatts2.

15. Takeshi Uemura, "Koizumi Shakes Establishment with Cabinet Selection Process," *The Daily Yomiuri*, October 3, 2002.

16. There is an ongoing debate about the future of LDP factions. They still define much of the party's politics, but they are weaker than they were in the twentieth century. Masami Ito, "LDP—A Party Defined by Factions," *The Japan Times*, October 15, 2008, retrieved November 23, 2008, from http://search.japantimes.co.jp/cgi-bin/nn20081015i1.html.

17. For an analysis of Gandhi's "survival strategy" as it reflected her leadership style, see Jana Everett, "Indira Gandhi and the Exercise of Power," in *Women as National Leaders*, ed. Michael A. Genovese (Newbury Park, Calif.: Sage Publications, 1993), 103–134.

18. Ibid., 131. It is plausible that Gandhi also shared the British view of a "loyal opposition," which in her view had been violated by her Indian opponents.

19. See, for example, Robin Jeffrey, *What's Happening to India: Punjab, Ethnic Conflict, and the Test for Federalism*, 2nd ed. (New York: Holmes and Meier, 1994).

20. B. D. Dua, "The Prime Minister and the Federal System," in Manor, 20–47, discusses in detail the use of President's Rule by all of India's prime ministers up to the 1990s.

21. Perhaps the best example of this was President Fakhruddin Ali Ahmed's role in the declaration of emergency that inaugurated the Emergency (1975–1977) when, in the middle of the night, he signed a proclamation of national emergency at the request of Prime Minister Indira Gandhi and one of her ministers, a proclamation that a majority of the Council of Ministers would likely have opposed. Manor, "Prime Minister and President," 124.

22. Manoj Mitta, "The President: Walking a Tightrope," *India Today*, May 31, 1996, 18–19.

23. On the 1998 and 1999 Lok Sabha elections, see Harish Gupta, "Narayanan to Go by Spirit of 'Letter', May Ask for Proof," *Indian Express*, April 21, 1999, retrieved December 28, 2008, from http://www.expressindia.com/news/ie/daily/19990421/ipo21060.html. For the 2004 election, see "Sonia Gandhi Meets President Kalam," *Indian Express*, May 18, 2004, retrieved December 28, 2008, from http://www.expressindia.com/news/fullstory.php?newsid=31547.

10

China:
The Party-State System

The choice of Hu Jintao as China's preeminent political figure in 2002 signaled the "Fourth Generation" of Chinese Communist leadership. The smooth transition from Hu's predecessor, Jiang Zemin, confirmed that the tumultuous succession politics described later in this chapter had been replaced by stability and legitimacy at the highest party levels. Nonetheless, questions still remained about China's political trajectory. Would the forces of economic competition, both domestic and global, stimulate political competition? Did the creeping rule by law presage a modern version of authoritarian legalism or a shift toward liberal democracy? How would the leadership handle the multiple problems caused by the breakneck economic growth, including a lagging rural sector and environmental degradation?

In the words of its constitution, the Chinese Communist Party (CCP) is "building socialism with Chinese characteristics." Since the launching of the reform period in the late 1970s, the *economic* achievements have been spectacular, although not without problems. The *political* changes have prompted scholars and "China-watchers" to be more ambivalent about the nature and scope of the accomplishments. Every country confronts these issues in different forms: the relationship between economic and political development, the link between law and liberty, and the sources of authority and legitimacy. For China, these issues lie at the core of the debate over democratization that has flooded the scholarly and popular literature on the People's Republic of China (PRC). This chapter explains the distinctive features of China's government and party structures to provide background on the debate about the country's future.

Although unique among the three countries compared in this book, China's party-state system existed in the USSR until 1991, as well as in other Communist states such as Vietnam, and also in Taiwan until the late 1980s (see Chapter 6). The implosion of most party-state systems has turned many scholars away from a comparative framework when examining China, but Chinese researchers have been preoccupied with understanding the dynamics that had so quickly led to the demise of the former communist governments. In retrospect, many of the policy initiatives taken by China's leaders in the past twenty years appear calculated to avoid the weaknesses found in the Soviet Union and other failed states.[1]

This chapter explores the evolution of the Chinese system since 1949, beginning with a description of the formal decision-making and administrative structures of the People's Republic of China and the Chinese Communist Party and the relationship between these two institutions. This is followed by a discussion of the philosophy behind this dual system and what the Chinese call the "leading role" of the party. Next, a historical overview of the major political periods since 1949 is presented. In the context of the dramatic shifts in political personalities and policy agendas during the twentieth century, the concluding section evaluates China's leadership and the party-state system in the twenty-first century.

The Party-State System

The term *state* as used here encompasses all the formal governing structures, both civilian and military, from the national to the local levels, in China. The state structures are described in the 1982 PRC Constitution, and the formal party structures are outlined in the 1982 Chinese Communist Party Constitution. As explained in Chapter 8, both of these constitutions have been amended, but the basic structures have not changed. The distinctive feature of the party-state system is the way in which political authority is shared between the institutions of the party and those of the state.

State Structures

As outlined in the PRC's Constitution, government at the national level is organized along the lines of a parliamentary system (see Figure 10.1). The National People's Congress (NPC) is "the highest organ of state power" (Article 57) and exercises the legislative power of the state. The NPC consists of approximately 3,000 deputies from the provincial level, as well as deputies from the armed forces. Normally, it meets annually, and between plenary sessions, its business is conducted by its Standing Committee. In principle, the NPC chooses and may remove from office China's top political officials, including the president and vice president, the premier of the State Council, the chairman of the Central

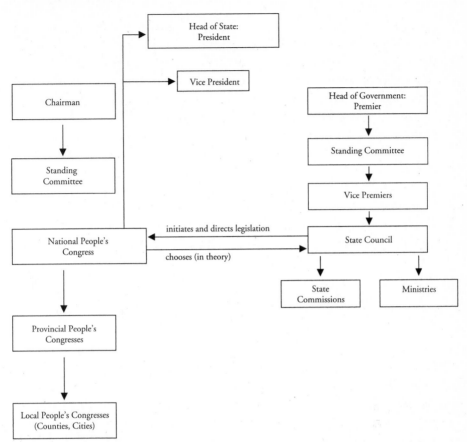

FIGURE 10.1 People's Republic of China, formal state structures

Military Commission, and the president of the Supreme People's Court. The president of the PRC serves as the symbolic head of state, and the premier of the State Council (the cabinet) is the head of government (Articles 62 and 63).

Because of the NPC's size and its relatively short meetings, its real authority is exercised by the Standing Committee, whose term runs concurrently with the term of the Congress. After the elections to the Eleventh NPC (2008), the Standing Committee had 175 members; its chairman is the head of the NPC, and along with the vice-chairman and secretary general, he handles the important day-to-day work of the NPC.[2] For the first thirty years of the PRC, the NPC was viewed as a "rubber-stamp" legislature, whose purpose was to add legitimacy (through unanimous approval) to policies determined elsewhere and to officials chosen elsewhere. In the 1980s, however, evidence began to accumulate that the Congress was asserting its constitutional mandate by demanding a role in policy deliberation, drafting major proposals, and even stalling initiatives sought by party officials. In the 1990s, the chairman of the Standing Committee and head of the NPC, Qiao Shi, took the position that some democratization should accompany economic modernization, and this led the NPC into greater prominence.[3] A number of indicators suggest that the NPC is emerging as a potential counterweight to top-down decision-making by the State Council and the monopoly over political debate held by the party. Increasingly, committees of the legislature solicit input from social groups, such as academics and representatives of labor, and Congress delegates have amended or revised government-proposed legislation.[4]

Effective executive authority at the national level belongs to the State Council, headed by the premier. The State Council may have as many as thirty core members, including the premier, vice premiers, state councilors, and ministers in charge of ministries and commissions. In addition, there are dozens of specialized state agencies directly linked to the State Council. Within the State Council is a Standing Committee that acts as an "inner cabinet" and comprises the most important members of the council. The State Council, like the cabinets in India and Japan, is the chief policy-making and administrative organ of the national government. It is the real center of state power, responsible for drafting laws, the budget, and the administrative plan and for submitting these to the National People's Congress for approval. It also oversees the implementation of all state policy.

In addition to the National People's Congress and the State Council, with their respective standing committees and the vertical hierarchies of the various state ministries, the national government structures include the Military Affairs Commission and the highest echelon of the judiciary, the Supreme People's Court and Supreme People's Procuratorate. None of these governing bodies is static. In particular, the state ministries, like those in India and Japan, may be merged, divided, and combined in different ways to reflect changing State Council priorities or to improve administrative efficiency in China's vast bureaucracy. In 2008, for example, a major reorganization of the State Council resulted in the creation of several "super-ministries."

Party Structures

The highest organs of power in the Communist Party are the National Party Congress[5] and the Central Committee elected by it (see Figure 10.2). The Party Congress has more than two thousand delegates and is held every five years (Article 18). Its main political role is to applaud decisions made elsewhere. The ses-

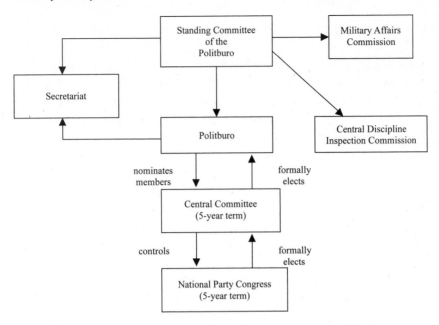

FIGURE 10.2 **Central organization of the Chinese Communist Party**

sions of the Party Congresses, which receive a great deal of media coverage, are numbered sequentially and legitimize major policy efforts or initiatives. The Twelfth Congress, for example, which met in September 1982, symbolized Deng Xiaoping's ascent to political primacy and approved the 1982 party constitution. Two decades later, the Sixteenth Congress (2002) introduced a new general secretary to the party, Hu Jintao, and ratified major changes to the party constitution. In 2007, Hu was reelected at the Seventeenth Congress, where his concept of "Scientific Outlook on Development" was enshrined in the constitution.

The executive bodies of the National Party Congress are more important than the Congress itself and in fact are the most important political bodies in China. The Central Committee members are nominally elected by the Party Congress and serve five-year terms. The Central Committee is itself large (more than 360 full and alternate members were elected in 2007) and meets only once or twice a year in plenary session. Its importance derives both from its constitutional authority and from the fact that most of its members hold other important positions, thus membership on the Central Committee is a way of gauging political influence. As noted, the Central Committee is (according to the party constitution) elected by the National Party Congress. In fact, the Political Bureau, which is formally elected by the Central Committee, actually determines the list of nominees standing for election to the Central Committee.[6]

The Political Bureau and its Standing Committee constitute the core of the CCP's power. The Political Bureau has averaged between twenty and twenty-five members; since 2002, its Standing Committee has consisted of nine members. Although the 1982 party constitution states that the Political Bureau and Standing Committee are elected by the Central Committee, the lists submitted for election are the result of careful behind-the-scenes negotiation and co-optation by those already in power. The composition of these top party organs signals to outsiders the relative strength of different leaders and their supporters.

There are three other important party organizations at the national level: the Secretariat, the Military Affairs Commission, and the Central Commission for Discipline Inspection. The Secretariat provides administrative support for the Central Committee and Political Bureau and is headed by the general secretary of the Central Committee, who is a member of the Political Bureau and, as a result of having control over party organization, is one of China's most important leaders.

The Military Affairs Commission, whose membership overlaps that of the government Military Commission, reports to the Political Bureau, oversees the armed forces, and makes national defense policies. In one form or another, it has existed since the 1930s and represents the party's control over the military. This control is exercised through the General Political Department, which is responsible for the political education of the troops. This function, along with the Military Commission's power to appoint and remove military personnel, explains its critical importance in Chinese politics. Consequently, the head of the commission is also one of the country's most important national leaders. For example, although Jiang Zemin retired as the secretary general of the party in 2002, he retained his position as chairman of the Military Commission until 2004. Hu Jintao then became the new chairman.

The Discipline Inspection Commission is responsible for party discipline, performance, and morale. This is the body charged with the faithful maintenance of party policy and ideology, which it does through a hierarchical system of regional and local commissions for inspecting party discipline. The Discipline Inspection Commission assumes particular importance during periods of party campaigns, such as the "rectification campaigns" described later in this chapter, and in recent years, it has played a role in investigating charges of corruption among party officials. In his policy speech to the Party Congress in 2007, Party General Secretary Hu made the fight against corruption one of his major themes.[7]

Party-State Interpenetration

The state and party institutions described in the preceding two sections are interconnected at all levels. In theory and in practice, the Communist Party has been the more important of the two since before 1949: The party initiates policy and controls its implementation through the complex state machinery. This is accomplished through a system of interlocking directorship, in which party leaders simultaneously hold government positions and direct government activity at each level. One of the most important signs of political liberalism in Chinese politics has been efforts to free government institutions from day-to-day party control.

Interlocking directorates exist on every level of the party-state hierarchy. The most important provincial, municipal, and county government officials are generally party members, presumably able to assure that party policy is correctly implemented. The higher the position, the tighter the party-state connection. Because the Political Bureau and its Standing Committee have small memberships, not every member of the State Council can simultaneously be a member of one of the highest party organs. However, top government positions, such as president, premier, and vice premier, are held by members of the Standing Committee.

Deng Xiaoping, after his leadership was confirmed with the adoption of the CCP and PRC Constitutions in 1982, pushed for a number of government reforms to accompany his strategy for economic modernization. One of his reform goals was the regularization of government administration to decrease the overlap in party and state personnel posts. Such regularization was intended to bring new blood into policy-making and administration at a time of aging leadership and also to help prevent the extreme concentration of power at the top that characterized China under Mao Zedong. Twenty-five years later, however, the lack of differentiation between party and state authority persisted, largely due to concerns over the erosion of CCP control throughout the political system.

To put this in a larger comparative perspective, it can be noted that it is common for the top political party leaders in many countries to also head the government; this is, in fact, one of the characteristics of a parliamentary system. Moreover, national party organizations often establish a functional structure that parallels the government ministries in order to maintain party expertise and better direct government policy (for the party in power) or critique and hold the government accountable (for opposition parties). However, below the ministerial level, the European principle of an independent civil service is the convention in a parliamentary system, and often regional governments are under the control of opposition parties.

In contrast, the party-state system that has characterized communist countries is distinctive due to the degree of overlap from the national to the local level. It differs also because of the underlying principle that neither the government leadership nor the bureaucracy should be independent of the party. Both civilian and military authority are to be directed by and held accountable to the Communist

Party, which, in theory, reflects the will of the people and the leadership of the revolution at all levels of government. Therefore the party in power does not change.

The next section looks at the philosophy behind one-party control. Discussion will include Lenin's theory of a communist party, which inspired the Communist Party of the Soviet Union and, after it, that of China. We will also examine the importance of "Marxism-Leninism and Mao Zedong Thought" as ideological principles that undergird the legitimacy of communist rule in China and that have persisted despite important accretions by Deng Xiaoping, Jiang Zemin, and Hu Jintao.

The Leading Role of the Party

Readers may recall from Chapter 6 that the Chinese Communist Party was founded shortly after World War I with the organizational assistance of the newly created Comintern (Communist International), which was controlled by the Soviet Union. The inspiration behind the Comintern was V. I. Lenin, best known as the leader of the 1917 Bolshevik Russian Revolution.[8] Karl Marx and Friedrich Engels bequeathed to the Russian and Chinese revolutions their analysis of class structures and interrelationships as a way of explaining the nature of socioeconomic change and political power, but Lenin provided the tools to create change and mobilize power under circumstances that Marx and Engels never foresaw. Lenin's ideas, transported to the Chinese Communist Party through the Comintern, helped the fledgling party build support and seize the initiative from the Kuomintang and supporters of the Republican revolution.

The Leninist Party

Lenin conceptualized a tightly knit political party as the hard-core group that would implement a revolution. Marx had argued that in capitalist societies the workers (or proletariat) would develop revolutionary potential as a result of their exploitation in the capitalist drive to maximize profit. Revolutionary potential would thus be greatest in the highly industrialized societies of advanced capitalism and would be expressed through spontaneous workers' strikes and demonstrations. But these signs of class struggle did not inevitably produce the conditions necessary for replacing the old order. Lenin understood that spontaneity would not build a new society, but he argued that organization, backed by theoretical understanding and education, would. Thus, his communist party was conceived as the leading edge, or "vanguard of the proletariat," whose primary purpose was to prepare the working masses for revolution by educating and organizing them.[9]

Lenin's model party had several key features, later adapted by the Chinese. The party served as a transmission belt, imparting the will of the leaders to the rank and file and others who supported the revolution's goals. Party leaders were expected to be professional revolutionaries possessing a Marxist understanding of social and political forces and prepared to commit their lives to the revolutionary cause. Another characteristic of the party was the insistence on discipline, both among the leaders and the followers.[10]

As the vanguard of the proletariat, the Leninist party both reflected and created the will of the masses through education. Education or "propaganda" (meaning the teaching of party doctrine) became one of the most important activities of party leaders and, more generally, party members. The importance attributed to education also helps explain the primacy of ideological pronouncements and movements within the CCP to purify or "rectify" the party's ideological line. As explained below, rectification campaigns and reeducation have been integral to CCP life since its early years.

The importance of education should not, however, blind one to the role of coercion throughout the revolutionary process. Overthrowing a government and even breaking up the apparatus of the old state are relatively easy tasks compared to transforming the social, cultural, and economic systems that undergird the state. In the language of the CCP Constitution, the party "is the vanguard both of the Chinese working class and of the Chinese people and the Chinese nation" and upholding the "people's democratic dictatorship" is part of its role.[11] This dictatorship is necessary to eliminate enemies of the revolution and deal with "contradictions" (conflicts) in Chinese society.[12] Justified by this necessity, Mao Zedong and other CCP leaders, like Lenin before them, could be—and often were—ruthless. Throughout the revolutionary process, the Communist Party thus maintains its "leading role," both in theory and in practice, so it is not surprising that one of the Four Cardinal Principles in the General Program of the party constitution is upholding the people's democratic dictatorship.

Marxism-Leninism and Mao Zedong Thought

Most of what Mao Zedong and the other early Communist Chinese leaders wrote and said about the desirability and inevitability of China's revolution owes its inspiration to the Marx-Engels theory of the nature of historical evolution and the importance of class structures and relations of production in socioeconomic change. To bridge the gap between revolutionary potential and the will to create a socialist society in China, Mao Zedong drew on Lenin's ideas and developed his own mixture of theory and practice. Maoism—or what the Chinese Communist

Party calls Mao Zedong Thought—has reinforced the leading role of the party and provides the ideological justification for the twists and turns of China's revolution. The General Program of the 1982 CCP Constitution explains Mao Zedong Thought in these words:

> The Chinese Communists, with Comrade Mao Zedong as their chief representative, created Mao Zedong Thought by integrating the basic tenets of Marxism-Leninism with the concrete practice of the Chinese revolution. Mao Zedong Thought is Marxism-Leninism applied and developed in China; it consists of a body of theoretical principles concerning the revolution and construction in China and a summary of experience therein, both of which have been proved correct by practice; and it represents the crystallized, collective wisdom of the Communist Party of China.

As China came to grips with the negative consequences of the Cultural Revolution and more generally with Mao's leadership, one of the greatest challenges confronting the party was to retain the legitimacy built up for the CCP and China's revolution by constant association with Mao Zedong. The problem was tackled in 1981, five years after Mao's death, when the party issued a lengthy document entitled "On Questions of Party History." After carefully sorting out Mao's history, the document concluded that he had made "gross mistakes," but that on balance "Comrade Mao Zedong was a great Marxist and a great proletarian revolutionary, strategist and theorist."[13] As was later explained, not every "word Mao uttered and every article he wrote, much less his personal mistakes, belong to Mao Zedong Thought." The party did not confuse all of Mao's personal acts with the sum of Mao Zedong Thought, the theoretical principles that had contributed so much to the success of the revolution.[14] The ability of the CCP to come to power and to maintain itself in power for more than sixty years has resulted not just from effective organization and ideology but also from the practical consequences of its policies. Its continued legitimacy thus depends on developments in all three areas. The next section summarizes the major policy shifts after 1949, paying particular attention to the implications of these shifts for China's party-state system.

The Evolution of Party-State Relations[15]

In surveying party-state relations from the 1950s to the 1980s, several questions stand out. Did the role of the Communist Party change as new political and legal institutions were put in place after the Communists captured power in 1949? What were the main conflicts inside and outside the party, including conflicts over the goals of the revolution, and how did the party leadership handle those conflicts? What role did the People's Liberation Army—the driving force behind the Communist victory—play in the implementation of these goals?

Restoring Order and Implementing Reform

The first years after 1949 were consumed by the overwhelming tasks of stabilizing the country and putting into place the new government institutions. Some features of this period have already been discussed. For example, Tibet was brought under Beijing's control in 1950, but Taiwan "escaped." China's reunification with Taiwan was delayed by the Cold War, which had developed in Europe after World War II and spread to Asia with the Korean War. The PRC intervened in Korea in late 1950 in response to the fear that American troops, which were pushing the North Koreans back and marching toward the Yalu River (the boundary between Korea and China), would invade China. Chinese successes in the war further legitimized the new government as responsible for the survival of the nation.

The early 1950s were also a period of close relations with the Soviet Union, with Russian textbooks used in the schools and Soviet advisers helping to build the new institutions of the state. By 1952, China was stable enough for the leadership to turn its attention to economic development, drawing on the Soviet national planning approach. The First Five-Year Plan, introduced in late 1952, followed the Soviet model by emphasizing heavy industry at the expense of agriculture and consumer goods. The desire to emulate the Soviet Union also meant that promising young Communists such as Jiang Zemin and Li Peng studied and trained in the USSR.

Consolidation of party rule during the early years entailed both conciliation and repression, much as it had in the Yan'an period of the 1930s and 1940s, when the CCP was building its organizational base. The party carried its strategy over into the early 1950s, encouraging "united front" groups and permitting the continuation of noncommunist "minority" and "democratic" political parties. At the same time, those who opposed the new order or were presumed to oppose it (such as landlords) were dealt with ruthlessly.

Within a month of promulgating the Agrarian Reform Law in 1950, the government also issued the Marriage Law. Both land and marriage reform characterized the "antifeudal" campaign of the CCP and were central to the goal of destroying the traditional culture and socioeconomic structures of prerevolutionary China. The dilemma over women's rights that had confronted party cadres during the Yan'an period reemerged, however. The landless, poor, and middle-class peasants whom the party was attempting to unite were divided across class ranks by attempts at marriage reform. The Marriage Law gave women equal rights with men in matters of marriage, divorce, choice of work, inheritance, and child custody, and a poor male peasant might find himself losing to his wife or even daughter-in-law some of the gains realized from agrarian reform. Although the Marriage Law was a landmark in the CCP's goal to improve the status of women, it fell short of revolutionizing that status when it appeared to conflict with objectives that seemed more central to maintaining popular (male) support in the conservative rural areas.[16]

The confidence of the new leaders in the combined successes of foreign and domestic policy, the elimination of opposition, and the inauguration of a strategy of economic modernization was signaled by the promulgation of the two constitutions discussed in Chapter 8, the 1954 state constitution and the 1956 party constitution. This confidence also manifested itself in a new phase of apparent liberalism and toleration of dissent. In May 1956, Mao Zedong appealed for intellectuals, who had been forced for several years to undergo self-criticism sessions over their antirevolutionary sentiments, to come forth with their criticisms and concerns about the government. Mao's invitation was couched in the slogan "Let a hundred schools of thought contend; let a hundred flowers bloom."[17] In response, intellectuals gradually came forward to criticize both party and government, mostly for the failure to achieve their professed goals. By 1957, it was apparent that there was, indeed, widespread dissatisfaction and resentment.

Whether Mao's Hundred Flowers Campaign was really a plot to flush out dissent or whether he was genuinely shocked by the extent of the dissent is debatable. The consequence, however, was a new campaign to weed out "counterrevolutionaries," launched after Mao issued his essay "On the Correct Handling of Contradictions Among the People" in June 1957. The essay harked back to his 1930s theory on contradiction, in which he distinguished between "nonantagonistic" and "antagonistic" contradictions. The former were part of the normal course of revolutionary change and reflected inevitable differences of opinion. The latter, however, reflected class differences and threatened the revolution itself. The dissenting intellectuals clearly fell into the second category. Millions of individuals were subjected to police interrogation, forced to criticize themselves for counterrevolutionary views, and "sent down" to the countryside for "reeducation," to learn from the peasants.

The Anti-Rightist Campaign, as this policy was known, was one of numerous such mass campaigns after 1949 that targeted specific groups in Chinese society, such as landlords, intellectuals, or Communist Party members themselves. As a method of control, these rectification campaigns were rooted in the experience of the Yan'an period and are noteworthy both as instruments of political control and as techniques of maintaining ideological conformity and party discipline.[18] The Anti-Rightist Campaign is also significant as a precursor of the massive attacks on all those deemed guilty of antirevolutionary thoughts or lifestyles that characterized the Cultural Revolution a decade later.

Reviving Revolution

The year after the Anti-Rightist Campaign, China embarked on a radical attempt to accelerate the revolutionary process. Abandoning the Soviet-inspired emphasis on centralization and heavy industry, the Great Leap Forward in 1958 called for extreme decentralization of industrial production at the same time that communes were introduced in the rural areas. Correct political thought, or "redness," became the motivation for greater economic productivity, whereas expertise was devalued as essential to the development process. Decentralization, communes, egalitarianism, and ideological motivation were the hallmarks of a new "Maoist model" of development. Although later discredited, this model captured the imagination of many outside China who saw it as an alternative to the Soviet and Western European capital- and technology-intensive approaches to modernization.

The communes merged the administrative unit at the township level with collectivized economic production. Large communes included as many as 50,000 people, whereas small communes in remote areas might have 5,000–6,000. Communes were intended to be self-sufficient, providing education and health care as well as political and economic direction for all households under their control. Because they were to represent an advanced stage of socialism, peasants were not permitted to own any private plots or even farm animals.

The communes remained for many years, but the most radical policies of the Great Leap Forward were abandoned between 1960 and 1962. The "Three Bad Years," as the period between 1958 and 1961 became known, was an economic disaster that opened the first major breach in the CCP leadership since the 1930s. More than 20 million Chinese died from starvation and illness stemming from malnutrition as a consequence of massive dislocations of agricultural production, failed crops, and accelerated work demands that undermined people's health. Meanwhile, in 1959, the USSR withdrew all of its aid, from blueprints to technical personnel to spare parts, in reaction to what Soviet leaders saw as irresponsible Chinese policies.

In 1959–1960, the CCP leadership divided over the Great Leap Forward and China's isolation in the wake of the Soviet withdrawal. For a decade, Mao Zedong, who had held both the top party and state positions, had dominated China's policy agenda. Now the Great Leap Forward had set China's modernization back years. Top CCP leaders who had been with Mao for two decades or more harshly criticized his policies, confirming Mao's growing suspicion that even veteran Communists could lose their revolutionary commitment. In his view, the establishment of China's socialist system had not yet eliminated "feudal" and antisocialist attitudes or behavior. Although some changes were made in the top leadership and for a time Mao's overwhelming domination of China's politics loosened, his conviction that too many in the party had been consumed by self-interest would lead him to unleash a massive attack against the CCP itself in a few years.

The Great Proletarian Cultural Revolution

The Cultural Revolution, like the Great Leap Forward, was a watershed of post-1949 Chinese politics. Although it was both a leadership struggle and a conflict over the meaning of revolution, the Cultural Revolution appeared as political madness to outside observers. The end of the Cultural Revolution overlapped with the struggle over the succession to Mao Zedong, and only with the death of Mao and the arrest of the so-called Gang of Four in 1976 could China move on to the reform era associated with Deng Xiaoping and his successors.

There is still much that is not known about the decisions that lay behind the start of the Cultural Revolution, but it seems clear that its roots were in Mao's preoccupations with the direction of Chinese socialism that had earlier prompted the Great Leap Forward and the divisions among Chinese leaders in the early 1960s. By 1965, there were four major groups of Chinese leaders.[19] Mao Zedong and those (including his wife, Jiang Qing) who shared his view of a revolution of ideological conviction ("reds") over technocrats ("experts"), pressed for another campaign to raise political consciousness. This group sustained the personality cult of Mao as the "Great Helmsman" of the Chinese revolution. A second group was dominated by CCP leaders such as Liu Shaoqi and Deng Xiaoping, who were Leninists in their commitment to party leadership and integrity. They were also pragmatists, believing in the importance of following socioeconomic strategies that would hasten China on the road to development. The third group, composed of government officials, shared with the party pragmatists the commitment to modernization. This group was headed by Premier Zhou Enlai, who ultimately chose to support Mao when the conflict between the radical Maoists and organizational pragmatists could no longer be avoided. The fourth group, the military, was itself divided between those who accepted the Maoist approach to development, notably Lin Biao, the defense minister and head of the People's Liberation

Army, and those whose primary concern was political order and a professionalized military.

In late 1965, Mao engineered the arrest of several top military and party officials whom he apparently believed were conspiring against him and who, in any case, were ideologically unacceptable. The conflict among the CCP leaders grew, and in spring 1966, Zhou Enlai allied himself with Mao's demands for a protracted campaign to eliminate "bourgeois ideology" in every aspect of culture. In the name of the CCP Central Committee, Mao declared the official opening of the Great Proletarian Cultural Revolution. Both Mao and Mao Zedong Thought were elevated as the source of all wisdom on the new revolutionary culture that, in and of itself, would assure the future of Chinese socialism.

Mao's long-standing obsession with "revisionism" within the Communist Party itself prompted his call, in August 1966, to China's youth to root out "old" culture and all those who represented or supported it. High-ranking government and party officials, including Liu Shaoqi and Deng Xiaoping, were removed from their posts and, along with their families, subjected to mass criticism and humiliation.[20] Millions of teenagers, dubbed Red Guards, "poured over the land, shouting down distinguished leaders, destroying precious art objects, and extolling puritan virtues."[21] Party committees joined in the attacks on teachers and school administrators, only to see students turning on party leaders themselves. Destroying the "four olds" (old ideas, old culture, old customs, and old habits) quickly became the excuse for attacks on anything and anyone deemed unrevolutionary by the Red Guards.

By mid-1967, the Red Guards had brought China to near anarchy. Marches, demonstrations, and study sessions gave way to mob violence and arbitrary, vicious attacks on anyone deviating from the Red Guards' unpredictable view of correct behavior. During the peak of the Cultural Revolution in 1966–1967, millions of young people poured into Beijing and other large cities, enjoying logistical support from the army. But by late 1967, the army gradually assumed control in an effort to restore order. With the party organization decimated, the PLA itself took over governing. By fall 1967, the PLA ruled directly in twenty-two of China's provinces.[22] This military prominence explains why Lin Biao, the leader of the pro-Maoist faction in the army, was designated Mao Zedong's "heir apparent" in the 1969 CCP Constitution described in Chapter 8.

For those who suffered during the Cultural Revolution, including the purged Deng Xiaoping and his son (who was thrown from an upper-story window and permanently crippled), the period from the beginning of the Cultural Revolution to Mao's death constitutes the Ten Bad Years. The disasters of the decade, including the destruction of the party and state bureaucracies, the derailment of economic modernization, and China's loss of international esteem, inspired the reform strategies after Mao's death.

Succession Politics: The Transition to Reform

From the late 1960s to the mid-1970s, the process of rebuilding both party and state structures proceeded slowly. Although a few ministries emerged relatively unscathed, many ceased to operate, as did the State Council itself. For a period, the integration and overlap of party and state structures was almost complete, as every government office was subjected to the control of a "revolutionary committee" whose leading member was also the party secretary.

In 1971, Lin Biao (Mao's "heir apparent") was killed in an airplane crash in Mongolia, apparently while trying to flee to the Soviet Union. Although the details surrounding this incident have never been verified, the party two years later charged that Lin had plotted to assassinate Mao Zedong and, with the help of other military leaders, to seize power in a coup d'état. Not surprisingly, the incident raised questions about the loyalty of the army and hastened the normalization process, in which party control over the military was reasserted.

The Lin Biao affair elevated Zhou Enlai as China's most important leader after Mao Zedong. Comparatively popular, Zhou was even featured on the propaganda posters that were widespread during the Cultural Revolution (and that are now part of the Maoist memorabilia for sale in China's urban street markets). Photo 10.1 shows such a poster: Zhou Enlai emulates a pose found in a popular painting inspired by Confucian values, in which a wise elder converses with a child—an ironic association during a period devoted to destroying "old culture." By 1973, Zhou had moved to rehabilitate old party cadres purged during the Cultural Revolution, including his former protégé, Deng Xiaoping, who had been held under house arrest for seven years.[23] Deng moved quickly to assume key posts and place moderates in party positions in order to position himself for the coming succession battle. However, when Zhou died in early 1976, Deng was purged again almost immediately by Maoist "radicals" in the CCP leadership.

The death of Mao Zedong in September 1976 produced the next spasm in the succession struggle. At the center of the struggle was the Gang of Four, composed of Jiang Qing and her three colleagues from Shanghai. Jiang claimed that on his deathbed, her husband said she should be the new party chair, but China's acting prime minister, Hua Guofeng, disputed the claim. One month after Mao's death, his wife and her colleagues were arrested, seemingly clearing the way for Hua, a compromise choice for the succession, to build his reputation as China's preeminent leader.[24] But in 1977, Hua acquiesced to Deng's return to leadership—a

PHOTO 10.1 Zhou Enlai poster from the Cultural Revolution. Photo courtesy of James W. Boyd.

major strategic mistake, for within three years Hua had been maneuvered out of all top party posts by Deng. The stage had been cleared for the reform period.

The Reform Period

Although associated with Deng Xiaoping, China's contemporary modernization strategy dates to Premier Zhou Enlai's 1975 proposal for comprehensive modernization in the four areas of agriculture, industry, defense, and science and technology by the year 2000.[25] The pragmatists' commitment to this program, known as the Four Modernizations, was opposed by those still wedded to the Maoist revolutionary model, but after the arrest of the Gang of Four, Hua Guofeng reintroduced Zhou's plan in 1978.[26] Although these plans went through numerous changes over the ensuing decade, they marked the beginning of China's reform period.

While Zhou was still alive and then again after his rehabilitation under Hua, Deng Xiaoping played a central role in the planning and implementation of the Four Modernizations. With the demotion of Hua and, in 1982, the adoption of the new party and state constitutions, Deng was secure in his position of preeminent leader. In the 1980s, he became known as the architect of China's "second revolution," and it was not until the Tiananmen events of 1989 that the issues of stable leadership and the direction of the revolution again moved to the forefront of Chinese politics.

The Tiananmen protests started as a rally demanding government reforms. But as thousands rallied in Beijing, protests spread to other cities. By May 13, around 3,000 students began a hunger strike. Within a week, more than a million people demonstrated in and around Tiananmen Square in support of the students. The situation threatened to get out of control, and on May 20, the government declared martial law. Both the causes of the protests and the government's responses were complex, but on June 3, troops were ordered into the square from three directions. They were met by thousands of citizens and hastily assembled barricades, and moved back, only to move in again with force. By dawn on June 4, the square had been cleared—at the cost of some 3,000 lives.

In retrospect, we can see that the events at Tiananmen Square reinforced the determination of the party leadership to safeguard the essential structures of the party-state system, even as much of that system—and especially its ideology—rapidly lost its relevance to the daily lives of most Chinese people. Nonetheless, the thrust of economic modernization which has defined China for the past three decades persists, leaving open the question of the long-term impact of these economic changes for the political reforms discussed in the next two chapters. For now, we turn to an assessment of the first half century of China's revolution under the "leading role of the party."

Assessing the Party-State System

Viewed retrospectively, the early phases of China's revolution were often a reaction to, or "correction" of, what occurred in a previous phase. Mistakes were made, then admitted, leaders differed over what—or who—was responsible, and policies were changed. Throughout the period, though, the same political problems recurred, albeit in new forms. These problems are both unique to China and shared with other developing nations, including India: maintenance of order, political legitimacy and stability, leadership succession, and tension between the central and regional governments. To these must be added the core issue that plagues countries that have endured massive revolution: When is the revolution judged complete, so that society can operate "normally"? By the 1990s, it seemed clear that normalization meant economic development while maintaining the "leading role" of the Communist Party.

The twists and turns in Chinese politics from the 1950s to the 1980s will not be replicated, but they do suggest some long-standing, unresolved problems, such as the tension between centralization and decentralization, an issue discussed in the next chapter. The question taken up here is what kind of leadership the reform period ushered in, and what outsiders can glean about changes in China's party-state system from that leadership.

Six characteristics of Chinese leadership and politics over the past half century stand out. First, top leaders, even at the regional level, have held both party and state positions, but the ultimate source of their influence continues to be their rank in the Communist Party hierarchy. Although there have been periodic efforts to separate party and state institutions, the integration of the two hierarchies, particularly at the top, persists.

Second, with the exception of the end of the Cultural Revolution and the Lin Biao period, China has been under civilian rule. Nonetheless, military support has continued to be essential for those who aspired to succeed Deng Xiaoping as China's preeminent leader. Thus it is not surprising that Hu Jintao assumed the chairmanship of the Central Military Commission after Jiang Zemin's retirement in 2004.

Third, the history of China's succession politics indicates that both personalism and factionalism have played important roles. Personalism in China has entailed the elevation of preeminent leaders, and it is typical of personalist politics that even as the "cult" of Mao Zedong was criticized and Deng Xiaoping undertook to prevent overconcentration of power in the hands of a single individual, Deng himself was elevated as a preeminent leader. As in many nation-states, acquiring and maintaining power in China relies on building personal loyalty within the party and state hierarchies, both of which are factionalized. Factionalism is discussed further in Chapter 12, but it may be noted here that it was widely presumed that the primary justification for expanding the CCP Political Bureau Standing Committee from seven to nine members in 2002 was to ensure that, although retired, Jiang had secured the promotion of several of his protégés to the party's most important body.[27]

Fourth, despite continuing differences over important issues in China's political and economic future, the backgrounds of the country's leaders reflect the importance attributed to technical expertise. With the passing of the last survivors of the Long March of the 1930s went those who supported Mao Zedong's emphasis on "redness" over "expertise." Modernization calls for leadership that understands the complex problems of economic growth. Differences over the speed or priorities of that growth have still occurred, but the commitment to modernization has framed the debate and differences have surfaced within the context of this commitment.[28]

Fifth, by the early twenty-first century it appeared that the leadership succession process had been regularized. Tiananmen Square marked the last major leadership convulsion up through the transition between Jiang Zemin and Hu Jintao in 2002–2004.[29] In contrast to the circumstances in which Jiang was elevated in the aftermath of Tiananmen, the succession process for Hu Jintao, his successor, was smooth.

Finally, one might ask how representative of the Chinese population as a whole China's leadership has been. The simple answer is "not very." Efforts have been made to recruit ethnic minorities into the CCP, but the twenty-five-member Political Bureau chosen at the Seventeenth Party Congress in 2007 included only one member from a national minority and none for its Standing Committee.[30] Minority CCP first secretaries in minority autonomous regions have also been scarce. Likewise, the top party posts have remained male preserves. The most important CCP organs, the Politburo, its Standing Committee, and the Secretariat, generally have had no female members, although one woman was chosen for the Politburo in 2007, and 18 percent of the delegates to the 2007 Party Congress were female. In short, the Chinese political system has shared with a preponderance of systems in the world the underrepresentation of women and minority populations in top political leadership.

Exploring Further

Among the works that treat the Cultural Revolution, see the poignant stories by Wen Chihua in *The Red Mirror: Children of China's Cultural Revolution*, ed. Bruce Jones (Westview Press, 1995), the contemporary novel by Dai Sijie, *Balzac and the Little Chinese Seamstress* (Knopf, 2001), and Xinran, *Voices from a Silent Generation* (Pantheon, 2008).

Notes

1. David Shambaugh contrasts the Western and Chinese discourses on party-state systems and details the preoccupation of the Chinese with understanding why the party-states in Europe collapsed. *China's Communist Party: Atrophy and Adaptation* (Washington, D.C.: Woodrow Wilson Center Press and Berkeley: University of California Press, 2008). See particularly chapters 4 and 5.

2. For information on the structure, personnel, and functions of the National People's Congress and other people's congresses, see the NPC website at www.npc.gov.cn/englishnpc/news/index.htm.

3. Murray Scot Tanner, "The Erosion of Communist Party Control over Lawmaking in China," *China Quarterly* 138 (June 1994), 381–403. See also Tanner's *The Politics of Lawmaking in Post-Mao China: Institutions, Processes and Democratic Prospects* (Oxford: Clarendon Press, 1999).

4. Suzanne Ogden, *Inklings of Democracy in China* (Cambridge, Mass.: Harvard University Press, 2002), 252–255; Michael William Dowdle, "Constructing Citizenship: The NPC as Catalyst for Political Participation," in *Changing Meanings of Citizenship in Modern China*, eds. Merle Goldman and Elizabeth J. Perry (Cambridge, Mass.: Harvard University Press, 2002), 330–349.

5. In order to avoid confusion with the National People's Congress, the National Party Congress will not be abbreviated as NPC.

6. The procedure for the past two decades is to present for election a list of nominees slightly larger than the number of slots to be filled. For the Central Committee elected at the Seventeenth Party Congress, the candidate list had about 8 percent more names than there were seats; the names were solicited through a series of nationwide interviews, according to the official news service, *Xinhua*. See http://news.xinhuanet.com/english/2007-10/21/content_6917379.htm, accessed November 5, 2008.

7. Corruption is an ongoing problem. In 2005, more than 110,000 party members (0.16 percent of the total membership) were punished; in 2006, the number dropped to 90,000. See the summary of Hu Jintao's speech at http://www.gov.cn/english/2007-10/15/content_776720.htm, accessed November 8, 2008.

8. See Alfred G. Meyer's classic study, *Leninism* (Cambridge, Mass.: Harvard University Press, 1957); also see Neil Harding, *Lenin's Political Thought*, 2 vols. (New York: St. Martin's Press, 1977).

9. See, in particular, pts. 2 and 3 of Lenin's classic work, *What Is to Be Done?* (first published in 1902).

10. Lenin's organizational theory was reflected in his conception of democratic centralism, which in principle encompasses both dissent and unanimity, free discussion and

enforced discipline, in the life of the party. Democratic centralism is one of the "four essential requirements" for "building the Party" as described in the General Program of the amended 1982 CCP Constitution: "Democratic centralism is a combination of centralism on the basis of democracy and democracy *under central guidance*" (emphasis added).

11. This phrase derives from "dictatorship of the proletariat," used by Marx, Engels, and Lenin to describe the form of state organization in which a newly victorious working class would use the coercive power of the state to suppress enemies of the revolution.

12. The significance of the term "contradiction" is explained in the essay "On Contradiction," claimed to have been written by Mao Zedong in 1937 during the Yan'an period but first published in 1952. The essay is reprinted in numerous anthologies. For a contemporary use of "contradiction," see the General Program of the 1982 CCP Constitution, as amended in 2007.

13. *Beijing Review* 24, no. 27 (July 6, 1981), 29.

14. Zhang Bizhong, "Differentiations Are Necessary," *Beijing Review* 24, no. 38 (September 21, 1981), 17.

15. There are many general histories of this early period. The following are recommended: Roderick MacFarquhar, ed., *The Politics of China, 1949–1989* (Cambridge: Cambridge University Press, 1993); Lucian W. Pye, *China: An Introduction*, 4th ed. (New York: HarperCollins, 1991); and Jonathan D. Spence, *The Search for Modern China* (New York: W. W. Norton, 1990), chaps. 19–24. Essential documents of the period are compiled and annotated in Harold C. Hinton, ed., *The People's Republic of China, 1949–1979: A Documentary Survey*, 5 vols. (Wilmington, Del.: Scholarly Resources, 1980).

16. Kay Ann Johnson, *Women, the Family and Peasant Revolution in China* (Chicago: University of Chicago Press, 1983), chap. 8.

17. The slogan alluded to the ancient Zhou dynasty period of the twelfth to third centuries B.C.E., when "one hundred contending schools" of philosophy, including the Confucian, Daoist, and Legalist, clashed. Pye, *China*, pp. 36, 244–246. For the text of Mao's original "One Hundred Flowers" speech, see Hinton, *Documentary Survey*, vol. 1, 341–349.

18. One of the most famous such movements was the 1942–1944 Rectification Campaign. The rectification method emphasized intensive education, small-group study, criticism and self-criticism, and thought reform.

19. See the discussion in Pye, 294–295; and Spence, 596–604. Tang Tsou analyzed intraparty factions (what he calls "informal groups") in *The Cultural Revolution and Post-Mao Reforms: A Historical Perspective* (Chicago: University of Chicago Press, 1986), chaps. 2, 3. The authors in MacFarquhar, *Politics of China*, also emphasize elite disunity.

20. Liu was head of state and a senior member of the Standing Committee of the Politburo. Deng was secretary general of the party and a vice premier under Zhou Enlai.

21. Pye, 298.

22. Ibid., 306.

23. Liu Shaoqi, who was purged (like Deng) in 1966, died in 1969.

24. Jiang and her three closest radical colleagues were dubbed the Gang of Four after their arrest, as part of the campaign to discredit them and the Maoist model. They were tried in 1980 and found guilty of a long list of counts related to their activities during the Cultural Revolution. Jiang Qing's death sentence was suspended in order to give her time to "repent." She committed suicide in 1991, while still under house arrest.

25. See Zhou's "Report on the Work of the Government," *Peking Review (Beijing Review)* 18, no. 4 (January 24, 1975), 21–25.

26. Hua Guofeng, "Report on the Work of the Government," *Peking Review* 21, no. 10 (March 10, 1978), 8–40.

27. Jeremy Page, "China Sets the Stage for a New Generation," *The Japan Times*, November 5, 2002; Susan L. Shirk, *China: Fragile Superpower* (Oxford: Oxford University Press, 2007), 50. For a detailed discussion of Jiang's manipulation of factions, see Guoguang Wu, *The Anatomy of Political Power in China* (Singapore: Marshall Cavendish International, 2005), chap. 3.

28. An example of intraparty differences bounded by the broad commitment to modernization is the 2008 debate over rural land-use reform. There was widespread agreement that rural development had lagged behind urban and industrial development and that rural discontent fueled social and political instability. At issue was the creation of a system to enhance farmers' ability to contract, lease, or exchange land rights, but there appeared to be disagreement within the leadership over the scope of the changes. Edward Wong, "Hints of Discord on Land Reform in China," *New York Times*, October 16, 2008; Jim Yardley, "China Enacts Major Land-Use Reform for Farmers," *New York Times*, October 20, 2008.

29. The original catalyst for the student demonstrations in May 1989 was the death of Hu Yaobang, the former general secretary of the CCP, who had been dismissed from his party post two years earlier. Students mourning Hu's death also used the occasion to demand government reforms. One of the casualties of their protests was Zhao Ziyang, then head of the CCP and the strongest supporter of the students within the top leadership of the Party. Deng Xiaoping reportedly called Zhao a traitor; Zhao was sidelined and troops brought in to quash the resistance. "The Shattered Dream," *Los Angeles Times*, June 25, 1989.

30. See the Congress website at www.16Congress.org.cn/english and http://news .xinhuanet.com/english/2007-10/21/content_6917665.htm, accessed November 8, 2008.

11

Levels of Government and Regionalism

This chapter examines the importance of subnational levels of government in the relationship between citizens and governments in India, China, and Japan. The first section summarizes federal and unitary systems, and the second examines Indian federalism, which has been molded and cross-pressured by the forces of both centralization and decentralization over the past half century.

The third section of the chapter discusses China's local and regional governments, with particular attention given to the decentralization of power that altered Chinese politics in the late twentieth century. Despite critical differences between India and China, these two Asian giants share many of the same problems that result when traditional societies undergo rapid change.

The last section of the chapter discusses Japan's levels of government. Japan has not experienced the kinds of pressures on local and regional governments that India and China have. Nonetheless, politics outside of Tokyo are far from static, and in the past decade, Japan has moved toward greater decentralization.

Federal and Unitary Systems

In a federal system, there are two levels of government with constitutional authority to make laws affecting citizens.[1] In a unitary system, that authority rests solely with the central government. Every country has more than one level of government, but in unitary systems, the regional and local governments may be created, changed, and abolished at will by the national government, and the powers of the subnational governments are those granted by the national government, which monopolizes sovereignty.

In theory, the distinction between federal and unitary systems is clear. In practice, the distinction is often murky, even messy. Constitutions typically list powers belonging to the central government and regional governments and may also enumerate shared jurisdictions. But dynamic socioeconomic conditions, along with shifting political values and judicial interpretations, influence the evolution of these jurisdictions in ways unforeseen by the drafters of the constitutions. This has happened in Canada and the United States as well as in India.

Evolution in federal systems has been matched by changes in unitary systems, where contemporary history provides examples of national governments attempting to centralize control over their country during some periods but decentralizing at others, or they may centralize in some spheres of activity (such as economic policy) but decentralize in others (social policy). Political and economic conditions often breed as many stresses in unitary systems as they do in federal systems. Such stresses are evident in China, for example, where economic reform policies have included substantial decentralization of policy-making and the introduction of what some scholars have called "market-preserving federalism" or "de facto federalism."[2]

Level-of-government relationships in India are especially complex. The national government, also known as the Centre or Union, has constitutional powers superior to those of the regional units, called states. The emergency powers and President's Rule examined in Chapter 9 are examples of the ultimate authority of the Union government. But states have become more important for a variety of reasons, creating tensions between the levels of government. It is to these dynamics that we turn next.

(Dis)Unity in the Indian Federation

To better understand the countervailing tendencies in Indian federalism, we need to review how India's Constitution designates the division of powers between the central government and the states. As explained in Chapter 8, the constitution has undergone substantial amendment over the years, with implications for relations between the national and state governments. In addition, political parties, specifically, and political participation, more generally, have also changed the Centre-state relationship.

Constitutional Provisions

Early in their deliberations, members of the Constituent Assembly concluded that a federal arrangement would best secure Indian unity and democracy. The country was too vast and too diverse, and the regions had too many distinct histories, to imagine that a centralized unitary system would be able to meet the challenges facing the nationalist leaders.

A federal arrangement was also consistent with India's long history. Readers may recall from Chapter 5 that ancient India had numerous great empires, but none of these encompassed the entire subcontinent. The empires had strong power centers but allowed peripheries to have legitimate power and responsibility for implementing decisions in ways appropriate to local conditions. The durability of village government, the *panchayat*, reinforced local autonomy.[3]

Indian federalism, variously described as centralized, cooperative, or quasi-federal,[4] is distinguished by a number of features, some of which it shares with other federations and some of which are unique. First, the constitution, in Article 1, characterizes India as a "Union of States"; nowhere does it describe the country as a federation or discuss federalism as such. Unlike the United States but like many other types of federal systems, Indian states do not have constitutions; there is only the national constitution.[5] Part Four of the Union Constitution describes in considerable detail the structure of government to be found in each state.

Dividing government functions between the Union and the states, the Seventh Schedule of the constitution contains detailed lists of the respective spheres of action of each level of government. Although the Union list is the longest and most comprehensive, the state list includes important and familiar (to North Americans) activities, such as the right to constitute and determine the powers of local government entities. A concurrent list details nearly fifty areas of shared jurisdiction. The national Parliament has residuary power, the power to make laws with respect to any matter not enumerated in the state or concurrent list.

Another important feature of Indian federalism is the distribution of financial power, an area of controversy in most federal systems. The constitution gives the most significant taxing powers to the Union government, those of income taxes, excise taxes, and customs duties. States may levy sales taxes and taxes on agricultural income, alcoholic beverages (an important source of revenue for many states), certain mineral rights, luxuries (including entertainment, such as movie tickets), and a number of other items. Together, these revenues have accounted for less than one-half of state expenditures. The remainder comes from taxes that are collected by the central government but are turned over to the states. In addition, the central government distributes grants-in-aid to poorer states as a way of compensating for regional inequities.[6]

In summary, the historical concerns about national unity produced a constitution in India that instituted some measure of regional autonomy balanced with superior authority for the national government. Chapter 9 also noted that the Rajya

Sabha, structured to represent state interests, is less powerful than the Lok Sabha. Only in a few instances that directly impinge on the states' authority does the upper house have the power to block lower-house action. The constitution authorizes the national Parliament to make laws regarding matters on the state list if approved by two-thirds of the voting members present and voting in the Rajya Sabha. This provision, along with the provision that Parliament may legislate with respect to any state matter when a proclamation of emergency is in effect, holds the potential for dramatically expanding the Union government's residual power.

Finally, the constitutional amending process also tips the balance of Indian federalism toward the center. Most of the constitution's provisions may be amended by the national Parliament alone, with the approval of the majority of both houses (including two-thirds of the members present and voting). This includes such important sections of the constitution as the enumeration of fundamental rights. However, amendment of those sections of the constitution pertaining specifically to the states, such as the Seventh Schedule lists, the representation of states in Parliament, and the relations between the Union and states laid out in Part Eleven, also require ratification by the legislatures of at least one-half of the states. Ironically, alteration of the boundaries of states or the formation of new states does not require formal approval of the states involved. These changes may be made solely under the authority of the national Parliament.

This discussion of the constitutional provisions pertinent to Indian federalism is essential to understanding how the government operates and what the political "ground rules" are. Neither the structures nor the ground rules are static, however. The next section examines the forces that demonstrate both the flexibility and the risks of India's federal system.

The Regionalization of Politics

When the Constituent Assembly was debating and drafting the Indian Constitution, its members were preoccupied with communal (Hindu-Muslim) conflict and the disastrous effects of Partition. But it was linguistic diversity that provided the first major challenge to the federal arrangement.

States' Reorganization. Most of the British-created regional units were linguistically heterogeneous, and prior to independence, the Indian National Congress had called for the formation of linguistically based provinces. But by the late 1940s, the most important Congress leaders were preoccupied with national unity and viewed the establishment of states along linguistic lines as threatening that unity by fostering subnational loyalties. Shortly after the constitution went into effect in 1950, however, demands by linguistic groups—demands that had never disappeared—escalated. In 1953, the state of Andhra Pradesh, with a Telegu-speaking majority, was created from the old British unit of Madras. The other part of Madras became Tamil Nadu (with a Tamil-speaking population).

Acquiescence to Telegu demands produced a clamor among other language groups for their own states. Reluctantly, Prime Minister Nehru appointed the States Reorganization Commission to examine the problem. The commission's 1955 report recommended that political boundaries be redrawn largely along linguistic lines, and the 1956 States Reorganization Act provided for fourteen states and six Union Territories (in contrast to the twenty-seven states that had existed in 1950). States reorganization in the 1950s, however, failed to appease all those making demands, and in the 1960s, the state of Bombay was divided into two new states (Gujarat and Maharashtra), and Punjab was divided into the new states of Punjab, Haryana, and Himalchal Pradesh.

The dynamic nature of India's territorial arrangements was again illustrated as recently as 2000, when three new states were established. In contrast to the earlier reorganizations, which had emphasized linguistic diversity, these new states were created in response to the demands of peoples in largely tribal areas who felt their interests had been ignored by their state governments. Uttaranchal was created out of the northwestern part of Uttar Pradesh, Jharkhand out of southern Bihar, and Chhattisgarh out of Madhya Pradesh (see Map 2.1).

Punjab. Nehru's fears that states reorganization would contribute to regionalism in Indian politics were probably well founded, although other factors that explain the growth of regionalism were and continue to be at work. The situation in Punjab, where there has been periodic pressure for a Sikh state, illustrates this complexity. A political party, the Akali Dal ("army of the faithful"), long argued for a separate nation-state. Originally, the Akali Dal couched its demand in linguistic, not communal (religious), terms, but it appealed primarily to Sikhs.[7]

In the 1980s, the situation turned violent, and Punjab quickly became one of the most dangerous threats to national unity and stability. The disintegration of the political situation resulted from the convergence of two independent developments.[8] The first was division between militants and moderates within the Akali Dal Party and within the Sikh community generally. A Sikh religious leader, Sant Jarnail Singh Bhindranwale, who saw as his mission the consolidation and purification of the Sikhs, emerged as an important militant leader.[9]

The second factor at work was the changed nature of center-state relations under Prime Minister Indira Gandhi. Prime Minister Gandhi's goal was to guarantee Congress preeminence in Punjabi politics by undermining the Akali Dal. To this end, her government encouraged Bhindranwale in the early 1980s as a way of dividing the Akali Dal, then changed its tactics when extremist Sikh attacks on Hindus began to threaten Congress support among Hindu voters. After the Centre imposed President's Rule in Punjab in 1983, Bhindranwale and Sikh terrorists set up their armed headquarters in the Golden Temple, the symbolic center of the Sikh religion in the city of Amritsar. When the prime minister ordered the Indian army to flush out Bhindranwale's sanctuary in "Operation Bluestar" in June 1984, Bhindranwale was killed, along with hundreds of his supporters and hundreds of Indian troops. Even among those Sikhs who had never supported the extremists' cause, Operation Bluestar was viewed as an assault on the essence of Sikhism. Five months later, Mrs. Gandhi was assassinated by two Sikh bodyguards, an act that in turn led to the massacre of thousands of Sikhs by mobs in New Delhi and elsewhere.

The events of 1984 left a sordid legacy in Indian politics, both in center-state and in communal relations. President's Rule, as suggested in Chapter 9, stymied the normal development of competitive elections in Punjab, and communal hatred grew unchecked. It was not until the late 1990s that the situation in Punjab stabilized, and political normalcy—in large part a response to the traumatic events of the 1980s—returned. The Akali Dal broke into factions, but largely reunified as the Shiromani Akali Dal. State elections held in 1997, 2002, and 2007 saw the Congress party and the Shiromani Akali Dal alternate pluralities, suggesting a pattern of alternation between the two dominant parties in the state might be emerging.

The example of the Akali Dal is extreme, but the role it has played illustrates an important political trend influencing Indian federalism. This trend is the regionalization of politics, which in turn reflects other political developments such as the decline of the Congress Party and the mobilization of voters around regional issues. The increasing importance of state parties—that is, parties within a particular state that have little or no national prominence—is one of the most salient aspects of the regionalization process.

State Party Systems. Paul R. Brass has categorized three types of Indian state party systems: those in which one party dominates, those in which one party dominates but there is institutionalized opposition, and those with competitive parties.[10] For many years, the first type was widespread, with a state-based Congress Party organization monopolizing power. Prime Minister Nehru's approach to center-state relations included negotiation with state party bosses in such a way as to maintain stability at the center and a measure of autonomy for the states. His daughter's efforts, when she was prime minister, to centralize control over state Congress machines ultimately undermined the party both nationally and regionally. By the 1990s, there were no longer any states where the Congress Party was predictably dominant.

In the one-party-dominant systems with institutionalized opposition, the dominant party is often still Congress, but opposition parties have been strong enough over time to alternate in power. As early as 1985, the Bharatiya Janata Party (BJP) was the main opposition party in three Indian states and eventually formed governments there, as it has in several other states since then. Thus as the electorate changes, so may the party systems, often becoming more competitive.

The states with competitive party systems frequently include Congress as one of the major parties, and Congress often forms the government; but alternation in power is a real possibility. The non-Congress parties illustrate the variety in Indian politics: They include the BJP, longtime regional players like the communist parties in West Bengal and Kerala, caste-based parties, and parties that have grown out of regional movements for cultural and linguistic identity, such as the Akali Dal in the Punjab.

State politics illustrate both the promises of and threats to Indian democracy. Politics at the state level is often the scene of political turmoil—enough to warrant the imposition of President's Rule, as we have seen. Caste and communal conflict typically play out at the local and state level and often result in violence. State boundaries mark a defined space within which a political party, movement, or government may engage in social engineering over a manageable territory. One of the clearest examples of this is found in the western state of Gujarat where, Hemant Babu has argued, beginning in the 1980s there was a systematic campaign to establish a "Hindu state." In the mid-1990s, the BJP came to power, eclipsing the Congress Party. A variety of Hindutva organizations, sustained by BJP tolerance, if not support, built a mass political base around the myths, language, and images of Hindu unity.[11]

In 2002, communal violence broke out in Gujarat, claiming about 1,000 lives and leaving thousands homeless. The BJP-led government was widely accused, both in India and abroad, of tolerating, even organizing, anti-Muslim pogroms. Although the chief minister was forced to resign, the BJP was reelected in elections held later that year and won almost two-thirds of the seats in the 2007 state assembly elections.

Despite this controversial illustration, some analyses of Indian politics suggest that the development of strong regional polities offers the best hope for national unity and democracy and reflects the spread of political participation to many groups formally excluded. Dennis Austin, for example, has maintained "guarded optimism" about India's future because the nation's extreme diversity makes it possible to insulate some regions from the instability of others.[12] Arendt Lijphart has argued that India's survival as a deeply divided, multiethnic democracy is tied to the degree of consociationalism it displays. Consociational theory views democratic stability in divided societies as linked to the degree and kind of power-sharing arrangements available to minority linguistic and religious groups. Thus, greater state autonomy and control over matters important to minorities would contribute to national stability. Although Lijphart's theory sets other prerequisites for consociational democracy, his is an argument for strengthening regional power sharing, not for encouraging greater centralization.[13] However, it is also true that the proliferation of regional parties has led to the formation of coalition governments (see Chapter 9), thus making it more difficult to formulate coherent national policies.

Regions and Regionalism in China

Although China is formally a unitary system, it shares with India the struggle to create balanced and efficient center-province relationships. The two countries also share many of the problems of large countries undergoing widespread socio-economic change, including regional imbalances in the distribution of wealth.

China is organized into twenty-two provinces, five autonomous regions, and four centrally administered municipalities (see Map 3.1). The most recent changes in boundaries were the separation of Hainan Island from Guangdong Province and the establishment of Chongqing municipality. The incorporation of Hong Kong in 1997 and Macao in 1999 as special administrative regions (SARs) also altered the administrative map. Beneath the provincial level are the local government entities: the cities, counties, and municipalities. The 1982 Constitution prescribes People's Congresses at each level as "local organs of state power" (Article 96). Executive authority is vested in provincial governors, municipal mayors, and chiefs in the townships. In general, the provincial and local government structures mirror those of the central government.

The provinces reflect China's traditional geographic and cultural regions, and as with India's states, they differ substantially in size, wealth, topography, and even language. The county, or *xian*, is the administrative subunit of the province, and there are approximately 2,000 of them. Since the late 1980s, governance has grown in so-called village committees, which are designed to encourage limited democracy, autonomy, and cadre accountability in China's more than 900,000 villages. Both village committees and neighborhood committees in the munici-palities have served to maintain state control at the grassroots level, but the committees are also potential targets of citizen pressures to address local concerns and thus serve as transmission belts to higher authority (see Chapter 12).

The powers of all regional units are delegated by the national government, and the highest-ranking regional authorities are appointed by the central government. Despite this, China is not as centralized as once believed. Provinces are especially important political players, and their power has grown since the 1980s, for several reasons. China's size and diversity contribute to regional forces that have always challenged national unity. The expanse and huge populations of some of the provinces have meant that the central government must rely on provincial governments to coordinate policy, as well as to deliver goods and services. The increased scope and complexity of the economy has added not only to the burdens but also to the leverage of regional and local officials responsible for implementing national policy.

The Impact of the Reform Period

Part of the post-Mao reform effort was to shift, or devolve, power from the national to the regional bureaucracies.[14] Crucial to the new development strategy was the decision to reorient the economy from national self-reliance to the international market. Earlier policies sought equalization of wealth between regions and classes, and capital investment was directed to underdeveloped inland provinces. But in the 1980s, the coastal regions, where commercial and industrial development had concentrated before 1949, were targeted for investment in order to expand China's export capacity. One result of this policy shift was obvious by the mid-1990s, when the coastal provinces, led by Guangdong, Zhejiang, and Fujian, experienced the highest rates of economic growth in the world.[15]

This devolution of power has led to new research on center-provincial relations, which, in turn, has recast the earlier interpretations of China as extremely centralized. Some scholars have described the new relations as Chinese-style federalism, for example. Western federalism is typically rooted in an explicit system for protecting individual and regional rights, has strong constitutional foundations, and is associated with democratization. In contrast, China's decentralization has been characterized by conditions that have required the allocation of responsibilities among different levels of government in order to implement the market reforms of the 1980s and 1990s.[16] Subnational governments were given primary authority over the economy within specified jurisdictions, including control of many state-owned industrial enterprises formerly controlled by the central government. Likewise, major construction or entrepreneurial undertakings required provincial cooperation to organize resources, including people. One consequence of this expanded role for subnational entities has been the increased bargaining between levels of government that became apparent within a decade after the reforms began.[17]

Three challenges in the evolving center-provincial relations are particularly pertinent in comparison with other countries. The first is to strengthen (or create) the institutions that provide enough central direction to maintain nation-wide coherence in implementing important policy objectives, while simultaneously permitting necessary regional flexibility. Expansion of local elections has been central to the reforms (see Chapter 12). Another element of this strategy has been to systematically train national leaders by recruiting or circulating them to the provinces. Promising candidates for national leadership positions are often transferred to local levels to acquire the practical experience deemed necessary for managing both party and state affairs in an increasingly complex economy.

As much as the goal at the central level is to strengthen linkages between the levels of government, by its very nature decentralization creates opportunities and incentives for a new-style, more independent politician to emerge. Even without the independent party or electoral bases that India's chief ministers or Japan's prefectural governors can claim, it is clear that a new political culture has emerged in many of China's regions, where provincial politicians attempt to build support and credibility less by pleasing central authorities than by using populist means—for example, by maintaining high public visibility, especially through media appearances.[18]

Fiscal Reform. The second challenge is managing the complexity of intergovernmental financial relations, which have changed substantially in China since the mid-1980s. During the period of centralized planning, the central government controlled fiscal policies at all levels of government. Beginning in 1980, the government undertook a number of reforms with the intent of decreasing costs to the central government and providing incentives to local governments to promote economic development. Budgeting, taxation, and revenue-sharing were all changed in order to give local entities more autonomy in controlling their revenue. At the same time, the central government gained more flexibility by devolving to local governments the responsibility to balance their own budgets. Although the collection of taxes was subject to unified national regulations, which gave the central government more control over this source of revenue, extra-budgetary income was under local control.[19]

The policy changes have had a number of effects, positive and negative, intended and unintended. To illustrate, by centralizing formal tax collection but negotiating revenue-sharing arrangements, the central government sought to increase transparency and predictability. However, no matter which form of rev-

enue-sharing has been used, and there have been several formulas, local governments always had to share the collected revenue with upper-level authorities of
the provincial and central governments. They often sought ways around the system, including "revenue hoarding" and the extra-budgetary extraction of revenue
from enterprises, including a variety of *ad hoc* charges.[20] Thus even as the central
government sought to increase accountability, one of the unintended consequences in many instances was to create the conditions for predatory behavior by
local officials—for some time a major source of grassroots political protests.

The reform also sought to increase tax revenues. Although the relative decline
in central government revenue was partially a result of privatization of enterprises
and a narrowing of the government's scope of responsibility, it also led to deficits
at a time when demands on government resources continued to grow.[21]

The third challenge of decentralization, and perhaps the most difficult, is to
reduce the growing gaps in social and economic welfare generated by rapid development. The ultimate success of China's development project may rely on the
ability of the party-state leadership to respond to the growing regional and class
disparities in well-being.

Regional Economies

As early as 1980, the central government designated "special economic zones"
(SEZs) on the coast, with incentives to attract foreign investment. The SEZs are
tax-free zones that provide customs exemptions and preferential treatment for foreign investors. Concentrated in coastal South China, the first four of the SEZs
helped make Guangdong and Fujian Provinces the richest in China, with their
growth rates around 20 percent in the early 1990s and per capita incomes 4 to 5
times higher than China's average. Along with coastal provinces further north
and the large metropolises of Shanghai, Beijing, and Tianjin, China's eastern
strip, which comprises 30 percent of China's population, became known as the
"Gold Coast" and accounted for almost one-half of the country's gross domestic
product (GDP) by the mid-1990s. This region also received approximately 80
percent of all foreign direct investment in China.[22]

There have been two repercussions of this economic boom that are pertinent
to the discussion of regionalism in China. The first has been the dramatic shift in
employment and population migration patterns. These regional disparities drove
millions of people to migrate to the richer provinces in search of opportunities.
It was estimated in the 1990s that the "floating population" of unemployed and
underemployed approached 100 million people. According to the 2000 census,
the southeast province of Guangdong alone had 21 million migrants, more than

a quarter of China's floating population at the time. This floating population was disproportionately made up of young males with modest educational levels (elementary to junior high school).[23] One of the concerns of the central government is the political consequences of unemployment. This has been an issue both in the northeastern "rustbelt," where many workers were laid off in the restructuring and closing of many former state factories, and again beginning in 2008, when the global economic recession affected the export-production factories in the southeast.[24]

The rapid growth also severely exacerbated the disparity in wealth between coastal and inland provinces, as well as the autonomous areas, where most of the minority nationalities live. The country's inland area, about 71 percent of the total, had been left out of the coastal boom. With a population of 29 percent of China's total, its share of the gross domestic product was less than 17 percent of the national GDP in the early twenty-first century.[25]

Although Guizhou is not typical of all the poor provinces, it illustrates the problems shared by poor regions in much of the world. The province is marked by a long history of relative geographic isolation and endemic rural poverty, and it has been stigmatized by its cultural identity as an area of minority nationalities, such as the Miao. Like many ethnic minority areas, in China and elsewhere, it has existed in a relationship of internal colonialism.[26] That is, Guizhou has been culturally, economically, and socially subordinate to and exploited by Han policies and peoples.

Fiscal decentralization during the first part of the reform period pushed Guizhou toward dependence on an inadequate local revenue base. Left to devise their own development strategies, Guizhou's political elites opted to capitalize (literally and figuratively) on the province's distinctiveness through a commodification of culture. "Cultural development has become something of a paradoxical idea, indicating the need to eradicate 'traditional thinking' while at the same time extolling ethnic tradition as a marketable commodity."[27] Thus Guizhou, like many poor countries, promotes ethnic tourism and traditional crafts, such as batik and embroidery, for wealthier urbanites.

In 1999, the Chinese government launched a policy for the "Great Western Development," with the intent of reducing the disparities between the coastal and interior provinces. The area targeted for development generally overlaps the traditional regions of "Outer China" described in Chapter 3, and includes the provinces of Gansu and Xinjiang in the northwest, Tibet and Qinghai in the west, and Yunnan, Guizhou, and Guangxi in the south. It will be recalled that these areas have concentrations of ethnic (and rural) minority populations.

Development in the interior is confronted by a variety of issues, ranging from lower education rates, cultural and ecological sensitivities, and physical inaccessibility. Although Western development represents a national priority, it is often left to local officials to devise and implement viable strategies. The primary capital investments by the central government thus far have been in the regions with the highest resource and strategic value, such as Tibet and Xinjiang provinces. In contrast, a province such as Yunnan suffers from geographic inaccessibility and poor infrastructure, poverty, and limited arable land.[28] Both the central and provincial governments plan the development of an industrial base, but tourism is a viable alternative, particularly in the short run. Thus the "commodification of culture" occurs in Yunnan, as it does in Guizhou, and women play a particularly visible role as ethnic cultural markers (see Photo 11.1).

PHOTO 11.1 Cultural presentation, Yunnan Province.
Photo courtesy of Martha A. Denney.

It is premature to assess the outcomes of the Western development efforts, and inevitably there will be benefits as well as costs, such as the erosion of traditional cultures and environmental damage. Assessed in comparative terms, the Chinese approach to development has much in common with those economic growth strategies pursued elsewhere that presume urbanization, industrialization, market competition, and, in recent decades, integration with the global economy. The winners thus far have been those in the "new economy," whereas the majority of the losers have been those in the old economy.

Crafting "Local Autonomy" in Japan

Decentralization of the Japanese state after World War II was one of the U.S. occupation's top priorities. SCAP officials saw greater local autonomy as a means to strengthen Japanese democracy by breaking up concentrated bureaucratic authority revolving around the prewar Home Ministry, which had appointed and overseen the prefectural governors. The 1947 Japanese Constitution confirmed the "principle of local autonomy" (Article 92), and the Local Autonomy Act of 1947 defined a two-tiered structure of prefectures and municipalities, separating local from national administration. The act also established the competencies and provided for the election of assemblies and chief executives (governors and mayors).

Although the true local autonomy envisaged by SCAP was unrealized, postwar Japan did institutionalize the separation between levels of government, and over the decades, prefectural and municipal officials have become more responsive to local constituencies. Urbanization and rapid economic growth created a host of problems, ranging from spiraling land prices to air and water pollution. These problems sparked grassroots protests and citizen pressures for ameliorative policies from local governments. Meanwhile, local elections for governors, mayors, and assembly representatives focused attention both on the problems and on alternative solutions. During the 1960s and early 1970s, local politics became more competitive; progressive parties cut off from national influence won local races. For example, by the early 1970s, major cities in Japan, including Tokyo, Osaka, Kyoto, Nagoya, and Yokohama, had elected leftist governors or mayors.

Japan is divided into forty-seven prefectures of varying sizes and types, including three municipal prefectures with large populations (Tokyo, Osaka, and Kyoto). There are approximately 1,800 municipalities (cities, towns, and villages), 13 of which are "ordinance-designated cities" that have increased local authority over public services such as social welfare and management of national and prefectural roads.[29] Like special administrative arrangements in other countries, including the centrally administered municipalities in China, these semi-autonomous cities and the municipal prefectures are designed to accommodate the complexities of providing services to urban agglomerations.

Despite the legal principle of local autonomy, it is generally agreed that the national government has been in a superior position and that Japan is properly classified as a unitary system. Nevertheless, the reality of intergovernmental relations is more complex than this observation suggests. The Local Autonomy Law, amended over the years, delegates a wide range of functions to local entities, ranging from regional development and management of water and power supply, sewage treatment, and transportation facilities to preservation of the environment and cultural properties. These are administrative responsibilities delegated by the national government, and local entities may also enact ordinances applicable within their own boundaries.[30] Laws passed in 1995 and 1999 sought to promote more deconcentration of authority and give additional resources to local governments.

As noted earlier, urbanization and industrialization have exacerbated numerous problems that local entities are under public pressure to address. For some time, Japan, like China, has been characterized by what Muramatsu Michio calls "administrative decentralization."[31] The old model of top-down policy-making has been modified in recognition of pressures on local governments, bottom-up demands on the national government, and complex horizontal linkages between various prefectures and municipalities. Although the Japanese government is still comparatively centralized, the past decade has seen growing pressure for decentralization.

We have already seen that intergovernmental finances are complex in India and China; Japan is no exception to this pattern. Local governments receive revenue through local taxes, fees levied for the provision of goods and services, and through transfers from the central government. Local government expenditure is high in comparison to the revenue-raising capacity of the prefectures, cities, and towns. On average, close to two-thirds of all public expenditures are made by local governments, but they raise only about 39 percent of the taxes, with the balance coming from national government transfers. These transfers take two forms: They are not only payment for functions that are assigned to local entities but also a fixed proportion of national income and sales taxes.[32] Without significant revenue-generating capacity, local entities exist in a kind of patron-client relationship with the central government.[33]

As in China and India, Japan's subnational politics continue to increase in importance. Although the prefectures and municipalities are no longer the place for progressive coalitions to try new policies (primarily because of the shrinking of leftist parties) regional politics can still be a lively affair. Numerous local politicians are not formally tied to any party, although many—such as Tokyo's controversial governor, Ishihara Shintaro—have been linked to the Liberal Democratic

Party (LDP).[34] Voter dissatisfaction with national politics since the early 1990s has often been reflected in the rejection of party-backed candidates in favor of electing independents to highly visible positions, such as governor. There are also increasing numbers of cases in which a governor may be in direct conflict with some aspect of national government policy. Many of the confrontations occur over environmental issues: The governor of Chiba Prefecture, which lies immediately to the southeast of Tokyo, called for canceling a land-reclamation project pushed for thirty years by the central government; to the northwest of Tokyo, the governor of Nagano Prefecture won election on a platform of opposing a dam planned by the central government; and further to the southwest, the governor of Mie Prefecture won support by opposing construction of a nuclear power plant.[35]

The next section discusses the unusual case of Okinawa Prefecture, which illustrates the maximum degree of political and legal authority that a prefectural governor may summon in a conflict with the central government. Although no other regional government has found itself in the same situation, the Okinawan case is important because of its international, as well as its national, implications.

Okinawa

The islands of the Ryukyu Archipelago, of which the largest is Okinawa, constitute Japan's far-flung southwestern Okinawa Prefecture. Okinawa's prefectural capital, Naha, is in fact closer to the capital cities of Taiwan (Taipei) and Korea (Seoul) than it is to Tokyo (see Map 3.1). In view of this geographic location, it is not surprising that the Ryukyus developed a traditional culture, including indigenous dialects, distinct from the rest of Japan.

Okinawa's strategic location meant that it bore an enormous burden during the Allied ground assault on Japan that began in April 1945. The battle(s) for Okinawa lasted almost three months and were among the bloodiest of the war. By August 1945, when the Ryukyu Islands were placed under U.S. military governance, 250,000 Japanese (including nearly 150,000 civilians on the islands) were dead; 12,500 Americans had been killed, and 37,000 had been wounded. Naha and other cities had been completely leveled; industry and agriculture had become nonexistent. All of this became part of the collective memory of Okinawans, influencing prefectural politics decades later.

The U.S. occupation of Japan lasted until 1952, but the Ryukyus remained under U.S. control until 1972. Military rule was a two-edged sword: The military authorities were responsible for rebuilding the islands' infrastructure and providing civilian jobs, but the redeveloped economy was heavily dependent on the American military presence. Homes were bulldozed and agricultural land confiscated to make room for expanding military bases and other facilities, especially as the strategic value of Okinawa was reaffirmed during the Korean and Vietnam Wars. Almost forty years after reversion of the Ryukyus, three-fourths of American bases in Japan and approximately 20,000 of American troops were still located in Okinawa Prefecture, which accounts for only 0.7 percent of Japan's total land.[36]

The right of the United States to occupy land in the prefecture dates from the postwar occupation period, but over the years, landowners increasingly protested the continued leasing of their property for American military facilities.[37] The landowners, along with many other Okinawans who resented both the American presence and the prefecture's treatment at the hands of a distant and often indifferent Japanese government, especially in negotiations over the future of the bases, pressured the provincial governor to represent their position more forcefully. In 1995, the base controversy exploded when three U.S. military men were arrested for abducting and raping a twelve-year-old Japanese girl. Over the course of the ensuing trial of the three men, tensions in the relations between Okinawa Prefecture and Tokyo were thrown into sharp relief, as were tensions in Japanese-U.S. relations.

In 1990, Washington and Tokyo had agreed to work toward returning many of the forty U.S. military sites in Okinawa to local control. In 1991, Okinawa's governor, Ota Masahide, threatened to withhold his signature from documents forcing local landowners to continue leasing land to the United States. He backed down when the central government agreed to secure base reductions from the United States. But in 1995, confronted, on the one hand, by a government slow or unwilling (from the Okinawan point of view) to defend the prefecture's position to the Americans and, on the other hand, by angry demands from his electors, Governor Ota was adamant in his refusal to sign similar documents again.

Ultimately, a prefectural governor's power is limited by both legal and political considerations. The prime minister of Japan is authorized by law to order the governor to sign the documents and if he refuses, to file a lawsuit against him. If the governor does not comply with a court order to sign, the prime minister can sign the papers himself. In 1995, both parties wanted to avoid such a deadlock and preferred negotiations. Governor Ota was strengthened in his position by popular outrage over the rape case and impatience over the central government's failure to move years earlier on the base issue. The central government, meanwhile, faced conflict with the United States over a number of issues and, like the U.S. government, had to balance multiple concerns while not appearing to capitulate to foreign pressure. Japan's prime minister at the time, Murayama Tomiichi, found himself in the ironic position of a long-time socialist who for years had opposed the U.S. military presence in Japan but who now headed a coalition government.

Forced to abandon his earlier pacifism, Murayama nonetheless hoped to appease simultaneously his coalition partners, the U.S. negotiators, conservative central government bureaucrats, Okinawans, and Japanese public opinion.

When a regional court ordered Governor Ota to sign documents extending the leases, he appealed to the Supreme Court. In September 1996, the dispute was resolved in favor of the central government when the Supreme Court dismissed the governor's appeal and he agreed to sign the documents. Two years later, LDP leaders at the central level backed an opposition candidate more favorable to Tokyo's position and succeeded in preventing Ota from serving a third gubernatorial term. The political status quo was further maintained as American plans to downsize its military installations limped along with the tacit approval of the central government.

Trapped by Japanese and American strategic concerns, Okinawa Prefecture also confronts economic disadvantages that consign it to relative poverty in Japan: resource scarcity, too few employment opportunities, and high transportation costs. In the first three decades after reversion, the prefecture received more than US$55.8 billion in government funds, but its unemployment rate was still twice the national average. As early as 1988, a free-trade zone was launched in Naha, the capital, in order to generate employment not linked to the bases.[38] This was followed by more than a dozen other tax-incentive schemes, and in 2002 the Diet passed legislation to give the prefecture "an array of dazzling financial and other incentives not seen anywhere else in Japan."[39] Successful realization of the legislation's goals, however, depends on conversion of some of the existing military bases, which has been very slow to happen.

Summary

Relations between levels of government have shown themselves to be dynamic and flexible in India, China, and Japan over the past half century. Nominally, India is a federal system, whereas China and Japan are unitary states. But Indian federalism is cross-pressured by a constitution that tilts the balance toward the central government and by regional developments that push the country toward decentralization, ranging from threats to its territorial integrity in the northwest and northeast to the growth of regional parties. In China, both the constitutional structure of a unitary system and the Communist Party guarantee central control, but economic policies have promoted decentralization. In Japan the unitary system was also altered in the 1990s by political and economic changes, together with laws to promote decentralization.

None of these trends is irreversible, although once regional governments and local politicians have developed a vested interest in controlling their own affairs with minimal interference from a higher level of government, reversing this course is likely to be as long and gradual a process as decentralization. Even in China, where the maintenance of strong central political control has been part of the government's agenda, reform policies have had a countervailing effect, and it seems likely that regional and local politicians will continue to try to maximize their political flexibility.

Notes

1. For helpful introductory analyses of federalism, see Daniel J. Elazar, *Exploring Federalism* (Tuscaloosa: University of Alabama Press, 1987), and Preston King, *Federalism and Federation* (Baltimore: Johns Hopkins University Press, 1982). Specifically for Asia, see Baogang He, Brian Galligan, and Takashi Inoguchi, eds., *Federalism in Asia* (Northampton, Mass.: Elgar Press, 2007).

2. Gabriella Montinola, Yingyi Qian, and Barry R. Weingast, "Federalism, Chinese Style: The Political Basis for Economic Success in China," *World Politics* 48, no. 1 (October 1995), 50–81; Zheng Yongnian, *De Facto Federalism in China: Reforms and Dynamics of Central-Local Relations* (London: Imperial College Press, 2007).

3. Romila Thapar, *A History of India*, vol. 1 (Baltimore: Penguin Books, 1966), 89–91, 144–145, and chap. 5.

4. Granville Austin, *The Indian Constitution: Cornerstone of a Nation* (Oxford: Clarendon Press, 1966), 187; Ramesh Thakur, *The Government and Politics of India* (New York: St. Martin's Press, 1995), 71–72; Robert L. Hardgrave Jr. and Stanley A. Kochanek, *India: Government and Politics in a Developing Nation*, 5th ed. (Fort Worth: Harcourt Brace College Publishers, 1993), 127, 131. See also David Taylor, "The Centre and the States: Evolution of a Union," introduction to Europa Publications Limited, *The Territories and States of India* (London: Europa Publications, 2002), 3–14.

5. The exception is Jammu and Kashmir, a north Indian state that theoretically has the right to determine its own constitution and that has a different status in the Indian Union.

6. M. Govinda Rao, "India: Intergovernmental Fiscal Relations in a Planned Economy," in *Fiscal Decentralization in Developing Countries*, eds. Richard M. Bird and François Vaillancourt (Cambridge: Cambridge University Press, 1998), 78–114.

7. The Punjabi language is the mother tongue of both Sikhs and Hindus (and before the nineteenth century, of Muslims as well), although Hindus increasingly have renounced Punjabi in favor of Hindi for political reasons. By Partition, only Sikhs wrote

Punjabi, using the Gurmukhi script in which their scriptures are written. Therefore, to claim a separate Punjabi-speaking state was effectively a religious (Sikh) demand as well. But after the horrors of Partition, any explicit demand for a religion-based state was unacceptable to the Congress leaders who dominated Union politics. Robin Jeffrey, *What's Happening to India? Punjab, Ethnic Conflict, and the Test for Federalism,* 2nd ed. (New York: Holmes and Meier, 1994), 69, 101–105. On the historical and social roots of Sikh nationalism, see Peter van der Veer, *Religious Nationalism: Hindus and Muslims in India* (Berkeley: University of California Press, 1994), 53–56, 73–77.

8. This analysis is derived primarily from Paul R. Brass, "The Punjab Crisis and the Unity of India," in *India's Democracy: An Analysis of Changing State-Society Relations,* ed. Atul Kohli (Princeton: Princeton University Press, 1988), 169–213; Paul R. Brass, *The Politics of India Since Independence* (Cambridge: Cambridge University Press, 1990), 170–178; and Jeffrey, chaps. 6, 7.

9. For an understanding of the socioeconomic and political conditions that encouraged support for Bhindranwale, see Joyce J. M. Pettigrew, *The Sikhs of the Punjab: Unheard Voices of State and Guerrilla Violence* (London: Zed Books, 1995).

10. Brass, *Politics of India,* 109–118.

11. Hemant Babu, "The Social Engineering of Gujarat," *Himal South Asia* (May 2002). The website "Countercurrents" has numerous resources devoted to the Gujarat case; see http://www.countercurrents.org/gujarat.htm, "Gujarat Pogrom."

12. *Democracy and Violence in India and Sri Lanka* (London: Royal Institute of International Affairs, 1994).

13. "The Puzzle of Indian Democracy: A Consociational Interpretation," *American Political Science Review* 90, no. 2 (June 1996), 258–268.

14. Dali L. Yang, *Beyond Beijing: Liberalization and the Regions in China* (London: Routledge, 1997), chap. 2.

15. Overall, China averaged between 9 and 10 percent annual growth rate from 1979 through 1994.

16. In "Federalism, Chinese Style," Montinola, Qian, and Weingast analyzed the characteristics of China's "market-preserving federalism."

17. Bargaining occurs not just between provinces but at the subprovincial level as well. See Kenneth G. Lieberthal and David M. Lampton, eds., *Bureaucracy, Politics, and Decision Making in Post-Mao China* (Berkeley: University of California Press, 1992), particularly pt. 4.

18. Hans Hendrischke, "Provinces in Competition: Region, Identity and Cultural Construction," in *The Political Economy of China's Provinces: Comparative and Competitive Advantage,* eds. Hans Hendrischke and Feng Chongyi (London: Routledge, 1999), 17.

19. Jian Zhang, *Government and Market in China: A Local Perspective* (Hauppauge, N.Y.: Nova Science Publishers, 2004), chap. 3. See also the studies done by the team led by Charles Pigott, "Issues Concerning Central-Local Government Fiscal Relations," in Organization for Economic Co-Operation and Development (OECD), *China in the World Economy* (Paris: OECD, 2002), 659–677.

20. Zhang, 63–65.

21. Total tax revenue as a percentage of the GNP declined from 23 percent in 1985 to approximately 10 percent a decade later. Roy W. Bahl, "China: Evaluating the Impact of Intergovernmental Fiscal Reform," in Bird and Vaillancourt, *Fiscal Decentralization*, 57–58.

22. Jan S. Prybyla, "All That Glitters? The Foreign Investment Boom," *Current History* 94, no. 593 (September 1995), 178.

23. Zai Ling, "Internal Migration: Policy Changes, Recent Trends, and New Challenges," in *Transition and Challenge: China's Population at the Beginning of the 21st Century*, eds. Zongwei Zhao and Fei Guo (Oxford: Oxford University Press, 2007), 201. The removal of government restrictions on travel facilitated migration.

24. Ching Kwan Lee, *Against the Law: Labor Protests in China's Rustbelt and Sunbelt* (Berkeley: University of California Press, 2007).

25. Ding Lu and William Neilson, "Introduction: West China Development—Issues and Challenges," in *China's West Region Development: Domestic Strategies and Global Implications*, eds. Ding Lu and William Neilson (Singapore: World Scientific Publishing, 2004), 1.

26. Tim Oakes, "Selling Guizhou: Cultural Development in an Era of Marketisation," in Hendrischke and Feng, *Political Economy of China's Provinces*, 31–76. See also the analysis by Chen Zhilong and Zhang Min, "Guizhou," in *Developing China's West: A Critical Path to Balanced National Development*, eds. Y. M. Yeung and Shen Jianfa (Hong Kong: Chinese University Press, 2004), chap. 19. In the mid-1990s, Guizhou's per capita GDP was only one-tenth that of Shanghai. Jiang Wandi, "Balance Reemphasized in Regional Development," *Beijing Review* 39, no. 4 (January 22–28, 1996), 20.

27. Oakes, 32.

28. Gan Chunkai and Chen Zhilong, "Yunnan," in Yueng and Jianfa, chap. 20.

29. "Saitama to Become 13th 'Semi Autonomous' City," *The Daily Yomiuri*, October 26, 2002.

30. Ian Neary, *The State and Politics in Japan* (Cambridge: Polity Press, 2002), chap. 9.

31. Michio Muramatsu, *Local Power in the Japanese State*, trans. Betsey Scheiner and James White (Berkeley: University of California Press, 1997), 2 and chap. 6. In administrative decentralization, the legal foundation for the division of power between central

and local authority rests with the central government, not the constitution (as is the case for federal systems).

32. "Local Government in Japan Today" (Sydney: Japan Local Government Center), online at www.jlgc.org.au (n.d., accessed November 25, 2002); Neary, 151–152.

33. "Japan's Regions, The Puzzle of Power," *The Economist*, March 8, 2008.

34. Ishihara, a conservative nationalist, served his first term as governor of Tokyo from 1999 to 2003 and was reelected in 2003 and 2007.

35. "The Day of the Governors," *The Economist*, June 16, 2001, 41–42; *The Japan Times*, September 2, 2002; David Pilling, "Tokyo Governor Threatens to Sue over Pollution," *The Financial Times*, April 2, 2003.

36. See Part III of "Measures for Defense of Japan," Ministry of Defense, Government of Japan, at www.mod.go.jp/e/publ/w_paper/pdf/2008/30Part3_Chapter2 _Sec1.pdf., accessed March 20, 2009.

37. During the first decade after reversion of the Ryukyus to Japan, the central government offered high rents to encourage landowners to sign leases permitting military use of their land. After 1982, an antimilitary campaign increased the number of antiwar landowners. By 1996, 2,937 landowners were refusing to sign lease contracts. *Japan Times Weekly, International Edition*, April 8–14, 1996.

38. "Okinawa's Free-Trade Zone Failing to Attract Companies," *The Japan Times*, September 13, 2002. Seventy-seven percent of the prefecture's revenue comes from the central government.

39. "Law for Okinawa's Prosperity," *The Japan Times*, April 6, 2002. The law is the Law on Special Measures for the Promotion of Okinawa.

PART FOUR

The Individual and the State

Most of us understand that the connections between individuals and the processes of governing are exceedingly complex. Part Four does not attempt to cover all aspects of these connections and processes. Rather, for our purposes, the discussion of these relationships is to emphasize patterns and raise questions. Since political leaders, government composition, and policy issues change frequently, even suddenly, Chapters 12–14 focus on patterns that are interesting and will be important over the next decade.

The organization and topics of Part Four reflect contemporary scholarly interest in understanding the multiple ways in which state institutions and policies influence (or mold) practices and values throughout society and also the ways in which those practices and values orient or constrain the state. Put simply, state-society relations are interactions, a "two-way street." Within this approach, three over-arching questions guide the discussion. First, how successful has been the push for economic development in Asia, and what have been the political and social consequences of development? Second, what does democracy mean and how does it work in Asia? Third, how do governments cope with the reality of being sandwiched between domestic and international pressures? All of these questions have been deeply affected by the forces of globalization that mark the twenty-first century.

Competitive multiparty systems and free elections are commonly seen as procedural prerequisites for democracy because they channel citizen preferences and hold governments accountable. Chapter 12 concentrates on the two oldest competitive-party systems in Asia, India and Japan, while asking what the prospects are for China. Entitled "The Decay of One-Party Rule: Elusive Democracy," the chapter examines the ways in which the authority of the Congress and Liberal Democratic parties, on one side, and the Chinese Communist Party, on the other, has been challenged and eroded. These studies raise the broader question of what can be learned about the role of parties and elections in linking individuals and states in Asia. Do political parties and elections foster citizen well-being over time, or are they a façade behind which elites manipulate political resources? Do they engender national community or fracture the polity, leading to cynicism or even violence?

Development has been an essential goal of governments around the globe, but often development policies have unintended consequences. Chapter 13, "Development, Democratization, and Governance in Asia," addresses the meaning of development and its implications for state-society relations. The process of development has contributed to the diversification of civil society and the emergence of new groups and political voices. The chapter pays particular attention to environmental issues to illustrate these changes.

Chapter 14 focuses on the implications of globalization in Asia, with particular emphasis on human security and the spectrum of violence. The second half of the chapter concludes our exploration of Asia by discussing the ways in which knowledge of Asian politics challenges our approaches to comparative politics and asks for a rethinking of concepts such as development and democracy.

12

Elusive Democracy:
The Decay of One-Party Rule

In democracies, political parties are central to civic life: In principle, they reflect the voters' preferences, provide alternative policy visions, and hold governments accountable. Parties are so useful to government legitimacy that even authoritarian states create parties to serve as conduits between citizens and governments. The structures and operations of parties tell us much about the dynamics of political systems.

The first part of this chapter compares the origins and structures of the Congress, Liberal Democratic, and Communist parties. The next section surveys the major opposition parties in India and Japan and the interparty relationships that contributed to the rise of coalition governments in the 1990s, the emergence of the Bharatiya Janata Party (BJP) and state-based parties in India, and the fragmentation of parties in Japan. The third section focuses on electoral systems, including village elections in China. Contested elections are central to democratic competition, but electoral systems themselves influence the nature of that competition and tell us much about the values that structure party representation.

The Congress, Liberal Democratic,
and Chinese Communist Parties

Although many European parties trace their roots to the first half of the nineteenth century, the earliest Asian parties appeared toward the end of that century. The predecessors of the contemporary Congress and Liberal Democratic parties date to the 1880s; the Chinese Communist Party, in contrast, was established shortly after World War I, as were other communist parties in Asia and Europe.

Origins and Structures

The origins of the Congress Party in India and the Communist Party in China are similar in several striking ways. Both had roots in the dramatic changes occurring in the two countries as their nationalist movements sought to cope with Western imperialism and the inadequacies of traditional social and political structures. Both Congress and the CCP were, in fact, the nationalist movements during much of their history, yet both parties borrowed heavily from Western ideas. Both were led by courageous and charismatic figures who were able to mobilize millions of Indians and Chinese on behalf of their parties. Neither party was monolithic during the early decades, as different leaders, strategies, and ideologies vied for dominance. Yet by 1950, Congress and the CCP were indisputably the ruling parties of their respective countries, each with a preeminent leader who commanded enormous authority within his party: Jawaharlal Nehru in the Congress and Mao Zedong in the CCP.

The critical differences between Congress and the CCP are most notable in the philosophies that have informed the parties' internal organizations and external policies. An obvious difference is Congress's commitment to electoral competition and other elements of political democracy during all but two of the years that it formed national governments. In contrast, the CCP operated under the Leninist norms of single-party monopoly of revolutionary momentum.

The history of the Liberal Democratic Party is very different from that of either the Congress or the CCP. Although the LDP has its roots in the political societies formed during the Meiji period, it took its contemporary form only in the 1950s. Ideology has seldom played a major role in determining either its leadership or its policies, and its legitimacy derived from the success of its economic development strategy, not from its origins in a mass-based nationalist movement. Nonetheless, it shares with the Congress Party the extensive internal factionalism that has resulted in the periodic splitting off of new political groups.

The Congress Party. Chapter 5 explained the evolution of the Indian National Congress from its founding in 1885 through the 1940s. Although often divided by philosophies, political strategies, and personalities during these decades, Congress outdistanced other parties established during the pre- and postindependence periods in popular support. The other parties did not seriously begin to challenge Congress until the late 1960s. From *swaraj* in 1947 until 1967, Congress enjoyed such majorities in the national legislature and in nearly all of the state legislatures that India became known as a one-party-dominant system.

Congress was the only party with a truly national presence until the late 1990s, when the Bharatiya Janata Party won electoral pluralities in the Lok Sabha.

This dominance was partly due to the party's legitimacy as a national movement, but its organizational reach and successful performance of interest aggregation were as important as this heritage. Political scientists consider a central characteristic of democratic political parties to be the ability to aggregate constituents' interests for the purpose of contesting elections and, if elected, to implement policies. Congress far surpassed its competitors in the performance of these functions. Drawing on the lessons learned during nationalist campaigns, Congress leaders at all levels became skilled at forging alliances among different social groups in order to win elections.

The early Congress leaders constituted a small, largely homogeneous elite, mostly upper caste and English-educated. But despite their similar status, these leaders frequently disagreed over policy priorities such as development strategies (see Chapter 13). Later, however, the primary goal of party officials became almost exclusively holding office. Patronage and the delivery of services to constituents—both possible because of Congress's near-monopoly of elected government positions—served further to maintain the party in power. Increasingly, the party attracted careerists who gained support by appealing to traditional, parochial loyalties, thus gradually building intraparty tension between the goals of modernization and change, on the one hand, and maintenance of the traditional social order, on the other.

The Chinese Communist Party. Like the Congress Party, the CCP has experienced internal tensions (see Chapter 10). China's size and diversity have contributed to regional pressures, and there have always been philosophical and policy differences within the party. In contrast to the Congress Party, however, the internal organization of the CCP places higher priority on the goal of maintaining internal cohesion. Different concepts of party membership lie at the root of the differences between the two parties.

Membership in India's Congress Party (like the LDP) requires only payment of a small subscription sum. There are no ideological or other requirements. Membership in the Communist Party provides a striking contrast. The first chapter of the CCP Constitution details the ideological and procedural requirements of party membership. New members must both apply and be recommended by two full party members. The application must be accepted by a general membership meeting of the party branch concerned and by the next-higher party level. New members then undergo a probationary period of one year (Articles 5–7).

Members at the lowest level of the party hierarchy are organized into units or cells of at least three full party members.

After 1949, CCP membership was the most important prerequisite for power and influence in China. Although members are ideologically directed to "serve the people wholeheartedly" and "not seek personal gain or privileges" (Article 2), CCP membership has conferred elite status. During the early decades, this status derived from the presumed higher levels of political education and commitment to the revolution's goals, along with the inherent authority conferred on the party and its members by virtue of the leading role of the party in China's governing system. Status has also derived from the relatively small proportion of China's population admitted to party membership. At the time of the Seventeenth Congress in 2007, there were more than 73 million members, about 5.6 percent of the population.

Although the CCP was reorganized and consolidated after the Cultural Revolution, the reform period brought a succession of new problems. One problem was the very rapid recruitment of new members after the Cultural Revolution, but many of the newer members were admitted using ideological standards that were subsequently rejected by the reform leaders during the late 1970s and after. With the emphasis on economic modernization came the concern that too many party members lacked the competence required by the new policies. In the late 1980s and the 1990s, party recruitment therefore focused on better educated, younger members.

Even more important problems have been corruption and abuse of authority from the local levels to the top of the CCP hierarchy. Maintenance of the party's recruitment standards and appeal has been an equally pervasive concern. By the mid-1990s, economic growth had not only generated corruption but had sprouted a new elite whose status derived from wealth rather than party membership (although membership frequently facilitated the accumulation of wealth). There were strong indications that fewer young people, especially those with higher education and skills and therefore other options, were attracted to joining the party. Jiang Zemin's push to open party membership to individuals from the private sector (the "new social stratum") led to CCP constitutional amendments in 2002 (see Chapter 8). This initiative was reinforced by Jiang's successors.[1]

The Liberal Democratic Party. The Japanese party system from the 1950s to the 1990s resembled the Congress system in some ways, most notably in the ability of the LDP to aggregate diverse interests through patron-client networks in order to sustain electoral dominance. In its origins, historical evolution, and policies, however, it is unique.

Unlike the Congress and Communist parties, the LDP is not rooted in a nationalist, revolutionary movement, although its predecessors can be traced back more than a century to the 1870s and early 1880s (see Chapter 7). Japan's political parties flourished in the 1920s but declined in the 1930s. In 1940, all parties were officially dissolved and replaced by the Imperial Rule Assistance Association. During the occupation period, parties were allowed to reestablish themselves almost immediately. By the end of 1945, three conservative parties, as well as the Communist and Socialist parties, had formed.

In the first decade after the war, both the conservative and leftist parties went through several organizational and name changes. The most important change was the merger in 1955 of the two largest conservative parties, the Liberals and the Democrats. However, from its inception, the Liberal Democratic Party has been a coalition of factions, as were its predecessors. Although there were and have continued to be some policy differences among individual LDP politicians, both ideology and policies have been fluid, usually characterized by general, middle-of-the-road positions permitting flexible, indeed multiple, interpretations. From the outset, the purpose of the LDP coalition was to assure conservative rule. In 1955, the clearest threat to this rule came from the imminent reunification of the Japan Socialist Party, which had split four years earlier. The move to consolidate conservative forces was strongly supported by business interests that then, as now, provided LDP financial support.[2]

Intraparty Factionalism

Factionalism is an important characteristic shared by the LDP, the Congress, and the CCP, although the nature of the factions differs in the three cases. Factions frequently are leader-follower, or patron-client, groups, and relations among members are often highly personalized. Factions play contradictory roles in party organizations: They make it possible to integrate divergent interests and groups, and they widen the base of political involvement, but well-organized factions may also pose a threat to party and government unity.

There are several general characteristics of intraparty factionalism. First, factions often operate in ways that suggest the carryover of traditional political values (such as group loyalty) into contemporary political party competition. Second, the personal ties that frequently define factions provide an alternative to other links, such as ideology or ethnicity, as a way to organize and mobilize people for political participation. Third, factional ties often operate "behind the scenes" to determine political influence and policy decisions, making it difficult for those outside the system to understand the political process. Finally, as noted earlier, factions may threaten party unity when strong leaders in opposition to the party mainstream leave the party and join the opposition.

LDP Factions. The structure of factions, including the importance of personal loyalty to a faction leader, suggests that this particular form of political organization is a good example of the way traditional values have carried over to contemporary politics in Asia. Readers may recall that loyalty was the central value of the Tokugawa system of social and political organization. Individuals were linked hierarchically through personal ties that provided group cohesion, but these same kinds of ties led to factional divisions among ruling elites. Thus, Japanese political parties originated in the disagreements among the oligarchs that arose shortly after the Meiji Restoration.

Some years ago, Japanese social anthropologist Nakane Chie analyzed the structure of groups throughout Japanese society.[3] She argued that the ranking of all members of the group in relation to each other and in accordance with the principle of seniority provides cohesion. Group leadership is restricted to one person, and all members of the group are linked in a relationship of superior-inferior status.

Originally, LDP factions consisted of Diet members "bound by the ties of obligation and debt that have long played an important role in Japanese political custom."[4] Faction members commit to the leadership of a senior party member who has developed close ties with other politicians, the bureaucracy, and the business community and has demonstrated his ability to raise money and dispense patronage. At the top echelon, party and Diet posts are apportioned to reflect the relative strength of factions within the ruling party.

Factions historically served as the campaign support organization from the grassroots to the national level. At the local level, personal support groups, called *koenkai*, have generally been organized to mobilize support for candidates. They represented the personal interest of the Diet member and in effect constituted the local organization of the LDP. *Koenkai* were justified not only by the cultural norms noted above but also by Japan's electoral system, in which LDP candidates competed against each in a single district.

Factions have tended to be stable for long periods, changing mainly when a faction leader retires from politics or dies; occasionally they may combine or reorganize. Within the faction, individuals advance through seniority as well as by ability, and in the Diet, seniority is based on the number of times a politician has been elected as a member of a particular faction. To change factions means a loss of seniority, so ambitious politicians are generally discouraged from changing factions.

Other Japanese parties have been factionalized, but LDP factions are the best known because of the party's long governing role. LDP factions were long criticized for contributing to the inordinate cost of Japanese elections, to influence peddling, and to other corruption-linked political practices. It was, in fact, public criticism of the connection between the electoral system, factions, and money politics that led to the long, drawn-out effort to reform electoral districts described later in this chapter. By the time Koizumi Junichiro (himself an LDP faction man) became prime minister in 2001, there were signs that factions might be fading. Koizumi bypassed faction leaders in making his cabinet appointments, and faction leaders complained of divisions within their own groups.[5] Although numerous observers predicted that factions would continue to wane after Koizumi, they had not disappeared by the end of the decade.[6]

Congress Party Factions. The durability of Japanese factions suggests that they reflect both cultural habits and political logic. The same is true of factions in India's Congress Party. Like the LDP, Congress has long been internally factionalized. Particularly during the first two decades after independence, factions within the Congress interacted in a way that provided built-in opposition, as well as accommodation of different ideological and policy stances. Thus, factions organizationally helped Congress build the consensus that led to its dominance both before and after independence.

Also like the LDP, factional competition within Congress determined the dynamics of the formal party structures that were described earlier:

> Factions contested for control of the important committees at each level through formal elections preceded by membership drives in which competing faction leaders attempted to enroll, even if only on paper, as many member-supporters as possible. Although the factional conflicts which developed often became intense and bitter . . . they also served to keep the party organization alive and to compel party leaders to build support in the districts and localities throughout the country.[7]

The nature of these factional conflicts varied from the local to the national level, and their effect on the party changed over time. Until 1967, their integrative functions outweighed their disintegrative threat. By their very nature, factions have been personalistic, often led by local "notables" whose original following came from caste or religious groups or from their control of private or public institutions, especially those with resources to distribute. But since their primary goal was to acquire political power in competition with other factions and external parties, faction leaders sought alliances across traditional group boundaries. Factional competition ultimately contributed to the secular nature of Congress politics: "By drawing in new caste and religious groups . . . factions politicized them in secular terms."[8]

Until his death in 1964, Nehru and his closest confidants controlled national politics largely by mediating factional conflicts at both the state and national levels. Mediation was, in fact, central to the ability of the Congress to maintain control. After Nehru's death, the party was torn by a succession struggle that involved his daughter, Indira Gandhi, and a number of faction leaders. This struggle was an important part of the history of Mrs. Gandhi's populist approach to mobilizing support in the 1971 elections, which in turn contributed to the dynamics that produced the Emergency described in Chapter 9. The Congress Party had split first in 1969, and it divided again in 1977, after the Emergency and in response to Mrs. Gandhi's handling of it.

Rather than using the mediating style of her father, Prime Minister Gandhi exerted control in a way that demanded loyalty to her personally. Factional conflict continued at the state and national levels, but the prime minister intervened by making decisions regarding matters such as the selection of state chief ministers on the basis of the degree of their loyalty to her. When Indira Gandhi was assassinated in 1984, her son Rajiv was automatically chosen as the new leader of Congress (I); despite early hopes that he would help revive Congress as a mass-based party, his approach to intraparty affairs largely duplicated that of his mother. Subsequently, when Rajiv's widow, Sonia, was elected to lead Congress, a faction opposing this "dynastic succession" left the party in 1999 to form the Nationalist Congress Party. One hundred twenty-five years after its founding, it could be said that the Congress "was no longer a party but an undifferentiated, unanchored medley of individuals sustained by patronage."[9]

In both the LDP and the Congress, intraparty factions have been responsible for much of the decision-making that occurs at both regional and national levels. Even when the two parties have dominated national politics to the extent that Japan and India were one-party–dominant systems, factional conflict decreed that party leaders had to take factional leaders and preferences into account when allocating posts and setting policy priorities. Both factional conflict and the necessity of accommodating faction preferences have been part of decision-making in the Chinese Communist Party as well.

CCP Factions. By the time of the Cultural Revolution, it became increasingly evident to scholars of Chinese politics that elite factions were responsible for conflict at the central government level. Although the details were not known, the purges of rival leaders during the 1950s and 1960s, as suggested in Chapter 10, could be explained by mutually reinforcing personal and ideological rivalries that took the form of factions. Analyzing Chinese politics after Mao Zedong's death in 1976, Lowell Dittmer argued that a cycle of elite conflict defined Chinese politics through the 1980s, a period that culminated in the removal of Zhao Ziyang in the wake of the Tiananmen events of 1989.[10] The factional conflicts in the 1970s and 1980s that Dittmer analyzed were based more on personal relationships than ideological differences, although other scholars have linked factions to broader conflicts within Chinese society brought on by economic reform.[11] Analyzing the history of factions, Jing Huang located their origins in the decentralized base areas established by the CCP during the civil war period.[12]

Succession politics are also linked to factional rivalry. The different scenarios regarding Deng Xiaoping's death and the dissolution of the ruling coalition that dominated top-level decisions for some fifteen years relied on assessments of the relative factional strength of the various contenders to succeed Deng. Much of the speculation surrounding the succession to Jiang Zemin addressed Jiang's ability to place his personal supporters in the Standing Committee of the Politburo, and thus to influence top-level decision-making even after he had retired.[13] More recently, scholars have argued that the nature of party leadership and factionalism gradually changed as Hu Jintao became more established. In contrast to the earlier patron-client relationships, those who have ties to Hu have career paths intersecting his, for example in provincial politics.[14]

In addition to those who hold formal positions, the political elite include the *mishus*, who are personal office secretaries found throughout China's political, economic, and military units. Their job is to serve their leaders in multiple capacities—as advisers, policy coordinators, speechwriters, administrators—doing anything that advances the interests of their mentors.[15] Leaders may have several *mishus*, who can become important political players in their own right over time. Typically, a *mishu* has not come up through the bureaucratic ranks but is recruited personally by his patron. But because of his importance in representing his boss at official functions, he is assigned bureaucratic rank, which he carries with him when he leaves his *mishu* position.[16] After a period of personal service, a leader will have his *mishus* transferred to other political posts, thus enhancing his influence.

The network of relationships found in the *mishu* system and more generally in factions is one example of the pervasiveness of *guanxi*, or personal ties, in China. Personal connections were important in prerevolutionary society, where they typically reflected family or clan ties. In modern China, *guanxi* includes a variety of interpersonal relationships and makes it possible to circumvent formal state or party strictures in order to acquire goods and services or just to get things done. *Guanxi* has contributed to corruption as colleagues and family members use their ties to profit from the economic opportunities that have opened up in the past thirty years, but connections also facilitate transactions in a society still marked by scarcity and bureaucratic encumbrances.[17]

Factionalism, Party Stability, and Decline

Numerous factors account for the decay in one-party rule, including organization and leadership weakness and the rise of competing social or political forces. Factionalism is important but must be assessed within this broader framework. In India, factions contributed to two major, formal splits in the Congress (1969 and 1977) and one smaller cleavage (1999). These divisions were both symptoms and causes of the weaknesses that in turn contributed to Congress's declining share of support, both in Lok Sabha and in state legislative elections. For example, in the 1996 Lok Sabha elections, the Congress share of the votes dropped more than 8 percent from its 1991 total. Exit polls indicated that both intraparty factionalism and the proliferation of regional parties were contributing to the erosion of Congress support. These political shifts, in turn, reflected profound changes in the electorate. "The rainbow of social communities brought together by the Congress (I) in the era of one-party dominance has not disappeared from the political horizon, but its slices are beginning to fall apart."[18] It was in this context that BJP-led governments came to power in the late 1990s.

During the same period that factionalism was contributing to the crumbling electoral fortunes of the Congress Party, factionalism led to the first non-LDP government in Japan since the establishment of the party in 1955. In 1992, the largest LDP faction, controlled by Kanemaru Shin, began to unravel. Kanemaru admitted receiving an illegal political donation and resigned as LDP vice president.

Kanemaru was the third major leader of his faction to be charged with large-scale corruption. His faction, more than any other, was linked to the kind of backroom political maneuvering and outright illegal campaign practices that were building public cynicism and discontent. It was the accumulated effect of the LDP's "politics as usual," joined by the latest Kanemaru scandal and the factional split, that produced major change in the 1990s. In June 1993, the government lost a vote of no-confidence, and in the ensuing House of Representatives elections, the LDP lost control of the lower house. In August 1993, the first non-LDP–led government in nearly forty years took office. This was to be the first of several coalition governments over the next several years, and in each coalition there were parties that were, in effect, either factional remnants of the pre-1993

LDP or the LDP itself. The Democratic Party of Japan (DPJ), which emerged in the early twenty-first century as a major challenger to the LDP, began as the result of a factional split in the LDP. Although LDP Prime Minister Koizumi discouraged factions, they reasserted themselves in the struggle to establish stable party leadership after Koizumi's resignation in 2006.

Factionalism has long been a source of weakness for the CCP. Factions contributed to political instability in earlier decades and still help account for the lack of transparency in party and government decision-making. The party officially prohibits factions but increasingly accepts that "interest groups" reflecting different policy positions may exist, and some observers have speculated that one future alternative for the CCP may be an intraparty organization resembling the LDP.[19]

Opposition Parties and Coalition Politics

In addition to the factors already discussed, another important reason for the ability of the Congress and LDP to dominate for so long was the weakness and general disunity of the opposition parties. Much of the debate about political parties in Japan and India focuses on the potential for a truly competitive national party. Would this be the Democratic Party of Japan (DPJ) in the former or the Bharatiya Janata Party (BJP) in the latter? Despite the significance of the DPJ and BJP, an important part of the political scenarios over the past two decades has been the weakness of other parties aspiring to national prominence (Japan) and the rise of regional parties (India) that was discussed at length in the previous chapter.

Japan: Parties of the Left and Center

Since the LDP began its long domination of Japanese politics in the 1950s, the country has had three types of opposition parties: those of the left (Socialists and Communists), those in the center, and those in the conservative opposition, consisting largely of former LDP factions and dissidents. Although their national electorate had shrunk dramatically by the early twenty-first century, the leftist parties provided the most enduring ideological opposition to the LDP. They originated in the flowering of parties early in the century and expanded their support as the working class itself grew, though they spent much of their early history underground.

Socialists and Communists. The Japan Socialist Party (JSP), created in 1945, has been marked by two kinds of divisions that have undermined its postwar promise to provide a progressive alternative to the LDP. The JSP, like its predecessors, was divided ideologically between left and right wings. The left and right wings of the party split in 1951 over the issue of the peace treaty with the United States, which the left wing rejected. It reunified in 1955, then divided again in 1960 when its right wing broke away. The second division of the JSP was factional. In fact, the JSP most resembled the LDP in its internal organization. The factions reflected historical divisions among smaller prewar parties, as well as the ideological cleavages just noted.

Through the 1970s and into the 1980s, the JSP received about 20 percent of the vote in Diet elections, although it often did better in local elections. But in the late 1980s, when the LDP was torn by scandal and voters hated a new LDP-imposed national consumption tax, the JSP benefited. The party made major gains in the 1989 House of Councillors elections, in which the LDP lost its majority. In the mid-1980s and again in 1990, the party modified its ideology to eliminate Marxist-Leninist references and to emphasize its social-democratic nature. It changed the English version of its name in 1991, and in 1996, its Japanese name, to the Social Democratic Party (SDP) in a bid to position itself as a more acceptable party in the post–Cold War era.

Despite these changes, the new Social Democrats failed to emulate their European social-democratic colleagues, who have formed numerous governments since the 1960s. Only when the LDP fractured in 1993 did they join a governing coalition, and when Socialist Murayama Tomiichi became prime minister in 1994, his eighteen months in office were marked by constant tension within his own party. The party's identity, especially in foreign policy, was destroyed when Murayama abandoned all pretense of opposition to the Self Defense Forces. Although some important steps were taken during the Murayama administration to address problems that the LDP had long denied, notably compensation for atomic bomb victims and "comfort women," the legacy of this period in government was further marginalization of the SDP.

The Japan Communist Party (JCP) is rooted in the proletarian politics of the post–World War I period. Established in 1922 (the year after the CCP's founding), the JCP enjoyed support from the USSR for several decades. The JCP is urban-based, and its strongest supporters have been those dissatisfied with the existing order. It has frequently criticized the close U.S.-Japan relationship and, along with the Socialists, has appealed to voters in the peace movement. Its showing in Diet elections has never surpassed 12 percent, although, like other leftist parties, it has often done better in municipal elections. This pattern seems unlikely to change: As the Social Democrats moved to the center and New Komeito (Clean Government Party) slipped into governing coalitions, the Com-

munists remained one of the few bellwethers of voter dissatisfaction with establishment parties. But the party confronts a dilemma that European communist
parties have also had to wrestle with: It has moderated its domestic and foreign
policies and conceivably might join a leftist coalition government, but (like the
Socialists) it has a declining membership and aging leadership. Any further mod-
eration of its policies means the party loses its remaining claim to distinctiveness.

Buddhists and "Democrats" in the Floating Center. The center of Japan's political party spectrum is fluid, consisting of a variety of parties that can realistically
aspire to share in governing only by joining a coalition. Of these centrist parties,
the most durable has been New Komeito, although in recent years attention has
focused on the Democratic Party of Japan (DPJ) as an alternative to the LDP.

Komeito was established in the mid-1960s as an offshoot of the Soka Gakkai,
the lay organization of the Nichiren Shoshu Buddhist sect described in Chapter
4. Soka Gakkai is a proselytizing organization committed to infusing politics with
its Buddhist values. Although formal Komeito-Soka Gakkai ties were severed in
1970, the original religious links made Komeito suspect for many Japanese even
as they made it more appealing to others. The party's constituents included many
alienated voters, including low-income, less educated, and female voters.[20] Ideologically, Komeito rejected both the extreme individualism of Western democracy
and Marxist collectivism, instead supporting strong welfare measures and traditional values.

Komeito's electoral fortunes have fluctuated since the 1960s. Although originally considered an opposition party during the period of LDP dominance, as
early as the 1980s it made clear its interest in a centrist-progressive alliance in order to govern. It joined the 1993 Hosokawa coalition government, then formally
disbanded in late 1994 to join with eight other parties and groups to form the
Shinshinto (New Frontier Party), which became the main opposition party for a
short time in the mid-1990s. In 1998, the party was reestablished as New Komeito and since 1999 has been a coalition partner in LDP-led governments.

New Komeito's legacy is important in two respects. First, its grassroots organization and appeal as a coalition partner rely heavily on the vote-mobilizing abilities of Soka Gakkai. Second, Soka Gakkai's strength raises questions about the
role of religion in Japanese politics. The question of whether Soka Gakkai exerted
improper influence in politics came to the fore in a 1995–1996 debate over revision of Japan's Religious Corporation Law, which provides tax benefits for officially recognized religious groups and generally limits government interference in
their activities. In 1995, the government proposed amending the law to tighten
registration and reporting requirements for religious groups. It argued that the

proposed changes would have made it easier to track the activities of the religious cult, Aum Shinrikyo, which was held responsible for the terrorist sarin attacks, including one in a Tokyo subway, in 1994 and 1995. Opponents argued that the amendments constituted a thinly veiled attack on Soka Gakkai's support for Shinshinto in the 1995 House of Councillors election.[21] Despite opposition, the amendments to the Religious Corporation Law passed the Diet in late 1995.

The Democratic Party of Japan (DPJ). The DPJ was initially created in the 1990s, and is a good example of a former LDP faction that has become a credible opposition to the LDP. Ozawa Ichiro, a long-standing LDP member of the House of Representatives, rose to become secretary general of the LDP by the late 1980s. He subsequently became a key player in the party's fractionalization and the efforts to create new parties in the 1990s, including the DPJ. The DPJ was reorganized in 2003 when it merged with the small Liberal Party. Ideologically, the party styles itself as socially liberal or center-left; it includes former members of the SDP who left the party in the 1990s, as well as former LDP members.

At its inception, the DPJ was largely a coalition of smaller parties opposed to the LDP. Its internal diversity is reflected in its internal factions and also in the difficulty it has had creating stable leadership. Between 2003 and 2008, for example, the party operated under five different presidents. In 2007, its then-president, Ozawa Ichiro, resigned after criticism that he had inappropriately considered joining a "grand coalition" to govern with the LDP (see Chapter 9). In the 2007 House of Councillors election, however, the party made a major breakthrough, winning a majority.

From its origin, the DPJ's distinguishing feature has been its drive to replace the LDP as the governing party, and its 2007 upper-house victory contributed to the inability of the LDP-New Komeito governing coalition to pass legislation. In early 2009, for example, it pursued a confrontational strategy of pressuring the government to call elections ahead of the normal expiration of the House of Representatives four-year term in the hopes of capitalizing on Prime Minister Aso Taro's unpopularity and popular dissatisfaction with the LDP.[22] It was not inconceivable that an LDP loss in the 2009 lower house elections could provoke the breakup of the party, only to be replaced by the DPJ, the party that most resembles it, and from which it was born.

India: The BJP—From Opposition to Coalition Governments

Japan's confusing array of parties is more than matched by India's. Over fifty recognized parties contested the 2009 Lok Sabha elections, and thirty-five parties were represented in the Lok Sabha after the 2004 elections, although nearly half of these held three or fewer seats. Added to this is the array of parties that are prominent in state-level politics, such as the Bahujan Samaj Party (BSP), the governing party in Uttar Pradesh, whose Dalit chief minister, Mayawati, was mentioned in Chapter 2. The BSP elected sixteen members to the lower house in 2004, although many state-based parties are represented only in their state assemblies. Photo 12.1 shows the party logo, an elephant, painted on a wall in the city of Varanasi (Banaras).

Together with the decline of Congress, two patterns in Indian parties stand out: the rise of the Bharatiya Janata Party as a national force and the multiplication of state-based parties. Parties have often drawn explicitly on traditional values or affiliations for their voter appeal, but by the mid-1990s, the Bharatiya Janata Party had captured attention for the way it built its appeal on a call for a *Hindu* India, or *Hindutva*.

PHOTO 12.1 Bahujan Samaj Party symbol, Varanasi. Photo courtesy of James W. Boyd.

The Bharatiya Janata Party (BJP). All Indian parties, to a degree, try to enhance their electoral appeal by referring to traditional cultural or religious themes. The BJP, in particular, benefited from the reaction against secularism that grew in much of India during the late twentieth century, and it has also successfully tapped nationalist sentiment. Nationalism marks the key elements of the BJP platform, including a strong defense posture as well as "cultural nationalism," which it defines as synonymous with *Hindutva*.[23] The BJP has long called for *swadeshi* (self-reliance) in India's economic development approach, and thus links its position to the movement developed in the early twentieth century by Indian nationalists. It is this *nationalist* platform as much as any specifically religious appeal that accounts for the breadth of its electoral reach.

From the date of its official establishment in 1980 onward,[24] the BJP systematically increased its percentage of votes in Lok Sabha elections from 7.4 (1984) to 25.6 percent in 1998, dropping back to approximately 24 percent in 1999. Although the BJP total dipped again in the 2004 elections, it remained one of India's two largest parties. But its support has always been concentrated in the north, west, and central states. For example, in the 2004 elections, it won at least 1 seat in 18 states, but 80 percent of its seats came in 7 states, where it contested most heavily (see the "seats contested" column of Table 12.1). In contrast, the Indian National Congress elected at least one member of parliament from every state.

A combination of factors accounted for the BJP's growth: the appeal of its clearly stated principles, the cohesiveness of its organization and apparent probity (especially in contrast to Congress), its effective grassroots mobilization (including the use of disciplined RSS members during elections), and its willingness to exploit religious sentiments.[25] The last two factors have been especially controversial, fueling the fires of those who attack the BJP as a right-wing, antiminority, chauvinistic party responsible for the 1992–1993 Ayodhya crisis and the 2002 attacks on Muslims in the state of Gujarat (see Chapter 11).

TABLE 12.1 Selected Results, 1999 and 2004 Lok Sabha Elections

Party	% of Votes Cast Nationally		% of Votes Won in Seats Contested		Number of Seats Won	
	1999	2004	1999	2004	1999	2004
Bharatiya Janata Party (BJP)	23.75	22.16	39.54	34.39	182	138
Indian National Congress (INC)	28.31	26.53	34.01	34.43	114	145
Communist Party Marxist (CPM)	5.41	5.66	35.16	42.31	33	43

Source: Adapted from the Elections Commission of India, www.eci.gov.in.

In anticipation of gaining a larger plurality in the Lok Sabha, the BJP advanced by eight months the elections due in 2004. To the surprise of most observers, its campaign emphasizing India's strong economic growth during the previous five years failed to persuade enough voters. It lost forty-four seats and was replaced by the Congress party at the head of the 2004–2009 coalition government. Postelection analyses suggested that the economic growth had benefited the urban middle and upper classes, whereas rural areas and agriculture had stagnated. Poor voters took their revenge, not just by returning the INC to power, but also by voting in greater numbers for leftist parties, such as the Communist Party (CPM).[26] Despite this setback, the BJP remained the only party large enough to challenge the Congress party in the 2009 election as a "national" party.

Coalition Partners: Class, Caste, and Region. Both the BJP and the Congress-led governments (1999–2004 and 2004–2009) ran close to their full terms, with the result that India enjoyed relative stability at the national level. Neither party seems likely to form a majority government in the foreseeable future; each has managed to lead a government in recent years only with the support of numerous smaller parties. As argued in Chapter 9, coalition governments are now the norm in India and likely to remain so for the foreseeable future. A confusing array of largely regional parties either supports or opposes the government. The most durable of these are two communist parties, the Communist Party of India (CPI) and the Communist Party of India Marxist (CPM), which split from the CPI in 1964; the regional culture-language parties and caste-based parties, ranging from two Tamil Nadu parties, to the little Sikkim Democratic Front and the Dalit-led Bahujan Samaj Party mentioned above. Even the class-based Marxist parties are largely regional parties: In 2004, thirty-eight of the CPM's forty-three Lok Sabha seats, for example, were won in the two states of Kerala and West Bengal.

Coalition Politics

The topic of coalition governments was introduced in Chapter 9. Here it is sufficient to review some of the practical implications for India and Japan. Due to the need for bargaining and compromise to hold a government together, a party that campaigned on one platform to attract votes may, once elected, moderate that platform to avoid alienating coalition partners. Such a strategy presents other problems, however. To illustrate, after 1999, Indian Prime Minister Vajpayee (BJP) was frequently caught between Hindu "hardliners" both inside and outside his party. It was in the interest of the BJP-led government to minimize communal violence, for example, by resisting some Hindu demands for immediate construction of a temple to Ram at Ayodhya. This very resistance by the government, however, may have had the unintended consequence of provoking Hindu nationalists to more violence in order to pressure the government. Consequently, another strategy for the Vajpayee government was to pursue less moderate policies in foreign policy (such as deployment of nuclear weapons or refusal to compromise on the Kashmir conflict) in order to appeal to broad national interests.

A different set of problems may be seen in Japanese coalition governments, where both interparty and intra-LDP negotiation and compromise result in near immobility. An illustration of this situation was the inability of the Japanese government to take the kind of initiatives—especially policies to enhance economic recovery—promised by Prime Minister Koizumi when he assumed leadership of a three-party coalition government in 2001, even though he was the strongest prime minister Japan has had for two decades.

In sum, by the late 1990s, the era of minority governments and coalition politics had become part of the political landscape of India and Japan, and it seemed unlikely that either the Congress or the LDP could resuscitate itself sufficiently to turn the clock back to a time of former dominance, although the two parties remained central to coalition arithmetic. Before discussing the role of electoral systems in these changes, this section closes with a look at China's "democratic parties" and the short-lived effort to establish a true opposition party.

China's Other Parties

The PRC's 1982 constitution, like its predecessors, acknowledges in its preamble the existence of "democratic parties" that are part of "a broad patriotic united front" under the Communist Party's leadership. The Chinese People's Consultative Conference serves as an umbrella, or "united front," organization for these parties. When the constitution was amended by the National People's Congress in 1993, the following sentence, which further acknowledges multiple parties, was added to the preamble: "Multi-party cooperation and the political consultation system *under the leadership of the Communist Party of China* shall continue and develop for the extended future" [emphasis added].

There are eight recognized small "democratic parties" in China, all dating to the pre-1949 period.[27] Since 1949, these parties have had no political freedom to deviate from "the leadership of the Communist Party," and they are incidental to China's political process.

More interesting for the long-term evolution of Chinese politics is the potential for independent political parties. Many Westerners see the existence of competition among multiple parties as a procedural prerequisite for democracy. However, the connection between political parties and democracy depends both on the nature of the parties and on the context in which they operate. The Chinese context is marked by three factors that argue against a competitive multiparty system: the organization and ideology of the CCP, a Confucian tradition that emphasized harmony, and the chaotic historical legacy associated with China's brief efforts to introduce European-style democracy after the 1912 Republican revolution.[28] Despite these factors, the ideal of an independent, opposition political party has its Chinese advocates, including those who launched the China Democracy Party (CDP) in 1998. Within six months, a coalition of intellectuals, students, and workers had established party committees in two dozen cities and provinces,[29] proclaiming their nonviolent commitment to a straightforward goal: "The CDP is a political party that calls for fair competition with the CCP."[30] By the end of 1999, all the major leaders of the CDP had been jailed on charges of conspiring to overthrow the government. Ten years later, Wu Bangguo, the chairman of the National People's Congress, reaffirmed the necessity of maintaining the CCP's monopoly on power in his comments to the NPC's 2009 session.[31]

Election Dynamics

In liberal democracies, political parties and elections are inseparable. A core rationale for political parties is to aggregate voter preferences in order to contest, and win, elections. Electoral systems set the rules for these contests, advantaging some kinds of parties over others. As an example, parties that may not have majority support anywhere but that have widespread plurality support (for example, one-third of the votes cast) typically benefit from the "first-past-the-post" (FPTP), single-member constituency (SMC) system that is used in the United States, Canada, Britain, and India. Small parties, especially those not regionally concentrated, prefer some kind of proportional representation (PR) system because it guarantees them legislative representation in approximate proportion to the votes they receive in the elections.

FPTP in India

Elections for the Lok Sabha (and also the state assemblies) are conducted under the FPTP system, first introduced by the British and maintained after independence. Voters elect a single member of Parliament from each district. Like Britain and Canada, but unlike the United States, candidates need not be residents of the districts where they run. By-elections (interim elections) are relatively common, and party leaders typically choose a safe constituency to run in, even when it means forcing the resignation of a colleague who already holds the district's seat.

Under the FPTP system, the highest vote-getter wins, no matter how low his or her percentage of the votes cast. A fragmented opposition benefits a dominant party like Congress, even though support for the latter may decline over time. Because part of the philosophy behind FPTP is to produce a stable governing majority (rather than to accurately represent the diversity of voter preference), it is possible for a party to win a considerably higher proportion of seats than votes. Thus, the FPTP system may inflate a party's majority, either when it has a plurality over a wide territory or when it is geographically concentrated. In 1999, for example, Congress won the largest percentage of votes, but due to its regional concentration of votes, the BJP won more seats.[32] In 2004, however, the percentages of votes received and seats won were very close.

Controversy in Japan

In Japan, the electoral system was blamed for the inordinate cost of Diet elections and, more generally, for contributing to political corruption. These problems were debated for twenty years before the rise of new governments in the wake of the LDP collapse in 1993 produced a political coalition that could effect reform. To understand the delay in reform, it is necessary to understand the logic of the old system.

For the 1993 election, there were 511 seats in the House of Representatives. These seats were divided among 130 multiple-member districts, most electing 3 to 5 representatives. In each district, voters cast their ballot for only one candidate, with the top vote-getters (the number depending on the seats to be filled) to be the winners. To win a majority in the House (and thus ensure the ability to form a government), a party needed a majority of 256 representatives elected from the 130 districts. This meant, in effect, winning an average of two seats in each district, necessitating competition between candidates from the same party. This intraparty competition helped perpetuate factionalism and money politics, especially in the LDP.

Proposals to change this system date at least to the early 1970s, but only in the early 1990s did financial scandals force LDP leaders to address electoral reform with concrete legislative proposals that, however, never made it through the Diet. Foot-dragging by some faction leaders over reform was an important reason for the LDP's fragmentation in 1992–1993, and the desire for reform was the most important bond holding the first non-LDP coalition government together in 1993. Cabinet members and party leaders agreed that the multimember constituency system should be replaced by a combined SMC-PR system, but disagreement centered on how many seats would be elected under each system. Two government changes occurred before any legislation was adopted. By the time the Murayama government took up the issue, the seat distribution had been renegotiated to 300 SMC and 200 PR from the originally proposed 250–250, because the LDP saw proportional representation as advantaging small parties at the expense of the larger parties that could field candidates in all constituencies. The new system was used in the 1996 House of Representatives election, although the reappearance of the LDP in governing coalitions resulted in another change to reduce the number of PR seats to 180.

Japanese voters now cast two ballots, one for a local district candidate and the other for a party in a nationwide constituency, in elections to both the lower and the upper house. The principal differences are in election timing (in the House of Representatives, variable with a maximum of four years, and in the House of Councillors, fixed six-year terms with triennial elections) and constituency size. Photo 12.2 shows a polling place for a House of Councillors election.

Local Elections in China

Chinese elections, held only at the local level so far, play a role very different from elections in India and Japan. Their purpose is to enhance the legitimacy and effectiveness of China's one-party system by portraying the government as more representative of popular interests and also by providing feedback on problems (with policies and officials) at the local level.[33] (Broadly speaking, of course, elections also help legitimize

PHOTO 12.2 Japanese election judges. Photo courtesy of James W. Boyd.

governing systems in liberal democracies.) Because China does not have a true multi-party system, elections do not serve to replace one governing majority with another. Whether they serve as an indicator of the decay or the revitalization of one-party rule is a more difficult matter to judge.

The principle of competitive elections in both party and state organs was introduced as part of the reforms of the late 1970s to early 1980s. Elections initially meant simply more candidates than positions, as well as (in principle) secret ballots. Even in the absence of competitive party politics, these were substantive—and substantial—reforms. The 1979 Election Law, followed by laws passed in 1987 and 1998, together with the provisions of the 1982 PRC Constitution, produced more competitive and transparent elections for village committees and local people's congresses. By the late 1990s, the government had undertaken a major effort to systematize electoral procedures throughout the country.[34]

The *intent* of the elections may have been to consolidate the party's position, but the *results* could be different. Assessing the results of the reforms is hard (and premature), partly because of the diversity of China's villages and towns and partly because the context in China has been changing so rapidly. Nonetheless, recent research has raised several provocative questions about political attitudes and participation in China as seen through elections. For example, it isn't clear what expectations voters bring to the ballot box. One study has found that people with a stronger democratic orientation were more likely to vote, whereas another study found that they were less likely to vote.[35]

A different question is whether voting will stimulate other forms of political participation. It seems clear that the formal legal and constitutional changes of the past three decades have gradually legitimized forms of political action quite different from the mass movements and campaigns of the Mao era. For some years, there have been reports of delegates to local people's congresses rejecting party-approved candidates,[36] and individual candidates persisting in their attempts to petition their way onto ballots despite the opposition of party officials.[37]

Finally, what will be the outcomes of thousands of elections, as they gather momentum across the country? One possibility is greater congruence of policy views between elected officials and electors and greater responsiveness of the former to the latter.[38] Rather different prospects are that villages will become increasingly fragmented, making coherent development policies more difficult, or that "money politics" and corruption will come to dominate the electoral process—much as it has in other countries: "As in the case of Western liberal democracies, nothing prohibits the electorates from reelecting corrupt village leaders."[39] A more optimistic assessment is that, over the long term, the elections help institutionalize the rule of law in China.[40]

Summary

It would be easy to conclude that the great political dreams of a half century ago in three of the world's most important nations have failed, largely because of self-interest, corruption, and factionalism in their dominant parties. Uncertain of their authority, CCP leaders called in the army to clear Tiananmen Square of protesters in 1989; the party itself admits thousands of members have been expelled for corruption. In India, the sorrow of Mahatma Gandhi over communal violence was reborn in the violence of Ayodhya and the domestic terrorism of the twenty-first century; cynicism about democracy and politics permeates public debates from slum corners to middle-class living rooms. In Japan, it took party leaders more than two decades to address the need for electoral reform, even as the momentum for political change that seemed so promising in the early 1990s drifted away within a few years.

Despite these and other signs of decay accompanying the legacy of one-party and one-party–dominant rule, the political dynamics are far more complex than is suggested by the overview of parties in this chapter. Parties and elections are central to the long-term viability of liberal democracies. But they alone, even when functioning well, do not tell the full story of democratic health. Democracy is more than party competition and electoral procedures. It is reflected in other modes of political participation and citizen behavior. It is sustained (or corroded) by other institutions, and is measured not just by procedural safeguards but also by substantive, socioeconomic progress.

All is not bleak: Local elections in China, however limited, are a wedge that pries open the CCP's political monopoly. In India, the chaos of political parties responds in some measure to the voices of millions of new voters, most of whom were subjects of, but hardly participants in, political decisions affecting them a half century ago. Meanwhile, in contrast to most of Asia, Japan—despite political immobility—remained a model of multiparty democracy.

Notes

1. The "new social stratum" includes private entrepreneurs, technicians and managerial-level staff in private or foreign-funded companies, and self-employed individuals. In 2007, it was reported that 3.18 million party members worked in private companies and that an additional 134,000 people from the "new social stratum" had applied for membership. Approximately one-third of the members accepted between 2002 and 2007 were college graduates. Report from the Press Center of the Seventeenth National CCP Congress at http://english.cpcnews.cn/92247/6279373.html, retrieved November 8, 2008.

2. Ronald J. Hrebenar, *Japan's New Party System* (Boulder: Westview Press, 2000), chaps. 3 and 4. For an analysis of candidate and party fund-raising, see Matthew Carlson, *Money Politics in Japan* (Boulder: Lynne Rienner, 2007).

3. Chie Nakane, *Japanese Society* (Berkeley: University of California Press, 1970). See the complementary analysis by Takeshi Ishida, *Japanese Society* (New York: Random House, 1971), chap. 7.

4. Koichi Kishimoto, *Politics in Modern Japan: Development and Organization*, 3rd ed. (Tokyo: Japan Echo, 1988), 102. For a timeline showing faction lineages from 1955 to 2001, see Ian Neary, *The State and Politics in Japan* (Cambridge: Polity Press, 2002), 68.

5. *The Daily Yomiuri*, November 23, 2002. Historically one of the most important incentives for faction membership has been a cabinet position, with prime ministers balancing their personnel appointments to reflect factional strength.

6. Masami Ito, "LDP—A Party Defined by Factions," *The Japan Times*, October 15, 2008, retrieved November 23, 2008, from http://search.japantimes.co.jp/cgi-bin/nn20081015i1.html.

7. Paul R. Brass, *The Politics of India Since Independence* (Cambridge, Mass.: Harvard University Press, 1990), 66.

8. Robert L. Hardgrave Jr. and Stanley A. Kochanek, *India: Government and Politics in a Developing Nation*, 5th ed. (Fort Worth: Harcourt Brace College Publishers, 1993), 199.

9. Ashutosh Varshney, *Ethnic Conflict and Civic Life: Hindus and Muslims in India* (New Haven: Yale University Press, 2002), 75.

10. Lowell Dittmer, "Pattern of Elite Strife and Succession in Chinese Politics," *China Quarterly* 123 (September 1990), 405–430.

11. See, for example, Susan L. Shirk, "The Politics of Industrial Reform," in *The Political Economy of Reform in Post-Mao China*, eds. Elizabeth J. Perry and Christine Wong (Cambridge, Mass.: Council on East Asian Studies/Harvard University, 1985), 216–220. Shirk linked factions to entrenched bureaucratic interests with different stakes in reform policies. See also her analysis in *The Political Logic of Economic Reform* (Berkeley: University of California Press, 1993).

12. Jing Huang, *Factionalism in Chinese Communist Politics* (Cambridge: Cambridge University Press, 2002), chap. 3.

13. David Shambaugh, *China's Communist Party: Atrophy and Adaptation* (Berkeley: University of California Press, and Washington, D.C.: Woodrow Wilson Center Press, 2008), 152–157; and Susan L. Shirk, *China: Fragile Superpower* (Oxford: Oxford University Press, 2007), 39–52.

14. Shambaugh, 155.

15. James C. Mulvenon and Michael S. Chase, "The Role of *Mishus* in the Chinese Political System," in *China's Leadership in the 21st Century: The Rise of the*

Fourth Generation, eds. David M. Finkelstein and Maryanne Kivlehan (Armonk, N.Y.: M. E. Sharpe, 2003), 140–151.

16. Personal *mishus* are overwhelmingly male, but a notable exception was Deng Rong, Deng Xiaoping's daughter. Wei Li and Lucian W. Pye, "The Ubiquitous Role of the *Mishus* in Chinese Politics," *China Quarterly* 132 (December 1992), 913–914.

17. Bruce Gilley suggests that because *guanxi* politics reflects cultural norms, it may persist even with democratization, as it has in Taiwan. *China's Democratic Future* (New York: Columbia University Press, 2004), 196. See also Doug Guthrie's discussion of the tensions between *guanxi* and efforts to establish rational and legal norms in China's new economy. *China and Globalization: The Social, Economic, and Political Transformation of Chinese Society* (London: Routledge, 2006), 103–112.

18. "How India Voted," *India Today*, May 31, 1996, 27.

19. John L. Thornton, "Long Time Coming: The Prospects for Democracy in China," *Foreign Affairs* 87, no. 1 (January/February 2008), 9.

20. Hrebenar, chap. 6. Komeito's successor, New Komeito, emphasizes its goal of representing owners and employees of small businesses and notes that Soka Gakkai, with its eight million households, constitutes its main support group. See the party's website at www.komei.or.jp/en.

21. *Japan Times Weekly International Edition*, December 11–17, 1995.

22. Hiroshi Oyama and Tetsuya Ennyu, "Stormy Waters Await Diet in Election Year," *Daily Yomiuri Online*, January 3, 2009, www.yomiuri.co.jp/dy/national/2009 0103TDY03103.htm, accessed January 4, 2009.

23. See the party's "vision document" prepared for the 2004 election at www.bjp .org/Press/mar_3104a.htm. The document is careful to specify that *Hindutva* respects India's multiple faiths and secular history; it also reiterates its commitment to building a temple to Ram at Ayodhya.

24. The BJP has an older lineage, of course. Its historical roots lie in nineteenth-century Hindu revivalism in opposition to British rule. As an electoral face of Hindu nationalism, it was created in 1952 as the Bharatiya Jan Sangh and participated in India's first coalition government in 1977. For the history of the movement and party, see Christophe Jaffrelot, *The Hindu Nationalist Movement in India* (New York: Columbia University Press, 1996).

25. Varshney, 76. The RSS (Rashtriya Swayamsevak Sangh) is the militant Hindu organization linked to the assassination of Mahatma Gandhi.

26. Zoya Hasan, "Indian Elections 2004: A Setback for the BJP's Exclusivist Agenda," September 2004, talk at the Centre d'études et de recherches internationales (Paris), accessed November 15, 2008, at http://www.ceri-sciencespo.com/archive/sept04/artzh.pdf.

27. Included in the eight parties is a remnant Kuomintang party (the KMT is Taiwan's long-term ruling party). For a history and description of the parties, see

english.people.com.cn/data/China_in_brief/Political_Parties/Democratic%20Parties. html, retrieved January 4, 2008.

28. Suzanne Ogden, *Inklings of Democracy in China* (Cambridge, Mass.: Harvard Asia Center and Harvard University Press, 2002), 42–48, 61–69, and chap. 7; Shao-hua Hu, *Explaining Chinese Democratization* (Westport, Conn.: Praeger, 2000), 23–27 and 44–54.

29. Teresa Wright, "The China Democracy Party and the Politics of Protest in the 1980s–1990s," *China Quarterly* 172 (December 2002), 906–927.

30. http://www.freechina.net/cdp/ (accessed March 5, 2003); see also the extensive report on the CDP at the Human Rights Watch website: www.hrw.org/reports/2000/china.

31. Michael Wines, "In China, No Plans to Emulate West's Way," *New York Times*, March 10, 2009.

32. A more striking example was the 1984 election held shortly after Indira Gandhi's assassination, in which her son Rajiv led the Congress to a victory of 48 percent of the vote—and a seat majority of more than 76 percent.

33. Jie Chen and Yang Zhong, "Why Do People Vote in Semicompetitive Elections?" *The Journal of Politics* 64, no. 1 (February 2002), 181.

34. For an explanation of the elections, see Ogden, chap. 6. In the late 1990s, the Chinese Ministry of Civil Affairs began a collaborative project with the Carter Center to improve election procedures; see www.chinaelections.org/en.

35. Compare the studies by Tianjian Shi, "Voting and Nonvoting in China: Voting Behavior in Plebiscitary and Limited-Choice Elections," *The Journal of Politics* 61, no. 4 (1999) 1115–1139; and Chen and Zhong, "Why Do People Vote in Semi-competitive Elections?"

36. John Pomfret, "Delegates Take on One-Party Rule in China's Heartland," *Washington Post*, March 4, 2003 (online edition).

37. Joseph Kahn "Democratic Hopes Test China's Political Limits," *New York Times*, March 2, 2003.

38. Melanie Manion, "The Electoral Connection in the Chinese Countryside," *American Political Science Review* 90, no. 4 (December 1996), 736–748.

39. Ogden, 209. Ogden points out that the combination of economic and political liberalization has facilitated the resurgence of "feudal" organizations (such as clans) and practices (including patriarchy, nepotism, and bribery) in village politics, 208–210.

40. Comments by Yawei Liu, Associate Director, the Carter Center, at the 16th Annual Meeting of the Association of Chinese Political Studies, Knoxville, Tennessee, April 4, 2003.

13

Development, Democratization, and Governance in Asia

Asian countries have had widely varying experiences with development. The one common characteristic across the region is a clear commitment to "develop" and "modernize." What this commitment means in practice, of course, shifts through time and across nations. This chapter explores the broad picture of the development experience in Asia. Several issues add to the complexity of this discussion, however. First, the meaning of development is controversial and therefore progress in meeting development goals is hard to measure. Second, ideas about development have always linked economics and politics, raising questions about the relationship between economic well-being and political freedom. In the twenty-first century, democratization has become part of our thinking about development, but disagreement over the connections between these two processes is persistent. Hence we should not be surprised that the contrasting patterns of progress in India and China lead to vigorous debate. The third issue is that though scholars and practitioners may debate development, ultimately the authoritative voice is that of political elites, for whom development is a pathway to legitimacy and power. However, one of the most important consequences of development in Asia has been the creation of new avenues for grassroots politics, with the result that government decisions may be challenged by those who are affected by them. Moreover, development policies often have unintended consequences, a point seen earlier in the case of China's one-child policy.

The first section of the chapter examines some of the well-known quantitative measures of development that emphasize economic well-being, including gross domestic product (GDP), poverty indexes, and human development indicators. This overview shows how international thinking about the nature of development evolved in the last half of the twentieth century. The second section approaches the debate over the meaning of development qualitatively by highlighting the relationship between political and economic factors. What can we learn about links between economic well-being and democratization by looking at the historical experience of India, China, and Japan? What does the discussion of "governance" bring to our understanding of development and democracy?

Measuring Development

What, exactly, is development? Throughout history, societies have always *changed*; does this mean they have *developed*? Most people would agree that *development* entails a certain kind of change, but embedded in the concept is the assumption of progress—that life will improve over time. The origins of the concept of development, both as historical reality and as aspiration, are found largely in the Western European experience with modernity over the past several centuries. From this experience we derive a number of assumptions that have come to dominate our worldview: Humans can alter their physical environments; all humans, not just the rich, have the right to improved material conditions; greater human productivity generates more material wealth and new technologies are an important way to increase productivity; governments bear some responsibility for crafting policies to improve the material lot of their citizens. Note that these are very general views and do not specify the kinds of governments that are most likely to generate growth or the best policies to pursue.

How to measure development? For much of the twentieth century, conventional thinking about development emphasized straightforward measures of the value of goods and services produced within economies. These measures rest on the assumptions derived from classical economics that development means quantifiable expansion in the size and complexity of the economy and that economic growth will "trickle down" to individuals. Although gross national product (GNP) and gross domestic product (GDP) require different calculations and yield different numbers, both rest on comparable assumptions about the central importance of overall economic growth as shown by increased productivity.[1] As measures of the economic conditions of a country and its population, such calculations assume that the higher the GNP or GDP, the better the quality of life a country and its citizens enjoy.

For several decades, scholars and practitioners have challenged the emphasis on single measures of economic growth, arguing that development is a complex, multifaceted process. For example, GNP and GDP are mean figures; they do not tell us the ways in which the distribution of wealth may be skewed or concentrated in particular regions or sub-populations of a country. Thus a country that is growing economically may still have huge pockets of poverty that could provoke political instability and eventually undermine its long-term development. Further, the measures exclude unpaid activity, including subsistence farming and family-maintenance activities such as child- and elder-care and housework. As a result, "women's work," in particular, is frequently uncounted or undercounted because it yields no monetary income. Finally, such measures cannot, by their nature, include qualitative factors that people value, such as many dimensions of the physical and cultural environments that enhance the human quality of life.

To address these kinds of limitations, a variety of more refined indicators that go beyond GNP and GDP have been devised to enhance our understanding of the multiple dimensions of development. One of the most extensive investigations focuses on poverty, using tools created primarily by economists. The well-known Gini coefficient or index, named after an Italian statistician, is a measure of the degree of inequality in a variable such as income.[2] Using the index, we can see that income inequality in a number of high-income countries such as France, Canada, and Norway has generally declined in recent decades, while it has noticeably increased in the United States.[3] One might ask, therefore: Has the United States become *more* or *less* developed? In Asia, Japan has comparatively low income inequality, and although it has gone up and down in certain periods, and is currently increasing, it is not dramatically different from what it was in the middle of the twentieth century. China, in contrast, has seen a substantial increase in inequality in the past two decades, despite impressive increases in GDP, and along with Nepal, now has the greatest income inequality among the developing countries in Asia.[4] The income trajectory for India also shows growing inequality. In India, for example, semi-skilled and unskilled workers live and work in the shadows of shiny new shopping centers, such as those found in the New Delhi suburb of Gurgaon (see Photo 2.1).[5] This is a common sight in many Asian cities and symbolizes the inequities of growth. Table 13.1 compares the most recent Gini coefficients for India, China, and Japan, with the United States and Norway added for purposes of comparison. Note that a number of zero (0) would be maximum equality and 100 maximum inequality; thus the higher the number, the greater degree of inequality.

By the 1970s, both quantitative measures such as the Gini index and qualitative evidence led to a reconsideration of the meaning of development and the reasons for the exclusion of millions of people from the benefits of economic growth. Concerns that the economic growth policies pursued during the past two decades had not eliminated widespread poverty, and indeed might have exacerbated it, led to a "basic needs" approach in the 1980s. This approach highlighted the provision of

TABLE 13.1 Gini Measure of Income Inequality

Country	Date*	Gini Coefficient*
China	2007	47
India	2004	36
Japan	2002	38
United States	2007	45
Norway	2005	28

* The most recent date of available information. All numbers are estimates.
Source: Compiled and adapted from Asian Development Bank (ADB), *Key Indicators of Developing Asian and Pacific Countries 2007* (Manila: ADB, 2007), 29, found online at www.adb.org/Documents/ Book/Key_Indicators/2007; and Central Intelligence Agency (CIA), *2008 World Factbook* (Washington, D.C.: CIA, 2008), found online at https://www.cia.gov/library/publications/the-world-factbook/.

adequate goods and services, ranging from food and shelter to public infrastructure. In the 1990s, development analysts sought to go beyond the basic needs approach to address poverty in the context of the broader social meanings of development. It is now safe to say that "the elimination of poverty is a key concern of all those interested in the development of poor countries, and now provides the main justification for promoting economic growth and development."[6]

The decade of the 1990s was remarkable for the expanded definitions of development and multiple measures of development that international organizations proposed. Together these definitions and new measures offer a more complex and comprehensive understanding of poverty and its implications for development. In 1997, the United Nations Development Program (UNDP) inaugurated the use of its Human Poverty Index (HPI) as a multidimensional composite index to combine different dimensions of human deprivation. The HPI, built on both the income and basic needs approaches, emphasizes four aspects of life: longevity, knowledge, economic condition, and social inclusion in its effort to understand both economic and social marginalization.[7]

Perhaps the best known indicator of poverty, and by implication, development, is the World Bank's "dollar-a-day" comparative measure of debilitating deprivation.[8] The appeal of this measure has been its simplicity as a slogan (and political exhortation), as well as a comparative indicator. For example, the first of the United Nation's eight Millennium Development Goals is to eradicate extreme poverty and hunger, by reducing by half "the proportion of people living on less than a dollar a day."[9] The dollar-a-day definition was adjusted in 2008 to set the poverty line at US$1.25. For students of development it's too soon to say if this adjustment will have any practical consequences, although it has already led to some revised poverty calculations for China. World Bank researchers concluded that by using the poverty line of $1.25, China's poverty rate was considerably higher than in past estimates. However, the data also suggested a larger reduction in the number of poor between 1981 and 2005 than previously assumed. So tinkering with the measure is unlikely to change our conclusions about the relative success of China's development strategy. It has succeeded in dramatically reducing the absolute level of destitution in China over the past quarter-century, even though millions of people are still extremely poor, as measured by their ability to consume.[10]

One of the most widely used measures of development is the Human Development Indicator, or HDI, introduced by the UNDP in its 1990 *Human Development Report*. The HDI has four components: life expectancy at birth; the adult literacy rate; combined primary, secondary, and tertiary school enrollment; and per capita GDP. Thus the HDI combines economic and social measures, as does the Human Poverty Index. The HDI was followed by the introduction of the Gender Development Indicator (GDI), which uses the same first three indicators, and the fourth is estimated earned income; all are adjusted to account for differences between men and women. The newest measure is the Gender Empowerment Measure (GEM), which the UNDP introduced in 1995.[11] The GEM is significant because it adds political indicators to the overall measure: The percentage of seats held in the national parliament by women, and the proportion of female legislators, senior officials, and managers, are part of the measure. Despite both conceptual and technical shortcomings in the measures, they illustrate the way in which the UNDP has progressively broadened its approach to development to accommodate social and political, as well as economic, criteria. The conceptualization of the HDI and GDI draws heavily from economist Amartya Sen's "capability approach" to development, which emphasizes the abilities of "persons to lead the kind of lives they value."[12]

Taken together, what do these measures tell us about development in Asia? Table 13.2 is a place to start. The table compares nine countries listed with several of the indicators discussed above: GDP per capita, absolute poverty (using the HPI), HDI, the HDI-GDI gap, and GEM. For purposes of illustration, the United States is listed along with eight Asian countries. In addition to India, China, and Japan, the table includes South Korea, the Philippines, Indonesia, Thailand, and Pakistan, countries representing different sizes, government types, and political histories and conditions.

The Political Economy of Development

The previous discussion of quantitative measures of development reveals two important dimensions of the efforts to define this complex process. First, the earlier

TABLE 13.2 Selected Development Indicators for Nine Countries

	GDP per capita (PPP US $) 2005	Human Poverty Index#	HDI Rank*	HDI Rank Minus GDI Rank*	GEM Rank*
China	6,757	11.7	94	1	57
India	3,452	31.3	132	0	—
Indonesia	3,843	18.2	109	1	—
Japan	31,267	—	8	-5	54
Pakistan	2,370	36.2	139	-7	82
Philippines	5,137	15.3	102	4	45
South Korea	22,029	—	25	-1	64
Thailand	8,677	10.0	81	0	73
United States	41,890	—	15	-4	15

The Human Poverty Index value is a percentage of the population. Empty cells means the data are not available in the UNDP database.

*Countries are ranked in the UNDP database according to a numerical value calculated from a basket of variables. The number of countries for which HDI, GDI, and GEM is available varies. The subtraction of the GDI rank from the HDI rank illustrates the discrepancy between the overall well-being of the population and that of females. There are 179 countries in the HDI database, 157 for GDI, and 93 for GEM.

Source: Adapted from databases in the United Nations Development Program, Human Development Report 2007/2008, http://hdrstats.undp.org.

assumptions that development was essentially an economic process have been modified to recognize its social and political dimensions. Second, the focus on national accomplishments has been complemented by asking questions about intranational development: Who has benefited and who hasn't? This question has led to greater efforts to disaggregate measures, for example by gender, race, or region. Disaggregating data, in turn, shines a light both on government policies and on the ability of those left out or disadvantaged to make their voices heard. Thus development often has the effect of restructuring the political relationship between policy-making elites and citizens. It is not surprising, therefore, that one of the central themes to emerge in discussions about development is the relationship between politics and economics. Does political change precede economic change or vice versa? Are authoritarian or democratic regimes, centralized or decentralized structures, better able to generate the desired change? These questions lead us to more qualitative explorations of the diversity in Asia's development experiences.

Idioms of Development and Political Legitimacy

Development in Asia is a normative mandate—that is, it carries positive connotations and, whatever its real-life failures, millions of people see it as something governments should be doing. Aside from its policy content, the commitment to development thus has implications for the way states are structured, from the priorities articulated by politicians to the size and organization of bureaucracies. In discussing this "normative privilege" of development, Sugata Bose uses the word "idioms" to include both the overarching goals of development (e.g., reducing poverty) and also the concepts of nationhood and the particular state forms favored by the ideology of development.[13]

Understanding the idioms of development requires some knowledge of a country's political history. To illustrate, the Indian commitment to national development emerged from opposition to British colonialism, even as postcolonial planners adapted some idioms of the colonial state, such as a centralized bureaucracy, for their economic development strategies after 1947. At the same time, these idioms did not go unchallenged, which helps explain India's postcolonial history of often unruly opposition to the central government. Mahatma Gandhi laid out his scathing critique of the Western idioms of development, particularly industrialization and centralization, as early as 1906 in his book, *Hind Swaraj (Indian Home Rule)*. During the 1930s, the leaders of the Indian National Congress contested visions of nationhood that were far more complex than a simple dichotomy between "Gandhian traditionalism" and "Nehruvian modernity" (see Chapter 5). In the end, the postcolonial leadership appeared to adopt a cohesive view of development that was grounded in industrialization and centralized planning, but in reality this view was the result of "the capture of centralized state power by the machine politicians among the nationalist elite."[14] Very quickly, the idea of development became an instrument of state legitimacy, and many of the pre-1947 aspirations, such as eradicating illiteracy, became secondary.

The case of China reflects its unique political trajectory and also serves to reinforce the comparative value of looking at development as an idiom that is used to enhance the legitimacy of political leaders and, more generally, that of the state. As in the case of India, China's commitment to development cannot be separated from the country's desire to reject Western colonialism and reassert a historic vision of Chinese greatness. But also, as in India, the question of *how* to achieve this was contested, particularly during periods of leadership struggles, such as the 1930s and the 1960s. The unabashed tilt in favor of the Four Modernizations and "market socialism" during the 1980s reflected the political supremacy of Deng Xiaoping. After the repression that followed the 1989 Tiananmen demonstrations, rapid economic growth and material consumption were reinforced as part of a national strategy to undermine political dissent and build international prestige and power.[15]

The historical context for Japan's development policies differed substantially from India's and China's. As explained in Chapter 7, the central purpose of the Meiji Restoration was to modernize Japan. This overarching goal justified the destruction of the Tokugawa political, social, and economic structures. Its successes were manifested in a wide range of development idioms, including a modern bureaucracy, formal constitution, *zaibatsu*, and a strong military. The costs, which are well known, resulted from the pretense that modern Japan was the harbinger of an East Asian renaissance. As both perpetrator and victim of World War II, the primary challenge confronting postwar leaders was economic reconstruction. This uncontested idiom became the raison d'être of the Liberal Democratic Party (LDP), which massaged political structures in a way that simultaneously consolidated the party's power (e.g., through the electoral system) and guaranteed consensus on the primary development priorities (for example, through systems of political-bureaucratic cooperation).

Democracy and Development

One of the most debated dimensions in the political economy of development is the role of democracy. Is democracy a necessary prerequisite to economic growth (or vice versa)? The historical experience of authoritarian Japan and China suggests that democracy, at least in the near term, is neither a precondition nor a guaranteed outcome of economic growth. However, the Chinese and Japanese cases are obviously very different, and in fact democratic India has enjoyed some notable development successes. These realities suggest that the democracy-development relationship is much more complicated than may appear at first glance. There are three clusters of questions that bear on the relationship. First, what is meant by "democracy" and "development"? We have already seen that development has had numerous interpretations over the years; concepts of democracy have been equally variable. Second, is political democracy inherent in the process of development? That is, are the two not just interrelated, but interdependent? This question is closely linked to the third question: What does the empirical evidence show about the historical relationship between the two? Despite considerable research on these questions, the answers are inconclusive.

A survey of the history of both development and democracy in Europe, Asia, and elsewhere makes it clear that the meanings of both terms vary through time and across geographic regions. To illustrate, Mao Zedong's strategy of development—

although discredited now—was once seen as a model of economic democracy for millions of Chinese because of its emphasis on national autonomy, egalitarianism, and rural advancement. Under Deng Xiaoping, however, development entailed an aggressive export economy, entrepreneurship, but at the cost of interregional and interclass inequality. By the post-Deng era, democracy came to include low-level, semi-competitive elections, greater rule of law, as well as increased media and cultural freedom. Under neither Mao nor Deng (nor Hu Jintao) have development and democracy been fused in the same manner as found in European social democracies, which include welfare "safety nets," low corruption, and competitive political parties and elections.

Thus even in any one country, democracy and development are multifaceted and change through time; countries are judged more or less democratic or developed depending on the criteria and the time period. These considerations make it more difficult to ascertain direct links between the two processes.

One school of thought argues that there is no necessary relationship between the two, however much one might like to think otherwise. For example, Deepak Lal, drawing on political and economic theory as well as empirical research, argues that there is no correlation between forms of government and economic performance. Where pluralism is the norm and pressure groups or NGOs (nongovernmental organizations) compete, there may be greater political freedom, but also more "rent seeking"—that is, behavior by special interests to acquire benefits or subsidies from governments (in the form of tax relief, favorable laws, or regulatory policies). Rent-seeking behavior may benefit particular groups, but not the taxpayers, consumers, and the economy in general. Pressure or interest groups are formed to serve self-serving goals, not the commonweal. Thus, argues Lal, they ultimately serve as a drag on economic efficiency. Moreover, competition for votes in elections, where promises almost always exceed means, often leads to larger governments and less efficiency.[16]

Arguing from a different perspective, legal scholar Amy Chua maintains that the promotion of democracy and markets—with the latter symbolizing the development idiom of international organizations and national governments since the 1980s—is frequently incompatible, particularly in newer nation-states. In her words, "The combined pursuit of marketization and democratization will often catalyze ethnic tensions in highly determinant and predictable ways and with potentially very serious consequences."[17] Her logic points to the tension between democracy, with its emphasis on majority rule, and the tendency of markets to concentrate wealth where there are no mediating institutions or ideologies to encourage some form of redistribution. More dangerous, she argues, is the reality that in much of the developing world, ethnic minorities have enjoyed economic domination over the majority of the population. In Asia, the most striking example of this is the role of Chinese minorities throughout Southeast Asia, and the case of the Tamils in Sri Lanka or certain castes in India could also be cited. Under circumstances of market competition, these minorities are well positioned to enhance their power and wealth. Under democratization, political leaders often appeal to long-standing resentments to build their own power bases. In the worst scenarios, violence against minorities (such as against the Indonesian Chinese in the late 1990s) is the result. A less pernicious illustration is the adoption of compensatory policies designed to favor certain ethnic groups (e.g., the Muslim majority, called *bumiputra*, in Malaysia[18]) at the expense of the entrepreneurial minorities (Chinese and Indian) and also at the expense of broad-base development.[19]

In contrast to Lal and Chua, many influential policy-makers assume that development is incomplete without democratization. Amartya Sen, for example, argues that the two phenomena are mutually constituted: Deprivations of freedom (such as denying political liberty and civil rights) do not help economic growth. He refutes the notion that there is a conflict between democracy and economic growth:

> The exercise of basic political rights makes it more likely not only that there would be a policy response to economic needs, but also that the conceptualization— including comprehension of "economic needs" itself may require the exercise of such rights. It can indeed be argued that a proper understanding of what economic needs are—their content and their force—requires discussion and exchange.[20]

Sen further contends that democracy has been especially successful in preventing disasters such as famines, although it is not a panacea. Democracy was central to India's commitment to eliminate famines, he argues, although it has not been equally successful in eliminating malnutrition.[21] Sen's position is noteworthy because he influenced the UNDP's crafting of the human development indicators, including those emphasizing the importance of gender equality.

In addition to the scholarly debates, it is important to recall that the connection between development and democracy is simultaneously a product of a country's history and cultural norms as well as the choices made by political leaders as they wrestle with the "idioms" of development explained in the previous section. For a fascinating example of the interplay between history, culture, and politics as it defines a new idiom of development in a tiny Himalayan country, see Focus Box 13 on Bhutan's Gross National Happiness.

BHUTAN'S GROSS NATIONAL HAPPINESS

Bhutan is a tiny Himalayan kingdom, with fewer than 700,000 people. To outsiders, it has seemed an idyllic "Shangri La." In the past decade, the government has led the country toward modernity, prodding it to alter many traditional economic and social patterns. Some changes have come rapidly: Television was introduced into the country only in 1999, but in less than a decade, satellite dishes and cell phones were widespread in the capital city, Thimphu, and in smaller towns. Still, most rural areas remain largely isolated due to the absence of communication and transportation facilities. The results of the encounter with development have been mixed, and many of the problems found in other newly developing countries are now appearing in Bhutan. Prominent among these problems are urban air pollution, alcohol and drug addiction, the erosion of traditional cultures, and a growing urban/rural gap.

In this context, the Bhutanese government's commitment to a strategy called Gross National Happiness (GNH) has inspired both skepticism and admiration. The obvious contrast with gross national product as a measure of progress inspires many observers to imagine that Bhutan offers an alternative to the often destructive and destabilizing development experiences of other Asian countries. At the same time, Bhutan is tiny, "walking between the giants"[1] (India and China). It has few natural resources other than water, much of the country is still inaccessible, and in the southwest of the country, Bhutan confronts a festering problem with a large minority of Nepalese descendants who are disaffected from the dominant Himalayan Buddhist culture.

Despite these hurdles, the fourth king (called *Druk Gyalpo*) Jigme Singye Wangchuk (r. 1972–2006) determined that Bhutan should change its long-standing policies of semi-isolation and modernize, but on its own terms. He proposed four tenets for GNH, inspired by Buddhist ideals of emphasizing the quality of life, rather than the quantity of material goods: sustainable and equitable development, preservation of cultural values, environmental conservation, and good governance. The government created a Gross National Happiness commission as a long-range planning body, and the GNH has inspired websites and international conferences. King Wangchuk also decreed the drafting of a new constitution, transforming Bhutan into a constitutional monarchy (see Focus Box 8); he introduced elections (see Photo 13.1) and, in

continues

continued

FOCUS BOX 13

celebration of the monarchy's centenary (2006), voluntarily retired and transferred power to his son, Jigme Khesar Namgyel. The coronation of the fifth
Wangchuk *Druk Gyalpo* took place in 2008.

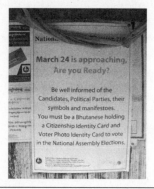

PHOTO 13.1 Election poster
in Bhutan, 2008. Photo courtesy of Dr. Mary Littrell.

Many of the observations are based on the author's visits to Bhutan in 2007 and 2008
and are adapted from Sue Ellen M. Charlton, "Constraints and Opportunities in
Bhutan's Democratic Development Strategy," *Journal of the Southwest Conference on
Asian Studies* 6 (2008), 106–131.
1. Dorji Penjore, "Security of Bhutan: Walking Between the Giants," *Journal of Bhutan
Studies* 10 (Summer 2004), 108–131.

Governance

The summaries of Lal's, Chua's, and Sen's positions are only a small representation of complex arguments, but they illustrate the debate about the linkages between democracy and development throughout Asia. One prominent strategy
offering an alternative approach is to focus on the nature of governance that exists
in a country. Many international organizations, including NGOs, increasingly
emphasize the quality of governance rather than democracy when comparing
countries. In much of the world, discussions are criticized for their reflection of
historical and cultural norms characteristic of Europe and North America. Moreover, scholars have long pointed out that government effectiveness—which is central to development—can be undermined by democratic process as varied as
elections and group politics (Lal's argument about rent-seeking) or ethnic tensions
(Chua's argument). In contrast, the concept of governance links key criteria of
both development and democracy by identifying multiple measures of government effectiveness in addition to traditional characteristics of democracy such as

accountability. There are innumerable definitions and measures of governance, but the World Bank Institute (WBI) definition illustrates the way in which criteria essential for both development and democracy can be accommodated, although a careful reading of the WBI approach shows how difficult it is to escape Western norms of democracy and market capitalism. To paraphrase the WBI, governance consists of the traditions and institutions for exercising authority in a country. It includes the process for selecting, monitoring, and replacing governments; the capacity of governments to formulate and implement sound policies; and the respect that both citizens and the state have for governing institutions.[22] For purposes of measuring the quality of governance, the WBI has identified six indicators: voice and accountability, political stability and absence of violence, government effectiveness, regulatory quality, rule of law, and control of corruption. A numerical "score" is computed for each of these indicators for each country in the database, including approximately twenty-five countries in East and South Asia.[23] The sources of information used for the composite measures are varied and include intergovernmental organizations (e.g., the Asian Development Bank), polls (e.g., Gallup), business assessments (e.g., Economist Intelligence Unit), and numerous NGOs (such as Freedom House and Reporters without Borders).

Governance measures are particularly useful for comparing countries such as India and China. To illustrate, India, which has dozens of political parties, regular elections, hundreds of NGOs, and largely free media, ranks much higher than China on voice and accountability measures. China ranks higher than India on political stability and absence of violence, and also ranks slightly higher on government effectiveness (see Table 13.3). Although ranking higher than China in terms of rule of law, India's composite score is lower than one would expect in a democracy and actually declined slightly between 1998 and 2007, suggesting perhaps that issues such as the Gujarat riots in 2002 have affected international judgments of legal processes in India.[24] Finally, one sees that corruption is widespread in *both* countries, although it appears to be marginally worse in China. The table includes Japan, which ranks much higher than either India or China on every governance measure.

One must be cautious about overstating conclusions from these data, as many of the sources used for the composite contain subjective elements. How, for example, does one actually *measure* corruption, when much of it is street-level? It is frequently taken for granted and almost never reported. But it is important to our thinking of both democracy and development. Corruption may not be seen as a measure of democracy in Western countries, yet it saps government legitimacy, subverts rule of law, and reinforces political and economic inequality. And although it may help sustain the economic survival of underpaid public officials (e.g., police

TABLE 13.3 Governance Indicators for India, China, and Japan: 1998 and 2007

Governance Indicator	Year	India		China		Japan	
		Percentile Rank	Governance (-2.4 to +2.5)	Percentile Rank	Governance (-2.5 to +2.5)	Percentile Rank	Governance (-2.5 to +2.5)
Voice and Accountability	2007	58.7	+0.32	5.8	-1.70	75.5	+0.93
	1998	58.2	+0.32	10.1	-1.38	75.5	+0.89
Political Stability	2007	17.8	-1.01	32.2	-0.33	88.0	+1.17
	1998	17.8	-0.87	41.8	-0.10	88.0	+1.18
Government Effectiveness	2007	57.3	+0.03	61.1	+0.15	89.1	+1.32
	1998	53.6	-0.17	47.9	-0.28	84.4	+1.08
Regulatory Quality	2007	46.1	-0.22	45.6	-0.24	83.5	+1.05
	1998	33.7	-0.39	40.0	-0.26	71.2	+0.65
Rule of Law	2007	56.2	+0.10	42.4	-0.45	90.0	+1.39
	1998	58.1	+0.16	41.0	-0.38	90.0	+1.47
Control of Corruption	2007	47.3	-0.39	30.9	-0.66	84.5	+1.20
	1998	48.1	-0.29	41.7	-0.38	86.9	+1.31

Source: Adapted from World Bank Institute, Governance Indicators website, at www.info.worldbank.org/governance.

officers) or be compatible with traditional cultural norms (such as *guanxi*), payoffs, both large and small, bypass more long-term productive investments.

A closer look at the criteria for voice and accountability in the context of changes in state-society relations highlights one of the unintended results of development, namely the creation of new opportunities for political activity. Increased political demands from below pressure governments as they are simultaneously pressured by the competitive forces of globalization.

Voice and Accountability

Voice and accountability refers to the ability of citizens to participate in selecting their government, as well as freedom of expression and association and a free media.[25] In surveying political parties and elections, Chapter 12 examined some dimensions of this indicator. This section looks at some of the informal dimensions of political participation that contribute to strengthening voice and accountability. In order to focus the discussion, first we look at the concept of civil society, which has been used by many scholars to understand state-society linkages. Following this, examples of environmental politics will illustrate the ways in which citizens exercise the opportunities available for freedom of expression and hold their governments accountable.

Civil Society. The term *civil society*, although often discussed in the context of democracy and development, is not synonymous with either concept. There are varying definitions of civil society, but generally it is understood as the arena of voluntary associations not regulated by the state or falling under the authority of the family. Thus an important indicator of the expansion of civil society is the growth of political structures and activities that function largely outside of state control. Both democracy and development are historically associated with increasingly complex and diverse societies, so it is not surprising that people may interpret an expanded civil society in this context.

The historical roots of civil society, both as concept and as reality, emerged in eighteenth-century Europe and reflected the decline of monarchical authoritarianism and the rise of early capitalism.[26] Theorizing about civil society revived in the 1980s following the emergence of dissident organizations in Eastern Europe. As the communist states of the region unraveled, the language used to discuss civil society took on clear normative overtones: "good" civil society had overturned "bad" communism.[27] Understandably, many people saw civil society and pluralist politics as mutually constituted. Despite the obvious links between the growth of new groups and movements and the rise of Western European democracies, the expansion of these autonomous spaces not under family or state control does not satisfy the procedural or substantive requirements of democracy. Much depends on the nature of a group or movement to provide opportunities for free engagement in political activity, which may not be feasible.

The use of a term such as civil society, which has clear historical and philosophical links to Western politics, in a discussion of Asian politics and development raises provocative questions about comparing political systems. The Western linkage of civil society with democracy assumes a society apart from the state as both historical reality and political ideal. Despite the many examples of such linkages, the presumption of autonomy or potential autonomy (for example, of political movements) persists. However, one must ask whether in China, for example, autonomous politics has been either the tradition or the modern reality *or* the ideal for most Chinese. To illustrate, one can make a case that Confucian theory posits a connected, interdependent political world from family to rulers. This is not to suggest that there was never dissidence or political opposition to rulers—clearly there was (and continues to be). We also know that Islamic political theory explicitly *rejects* the ideal of autonomous (or separate) spheres of state and society, with religion the defining feature of the latter. Thus Euro-American assumptions about the transportability of the notions of an autonomous political sphere may be unrealistic, as well as unwarranted. Recognition of these alternatives, however, is not an argument for repressive politics; rather, it is a call for caution in assessing the way in which political activity occurs in contexts very different from our own.

Environmental Voices
Transforming Asian Politics

Political activity takes many forms throughout Asia, but in focusing on environmental politics, one can see more closely the relationship between development and democracy, and the challenges to governance that countries confront. Here the focus is on the domestic dimensions of this challenge; the next chapter looks at the transnational implications.

India, China, and Japan have all achieved remarkable feats of development, given the challenges each has faced: Western imperialism, colonialism, war, population pressures, ethnic and linguistic diversity, scarce natural resources—to name a few. The environmental effects have been severe, even devastating in some instances. Hence it should not be surprising that environmental degradation sparks political protest when people's lives are directly and intimately bound up with the quality of land, water, and forests on which they depend.

India

Two decades ago, Indian political scientist Rajni Kothari drew attention to the importance of voice and accountability by pointing to the contradiction between an idiom of development that professes to benefit all citizens and the reality of development policies that advantage economic and political elites and largely ignore the poor (or leave them worse off). Kothari's argument raises questions about many countries where development in the name of the poor proceeds largely without reference to their real interests. Organized politics, especially political parties, are part of the problem, Kothari argued, and their decline, along with the absence of effective government in many parts of India, has created a new political space. Grassroots movements have started to occupy this space, transforming the nature of politics.[28]

Kothari's argument is more persuasive in India, which arguably has more political action groups, nongovernmental organizations, and grassroots movements than any other country in the world.[29] India, after all, is not just a country of enormous diversity; the effects of its development policies have been felt unevenly, and its comparatively open political system offers multiple opportunities for organizing. Moreover, Mahatma Gandhi's own philosophy of collective action—*satyagraha*—established a tradition of legitimacy for protest movements.

The best known example of environmental protest that illustrates the linkage between uneven economic growth, Gandhian norms, and a movement that endeavors to give voice to the poor while holding the government accountable, is the Narmada Bachao Andolan (NBA, Save the Narmada Movement). The idea of damming the Narmada River system predates independence. Planning by the Union government began in the late 1950s under Prime Minister Jawaharlal Nehru, who had long supported the development idioms of industrial growth and centralized planning. The Narmada River basin drains from three states—Gujarat, Maharashtra, and Madhya Pradesh—and the project is designed to control the waters of the Narmada and its 40-odd tributaries through 30 large (with Sardar Sarovar the largest), 135 medium, and innumerable small dams. The Sardar Sarovar project (SSP) includes a 455-foot dam, reservoir, and elaborate canal system and has displaced thousands of people, with some estimates claiming that when the entire project is completed, at least 300,000 Indians will have been displaced.[30]

Because the river basin drains from three states, one of the earliest problems to be resolved was to decide how the waters impounded by the various dams would be shared by the states. In order to resolve the interstate dispute, the Union government set up a Water Disputes Tribunal in 1969. After ten years of delays and deliberations, the tribunal made its allocations, after which the final planning phase began. As construction finally got under way in 1987, a dispute arose between Gujarat and Madhya Pradesh over resettlement of the people displaced by the project. Although the issue was nominally resolved through mediation by the central government, critics of the project argued that no systematic resettlement plan had been developed either by the states or by the central government, partly because no one knew exactly how many people would be displaced.

The Narmada Bachao Andolan took the lead in protesting the SSP and defending the rights of the displaced villagers, many of whom are *adivasis* (tribal peoples). In 1991, using tactics consistent with India's cultural and political traditions, Medha Patkar, the head of the NBA, and more than six thousand farmers and *adivasis* undertook a 125-mile march from Madhya Pradesh to the dam site in Gujarat, a march modeled after Gandhi's famous 1930 Salt March. The leaders of the movement also fasted when denied permission to cross the Gujarat border. This early protest would be followed by many others: Medha Patkar conducted a hunger strike in 2006, and in July 2008 and again in November 2008, thousands of people demonstrated over the inadequacy of resettlement efforts for those displaced by the Sardar Sarovar project.[31] Despite these activities and numerous court cases resulting from the protests, work on the SSP has continued and resettlement issues are still unresolved.[32]

The rhetoric and strategies associated with both electoral politics and economic modernization have increased people's expectations. Local and regional elites who have resources (such as landowning castes) are able to use informal party and government networks to achieve their goals, but those without such resources typically resort to protest methods, such as marches, sit-downs, general strikes, and sometimes violent confrontation. Social action and environmental rights groups have increased steadily in India since the 1970s, most focusing on specific regional issues (such as the SSP). Many mobilize along ethnic, caste or class, or gender lines, and they are inspired by a range of philosophies, including Gandhian social transformation, Marxist-Leninist class-based resistance, and feminist consciousness-raising. In urban areas, citizens' groups have formed in response to deteriorating environmental conditions and ineffective local governments. Sometimes they perform tasks under the official purview of the local governments (such as garbage collection). In other instances, they form primarily to launch collective protests to public officials.[33] Some groups have been durable, building an organizational infrastructure and a core leadership that enables them to respond to changing political contexts, and a number of them—including the NBA—have wide international following. However, despite Rajni Kothari's optimism, noted earlier, there is little evidence yet that these social movements have significantly altered the overall development priorities of the central or state governments. Nonetheless, individually and collectively, they have had piecemeal successes and clearly represent a dynamic part of the voices in India's civil society.

China

Like India, China also has had its anti-dam protests, the most famous of which was opposition to the construction of the Three Gorges Dam across the Yangtze River.[34] China's nascent political liberalization in the 1980s encouraged much of this debate about the dam project, and in early 1989, a book edited by Dai Qing (later translated into English under the title *Yangtze! Yangtze!*) was published in China. It summed up the controversy over Three Gorges, served as the rallying cry for the groups opposed to the project, and contributed to the decision later that year to postpone construction for a time. The book was banned after the democracy movement in May-June 1989 as allegedly "contributing to the political turmoil in Beijing," and some 30,000 copies of its Chinese edition were destroyed.[35] During this same period, well-known opponents of the dam in the environmental and scientific communities were excluded from decision-making related to the project. This opposition was manifested even in the National People's Congress, where more than 30 percent of the delegates either voted against the project or abstained in the final vote for approval. Despite the protest, the displacement of more than one million people, and ongoing charges of environmental damage, construction of the dam continued until its completion in 2008.

The outcome of the anti–Three Gorges protest might suggest that China is still a long way from experiencing greater voice and accountability. In fact, however, the complexity of China's civil society and consequently the dynamics of environmental politics have changed noticeably since the 1980s. Several factors have contributed to the expansion of environmental protest. Energy and water shortages mean that the government maintains its commitment to large-scale projects (such as dams) deemed necessary to meet demands for power and also (in the case of factories) provide employment. The growth of social inequalities and continued displacement of large numbers of people for the construction of factories and dams, often accompanied by unauthorized but tolerated land-grabs, generate resistance by farmers, in particular. Increased contact between Chinese and international NGOs brings ideas, strategies, and money to some environmental causes. In all of these changes, the growth of technology has been an important factor.

Many of the "mass incidents" (social protests) reported by the Chinese government, particularly in cities, involve workers displaced by the disappearance of their jobs in the switch to a market economy.[36] Some of these protests overlap those linked to environmental problems, for example, when people are coerced off their land in areas slated for "development," such as the building of polluting factories. But an increasing number of "mass incidents" that are reported in detail are specifically generated by real or anticipated environmental damage resulting from China's growth.[37] An unintended consequence of the speed of growth, and the concomitant widespread adoption of new technologies, has been the use of the Internet and cell phones to organize protests against construction projects, pollution, and food safety.[38] In late spring 2007, for example, thousands of people demonstrated at Xiamen, Fujian Province, against the construction of a chemical factory, claiming a risk of air and water pollution. In response the local government called a halt to the project in order to reassess the environmental effects of the factory. The event was covered by numerous bloggers and a video was posted on YouTube.[39]

Periodic scandals about food quality focus attention on one of the unanticipated costs of rapid economic growth in a country seen as authoritarian: lack of government oversight. China, like India, confronts water supply and quality issues that threaten crops, health, and exports.[40] In 2007–2008, for example, pollution of China's lakes generated both protest and a government response in the form of a plan to remove algae and other pollutants from the lakes.[41] In recent years, Dongting Lake (Hunan Province) and Tai Lake (Jiangsu Province) have become well known both inside and outside China for their pollution stemming from human and industrial waste. In 2007, a local activist, Wu Lihong, who had been campaigning against the pollution of Tai Lake, was arrested, although two years earlier he had been nominated by the Jiangsu provincial administration for an environmental award.[42]

Between the high-profile environmental activists such as Wu Lihong and the quasi-spontaneous demonstrations such as that at Xiamen, China has experienced a significant growth in the number of environmental NGOs: Green Earth Volunteers, the Institute of Public and Environmental Affairs, the Beijing Global Village, and Friends of Nature are examples of these. Although in some instances NGOs receive international financial support (as they do in India), their most significant support comes from urban, middle-class, and increasingly cosmopolitan Chinese citizens.

Both urban and rural protestors turn to a combination of law, tradition, and ideological exhortation to pursue their causes—a combination that suggests a distinctive Chinese form of civil society may be developing. Kevin J. O'Brien, for example, has defined this form of protest as "rightful resistance"—popular action that employs laws, public policies, and even dominant values to pressure political elites to do what they are supposed to do, whether that might be implementing a policy or curbing abuses of power. In O'Brien's words, "It is a sign of growing rights consciousness and a more contractual approach to political life. It appears as individuals with new aspirations come to appreciate common interests, develop an oppositional consciousness, and become collective actors in the course of struggle."[43] In her study of labor protest in China, Ching Kwan Lee has noted that along with workers and peasants, urban middle classes are becoming more open and organized; they work through and around the law and may appeal to the very ideology that originally provided the legitimacy for China's party-state. She quotes one angry interviewee whose home was destroyed to make way for the 2008 Olympics:

> Many demolition workers . . . surrounded my house. I wrote on the walls of my house in big characters, "The Communist Party and the Eighth Route Army didn't take away a single pin or a penny from ordinary people," "Equality to all before the law" . . . My two brothers are soldiers serving the Party and protecting our country. Ironically, I cannot even protect our own family home . . . Is this country ruled by the communists? How come the government has become like the nationalists?[44]

The dominant development idiom in China is a commitment to rapid growth, despite the environmental costs. This does not imply that the government is disinterested in these costs; in fact, increasingly the government recognizes the long-term risks to economic growth posed by environmental degradation. More important from a government and party perspective is the threat of social instability, which is increasingly a by-product of the national development strategy. Put differently, China's increasingly complex civil society—if not a Western model of democracy—offers more political voices demanding public accountability. In this way, the developmental impulse and the environmental crisis it has generated will be moderated by democratic trends: "New voices will be able to challenge damaging development by making the costs better known."[45]

Japan

Despite the many differences between Japan and China, they share some similarities that enrich our understanding of the dynamics of state-society relations and the effects of development on these dynamics. One obvious similarity is the dominant role of the central government in defining the overarching postwar development idiom: expand economic production and the infrastructure necessary to support it. A second similarity is the way in which government has molded civil society. The state-society relationship obviously has not been identical in the two countries, but in both instances Japan and China offer examples of top-down management, co-option, and collaboration. Consequently, the structures and organizations of civil society organizations (CSOs) contrast with the Indian patterns. In turn, they broaden our understanding of the complexity of civil society and its implications for development and environmental activism.

Social scientists have long noted how influential the state is in determining the kind of civil society that develops in a country. The term *corporatism*, for example, has been used to describe institutional arrangements in which states establish regularized channels of access for the primary functional groups in a capitalist economy, particularly business, labor, and agriculture. The original ideas of corporatism derived from nineteenth- and twentieth-century ideas of organic, cooperative societies, but the term came to be applied to a wide range of political structures for organizing state-society relationships. The significance of the corporatist literature is that it provided an alternative to the dominant pluralist (typically American) assumptions that nonstate associations and interest groups are autonomous and encouraged scholars to look for more complex and subtle linkages. With new analytical perspectives, cases like Japan have been incorporated into a broader understanding of civil society.

State-led corporatist impulses were central to the modernizing strategy of twentieth-century Japanese governments, both before and after World War II. Sheldon Garon has developed the concept of "social management" to explain a pattern of Japanese governance in which the state constructs an ideology, promulgates policies, and establishes institutions that shape how ordinary Japanese think and behave. In this endeavor, the government agencies maneuvered to transform Japanese citizens into active participants in the state's projects of modernization.[46]

States shape civil society in multiple ways, some of them transparent, others not. Robert Pekkanen has explored these strategies in order to explain a seeming paradox in Japan: There are many small local groups and associations but few large, professionalized groups able to influence policy-making in the way that American interest groups do, for example. He finds the explanation for this "dual civil society" primarily in the country's regulatory framework, including law and resources.[47]

These arrangements illuminate several features of environmental politics in Japan. The term "citizens' movements" is associated largely with a type of social movement that arose in the 1960s primarily "to protest the rapid economic growth policies of government and their consequences at the local level, particularly pollution and the deterioration of the quality of life."[48] There were also antiwar, civil rights, and consumer rights groups, but the environmentally oriented groups have received most of the scholarly attention because they raised critical questions about the course of Japan's development and had an impact at the local level. Detailed research on the movements has suggested that they were influenced by postindustrial values and concern over the discernible effects of industrial pollution, but that as important as the intensity of the pollution problem was the preexisting network of community associations at the local level, including neighborhood associations.[49]

Citizens' movements declined in visibility and numbers in the 1980s, leading some observers to claim that their progressive gains were not sustained and that they had been co-opted by various state agencies.[50] In his study of Oita Prefecture on Kyushu Island, Jeffrey Broadbent explained these dynamics in the context of postwar Japanese politics, where the state "has favored soft means of social control."[51] Postwar development relied on the ability of the Liberal Democratic Party to drain surplus profit from the corporate world, which depended in turn on the continued expansion of the Japanese economy. This reliance reflected the structural dominance of the corporate world over the LDP. With close links between business, LDP politicians, and state agencies, a "Triple Control Machine" operated to control or co-opt local grassroots movements.[52]

The patterns of control and cooptation described by scholars such as Broadbent and Garon suggest that Japan bears strong resemblance to the state-led civil society Michael Frolic sees in China: "It is created by the state, principally to help it govern, but also to co-opt and socialize potentially politically active elements in the population."[53] However, changes in Japanese politics during the 1990s have led others to observe that a civil society with greater autonomy may be emerging, and that environmental politics is especially illustrative of these changes.

One of the best known protests of the late twentieth century was controversy over damning the estuary of the Nagara River on Honshu Island. This case demonstrates not only energy of environmental movements in Japan but also the obstacles they confront in trying to realize policy objectives. Plans to construct the dam dated to the 1960s, but active planning only began in 1988, after settlement of lawsuits brought by fishing interests opposed to the project. In the late 1980s, a new movement, the Society against the Nagara River Estuary Dam Construction (SANREDC), formed to prevent the construction. SANREDC was very successful in mobilizing citizen support and media attention throughout Japan, but ultimately it failed to stop the construction, which was completed in 1996.

From one perspective, the unsuccessful campaign resembles other failed protests in Asia (including the Three Gorges and Narmada cases): It is exceedingly difficult to stop or redirect "development" projects to which the government is committed and from which politicians stand to benefit. However, there are different lessons to be gleaned from this illustration, two of which stand out. One is that despite the absence or relative weakness of large, well-financed national environmental organizations in Japan, local movements have been growing, many of them successfully forming coalitions across the normal boundaries of interest groups. SANREDC, for example, brought together local residents, fishers, outdoors enthusiasts, scientists, and celebrities. The second key point is that the images and rhetoric used by SANREDC linked protest grounded in domestic political issues (such as corruption in public-works projects) and the global environmental movement. SANREDC organizers connected with anti-dam protestors in other countries, including the Narmada Bachao Andolan and the U.S.-based Friends of the Earth, and Dai Qing was one of the international activists who participated in a SANREDC activity.[54]

Summary

The central questions explored in this chapter are the meaning of development and the relationship between socioeconomic change and political change. The meaning of development is contested; hence it is not surprising that environmental movements emerged in the second half of the twentieth century to challenge state-led projects. Put simply, development has altered the state-society relationship in all three countries—indeed as it has elsewhere in Asia, including tiny Bhutan. The experiences of India, China, and Japan suggest that development has contributed to more multifaceted, complex civil societies by stimulating political expression and (notably in China) creating space for grassroots movements. These changes have in turn enriched understanding of the meaning of civil society and broadened it beyond its conventional use in Western democracies.

What have these changes meant for the evolution of governance in Asia? Although not discussed in this chapter, some elements of governance have altered little, a notable case being levels of corruption. In terms of the primary focus of the last section of the chapter, voice and accountability, it seems obvious that—despite the failings of environmental and other nongovernmental movements—citizens are far from passive. In this regard, they join citizens from around the globe whose lives have been altered by globalization. The next chapter looks more closely at these global changes.

Notes

1. GNP is the total value of goods and services produced in a nation and by its citizens abroad, whereas GDP is the value of goods and services produced in a country,

with exports (minus imports). *Per capita* GNP or *per capita* GDP is found by dividing the total GNP or GDP by the number of people in the economy.

2. The index is not a perfect measure of egalitarianism because although it is used for income ratios, there are elements of wealth that it does not include, such as that from underground, informal, and subsistence economies.

3. For details on the United States, see *The Changing Shape of the Nation's Income Distribution* (Washington, D.C.: Census Bureau, 2000), retrieved June 20, 2008, at www.census.gov/prod/2000pubs/p60-204.pdf. Changes in data collection methods during the early 1990s mean that the results before and after 1992 are not precisely comparable.

4. Asian Development Bank (ADB), *Key Indicators of Developing Asian and Pacific Countries 2007* (Manila: ADB, 2007), 29, retrieved December 4, 2008, from www.adb.org/Documents/Book/Key_Indicators/2007.

5. The case of Gurgaon is also featured in Somini Sengupta, "Inside Gate, India's Good Life; Outside, the Servants' Slums," *New York Times*, June 9, 2008; and Somini Sengupta, "Thirsting for Energy in India's Boomtowns and Beyond," *New York Times*, March 2, 2008. Sengupta's emphasis is on the huge discrepancy between rich and poor in access to water and electricity.

6. Frances Stewart, Caterina Reggeri Laderchi, and Ruhi Saith, eds. *Defining Poverty in the Developing World* (Houndmills: Palgrave Macmillan, 2007), 1.

7. United Nations Development Program (UNDP), *Measuring Human Development: A Primer; Guidelines and Tools for Statistical Research, Analysis and Advocacy* (New York: UNDP, 2007), chap. 2, 48–50, available online at http://hdr.undp.org/en/media/Primer)_ch2.pdf (retrieved June 20, 2008). Social inclusion refers to long-term unemployment (one year or longer).

8. *World Development Report—1990: Poverty* (Oxford: Oxford University Press, for the World Bank, 1990), http://go.worldbank.org/EXWOKFLSZ0, retrieved June 20, 2008.

9. See www.un.org/millenniumgoals.

10. Martin Ravallion, Shaohua Chen, and Prem Sangraula, *Dollar a Day Revisited*, World Bank Policy Research Working Paper 4620, May 2008; and Shaohua Chen and Martin Ravallion, *China Is Poorer Than We Thought, But No Less Successful in the Fight Against Poverty*, Policy Research Working Paper 4621, May 2008, retrieved from www-wds.worldbank.org, June 12, 2008. The researchers use a benchmark of 2005 parity purchasing power.

11. HDI, GDI, and GEM are explained further in UNDP, *Measuring Human Development: A Primer*.

12. Amartya Sen, *Development as Freedom* (New York: Anchor Books, 1999), 18. Sen's conceptualization emerged from his work on development and inequality (income,

racial, gender, and so on), and over the past two decades it has acquired enormous influence. See also Martha C. Nussbaum, *Women and Human Development: The Capabilities Approach* (Cambridge: Cambridge University Press, 2000).

13. Sugata Bose, "Instruments and Idioms of Colonial and National Development," in *International Development and the Social Sciences: Essays on the History and Politics of Knowledge*, eds. Frederick Cooper and Randall Packard (Berkeley: University of California Press, 1996), 46–47.

14. Ibid., 52.

15. Viewed historically, China has employed several idioms of national development that have become popular exhortations, from Mao's "Great Leap Forward" through the Four Modernizations, to Jiang Zemin's "Three Represents" and Hu Jintao's "Scientific Outlook on Development" (see Chapters 6 and 10).

16. Deepak Lal, "Is Democracy Necessary for Development?" in *Development and Democracy: New Perspectives on an Old Debate*, eds. Sunder Ramaswamy and Jeffrey W. Cason (Hanover: Middlebury College Press, 2003), 17–42; and Deepak Lal, with H. Myint, *The Political Economy of Poverty, Equity and Growth—A Comparative Study* (Oxford: Clarendon Press, 1996).

17. Amy L. Chua, "Markets, Democracy, and Ethnicity," in Ramaswamy and Cason,145; and Amy L. Chua, *World on Fire: How Exporting Free Market Democracy Breeds Economic Hatred and Global Instability* (New York: Doubleday, 2003).

18. The *bumiputra* (or *bumiputera*), or "sons of the soil," comprise a little over half of Malaysia's population. The remainder of the population includes ethnic Chinese and Malaysians of Indian descent. The Malays historically have been poorer and since the 1970s, the government has crafted preferential policies (the "New Economic Policy") in education, jobs, and housing to improve their status and economic conditions.

19. Chua, *World on Fire*, 35–36 and 270–272. Chua acknowledges that the New Economic Policy (see n. 17) has improved the economic condition of Malays.

20. Sen, 153.

21. Ibid., 154–155 and 178–184.

22. The home webpage for the World Bank Institute (WBI) is http://info.world bank.org/governance/wgi/index.asp. The website contains numerous links to databases and reports. Among the more useful of the many sources dealing with governance, see the Canadian-based Institute on Governance (www.iog.ca); the Global Development Research Center (www.gdrc.org); "What is Good Governance," at the U.N. Economic and Social Commission for Asia and the Pacific, retrieved December 10, 2008, from www.unescap.org/pdd/prs/ProjectActivities/Ongoing/gg/governance.asp.

23. There are more than 200 countries in the primary database, although information on some countries may be missing.

24. See the explanation of Gujarat in chapter 11. For the aggregate indicators on India, as well as the sources used to compile the indicators, see http://info.world bank.org/governance/wgi/pdf/c104.pdf, accessed November 25, 2008.

25. Definitions and data are available at Daniel Kaufmann, Aart Kraay, and Massimo Mastruzzi, *Governance Matters VII: Aggregate and Individual Governance Indicators, 1996–2007,* World Bank Policy Research Working Paper No. 4654. Available at SSRN http://ssrn.com/abstract=1148386, pp. 7ff, retrieved June 24, 2008.

26. Michael Ignatieff, "On Civil Society," *Foreign Affairs* 74, no. 2 (March/April 1995), 128–136. A useful overview is provided by Frank Schwartz, "What *Is* Civil Society?" in *The State of Civil Society in Japan,* eds. Frank J. Schwartz and Susan J. Pharr (Cambridge: Cambridge University Press, 2003), chap. 1.

27. B. Michael Frolic, "State-Led Civil Society," in *Civil Society in China,* eds. Timothy Brook and B. Michael Frolic (Armonk, N.Y.: M. E. Sharpe, 1997), 47–48 and 50.

28. Rajni Kothari, *State Against Democracy: In Search of Humane Governance* (Delhi: Ajanta Publications, 1988), chap. 3.

29. See the following NGO websites for partial listings: www.ngosindia.com and www.indianngos.com. By one estimate there are more than one million NGOs in India, although many are miniscule one- or two-person operations. About one-half are registered with the government. Rita Anand and Umesh Anand, "India Needs Its NGOs," *Harvard International Review,* January 8, 2007, accessed December 3, 2008, at www.harvardir.org/articles/1465/3/.

30. Estimates of the number displaced vary considerably. A comparable treatment of estimates for people displaced by dams throughout India and in other countries (including China) is in Patrick McCully, *Silenced Rivers: The Ecology and Politics of Large Dams* (London: Zed Books, 2001), appendix 3.

31. Press releases dated July 12, 2008, and November 6, 2008, from Friends of the River Narmada, accessed December 5, 2008, at http://www.narmada.org/nba -press-releases/november-2008/Nov6.html.

32. Official information on the project may be found at www.sardarsarovardam .org, and information from those supporting the NBA (Friends of the River Narmada) is at www.narmada.org.

33. Bharat Dahiya, "Understanding Local Politics, Democracy and Civil Society: Environmental Governance in Urban India," in *Rethinking Indian Political Institutions,* eds. Crispin Bates and Subho Basu (London: Anthem Press, 2005), 107–124.

34. Both the Narmada and Three Gorges cases were analyzed in the 2nd edition of *Comparing Asian Politics,* 274–284.

35. Audrey R. Topping, "Damming the Yangtze," *Foreign Affairs* 74, no. 5 (September/October 1995), 143. The book is *Yangtze! Yangtze! Debate over the Three*

Gorges Project, trans. Nancy Liu et al. (London: Earthscan Publications, 1994). Dai Qing was also imprisoned for ten months.

36. See the detailed study by Ching Kwan Lee, *Against the Law: Labor Protests in China's Rustbelt and Sunbelt* (Berkeley: University of California Press, 2007).

37. The Chinese government openly acknowledges the problem of "mass incidents" and exhorts measures to deal with them. For example, "Official Calls on Prompt Measures to Address Local Complaints," *China Daily*, November 24, 2008, accessed December 5, 2008, at www.chinadaily.com.cn/china/2008-11/24/content_7235624.htm.

38. "A Lot to Be Angry About," *The Economist*, May 3, 2008, 49.

39. The nine-minute video may be found at www.youtube.com/watch?v=gDewvxALlbc, accessed December 5, 2008.

40. See the *New York Times* series entitled "Choking on Growth," including the article by David Barboza, "China's Seafood Industry: Dirty Water, Dangerous Fish," December 15, 2007; and World Bank, East Asia and Pacific Region, *Water Pollution Emergencies in China: Prevention and Response*, June 2007, available at http://siteresources.worldbank.org/INTEAPREGTOPENVIRONMENT/Resources/Water_Pollution_Emergency_Final_EN.pdf.

41. "China Sets Timetable for Pollution Control in Major Lakes," accessed June 20, 2008, at http://english.gov.cn/2008-01/22/content_865716.htm.

42. "Chinese 'Environmental Activist' Sentenced to 3 Years in Prison on Extortion Charges," *People's Daily Online*, August 11, 2007, accessed June 20, 2008, at http://english.people.com.cn/90001/90776/6237113.html.

43. Kevin J. O'Brien, "Rightful Resistance," *World Politics* 49, no. 1 (October 1996), 34. See also Kevin J. O'Brien and Lianjiang Li, *Rightful Resistance in Rural China* (New York: Cambridge University Press, 2006).

44. Quoted in Lee, 261.

45. Bruce Gilley, *China's Democratic Future: How It Will Happen and Where It Will Lead* (New York: Columbia University Press, 2004), 207.

46. Sheldon Garon, *Molding Japanese Minds: The State and Politics in Everyday Life* (Princeton: Princeton University Press, 1997).

47. Robert Pekkanen, *Japan's Dual Civil Society: Members Without Advocates* (Stanford: Stanford University Press, 2006), 16–19 and chap. 3. For related analyses, see the essays in Schwartz and Pharr, *State of Civil Society in Japan*.

48. Ellis S. Krauss and Bradford L. Simcock, "Citizen's Movements: The Growth and Impact of Environmental Protest in Japan," in *Political Opposition and Local Politics in Japan*, eds. Kurt Steiner, Ellis S. Krauss, and Scott C. Flanagan (Princeton: Princeton University Press, 1980), 190.

49. Krauss and Simcock, 206–208; and Jack G. Lewis, "Civic Protest in Mishima: Citizen's Movements and the Politics of the Environment in Contemporary Japan," in Steiner, Krauss, and Flanagan, *Political Opposition*, 288–289.

50. Beverly Smith, "Democracy Derailed: Citizens' Movements in Historical Perspective," in *Democracy in Contemporary Japan*, eds. Gavan McCormack and Yoshio Sugimoto (Armonk, N.Y.: M. E. Sharpe, 1986), 157–172. See also Hidefumi Imura, "Japan's Environmental Policy: Institutions and the Interplay of Actors," in *Environmental Policy in Japan*, eds. Hidefumi Imura and Miranda A. Schreurs (Cheltenham: Edward Elgar, 2005), 49–85.

51. Jeffrey Broadbent, *Environmental Politics in Japan: Networks of Power and Protest* (Cambridge: Cambridge University Press, 1998), 185.

52. Ibid., chap. 6.

53. Frolic, 56.

54. Kim Reimann, "Going Global: The Use of International Politics and Norms in Local Environmental Protest Movements in Japan," in *Local Environmental Movements: A Comparative Study of the United States and Japan*, eds. Pradyumna P. Karan and Unryu Suganuma (Lexington: University Press of Kentucky, 2008), 50–54.

14

Asian Politics and Global Transformation

The previous chapter emphasized the importance of economic development as an important goal of Asian states and pointed to some of its political consequences. The primary goal of this chapter is to stimulate additional thinking about political change in Asia with attention to two questions important to the study of comparative politics. The first question is how the processes of globalization have affected domestic and transnational politics, and the second is how political thought or institutions in Asian countries have influenced—or might influence—issues in comparative politics. Discussion of these questions raises controversial points and calls for examples beyond the borders of India, China, and Japan but also provides the opportunity to review the central themes of the book.

Globalization

Globalization may be taken to mean several things, but the word is used most commonly to describe the creation of an international market economy marked by theories of capitalist production, integrated markets (with free movement of capital, labor, and goods), and an emphasis on material consumption. The values, institutions, and consumer patterns in this global economy emerged primarily from North America and Western Europe, with the United States playing a leading role. The newspaper advertisement in Photo 14.1 illustrates the global reach of Western companies in a Malaysian context. The political dimensions of globalization are also deeply influenced by the West: the spread of democratic norms, the expansion of international nongovernmental organizations (NGOs), and the role of intergovernmental organizations (IGOs) such as the World Bank.

PHOTO 14.1 Newspaper advertisement—
Western reach in a Malaysian context. Photo
courtesy of James W. Boyd.

Despite the Western imprint on globalization, non-Western states and societies are much more than passive receptacles of foreign values, practices, and institutions. Nowhere is this more evident than in Asia, where states have crafted their own answers to the age-old questions of government, as well as adopting and adapting Western institutions.

Globalization, however the term is used, is apt to be controversial, and for many the word itself has become value-laden. Defenders point to the material well-being that results from economic competition, arguing that free markets offer better lives to more people. Detractors note that (as in other transformations) there are winners and losers and emphasize the global forces that erode national sovereignty and indigenous cultures and further impoverish people who have few resources enabling them to compete in a global marketplace. Post–World War II Japanese leaders and post-Mao reform leaders in China opted to join the global economy as part of their development strategies, although the Chinese have been slow to accept many of the postwar political arrangements. Indian governments since the early 1990s have opened their economy to international trade and investment, but the global economy remains exceedingly controversial among trade unions, the intellectual and political elite, and many grassroots organizations. Many believe that opening the Indian economy to international competition contributes to unemployment and environmental damage and is also destructive of Indian culture.[1]

The discussions that follow raise questions about the connections between global integration and politics in Asia. Three preliminary observations are in order: First—as emphasized in Part One of this book—Asian political systems have long been molded by the confluence of indigenous, intra-Asian, and Western influences. Second, the foreign and the indigenous have often coexisted in tension, so when this tension occurs in the twenty-first century, we need to remind ourselves that it is not uniquely the result of the recent forces of globalization. Finally, we should reserve normative judgment about Asian politics until we examine the theories and values that we bring to our *own* study of politics. The matter of human rights illustrates both the complexities of globalization and also the importance of reserving (but not abandoning) judgment.

The Confluence of National, Transnational, and Global Politics

The changes described earlier in this book have altered politics in multiple ways. It has already been emphasized that government policies may have unintended effects and that governments are "sandwiched" between subnational and supranational political and economic pressures. In order to further illustrate these points and to illustrate some of the new forces that are reshaping the political terrain in Asia, the following sections look at the growth of consciousness about human rights and some of the tensions this growth has engendered.

Individuals and Communities

Since the crafting of the Universal Declaration of Human Rights in 1948, the belief that human rights should be accessible to all people has become a global reality, even when the belief is honored only in the breach. Numerous IGOs and NGOs are dedicated to pursuing human rights; the media track real and alleged abuses of rights; people are mobilized, insurrections mounted, and wars fought in the name of freeing people from oppression and securing human rights. Universal commitment, however, is not matched by universal agreement on exactly which rights should be accessible to all, whether some rights are more critical than others, or how to resolve conflicts between rights.

Americans tend to interpret rights in individual and procedural terms. When addressing the political dilemma of balancing the individual and the community, for example, Americans are more inclined to think first in terms of what they, as individuals, should be free to do. Many of the most important public policy debates in the United States embody the philosophical tension between definitions of rights that privilege individuals and those that emphasize the community. The debates over affirmative action and guns (free versus controlled access) are illustrations of this tension.

In contrast to the American tradition, community (variously defined as family, caste, clan, or religious or ethnic group) historically has been more important in Asia—just as it has been in many other places in the world. The infusion of Western values, including procedural norms of democracy and individual-based rights, has tended to undermine Asia's social and political traditions, with both positive and negative effects. The Shah Bano case described in Chapter 8, for example, illustrated the way in which a Muslim woman, pursuing her rights after divorce, stimulated communal tension between Hindus and Muslims. The case highlighted the diverse ways in which the matter of rights generates political conflict. Did Muslims as a community have the right to state protection for their separate laws and customs—however onerous they might be for an elderly, poor woman? Or did Shah Bano have the right to pursue her case for restitution—as an individual—through the courts, however threatening her cause was to community identity? Women's groups, including Muslim feminists, complicated the debate by pointing to the structural inequality between women and men that the case highlighted: Muslim community rights were defined by conservative, male clerics; the civil decision-makers were male; and single (divorced or widowed) women are socially stigmatized and economically disadvantaged throughout India. Taken together, these issues illustrate the intertwining of indigenous, intra-Asia, and Western political norms.

The tensions in India are but one example of the transformation of our rights consciousness that began with colonialism, was bolstered by European and American economic prowess in the twentieth century, and has accelerated with contemporary political and economic globalization. Two characteristics of this process warrant emphasizing because they tell us much about the political world we have inherited and are likely to bequeath: American influence on political rights and the growth of IGOs and NGOs.

Political Rights and American Influence

The primary American contribution to a nascent international human rights regime has been to propagate basic concepts stated in the U.S. Bill of Rights and that constitute the distinctive theory of American democracy. These include civil liberties such as freedom of speech and assembly, as well as rights to due process in legal proceedings, and the procedural norms of democracy, including the right to free elections. The continued relevance of these rights everywhere, including Asia, calls for little debate. The most egregious case of widespread rights abuses in Asia is probably Myanmar (Burma), where Nobel laureate Aung San Suu Kyi has struggled since 1988 against a military government that has tried to strangle her opposition political movement. Civil liberties routinely accepted in neighboring India are nonexistent in Myanmar. Freedom of information is denied in what one NGO called "the world's largest prison for journalists."[2] There is no independent judiciary. Forced labor, torture, and the repression of ethnic minorities (including the use of systematic rape) have been documented.[3] Under circumstances like these, few people are prepared to argue that the long-standing Western support for internationalizing norms of political liberty is undesirable.

Other situations are more debatable. In the case of abortion, for example, several American administrations worked to internationalize proscriptions against abortion by withholding funds from family planning programs. This is a controversial stance both because there is no consensus within the United States on the matter of the rights being protected and also because many countries disagree with the American position, making it difficult to argue that there is a Western or international consensus on the issue. American foreign policy on abortion is just that—American foreign policy; it is not indicative of the globalization of human rights. This is one reason that China's periodic criticism of American interference in its domestic affairs is often received more sympathetically by other countries than similar complaints from Myanmar's generals.

IGOs and NGOs

The second characteristic of the emerging global rights consciousness is the central role played by international and nongovernmental organizations. The United Nations system, in particular, has provided the context for establishing, however haltingly, an international rights regime, beginning with the Universal Declaration of Human Rights. Through the U.N. machinery, a series of wide-ranging treaties or conventions has established ideal performance standards that all governments should strive for in protecting human rights. These agreements gradually create popular expectations as well as policy benchmarks, even though they are rarely enforceable or are not ratified by all U.N. members.[4] The treaties are cited by groups around the world in a manner that recalls "rightful resistance" in China, where individuals and groups point to laws and the Chinese Constitution in order to enhance the legitimacy of their demands for justice.

Much of the momentum in this movement has been sustained by NGOs. Although the most powerful of these are based in Western countries, Asian-based NGOs have multiplied in the last three decades—sometimes with Western financial or organizational assistance, but often on their own. Whereas NGOs in China find it difficult (but not impossible) to challenge the government on rights issues, a wide diversity of Indian groups has long fought for the integrity of the fundamental rights promised by the Indian Constitution. As the previous chapter suggested, the development of Japanese NGOs has been uneven, but since the 1990s, it has been on the rise, often with support of activists from elsewhere in Asia. Anti-dam activists in Japan received support from environmental activists in both India and China.

Since the 1970s, NGOs, IGOs, and national governments have increasingly worked together on rights issues, often behind the scenes. Major international conferences sponsored by the United Nations to examine issues such as the rights of indigenous peoples, the disabled, children, or women, are structured with a parallel conference of nongovernmental organizations. Government and NGO representatives engage in a tug-of-war to set their agendas and draft documents, but the overall consequence is to highlight specific clusters of problems and recommend solutions. To cite a well-known example, the four United Nations Conferences on Women (1975, 1980, 1985, and 1995) drew increasing numbers of NGOs to participate in forums that ran parallel to the intergovernmental conferences. By the time of the Fourth World Conference on Women in Beijing (1995), approximately 30,000 individuals attended the NGO forum. Many of the Chinese women who attended or otherwise learned of the conference saw the panels, debates, and flea market of ideas as reflecting their concerns about women's rights. It would be an exaggeration to suggest that the conference transformed Chinese politics, but it is reasonable to surmise that the event legitimized efforts to draw attention to the problems of Chinese women in the reform period. The leaders of the All-China Women's Federation, for example, have used the platform issued by the Fourth U.N. Conference to press their own agenda on women's rights at the highest level of government.[5]

The transmission belts of globalization are not solely IGOs and NGOs, or even corporations and the Internet, but thousands of individuals on the move, including scholars, journalists, and study-abroad students, all of whom have the potential to magnify our rights awareness. Even before the Internet, modern travel often linked groups in ways that brought their voices into international debates about the meaning of rights and the best way to secure them. Years before Indian villages were "wired," for example, a young Indian lawyer made her way to a conference in Washington, D.C., to explain how her pro bono work helped poor village women pursue their rights through a ponderous court system. The global link for her was an American sociologist doing work on village development in South India and an NGO that purchased the lawyer's plane ticket.

To use a different illustration, efforts are made to introduce tourists in Cambodia to the problems of the 160,000 victims of land-mine explosions who have lost limbs. As tourists flock to Siem Riep to view the celebrated Angkor Wat ruins, they can visit a small gift shop run by an NGO, where the proceeds of purchases help land-mine victims and enhance awareness of the lingering costs of the political repression that ravaged the country under the Khmer Rouge during the 1970s.[6] In this way, the transnational flow of information and resources gradually changes both domestic and international politics.

Identity Politics and Cultural Rights

However worded, the essential criticism of globalization is that it erodes national sovereignty and ultimately national identity. From the perspective of the nation-state and its government, signing treaties and joining international organizations entail some loss of control over domestic economic and political life. National governments respond differently to this erosion of control, depending on their calculation of costs and benefits and the resources they can muster to advance their positions.

Even a casual reading of world history shows us that there is nothing sacred about national boundaries or even the nation-state as understood today. Nevertheless, as Part Two emphasized, constructing and defending the nation-state has been one of the central preoccupations of Asians in the modern era. Early European advocates of dissolving empires (such as the Austro-Hungarian and Ottoman empires) in the name of nationalities were followed by Asians who, like Africans later, challenged the British, French, Dutch, and American empires in the name of liberating the Indian subcontinent, (French) "Indo-China," Indonesia, and the Philippines.

Asian nation-states, like their predecessors, have been built by eradicating, absorbing, or altering indigenous and regional cultures, always at some cost to indigenous peoples, such as the Ainu or Okinawans in Japan. It is one of the realities of modern history that even the great anticolonial independence movements after World War II did not assure national unity. Partition in 1947 and later Pakistan's 1970–1971 civil war have scarred the Indian subcontinent for more than a half century. Pakistan's national aspirations are warped, like Afghanistan's, by regional cleavages and the enduring power of preindependence ethnic and tribal loyalties. The conflict in Kashmir is a constant reminder of the difficulty of guaranteeing national boundaries, identity, and stability. India struggles at both its western and eastern borders with ongoing secessionist movements. The "underside" of globalization, the international arms and drug trades, as well as terrorist networks, feed the regional tensions. In all of these circumstances, and in every country, preservation of human rights—however defined—quickly succumbs to the drive for territorial integrity of the nation-state.

Elsewhere in Asia, postcolonial nation-states struggle to maintain their hegemony over movements for local cultural identity (particularly preservation of language and religion), autonomy, or outright secession. Singhalese and Tamils have fought a civil war in Sri Lanka for over a quarter century; Tibetans and Taiwanese in very different ways have struggled for autonomy, challenging China's definition of national unity; East Timor finally won its independence from Indonesia in 2002, after nearly twenty-five years of fighting; and early in the twenty-first century, a resurgence of Muslim identity, in some cases with financial and political support from international groups, strengthened old secessionist movements in the southern Philippine island of Mindanao. In Mindanao, as in Sri Lanka, Tibet, and Kashmir, both alleged and very real abuses of basic human rights periodically escalated.

Although these movements and wars capture headlines, the issues of national identity are as much about culture as about territorial integrity. Whether in simple propaganda or complex philosophical treatises, people wrestle with assertions of identity and claim the right to cultural integrity. Symbols assume paramount significance: McDonald's becomes the sign of all things evil in foreign investment (Others) and flags the sign of all things great about one's own country (Us). Partisans of India's Hindutva movement, for example, appropriate the symbol *Om* (*Aum*) for the ancient, sacred Sanskrit mantra; flags reflect their political mobilization (see Photo 14.2).

A prominent Indian historian, Romila Thapar, has condemned this cultural nationalism as producing a "sledgehammer history" of India that has sought to capture the educational system at every level. The core dilemma of what it means to be Indian is resolved in favor of a claim "that the Hindus have had an unbroken, lineal descent for five thousand years. In order to maintain that the Hindus are Aryans and all others are non-Aryan and therefore foreigners, it has to be ar-

PHOTO 14.2 **Party appropriates sacred Hindu mantra "Om" ("AUM"), Rajasthan. Photo courtesy of James W. Boyd.**

gued that the Aryans and their language Indo-Aryan, are indigenous to India." Thapar observes that this kind of exercise recalls the Nazi abuse of archaeology in the 1930s to prove the Aryan origins of the Germans and links this new history to economic globalization, which generates the consumer aspirations of India's huge middle class.

> But . . . for the majority . . . these aspirations are not met, and there is a widening disparity between the suddenly affluent fraction and the rest who remain on the margin. The latter are caught up in intense competition over employment and suffer from insecurities with the breaking down of earlier forms of broad-based community living. The propagation and glamourising of hate . . . serves to heighten the uncertainties. The new communities created by globalization are supposed to be modern but where modernization fails them they use religious identities as a cover for a barbaric cult of terror and fear.[7]

Even in societies that are more homogeneous than India, the processes of globalization revive concerns over national identity in ways that are both blatant,

as when foreign companies move into the domestic market, and subtle, even un-
conscious, such as rethinking the meaning of national history and identity.
Chapter 1 noted that Chinese and Japanese see the events of World War II
through different lenses, and that particularly in Japan, there are also conflicting
domestic interpretations of the war. The conflict in the Japanese interpretations
reflects the tension in the national memory between definitions of Japan as victim and Japan as victimizer.

Underneath this tension in historical memory is the challenge to theories of
Japanese uniqueness, or *Nihonjinron*, provoked by globalization, which was explained in Chapter 7. Despite the stability marking Japanese history since 1945,
change was obvious in small and large ways by the twenty-first century. Some of
this resulted from the pervasive globalization of consumption patterns. Coffee, in
the 1980s an expensive luxury, had become competitively priced and ubiquitous.
Blond hair in Japan is no longer a dependable mark of foreigners. Other changes
reveal the shift in fundamental values, often reflecting the permeation of international human rights norms: People with disabilities, once hidden, are increasingly
visible, acknowledged, and supported. Thus at the same time that they "reproduce globalization through consumption,"[8] changes in diet, dress, and personal
behavior heighten awareness of the ways in which Japan has changed. "With such
imports come threats to a sense of cultural identity and the feeling that the geo-
graphical and psychic boundaries so jealously guarded since at least the early
Tokugawa have become so porous as to have almost disappeared."[9]

Japan, of course, has been an aggressive contributor to globalization, whether
through its own multinational corporations, foreign investment, and foreign aid,
or through its cultural exports, from *anime* and *manga* to religions and sushi. Political conservatives, however, typically focus on the threat to identity rather than Japan's role in defining and extending processes of globalization. The stance of
conservatives, in turn, raises questions about the trajectory of Japanese history over
the past half century and the directions it will take in the twenty-first century.

Although conservative interpreters of Japanese identity often seize the headlines, it is worth noting the longer-term, more subtle changes that have occurred
in Japan's relationships with its Asian neighbors. One illustration of these
changes was observed earlier: Scholars, lawyers, and human rights activists
joined together in the 1990s to bring to public attention the history of military
sexual slavery—and Japanese were active participants in this process.

More recently, a team of Japanese, Chinese, and Koreans gave us a "microcosm"
and "window" into the issues of historical memory in Asia. Readers will recall the
textbook debate highlighted in Chapter 1, and in particular the conflicts between
Japanese and Chinese interpretations of historical events such as the Nanjing Mas-

sacre. The 2002 Japanese Ministry of Education approval of a right-wing text for use in the middle schools prompted a trinational forum that led to the decision to collaborate on a history text. Although it took almost a year to agree on the outline, the book (designed as a supplementary teaching resource) was completed in 2005. The significance of this effort goes beyond its role in illustrating transnational cooperation to the awareness it provoked among the participants themselves. Although they were, by definition, committed to international understanding, they discovered their "own-history-centeredness," that is they came to understand the nature of their *own* national lenses and, in effect, relearned history.[10]

The individuals engaged in these kinds of efforts are largely self-funded, and although they may have government connections (especially true for the Chinese participants), they reflect the dynamics of complex civil societies in the twenty-first century. Governments as well often show the impact of similar changes. For example, the old museum at Hiroshima emphasized Japan as the victim of nuclear devastation. But the museum was expanded, and new exhibits were added to show the role of Hiroshima as a major military and industrial center in the war, so now visitors are given a context that helps explain why the city was targeted by the United States.

Human Security in the Twenty-first Century

In 1994, the annual report of the United Nations Development Program (UNDP) emphasized the theme of human security, as meaning "freedom from fear and freedom from want."[11] In elaborating on the concept, the UNDP summarized much of the thinking about development that Chapter 13 explained: Sustainability, equity, basic human needs, and the "universalism of life claims"— all are central to human security.[12] The report elaborated further by defining the various dimensions of human security: economic, food, health, environmental, personal, community, and political. Two dimensions of the UNDP approach stand out. First, human security is seamless, that is, it embraces conditions from the individual or personal through the national and global. The second key dimension is the multidimensionality of the security concept. One can no longer think of security solely in military terms, for ultimately the human condition embraces more than violence—it demands that we address the social, economic, and political conditions under which we live. Thus many of the concepts discussed in the previous chapter are relevant here, including the nature of development, the quality of governance, and the pressing issues of the environment.

Although the UNDP approach reinforces our understanding of the interconnected nature of security, in this section we draw attention specifically to issues of physical security, including military security and the reality of violence. Looking back over the post–World War II period, a number of Asian countries stand out for the number and duration of international and intrastate conflicts they have been involved in: Burma/Myanmar, India, Vietnam, Indonesia, and Thailand all rank in the top two dozen conflict-prone states.[13] Although the number of international conflicts declined toward the end of the twentieth century, in retrospect, it was a century of violence, and Asia was no exception: "In the second half of the century, most of the killing took place in the developing world, especially Asia."[14] From West to South Asia, the Chinese Civil War, the Korean War, the Vietnam War, the Iran-Iraq War, and wars in Afghanistan accounted for one-half of all battle deaths between 1946 and 2002 (that is, before the U.S. invasions of Afghanistan and Iraq).[15] As of 2007, there were four major armed conflicts, all of which had endured decades and caused more than 150,000 battle-related deaths (see Table 14.1).

The specter of a nuclear conflict in Asia, where China, India, and Pakistan all possess nuclear weapons, contributes further to the overall picture of human insecurity (see Focus Box 14). The most dangerous areas are South Asia, where India and Pakistan confront each other, and Northeast Asia, where the division between North and South Korea persists, and North Korea seeks to develop its nuclear potential. This scenario is one of the primary justifications for the Japanese argument that it is time to reassess the country's nonnuclear status and also its constitution—particularly Article 9. Given the historical dynamics between the countries of East Asia, however, any significant shift in Japanese policies is bound to have a ripple effect on the Korean peninsula, in China, and certainly also in China-Taiwan relationships.

If one were to add to this picture violence not related to war but which often results in death (personal violence, including rape and murder, political violence, and so forth), Asia does not appear to be a very secure region. Moreover, in the

TABLE 14.1 Major Armed Conflicts in Asia

Country	Location of Conflict (Territory)	Year Conflict Originated	Total Battle- Related Deaths
India	Kashmir	1977	29,300
Myanmar	Karen State	1948	20,100
Philippines	Mindanao	1968	38,600
Sri Lanka	"Tamil Eelem"	1976	64,400

Source: Adapted from SIPRI Yearbook: Armaments, Disarmament and International Security (Oxford: Oxford University Press, 2008, for the Stockholm International Peace Research Institute), Table 2A.3.

FOCUS BOX 14

NUCLEAR ASIA

In February 2009, Abdul Qadeer Khan was released from house arrest in Pakistan. Considered a national hero in his country for building Pakistan's nuclear program, Khan admitted in 2004 that for two decades he had sold nuclear technology and equipment to such countries as Libya, Iran, and North Korea. Thus he played a pivotal role in "nuclearizing" Asia from west to east. To European and North American governments concerned about nuclear proliferation, he remains a pariah.

Although nuclear power is central to the strategy of such countries as South Korea and Japan to increase domestic energy supplies, nuclear weapons are one of the most important sources of tension in Northeast, South, and West Asia. The six-nation group (China, South Korea, Japan, North Korea, Russia, and the United States) that has intermittently, from the Clinton and Bush to the Obama administrations, negotiated to persuade North Korea to terminate its nuclear aspirations has largely failed. In 2006, North Korea tested a small nuclear device, and in 2009, it claimed to have "weaponized" enough plutonium for several nuclear bombs. On the other side of Asia, both threats and offers of negotiations similarly failed to dissuade Iran from developing its nuclear capability.

The situation in South Asia presents somewhat different problems: both India and Pakistan are acknowledged nuclear powers, and the ongoing conflicts over Kashmir and the terrorist attacks in India have increased tension between two countries that have fought three wars since independence. Neither has signed the Non-Proliferation Treaty (NPT) that has been in effect since 1968; both argue that the treaty's restrictions on nuclear states supplying technology to nonnuclear states constitute an unequal system. Questions about the long-range stability of Pakistan raise further issues about the degree of control the government is able to maintain over technology, fuel, and the weapons themselves.

The most important development in recent years is the U.S.-India Nuclear Cooperation Accord and Non-Proliferation Enhancement Act that the two countries signed in 2008. Despite the fact that India has refused to sign the NPT and has agreed to place only eight of its fourteen nuclear reactors under international inspection, the United States, under President George W. Bush, pushed for the accord. Critics claim that the act sets a bad precedent, essentially rewarding India although it has disregarded the NPT. Supporters point to

continues

┌───┐
│ *continued*   **FOCUS BOX 14**   │
│   │
│ the country's desperate need for energy: India wants to increase its nuclear │
│ power generation from 3 to 20 percent of its total within the next three de- │
│ cades. Although it isn't argued publicly by either government, both Americans │
│ and Indians presumably see this enhanced capability as a counterweight to │
│ China. Clearly for the United States, concern about the overall stability of the │
│ region was a motivation to conclude the agreement. For Indian Prime Minister │
│ Manmohan Singh, who staked the life of his coalition government on the │
│ agreement in 2008, U.S. congressional approval was a major political victory. │
│   │
│ ─── │
│ I am grateful to Robert M. Lawrence for his insights on this topic. │
└───┘

twenty-first century, Asia has become one of the most important centers of human trafficking, primarily for sex. Statistics vary widely as to the number of people trafficked, both within and across borders, but the most vulnerable to trafficking are overwhelmingly women and girls. Trafficking is clearly linked to issues of development, for it is typically (though not always) the poorest individuals who are most prone to exploitation. Moreover, "armed conflicts create new opportunities for traffickers. War torn countries may be used as transit routes, while mass displacement and loss of livelihoods create a huge potential supply of victims."[16] Cambodia, Thailand, India, and Nepal have all been implicated as major centers of trafficking.

Some might assume that the greater the public expenditure in areas that contribute directly to human development and the lower a government's military expenditures, the more likely we would be to see reduced levels of violence. The patterns are not so clear, however, as Table 14.2 suggests. India spends more on education than Japan but achieves less, for a variety of reasons. Singapore and Vietnam devote the highest percentage of their GDP to military expenditures, yet neither state is currently engaged in a conflict. Japan's high expenditure on public health reflects both a higher level of development but also higher expenditures due to an aging population. Despite the limitations of statistics such as these, the data remind us that government priorities are subjected to multiple competing pressures and policies must be understood within the context of historical trends.

Despite this comparatively bleak assessment of security issues in Asia, all of which recall historical trajectories elsewhere in the world, it is appropriate to remember that which is uncommon—or unique—about the Asian experience, and how we can learn from this experience.

TABLE 14.2 Public Expenditure on Health, Education, and the Military

Country	Public Expenditure on Health (% of GDP)—2004	Public Expenditure on Education (% of GDP)— 2002–2005*	Military Expenditure (% of GDP)—2006
India	0.9	3.8	2.7
China	1.8	1.9	2.1
Japan	6.3	3.6	1.0
Indonesia	1.0	0.9	1.3
Korea (R.O.K.)	2.9	4.6	2.5
Pakistan	0.4	2.3	3.2
Philippines	1.4	2.7	0.9
Thailand	2.3	4.2	1.1
Singapore	1.3	3.7	4.7
Vietnam	1.5	N/A	5.6
United States	6.9	5.9	4.0

* Data are from the most recent year available during the period specified.

Source: Compiled from the United Nations Development Program, *Human Development Report 2007/2008*, at http://hdr.undp.org/en/ (public expenditures on health and education); *SIPRI Yearbook of Armaments, Disarmament and International Security* (Oxford: Oxford University Press, for the Stockholm International Peace Research Institute, 2008), 229–230 (military expenditure except for Vietnam); and International Institute for Strategic Studies (IISS), *The Military Balance 2008* (London: Routledge, 2008), accessed November 21, 2008, at http://www.iiss.org (for Vietnam's military expenditure).

Learning from Asia

Boundaries of the Social Sciences

Contemporary social science, including political science, is grounded in Western thought systems that bring with them assumptions about human agency, society, and nature. Asian thought systems have long challenged these assumptions in a manner that has profound implications for our understanding of reality, including social reality. A common example is that of medicine, where Chinese practices, including acupuncture, have stretched the boundaries of Western scientific approaches to health. Similarly, traditional Indian, Chinese, and Japanese philosophies, when taken seriously, force us to reappraise the connections between individuals and communities that are central to most Western thinking about politics.

One of the most provocative ways in which the Asian traditions expand the boundaries of the "social" is in the relationship between nature and humans.

Contemporary philosophers and ecologists have challenged the dominant instrumental view that there is a clear hierarchy between nature and humans and that progress is defined in terms of the ability of humans, through technology and social organization, to control nature. These views are central to the development experience of the past three centuries and define the way in which socioeconomic systems (whether capitalist or communist) approach the environment.

The argument that we can learn from Asia about the environment does not rest on the physical evidence of development, which obviously has wrought as much environmental degradation in the East as in the West. Rather, it rests on the subtle, but influential, contributions of Asian thought to questioning old "givens" about human well-being—what it means and how societies should achieve it. To cite one well-known (and exceedingly controversial) example, Indian physicist and philosopher Vandana Shiva has argued that development approaches in the so-called Third World replicate Western economic and scientific beliefs that destroy the environment. She further argues that the Western approaches are philosophically grounded in an epistemological tradition of dominance and a reductionism which reduces both the capacity of humans to know nature and "the capacity of nature to creatively regenerate and renew itself by manipulating it as inert and fragmented matter."[17]

In Japan, the worldview of Shrine Shinto also offers a different approach to nature, one that assumes that humans are embedded in and participate in nature. Shrine rituals permit participants to tap into the *ki*, or universal energy of all life forms.[18] Individual shrines encourage humans to connect to a specific place and specific *kami* that are embodied in trees and water, for example, and that link us with an immense life force. Although Shrine Shinto is related to State Shinto, which is explicitly political (see Chapters 4 and 7), John Clammer has maintained that the worldview of Shrine Shinto has the potential to be politically subversive. The principal focus of a shrine is nature and the cosmos; it "points to a mode of thinking, organization and rootedness in the universe."[19] Human interests, including politics, exist within this much broader context, and Clammer has argued that a rethinking of the animism in Shinto "reflects a deep ecological consciousness: one which sees the environment not merely as object, but as something inseparable from the species-being of humanity."[20]

Ideas such as these are embedded in a cultural experience profoundly different from the dominant thought patterns in modern Europe or North America. Western social sciences rest primarily on an ontological dichotomy or division between humans and nature, natural and supernatural, but other thought systems, including many among indigenous peoples around the world, challenge that division.

Rethinking Development and Democracy

If some Asian values are cause for questioning the environmental impact of Western development models, Asian experiences with economic growth open different questions. Put bluntly, the central question is why some countries have modernized successfully—even spectacularly—and others not. The answer lies in some combination of resources, culture, institutions, and policies, all of which have been explored by scholars and practitioners of development. Of these, the most provocative factor is culture because it seems so obvious, but at the same time it is "slippery," that is, hard to define and harder to quantify. Are the cultural differences that obviously exist between Asia and Europe, as well as among Asian countries, sufficient to explain differences in development experiences? Few think culture is a sufficient explanatory factor, although it may be a necessary one.

Culture is not static; it evolves in response to indigenous and exogenous forces, as a result of formal government initiative and informal shifts in popular tastes. It is reasonable to assume, therefore, that culture influences development patterns in two fundamental ways: It sets the context within which economic and political change occurs, and it is also a potential tool to be used in the crafting of development strategies.

In East Asia, the cultural norms most frequently explored in understanding development are linked to Confucianism, which influenced not only China, but also Korea, Japan, Taiwan, Singapore, and Vietnam. As a moral and political philosophy, Confucianism emphasizes hierarchical reciprocal relationships, deference to authority, and bureaucratic privilege, all of which have persisted to varying degrees in East Asia. Other prominent cultural patterns, such as group orientation, have fused with Confucian practices to become politically important, as illustrated by the factionalism that dominates Japanese political parties.[21]

By the 1980s, it had become common to argue that these cultural attributes were instrumental in facilitating the rapid modernization of Japan, South Korea, Taiwan, Hong Kong, and Singapore, by establishing, for example, a respect for authority and high emphasis on education.[22] References to an "East Asian development model" spread. Although subsequently challenged—partly as a result of the region's economic problems in the 1990s—the focus on this development model challenged conventional thinking about development.

Through the 1970s, two competing theories dominated social science analyses of development. One assumed that the experience of Western Europe would be replicated for "late comers" to modernization. Development would be promoted by capitalism, "modern" (secular) cultural values and social structures, and, for some theorists, Western-style democracy. Many theorists also assumed an inherent conflict between growth and equity.[23] The alternative "dependency" theorists criticized the assumptions of a European pattern by emphasizing the position of developed and "underdeveloped" economies in a world economic system dominated by Western Europe and North America. The latter, the "core" of the system, is seen as exploiting the "periphery" in a relationship of dependency.

The economic success of several East Asian countries challenged these two theories in several ways. First, development in countries such as Japan, South Korea, Taiwan, and Singapore did not follow the Western historical trajectory. The East Asian experience also challenged the assumptions about conflict between growth and equity because these countries seemed to have experienced less class inequality (or experienced it for a shorter period) than European countries during their periods of rapid industrialization. These same East Asian countries, however, also undermined dependency theory because the export policies pursued as part of their growth strategy reflected the reality that these countries were economically dependent on the core, but they achieved remarkable rates of economic growth despite that dependence.

The main value of hypothesizing an East Asian development model was not that it led to better prediction or was any more consistent throughout the region than its predecessors. Yet it did stimulate a new debate about the diversity of variables that produce development, the relationship between these variables, and ultimately the meaning of development itself. In particular, the dominant role that government played in East Asian development contributed to studies of "state-led development" and helped to generate a reconsideration of the role of state institutions in political processes.[24]

The persistence of traditional cultural norms in the rapidly growing Asian states also encouraged scholars and practitioners to consider the possibility of several models of development and to suggest that "modern" might not be synonymous with "Western." Samuel Huntington emphasized this point:

> The image of the developed Western society . . . may not constitute a meaningful model or reference group for a modern Islamic, African, Confucian, or Hindu society. Throughout the non-Western world, societies have judged themselves by Western standards and found themselves wanting. Maybe the time has come to stop trying to change these societies and to change the model, to develop models of a modern Islamic, Confucian, or Hindu society that would be more relevant to countries where those cultures prevail.[25]

The above quotation raises (but does not answer) the question of what a relevant non-Western development model might look like. As Chapter 13 noted, from the Great Leap Forward through the Cultural Revolution, Maoist China prioritized an unconventional idiom of development, one that emphasized national self-reliance, economic decentralization, communal structures, and class and gender equality. But the political and cultural extremes of that era, along with economic failures, led to the reform period of the late 1970s. Since then, Chinese policies have recalled the early phases of other East Asian development paths by combining rapid, export-oriented growth with political authoritarianism, leaving open the question of whether China might gradually democratize as South Korea and Taiwan have.

Does India, a democracy from independence, offer another model? India, like China, emphasized national self-reliance, although its early policies were deeply influenced by Western thought. Prime Minister Jawaharlal Nehru, who more than any other leader crafted the early vision of modern India, believed that India could follow three goals simultaneously: industrialization directed by the state, constitutional democracy, and economic and social redistribution. With these goals, his project was close to European social democracy, and he refused to make the "stark choice" between development and democracy.[26]

For the first quarter-century after independence, India appeared to have plotted a workable alternative path to development, one that made impressive gains in building an industrial infrastructure, encouraged agricultural modernization through the "Green Revolution" of the 1960s, avoided the polarity of Cold War politics, and maintained both a secular democracy and cultural integrity—without the violence and repression that marked China during the same period.

In their analysis of the Indian path, Lloyd I. Rudolph and Susanne Hoeber Rudolph attributed much of India's success to the one-party–dominant system under which the Congress Party maintained moderate policies and an ideological commitment to secular democracy. The Rudolphs used the metaphor of Lakshmi, the Indian goddess of good fortune and prosperity, to symbolize the aspirations of many Indians, and as an indigenous figure, uniquely represents the interplay of party politics, state policies, and social forces that characterized India's accomplishments and failures. Lakshmi's image and name are still widely used in advertising, as shown in Photo 14.3.[27]

Both the metaphor of Lakshmi and the Rudolphs' analysis are helpful in understanding early Indian development efforts in the context of India's complex cultural traditions and social structures. The contradiction between wealth and poverty and the divisive politics of religion and region prevalent since the 1980s suggest, however, that this model is unsuitable for other countries. Nonetheless, India arguably contributes more to our comparative exploration of persistent political dilemmas than any other Asian country. India has eschewed both communist

PHOTO 14.3 Advertising: Mahalakshmi. Photo courtesy of James W. Boyd.

and military rule, which have been tried in countries as diverse as the former Yugoslavia and Soviet Union, as well as Thailand, Pakistan, and Indonesia. Most of all, India continues to grapple with the issue that dominated Nehru's early thinking: How to avoid the "stark choice" between development and democracy.

Conclusion

By exploring the relevance of globalization for Asia and the multiple ways in which the study of Asia enriches comparative politics, this chapter can only raise more questions than it answers. So it is with the book as a whole, which is intended as a bridge to further thinking about Asia in the context of the political climate of the twenty-first century. The world in which the political, social, and economic transformation of Asian countries is occurring is very different from the world in which European countries—or Japan for that matter—modernized earlier. One of the most important differences is that the nation-state, as a form of political organization, is increasingly undermined by global forces at the same time that nationalism, as a source of political identity, appears to enjoy new life.

It is perhaps a historical irony that a global economy coexists with a nation-state organization that is defined by the efforts of the state to secure territorial integrity and national identity. The tension between the policies governments follow in order to compete in and secure benefit from global transactions, on the one hand, and the desire to monopolize political control within the national boundaries, on the other, is amply illustrated in China. In different ways, India also struggles with the global economic momentum and, perhaps even more than China, with the regional and international pressures on its territory that have escalated with the conflict in Kashmir. The worst scenario for India, like Pakistan, in the twenty-first century is disintegration of the country into a series of civil wars or wars of secession that, given the international relations of the subcontinent, would likely mean international conflict as well.

Viewed historically, both the international relations and the domestic politics of Asia reflect choices and organizations that have evolved during a period of dramatic political change that dates back roughly 150 years. The middle of the nineteenth century was replete with harbingers of the massive transformation of Asia, but it would have been impossible to imagine the complexities that we confront in the early twenty-first century. The most important difference, of course, is that in this century—unlike the nineteenth—Asians are writing their own history.

Notes

1. For an extreme version of this position, see the writings of novelist and political activist Arundhati Roy.

2. Reporters without Borders, *2002 Asia Annual Report* (section on Burma), found at www.rsf.org. Radio, television, and all daily newspapers are run by the military government.

3. See, for example, the annual reports of Human Rights Watch/Asia at www.hrw.org and Amnesty International at www.amnesty.org.

4. For example, the United States has not ratified two treaties that have been ratified by the vast majority of countries: the 1989 Convention on the Rights of the Child and the 1979 Convention on the Elimination of All Forms of Discrimination Against Women.

5. "Women and Violence," Comments by Deng Li, Deputy-Director of the ACWF Legal Department, China-U.S. Conference on Women's Issues, Beijing, October 2002.

6. The Khmer Rouge was a radical communist movement that captured the Cambodian government in 1975, proceeding to establish an agrarian society by evacuating cities, closing factories and schools, and killing skilled workers and intellectuals. In 1979, Vietnam invaded Cambodia and deposed the Khmer Rouge government, but not until the late 1990s did the remnants of the movement dissolve. An estimated 1.5 million people were killed or died as a result of Khmer Rouge rule.

7. Romila Thapar, "History as Politics," *Outlook India*, May 1, 2003; online edition at www.outlookindia.com.

8. John Clammer, *Japan and Its Others: Globalization, Difference and the Critique of Modernity* (Melbourne: Trans Pacific Press, 2001), 17.

9. Ibid., 5.

10. The term and the description of this process are from Lonny Carlile, "Reconciling History: Political Context and Dynamics of Common History," Presentation to the Japan Studies Association conference, New Orleans, January 10, 2009. The participants came from Japan, China, and Korea.

11. UNDP, *Human Development Report 1994: Towards Sustainable Human Development* (Oxford: Oxford University Press, for the UNDP, 1994), 24.

12. Ibid., 13 and following.

13. Human Security Centre (University of British Columbia), *Human Security Report 2005: War and Peace in the 21st Century* (Oxford: Oxford University Press, 2005), 26–27.

14. Ibid., 29.

15. Ibid.

16. Ibid., 88.

17. Vandana Shiva, *Staying Alive: Women, Ecology and Development* (London: Zed Books, 1989), 22.

18. In popular Japanese psychology, *ki* has a variety of translations referring to "mind" and "spirit." Principles of *ki* or *qi/chi* (in Chinese) are central to practices of mental-physical discipline, including tai chi, qigong, and the martial arts, such as aikido.

19. Clammer, 235.

20. Ibid., 238–239.

21. See the discussion in Robert W. Compton Jr., *East Asian Democratization: Impact of Globalization, Culture, and Economy* (Westport, Conn.: Praeger, 2000), chap. 2.

22. Some observers noted the irony of this reassessment of Confucianism, which earlier had been blamed for hindering development in Asia, especially China. The

classic critique of Confucianism as a hindrance to modernization is found in the writing of the great twentieth-century sociologist Max Weber. For a careful analysis of Weber, Confucianism, and traditional culture in East Asia, especially Japan, see Winston Davis, "Religion and Development: Weber and the East Asian Experience," in *Understanding Political Development*, eds. Myron Weiner and Samuel P. Huntington (Boston: Little, Brown, 1987), 221–280.

23. Samuel P. Huntington, "The Goals of Development," in Weiner and Huntington, *Understanding Political Development*, 11–13.

24. See, for example, David Waldner, *State Building and Late Development* (Ithaca: Cornell University Press, 1999), chap. 6.

25. Huntington, 25.

26. Sunil Khilani, *The Idea of India* (New York: Farrar, Straus and Giroux, 1999), 76, 80.

27. Rudolph and Rudolph were explicit about the importance of Lakshmi to their analysis, in which they endeavored to emphasize both the unique elements and the comparative utility of a complex country. In this way, Lakshmi enabled them to bridge East and West, the universal and the particular. *In Pursuit of Lakshmi: The Political Economy of the Indian State* (Chicago: University of Chicago Press, 1987), 393.

Glossary

Ainu Indigenous people of the northern Japanese island of Hokkaido.

Akali Dal Sikh political party in Punjab state.

All-India Muslim League Established in 1906 to promote Muslim interests in Indian nationalist movement; later led by **Jinnah**.

Amaterasu Omikami Legendary sun goddess marking the origin of the Japanese imperial line.

Ambedkar, B. R. (1891–1956) Indian nationalist and leader of the untouchables; critic of Hindu caste structure.

Arya Samaj Indian nationalist organization founded in 1875; sought to restore ideal Hindu Aryan past.

Ayodhya North Indian town; legendary birthplace of Hindu god **Rama**; location of Muslim mosque destroyed in 1992, leading to Hindu-Muslim conflicts in India.

Backward Classes (BCs) Socially and economically disadvantaged Indians; includes **Scheduled Castes and Tribes**, as well as lower strata of Shudras (see *varna*), the latter also called Other Backward Classes (OBCs).

Bharat, Bharatiya Original name in Sanskrit and Hindi for India, after one of the early Aryan tribes that invaded the subcontinent around 4,000 years ago.

Bharatiya Janata Party (BJP) Indian People's Party.

Boxer Uprising (1899–1900) Based in Shandong Province; an attack on foreign, especially Christian, presence in China.

Brahman Ultimate reality or One in philosophical Hinduism.

Brahmin Member of the highest *varna* in India; traditional priestly caste (may also be spelled "Brahman").

British East India Company Founded in 1600 for trade in India; gradually became the de facto ruler of India until control was officially assumed by the British Crown in 1858.

Burakumin Literally, "hamlet people"; traditional, pejorative name, *eta*; indigenous "subclass" of Japan.

caste Inherited social, ritual, and class distinctions characteristic of Hindu society in India. See also *jati* and *varna*.

Chiang Kai-shek (1887–1975) Leader of **Kuomintang** after death of **Sun Yat-sen**; president of the Republic of China.

civil society Political arena of voluntary associations not under the control of the state or family.

collective responsibility Principle of parliamentary government found in India and Japan, under which government ministers share responsibility for defending government policies.

comfort women Euphemism for women forced to provide sex for the Imperial Japanese Army during World War II.

communalism Indian term for loyalties to and tensions between communities of faith, particularly Hindu and Muslim.

communes Administrative and economic unit found in China from 1950s to 1970s; ranged in size from 5,000 to 50,000 people.

Confucianism System of Chinese ethics, government, and social order derived from the teachings of Confucius (551–479 B.C.E.).

Congress Party Successor to Indian nationalist movement, the **Indian National Congress**; dominant party in India from 1947 until mid-1990s.

Constituent Assembly (India) Legislature responsible for writing India's Constitution, 1947–1949.

Cultural Revolution Also called "Great Proletarian Cultural Revolution," peak years 1966–1969. Maoist-inspired campaigns to eliminate so-called revisionists in the party and "feudal" elements in Chinese culture. **Red Guards** mobilized for leading role.

Dalai Lama Literally, "grand priest." Tibet's traditional spiritual and political leader; currently Tenzin Gyatso.

dalit "Oppressed" or "downtrodden"; contemporary name for former untouchables; signifies commitment to political activism.

declining sex ratio Decline in the proportion of females to males in a population.

democratic centralism Leninist organizational principle for Communist Party, found in CCP; presumes consultation and exchange of views before decisions are taken, then centralized control is enforced.

Deng Xiaoping (1904–1997) Long March veteran and top Chinese leader after 1978; credited with China's policies of economic modernization.

dharma Sanskrit term referring to the sacred law governing the universe as well as to codes of conduct governing relations between social groups and religions; central to the Hindu worldview.

Diet Japanese national parliament.

Directive Principles of State Policy Socioeconomic goals found in Part 4 of the Indian Constitution.

Dravidian Language grouping and peoples based in South India; linguistic and cultural heritage distinguished from Sanskrit-based languages and culture of North India.

dynastic cycles Classical Chinese theory that imperial rule moved in cyclical fashion, with socioeconomic and political well-being followed by the decline and ultimately the fall of a dynasty. See **Mandate of Heaven**.

Edo Traditional name for Tokyo; on the Edo period, see **Tokugawa period/shogunate**.

Emergency, the Period from 1975 to 1977 when the government of Prime Minister **Indira Gandhi** invoked a state of emergency in India, suspending constitutional civil rights protection.

extraterritorial jurisdiction Characteristic provision of unequal treaties that China was forced to sign with foreign states, under which foreign residents of China were governed by the laws of their own states (nineteenth century).

Four Modernizations China's program of modernizing agriculture, industry, defense, and science and technology, begun in late 1970s, for which **Deng Xiaoping** was given credit.

fusion of powers Characteristic of parliamentary systems, in which cabinet government is drawn from and reflects the majority of the legislature, hence, legislative and executive branches are "fused."

Gandhi, Indira (1917–1984) Daughter of **Jawaharlal Nehru** and prime minister of India, 1966–1977 and 1980–1984.

Gandhi, Mohandas K. (1869–1948) Indian nationalist leader known for his philosophy of nonviolence and his efforts to reform Hinduism. Called Mahatma, meaning "the Great Soul."

Gang of Four Group of radical leaders, led by **Mao Zedong**'s wife, Jiang Qing. Rose to prominence during the **Cultural Revolution**; were arrested and imprisoned shortly after Mao's death.

Gender Development Indicators (GDI) HDI indicators disaggregated by gender.

Gender Empowerment Measure (GEM) Indicators of political empowerment of women and men constructed by the United Nations Development Programme.

Government of India Act (1935) British reform of India's political institutions; many provisions were carried over to independent India's Constitution.

Great Leap Forward Maoist campaign (1958–1959) for accelerated economic production and ideological "redness"; disastrous human and economic consequences.

guanxi "Personal connections"; found throughout Chinese politics.

Gupta period Along with Mauyra, major ancient North Indian empire, ca. fourth to sixth century C.E.; India's "golden age."

Han Ethnic majority (approximately 90 percent) of Chinese population; name derives from Han dynasty (206 B.C.E.–222 C.E.).

harijans "Children of God"; Gandhi's term for untouchables.

Hinduism Dominant worldview of approximately 85 percent of Indians; caste system intrinsic to Hindu social structure.

Hindutva Concept of a Hindu India, supported by **Bharatiya Janata Party**.

Hirohito Personal name of the Emperor Showa (literally "Enlightened Peace"); reigned 1926–1989.

Hu Jintao China's preeminent political leader, chosen for two terms: 2002–2007 and 2007–2012.

Human Development Indicators (HDI) Indicators from the United Nations Development Programme to measure development within the nations of the world.

Hundred Flowers Campaign The 1956 invitation by CCP leaders for criticism of government and revolution; followed by purges and "reeducation" of dissenters.

IGO Intergovernmental organizations; international organizations whose members are nation-states or other international organizations.

Imperial House Shinto Ancient Shinto rituals performed by and for the imperial family.

Imperial Rescript on Education (1890) Required reading of all Japanese schoolchildren as part of their moral education; symbolized conservative, Confucian reaction of late Meiji period.

Indian National Congress Also called "Congress." Founded 1885; most important nationalist movement from 1880s until independence, when it became the **Congress Party**.

interlocking directorship Found in **party-state systems**, in which party leaders simultaneously hold government positions.

Islam "Submission" to God's law or command; the Muslim religion.

Jainism An Indian religion with less than 1 percent of the population as adherents; originally a movement to reform Hinduism.

jati Endogamous, ritual, occupational subdivisions of *varna*, Indian castes.

Jinnah, Muhammad Ali (1876–1948) Prominent Indian nationalist leader; president of Muslim League and founder of Pakistan.

kami Sacred spirits found in indigenous Japanese belief system of **Shinto**.

keiretsu Japanese company networks joined by common links to banks and trading companies.

ki (also *qi* or *chi*) East Asian concept of spiritual and physical energy that pervades life.

koenkai Local-level, quasi-permanent organizations that provide support for LDP politicians in Japan.

kokutai National polity or essence; theory of the essence of the Japanese state developed in eighteenth and nineteenth centuries. Emphasized uniqueness of Japanese imperial tradition; foundation of twentieth-century Japanese nationalism.

Komeito (New) Clean Government Party; Japanese political party created in 1960s; affiliated with **Soka Gakkai**, Buddhist lay organization.

Kuomintang (KMT) Nationalist Party (successor to **Tongmeng Hui**). (In Pinyin, Guomindang [GMD].)

Liberal Democratic Party (LDP) Dominant governing, conservative party in Japan after 1955.

Lin Biao Former Chinese vice premier and defense minister; rose to top leadership during the **Cultural Revolution**, named "heir apparent" to **Mao Zedong** in 1969 CCP Constitution; allegedly died fleeing the country in 1971.

Lok Sabha House of the People; lower house of Indian parliament.

Long March Yearlong, six-thousand-mile march (1934–1935) of Communists from their bases in southwest China to Shaanxi Province in the North. Consolidated Communist Party leadership.

Malthus, Thomas (1766–1834) Argued that Chinese population would outstrip food production in *An Essay on the Principle of Population* (1798).

Mandate of Heaven Classical Chinese imperial theory that the emperor reflected the will of heaven in his rule but through misrule could lose this mandate. See **dynastic cycles**.

Mao Zedong (1893–1976) Preeminent leader of Chinese Communist movement.

May Fourth Movement Name taken from Beijing demonstration against results of Versailles Conference, May 4, 1919; became major intellectual and political movement in post–World War I period.

Meiji Constitution (1889) Part of conservative reaction to Meiji borrowing; established governing institutions for Japan, including the sacred role of the emperor, that remained in place until 1945.

Meiji Restoration (1868–1912) Period of rapid modernization in Japan, named after the Meiji emperor (reign name: "enlightened rule") who was "restored" to the throne after the **Tokugawa shogunate.**

Middle Kingdom "Central country" *(Zhongguo);* traditional name for China; reflection of the belief that inferior peoples and cultures surrounded the Chinese.

Morley-Minto Reforms (1909) Important British reforms in India; created separate Muslim and Hindu electorates.

Mughal Empire Muslim empire in North India (sixteenth to nineteenth centuries).

national minorities Government-designated ethnic minority groups in China, many of which live in autonomous regions.

National People's Congress National legislature in China.

Nehru, Jawaharlal (1889–1964) Leader of Indian nationalist movement; supporter of secular constitution and strong central government; first prime minister of India; father of **Indira Gandhi.**

new religions Japanese sects and movements derived from Buddhism and Shinto; developed in the nineteenth and twentieth centuries, attracting millions of followers. See **Soka Gakkai.**

nihonjinron Debate about the nature and meaning of Japanese national identity.

nongovernmental organizations (NGOs) Private or voluntary associations important in both domestic and international politics.

Operation Bluestar Attack by Indian army on Sikh terrorists in Golden Temple in Amritsar, Punjab (1984). Led to assassination of Prime Minister **Indira Gandhi.**

Opium War Between China and Britain (1839–1842); British victory became a source of Chinese humiliation and motivated the Chinese nationalist movements of the nineteenth and twentieth centuries.

Orientalism Western cultural and intellectual views regarding the nature of Eastern ("Oriental," or Asian) history and culture. Also title of book by Edward Said, who argued that orientalist constructs reflect Western domination of the East.

outcastes Pejorative term for Indians outside the four *varna*; see *dalit,* **untouchables, Scheduled Castes and Tribes.**

panchayat Village government in India, both traditional and contemporary.

Parsis Indian Zoroastrians, found primarily in Mumbai region.

Partition Division of the Indian subcontinent into the independent states of Pakistan and India in 1947.

party-state system Form of governance characterized by penetration and control of state institutions by a single, dominant party (such as in China).

patriarchal Characteristic of family and social organization in which the father or eldest male monopolizes property and legal and political authority.

patrilineal Designating descent and kinship through the male, or father's, line rather than the mother's.

President's Rule Indian constitutional procedure by which the central government, under presidential authorization, assumes direct control of a state government.

private sphere Domestic, household, family space, to which women are often confined in traditional societies. See **public sphere.**

productive activities Production for exchange, often takes the form of paid work.

public sphere Social space outside the household; viewed in many traditional societies (including China, Japan, India) as a male preserve.

purdah Literally, "curtain"; seclusion or veiling, or both, of Muslim and Hindu women.

Qing dynasty (1644–1912) Last Chinese dynasty. Also known as Manchu dynasty.

Raj Literally, "rule"; usually refers to the British Empire in India.

Rajya Sabha Council of States; upper house of Indian parliament.

Ram, Rama Indian god, hero of the classical epic, the *Ramayana.* Reputed to have been born at **Ayodhya.**

rectification campaigns Chinese Communist Party method of maintaining political control and ideological discipline; typically involves self-criticism, reeducation, and purges.

Red Guards Young people, primarily teenagers, called to play a leading role in the **Cultural Revolution** by attacking anything connected with prerevolutionary society and culture.

reproductive activities Activities that assure the survival and well-being of the household and family, including procreation and tasks such as food procurement and preparation, child and elder care, and cleaning.

reservations Indian policy of establishing quotas in state or national government agencies and other public bodies (such as universities) for **Backward Classes** and **Scheduled Castes and Tribes.**

residuary power The power of a national or regional government to make laws with respect to any matter not enumerated in the constitution of a federal system; this power belongs to the Union, or central government, in India.

Ritsuryo System of centralized rule, derived from a Chinese model, in Japan from seventh to tenth centuries. Comprehensive legal code placed sovereign at apex of rule.

romanization The respelling in the Roman alphabet of words or text from another alphabet (necessitates **transliteration** from another alphabet).

Roy, Rammohun (1772–1833) Indian intellectual and civil servant; open to Western thought and Christianity but committed to regeneration of Hinduism; a founder of Indian national movement.

Russo-Japanese War (1904–1905) Japan's defeat of Russia confirmed the former's status as a modern military power and assured Japanese interests in Korea and Manchuria.

samurai Class of warrior-administrators during **Tokugawa shogunate**; also called *bushi* ("military gentry").

Sanskrit Ancient Indo-European language forming the basis for contemporary spoken languages in North India.

sati Self-immolation of a Hindu widow on her husband's funeral pyre.

satyagraha Gandhi's concept of "soul force" and nonviolent resistance.

Scheduled Castes and Tribes Castes and tribes outside four traditional Hindu *varna*. Originally listed by the British, subsequently included in the Indian Constitution. Given preferential treatment in government policies. See **reservations**.

Self Defense Forces (SDF) Armed forces of Japan.

Sepoy Mutiny (1857–1858) Revolt of Indian soldiers against the British.

Shah Bano case Indian court case involving rights of a divorced Muslim woman; raised issues of community versus state law.

Shinto Literally, "the way of the *kami*"; indigenous Japanese religion.

Sikhs Followers of the Sikhism religion, founded in the sixteenth century; especially important in the northwest Indian state of Punjab.

Sinitic Technically, a branch of Sino-Tibetan languages, including Chinese and its dialects. More generally, a synonym for Chinese.

Sino-Japanese War (1894–1895) Conflict primarily over control of Korea. Japan demonstrated the weakness of the **Qing** state by inflicting decisive military defeat.

Soka Gakkai Proselytizing Japanese "**new religion**," linked to Nichiren Shoshu Buddhism and to **Komeito**, the Clean Government Party.

special administrative region (SAR) PRC administrative subdivision designed for Hong Kong after 1997 and Macao after 1999; Hong Kong SAR, Macao SAR.

special economic zones (SEZs) Chinese coastal enclaves established to attract foreign investment with preferential treatment for foreign investors.

State Shinto State ideology fostered during the Meiji period; emphasized national unity focused on devotion to the emperor. Peaked during Word War II.

states reorganization Process of redrawing the boundaries of the states in India to conform to linguistic or ethnic communities.

Sun Yat-sen (1866–1925) Nationalist leader of Republican revolution in China; founder of **Tongmeng Hui**.

Supreme Commander for the Allied Powers (SCAP) Occupation headquarters for Japan (1945–1952); the term referred to both General Douglas MacArthur and his headquarters.

swadeshi "Self-reliance"; philosophy and strategy developed in early twentieth century by Indian nationalist movement.

swaraj "Self-rule"; central tenet of Indian nationalist movement.

Taiping Rebellion (1850–1864) Massive rebellion against **Qing dynasty**, centered in southeastern China.

Taisho democracy Japanese period (1920s) when political parties flourished; named after Taisho emperor, who reigned 1912–1926.

Tiananmen Square Huge public square in central Beijing; site of student-initiated democracy movement suppressed by Chinese government in June 1989.

Tilak, Bal Gangadhar (1856–1920) Leader of extremist wing of Indian nationalist movement; opposed to Western influence and British rule; proponent of traditional Hindu values.

ti-yong **ideology** Characterized nineteenth-century reform efforts in China: adopt Chinese learning for the essence (*ti*), Western learning for practical use (*yong*).

Tokugawa period/shogunate Japanese period of military rule, 1600–1867; named after Tokugawa Ieyasu, first shogun or military ruler of the period. Also called **Edo** period.

Tongmeng Hui Organization that sparked revolution against **Qing dynasty**; known also as Alliance Society or United League.

Tongzhi Restoration Effort at moral and political reform of the **Qing dynasty**, named after the reign title of the Emperor Tongzhi (1861–1875).

transliteration The writing or spelling of words from one alphabet in another alphabet in a way that represents the same sounds.

Treaty of Nanjing (1842) Marked end of **Opium War** and set pattern for unequal treaties that China was forced to sign with foreign states. Island of Hong Kong ceded to Britain.

united front Collaborative **Kuomintang**-Communist strategy against the Japanese in late 1930s. More generally, Communist term for cooperation with non-Communist organizations.

untouchables Outdated, pejorative term for *dalits*.

Urdu Language used by Indian Muslims and formerly by Mughal rulers; emerged from Hindi, Persian, and Arabic, but is written in Arabic script.

vanguard of the proletariat Lenin's term for the Communist Party, conceived as the leading edge of the working class.

varna Sanskrit word meaning "color"; name for the four broad caste groupings in India (**Brahmins**, Kshatriyas, Vaishyas, Shudras).

xian Administrative subunit of Chinese provinces.

Yasukuni Shrine Large Shinto shrine in Tokyo commemorating the spirits of those who died fighting for Japan.

Yuan Shikai Qing general; president and military dictator of Republican China, 1912–1916.

zaibatsu Japanese industrial and financial conglomerates developed during Meiji period and broken up during U.S. occupation.

Zhou Enlai (1898–1976) Early leader of **May Fourth Movement** and CCP; **Long March** veteran; after 1949, premier of PRC.

Zoroastrianism Ancient Persian religion; established in India by Zoroastrians who fled Persia to escape conversion to Islam.

About the Book and Author

Comparing Asian Politics presents an unusual comparative examination of politics and government in three Asian nations: India, China, and Japan. Sue Ellen M. Charlton artfully points out both the unique and shared features of politics in these Asian countries. The author examines the links between politics and each nation's distinctive cultural and historical contexts and, at the same time, demonstrates the intermingling and grafting of Asian traditions with the influence of Western values and institutions.

National identity, political cohesion, and socioeconomic change emerge as central to how politics has developed in each nation-state. Charlton provides insight into such topics as the significance of constitutions in the political process, the parliamentary system in Asia, the regionalization of politics and the importance of levels of government, the decay of one-party rule, state authority, the development of grassroots politics, and the impact of globalization. Selected public policy questions for each country are introduced early in the book in order to acquaint readers with political controversies that are important both domestically and internationally. Often these focus on the role of ethnic minorities, women, and regional groups in Asian political processes.

Unlike many comparative studies, this book not only illuminates the politics of India, China, and Japan in relation to one another, but it also suggests to readers how their own experience of politics can be informed by understanding the politics and government of these three Asian nations.

Sue Ellen M. Charlton is professor of political science at Colorado State University.

Index

Page located in **bold** indicates map, chart, or photograph

Japan *(continued)*
nongovernmental organizations in, 332
Okinawa, 262–264
opposition parties and coalition politics,
281–284, 288
political relationships in contemporary, 7
population, 21, 55, **73**, 73–78, **77**
postwar occupation of, 165–166
prefectures and municipalities of,
260–261
Prince Shotoku's constitution, 87
recasting as peace-loving nation, 168
recessions of 1990s/2000s and
employment, 77–78, 151, 167, 168
reconstruction of after WWII and
Cold War, 166
religion/new religions in, 86–89, 90–91
retaining of emperor after WWII,
166, 167
textbooks in, 12, 167, 336–337
as unitary system, 261
vulnerability of and reliance on
imports, 76
See also Japanese Constitution of 1947;
Meiji period in Japan; Self Defense
Forces (SDF); Shinto; Tokugawa or
Edo in Japan; Yasukuni Shrine
Japan, parliamentary system in
coalition governments, 218–219
constitutional monarchy, 205–206
Imperial House, 209–211
inspired by British model, 201–202
lower legislative house more
powerful, 202
major institutions of government of
Japan, **203**
prime minister and cabinet in, 205–206
prime ministers of, 211–213
role of emperor in, 206, 208–209
Japan Communist Party (JCP), 164, 275,
282–283
Japan Socialist Party (JSP), 275, 281–282
Japanese Constitution of 1947, 167,
184–189
amending/approval by Diet, 186, 187
description of contents of, 186–187
equality of sexes, 78–79

evolution of and legitimacy, 186–188
judicial review, 188–189
local autonomy, 260
no-war clause (Article 9), 185, 186,
188–189, 338
preservation of emperor, 185, 186
Research Commission on the
Constitution to examine revision,
187–188
"stealth approach" to constitutional
revision, 188
Yasukuni Shrine controversy, 170
Japanese language, **15**, 15–16
Japanese Society for History Textbook
Reform, 167
Jati, 29–30, 33, 354
Jiang Qing, 236, 238, 353
Jiang Zemin, 195, 233, 241–242, 274, 279
Jiangxi (Kiangsi), 139, 140, 141
Jigme Khesar Namgyel, 308
Jigme Singye Wangchuk, 179, 307–308
Jing Huang, 279
Jinnah, Muhammad Ali, 112, 351, 354
Jiyuto (Liberal Party), 158
Judicial review, 184, 188–189

Kalam, A. P. J. Abdul, 207
Kamakura period, 92
Kami, 15–16, 87, 89, 210, 342, 354
Kamikaze ("divine wind"), 154
Kanemaru Shin, 280
Kashmir, 35, **121**, 285, 334, 347
confrontation in, 1, 43, 120–122, **123**
surrender to British by Sikhs, 108
Keiretsu, 166, 354
Kenji Hayao, 212
Kerala, 27, 41
Khan, Abdul Qadeer, 339
Khan, General Ayub, 118
Ki (also *qi* or *chi*), 342, 354
Kim Il Sung, 161
Kim Jung Il, 161
Koenkai, 276, 354
Koizumi Junichiro, 211, 212–213, **213**,
277, 281, 288
Kokoro (heart-mind), 167
Kolkata (Calcutta), 106